AN ODYSSEY

Between the
CARTWHEELS

Second book in the
CARTWHEELS QUADRILOGY

Lawrence
WINKLER

Note for Librarians: A cataloguing record for this book is available from Library and Archives Canada at www.collectionscanada.ca/amicus/index-e.html

Cover Image:
Shaunl, www.istockphoto.com (Image ID: 64996617)

Cover Design:
Jenny Engwer, First Choice Books

Book Images:
"Carpenter" courtesy of
Tim Dowley Associates Limited
44 Carson Road, West Dulwich London, SE21 8HU

ISBN – 978-1-988429-06-9

Printed in Canada ♻ on recycled paper

 FIRST CHOICE BOOKS

firstchoicebooks.ca
Victoria, BC

10 9 8 7 6 5 4 3 2 1

For Rhea and Rose

Spokes

If I Forget Thee O Jerusalem
Collectivism by Candlelight
Travels with the Anointed
In the Middle of the Wine-Dark Sea
The Air Between the Columns
Songs of the Sirens
Hash as to Ashes
Suckling the Wolf
Stendhal Syndrome
The Most Serene Republic
Michelin Star
Damascenery
Gates of Paradise
Atlas Shrugged
Querencia
Shadow on the Moon
A Whale Stranded
Entre-deux-Mers
Canton Ease
Aérospéciale
Rundai
Tapestry
Guinness Record
Óst na nOileán
The Tinker's Tapeworm
Skye Lark
Drifter
Schotel of Mosselen
Stroopwafel
Die Sündige Meile

Sam and Millie were sitting on the picnic table under the Otama night sky.

Clouds rolled across the full moon, platinum floodlight patchdancing on the wide expanse of ocean below.

Orion hung upside down above them.

"Were you the constellation or the myth, Uncle Wink?" Sam asked.

"The myth." he said.

"What were you in the myth, Uncle Wink?" asked Millie.

"The hero." he said.

Between the Cartwheels

is an inaccurate name for this story, of course. I wasn't really between the cartwheels. I was actually on a new one. You can't be between four of anything, if you're on, and one of them. And I was on the Grand Tour, the grand turning clockwise through Europe, spinning the history of Western Civilization forward, and the travels of Benjamin of Tudela in reverse. I was entering the realm of the cartwheel chandelier, the cartwheel ruff, and the cartwheel tuppence. This was the second cartwheel, and hammered between the Fertile Crescent and Eastern Block, it was also the land of Catherine's wheel, my breaking wheel. I needed to keep up the revs. Push on through to the other side. *Between the Cartwheels*, it is.

If I Forget Thee O Jerusalem

'Can you loosen Orion's belt?'
Job 38:31

The shopkeepers had awakened. The rolling thunder of metal accordion doors resonated through the stone bowels of the old city. I watched the sunrise on the Western Wall, trying to burn off the tribal memory of a thousand distant atrocities. But the heat and light was unable to penetrate the closed eyelids of the bearded Haredim, bobbing and swaying in front of the giant Jerusalem stone blocks. After all the random twists of fate over the previous three millennia, they were still hooked through their trout gills, spiraling along the remnants of Herod's temple.

The Rabbi of Lodz, on first seeing the Auschwitz crematoria belching fireballs and smoke, had turned to his flock in dismay. "There is no God." He said. But the bobbing and swaying continued anyway. There is no worse addiction than Rapture.

Extending fingers pushed paper prayers into the cracks of history and limestone. And the prayers that went into and through the crevices, pushed their own fireballs and smoke, into and through the tent that once stood high upon the Temple Mount, into and through the 'Holy of Holies,' the inner sanctuary of the tabernacle, into and through the Ark of the Covenant, containing the spiritual point from which reality emerges- and the Sinai treasure of Ten Commandments. I pressed my own paper prayer into a fissure, and covered it with my palm so it wouldn't escape.

My trip across the Sinai had been thirty-eight years shorter than Moses took, but I wasn't carrying the spiritual point from which reality emerged. I was carrying Serendipity, Diogenes and the Gold Kazoo- my backpack, tent, and sleeping bag- not as much baggage, and far less than I started

1

with. Most of that had baked off above the long hot roads of South America and Africa, in return for clarity. The disasters forecast by the colleagues I left behind had not come to pass, although there had been moments of terror and exhilaration. Eighteen months after I first carved an arc in the air with my thumb, I had arrived in the land of my forefathers. Jacob, the most ancient, had been 'a quiet man, a dweller in tents.' I was as free then, as I would ever be again.

It was dawn in Jerusalem. Faith hovered over the towers. After being destroyed twice, besieged 23 times, attacked 52 times, and captured and recaptured 44 times, it had no choice. I had yet to wash in the waters of the Gihon Spring, which founded and sounded S-L-M... Sa-La-eM... Salem... Salaam... Shalom... Yarushalaim... *Jerusalem*.

Before the Israelites arrived in 1000 BC, the local God of Dusk had been called 'Shalim.' After they arrived, Shalim left town with the last of the Canaanite light. The men and daggers that David sent up into the city, through the water shaft of the Gihon Spring at night, produced the City of David by morning. With Goliath slain and his Psalms recorded, King David was primed for a noble legacy. Until he sent out a Hittite soldier to die in battle, in order to steal his wife. And Bathsheba begat Solomon, and Solomon begat the First Temple. And the daughters of Jerusalem came outside with borrowed white garments, and danced in the vineyards, until the Age of Festivals gave way to the Age of Lamentations.

My own lamentation was for the shower I hadn't been able to access in the last three days. The cheapest place to sleep in Jerusalem was the Muslim Quarter. The thirty shekels I had paid for a bunk upstairs in the *Lemon Tree* hostel, and the thirteenth century Mamluk character of the house it was converted from, also bought me its 13th century water supply. When I asked the two owners if and when I would be able to bathe, their eyebrows rose in unison. *Insha'Allah.* They were more interested in the plumbing of the female Swedish

2

travelers, lavished with Arab sweetmeats and sweeter nothings. Water magically appeared in their shower stalls, and they reemerged clean and unbaptized, wearing the latest keffiyeh fashion statement. Like their ideology.

The other travelers in the *Lemon Tree* were a diverse lot. Eli was a Bavarian, who wandered into Jerusalem in a random search for drugs. With all the other visions that were possible in that town, it wasn't something he should have been trying to turbocharge. There was Nikki, a shorthaired Aussie pothead, who always dressed in black drapery, and far too much matching mascara. She was unreachable, having come to Jerusalem to find the Messiah, and finding far too many to reckon with. Matt was a Vietnam vet from Pennsylvania, excessively calm for whatever quest he was on. Sam and Lucy were happily Born Again, careening headlong into full-blown Jerusalem Syndrome. There was English Ken, who obviously didn't believe in anything, and was definitely running from something. He was still likeable in a simple way, but with a forced congeniality and shallow smile, which inspired you to push your money belt just that little bit further, into the pillowcase your head lay on.

And then, there was me. I had wound down to neutral. I needed a wash. The Talmud said that there were three gates to purgatory, and one of them was Jerusalem. There I was, in all my aromatic Aramaic glory- waiting for Steve and redemption.

*   *   *

'In the third year of the reign of Jehoaikim king of Judah came Nebuchadnezzar king of Babylon unto Jerusalem, and besieged it.'
Daniel 1:1

I remember the light streaming into the *Lemon Tree* courtyard in the morning, the oily smell of Turkish coffee, and the guttural Arabic of the owners, giving orders with a flick of the back of one hand, and the metronome *clack-clack-clack* rhythm of their colliding amber worry beads with the other. The collision of sunlight with Jerusalem stone is a photosynthetic reaction, the end product of which is Religion. No chlorophyll is involved. Nothing green influenced the carbon-based forces of the three monotheistic cults that evolved in the desert. The absence of other life was actually essential- no animistic distractions to interfere with a supplicant and the space between the sand and the twilight he prayed to. There was the occasional desiccated shrub, camped in the interstices of a rock wall, or cobble path, but most of what held the limestone spaces of the city together was an unstable amalgam of blood and dust. Jerusalem was built with blood and dust. It flowed on the lips of the Crusader, the 'Next Year' of every Jew, the Moslem flight path to paradise, and in the spinal arteries of every invader- Egyptians under Sheshonk I, followed by Shalmaneser III of Assyria, by the Philistines, the Arabs, the Ethiopians, by Hazael of Aram Damascus, and then by Nebuchadnezzar, who destroyed Solomon's Temple, slaughtered the King's descendents in front of him (before removing his eyes so that would be the last thing he ever saw), and then dragged him and the entire population of the city to Babylon. Seventy years later, Cyrus II of Persia allowed the Jews to return to Judah and rebuild the Temple. Some decided that the traffic in Jerusalem wasn't worth the commute, and formed ascetic communes near the Dead Sea. Their culture was governed by solemn rules, against anger, swearing oaths, and owning money and personal property. It was like marriage, but that was forbidden as well. The Essenes had plenty of time to write about their Rapture.

Two thousand years later, I was watching a holographic projection at the Israel Museum.

"She really moves, doesn't she?" It was Bork, the Dutchman who had boiled our salad in Nairobi. And we laughed, and ran as hard as we could, to catch a glimpse of the Dead Sea

Scrolls, before the Shrine of the Book catacomb, in which they were housed, closed. I went to see the fragments of the Book of Enoch, left out of the Bible by Constantine, and known to exist only in Ethiopia, before their rediscovery in 1947 by a young Bedouin boy, chasing his escaping goat into the cliff-top caves of Qumran.

'Scapegoats' had been sent out by the high priests of the Tabernacle, into the desert wilderness for centuries. They had carried away the accumulated sins of the Israelites, on every annual Day of Atonement since the Exodus. This one was bringing some of them back.

'And he shall take the two goats, and present them before the Lord at the door of the tabernacle of the congregation.
And Aaron shall cast lots upon the two goats; one lot for the Lord, and the other lot for the scapegoat.
And Aaron shall bring the goat upon which the Lord's lot fell, and offer him for a sin offering.
But the goat, on which the lot fell to be the scapegoat, shall be presented alive before the Lord, to make an atonement with him, and to let him go for a scapegoat into the wilderness.'

Leviticus 16:7

According to the Book of Enoch, the fallen angel scapegoat-spirit, *Azazel*, had been bound and hung upside down in the sky for all to see:

'These are of the number of the stars of heaven, which have transgressed the commandment of the Lord, and are bound here till ten thousand years... This place is the prison of the angels, and here they will be imprisoned for ever.'

Book of Enoch, Chapter XXI

Azazel became the constellation, Orion. No one knows why the Hebrew University of Jerusalem group, dedicated to the study of the Dead Sea Scrolls, is called the Orion Center. But Azazel's descendents were called the *Nephilim*, from *Nephili,* which means 'fond of spinning.' I found it reassuring that, with all the sins of humanity escaping into the desert, even without a map, it was still possible to follow Orion's Cartwheels.

The Book of Enoch was written before the Flood. If there was any water in the Holy Land, I continued to find no evidence of it at the *Lemon Tree*. Dry channeling Moses, I was becoming like my own ancestral Passover- a little sour, a little salty, a little bitter, and, without the prospect of a shower, in the land of milk and honey, only a little sweet. I asked the Arab owners again. *Allahu A'lam*. Whenever the answer was no, or unknowable, God was to blame.

I left, and made a game of dodging the shafts of light penetrating onto the long underground steps, in the covered maze of the old city, as I raced to swallow the big gulps of air, waiting for me at the top outside the gates. I bought a sweater and a leather bag, and spent an afternoon sewing the strap back on, over hummus and slow mint teas, in the Open Sesame café. Nikki and Sam and Lucy would join me. English Ken arrived for a hubble-bubble and too many beers. We spoke of our plans. Steve of the Jacuzzi wouldn't arrive in Israel for another month. I had intended to work on a Kibbutz after I finished the sights of Jerusalem. When that time would come, English Ken volunteered to volunteer with me. But I was still only part way through the layered history and geography of the place. I had yet to watch that sunrise on the Western Wall, although I could imagine what it would have looked like as the Second Temple, before the Great Revolt, and its destruction by the Roman's, in 70 AD. As the result of the revenge of Titus, a commemorative Arch was constructed in Rome, Israel was scattered to the winds for the second time, and I was born in one of the lands of exile, two millennia later. I still remember the last words of the last Day of Atonement incantation that I was taught to pray for, every year as a child- *'Next year in Jerusalem'*- resting on the lips of the fallen angel goat that escaped.

*　　*　　*

'Jerusalem! Jerusalem!
Thou art low! thou mighty one,
How is the brilliance of thy diadem,
How is the lustre of thy throne
Rent from thee, and thy sun of fame
Darken'd by the shadowy pinion
Of the Roman bird, whose sway
All the tribes of earth obey,
Crouching 'neath his dread dominion,
And the terrors of his name!'
Alfred Tennyson, *The Fall of Jerusalem*

As bad as Titus had been, Hadrian was worse. He rebuilt
Jerusalem as a pagan city named Aelia Capitolina, killed a half
million Judeans, and banned the survivors from reentering
the walls. A few years later, he constructed a large temple to
the goddess Aphrodite, which ultimately became a shrine to a
dead Jewish carpenter from Nazareth. I walked his path
backwards, down the Via Dolorosa, through the history of
Byzantium and four Arab Caliphates, to the Church of the
Holy Sepulcher.
I arrived at a brooding lineup of elbows and utterances.
Whoever these glum disciples were, they were not adherents
of Venus. All lightness of being was suffocated by the dense
darkness of the ringed interior chamber. The pilgrims
polished the Stone of Anointing slab with their bodies, jostled
the Eastern priests, and filed singly, for the brief moment
they were allowed past a wax virgin draped in a costume
jewelry window display. They pushed me along, and through
the sphincter of the Edicule. Gravitational force made escape
impossible. There was no oxygen. The tiny marble space of
the tomb of Jesus held a silver plate, an Orthodox Icon
painting, and a transparent electric light bulb, with a single
vibrating crooked filament. I had expected an illuminated
Rapturous exhilaration, but I was extruded across a
claustrophobic event horizon of oppressive kitsch. The same
Crusaders that had rebuilt the Church of the Holy Sepulcher,
had placed all the Jews of Jerusalem in the city's synagogue,

and burned it down. It would require a Moslem reconquest for the worship of all religions to be again permitted in the Abode of Peace. Even with the Ottomans in power, the continuing tensions among the Greek Orthodox, Catholic, Armenian, Coptic, and Ethiopian Churches ran so high, that the keys to this Black Abbey of Zombies had to be safeguarded by a pair of neutral Moslem families.

Just before Saladin reentered Jerusalem in 1187, and a hundred years before Marco Polo, a Wandering Jew named Benjamin of Tudela began an epic journey from Spain to the Middle East. He took the long road home, visiting over 300 cities in the known medieval world. His description of Jerusalem was that of 'a small city full of Jacobites, Armenians, Greeks, Georgians, and two hundred Jews dwelling in a corner under the Tower of David.' Without ever having heard of him, I would end up recreating his route backwards across Southern Europe, eight hundred years later. Without realizing it, I would be tracing my own Grand Tour of the forward history of Western Civilization, from the Fertile Crescent through Greece and Italy, to Spain and beyond. Unlike the ritual Grand Tours of upper class English gentlemen, hunting souvenirs with their Cicerone *bear-leaders*, valets, coachmen, cook and Cook's Tours, I was on a vision quest. Mine was not a liberal education rite of passage; like Benjamin of Tudela, I was engaged in a rite of personal devotion.

*   *   *

'Jerusalem has four gates- the gate of Abraham, the gate of David, and the gate of Gushpat, which is the gate of Jehoshaphat, facing our ancient Temple, now called Templum Domini.'

Benjamin of Tudela, *The Travels of Benjamin*

Jerusalem had no gates. For three hundred years, after the city walls had been razed by the Ayyubud Sultan of Damascus in

1219, Jerusalem had no gates. There had been an enfeebled attempt to rebuild the ramparts by Frederick II of German, but this was smashed by the Emir of Kerak; later efforts made by other Christians, were destroyed by the Tatars, the Egyptians, the Mongols, and then, in the middle of the thirteenth century, by the Mamluks, who built the *Lemon Tree* hostel. I had yet to wash in the waters of the Gihon spring.

It was the Ottomans, under Suleiman the Magnificent, who finally rebuilt the walls and portals of Jerusalem. Suleiman had been infatuated with a harem girl named 'Roxelana,' the daughter of an Orthodox Ukrainian priest. If his poetry was any indication, he was smitten hard:

'Throne of my lonely niche, my wealth, my love, my moonlight.
My most sincere friend, my confidant, my very existence, my Sultan
The most beautiful among the beautiful...
My springtime, my merry faced love, my daytime, my sweetheart, laughing leaf...
My plants, my sweet, my rose, the one only who does not distress me in this world...
My Istanbul, my Caraman, the earth of my Anatolia
My Badakhshanmy Baghdad, my Khorasan
My woman of the beautiful hair, my love of the slanted brow, my love of eyes full of mischief...
I'll sing your praises always
I, lover of the tormented heart, Muhibbi of the eyes full of tears, I am happy.'

Israel was moving from the land of poetry to the land of prose, but I was still with Suleiman. The poetry was just outside the Damascus gate, which he had constructed in 1542. Her name was Miriam, with beautiful hair and mischief eyes. She was a teacher from Germany. Her mother was German. Her father had been Jewish. She was at the Damascus Gate, searching for the meaning of that. Miriam was wrestling with three demons. The first was a simple question of identity. What tribe are you, if your parents are from different tribes? I had seen this confusion in the

Mestizos of Latin America. How do you feel if one side of your family had conquered the other, with unspeakable cruelty.

"At least we married ours." One Spaniard said to me months later. The second demon was what she wasn't, and could never become, without an artificial conversion. According to the traditional Judaic definition, children are Jewish because their mothers are Jewish, not their fathers. Jewish husbands that allowed their non-Jewish wives to retain their religion, as did the wives of King Solomon, were blamed for the fall of Israel. Miriam's mother was German, and there was already more than enough blame to go around. Finally, and most traumatic, was the magnitude of the viciousness, inflicted on one tribe by the other. The Nazis called the children of these mixed marriages 'mischlinge.' *Mongrels.*

But Miriam was the most beautiful mongrel of the mongrel tribe, and I was smitten hard. We went to small vegetarian restaurant, and spoke of love and water.

"You could use a little of both." She said. I told her how long I had been waiting for the water.

"Next year in Jerusalem." She said. And invited me to use her shower at the Holy Land East Hotel.

"In Israel, in order to be a realist you must believe in miracles." I said. And we left to create one of our own.

The days flew barrel rolls. I slept in the Lemon Tree, but I dreamt in the Holy Land East. One morning, Miriam and I visited the Temple Mount, where the world had expanded into its present form, and the dust had been gathered to create Adam. In that more innocent time, we were allowed to enter the Dome of the Rock, ushered in by an Arab guide, who gently corrected any detectable biblical or political inaccuracy. He took us over to view the Foundation Stone that lay over the Well of Souls. It was here where Adam, Cain, Abel and Noah had made offerings, here where Abraham almost sacrificed his son, Isaac, here where Jacob dreamt about his Holy Land angels, here where David bought the threshing room floor, here where the Holy of Holies stood, and here, of no small consequence, here where Mohammed ascended to Heaven. Here was, in the standard real estate parlance of our time- location, location, location.

Miriam and I walked out of the cobbles of the old city, and into the Orthodox streets of Me'a She'arim. We entered an Eastern European ghetto, frozen in a different time and space.

'Please do not pass through our neighborhood in immodest clothes.' Pleaded the black and white and red print entrance sign. The whole place seemed to be pleading. Bodies, transplanted from the Pale of Settlement to the overheated Middle East, pleaded for release, from wigs and thick black stockings and beards and black frocks and fur-trimmed hats. Minds, stuck in the medieval mire of caged self-loathing, pleaded for the return of the Messiah, so as to avoid any risk of new thoughts or experience. The Haredim pleaded for exemption from military service, for public welfare to support their large families and to be left alone to study Torah, to the exclusion of any other activity. Some, the Neturei Karta, even pleaded with Arafat to eradicate the evil State of Israel that supported them, in the bizarre belief that its existence and self-determination was impeding the arrival of the Messiah. They pleaded for permission to be killed. Was it these Jews that Hitler met in the streets of Vienna, that caused him to ponder his two questions. *Is this a Jew? Is this a German?* If he had met Miriam instead, would he have painted his abysmal watercolors a while longer?

On her last evening in Jerusalem, I took Miriam to the Sea Dolphin fish restaurant, long before anyone knew the menu could be translated into Russian, and too many shekels could be spent in one night. It was still more shekels than I really had to spend, but it was the Last Supper for my love of the tormented heart. The taste of that succulent trout with olives and nuts is still on my tongue.

She stopped me as I left the Holy Land East early the next

morning.

"Remember the Dome of the Rock." She said.

The desk clerk stopped me as well, demanding more shekels to let me out.

And that's how I remember the dawn of my time between the cartwheels, watching the sunrise on the Western Wall, and wondering how a trout gets to Jerusalem.

'And Zion's daughter is left abandoned like a hut in a vineyard, or like a shelter in a cucumber field, like a city under siege.'

Great Isaiah Scroll, *Dead Sea Scrolls*

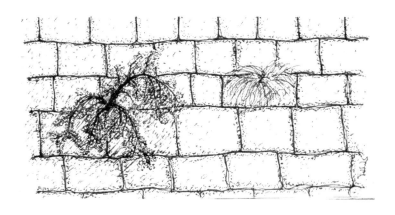

Collectivism by Candlelight

'Then I came to them of the captivity at Tel Aviv, that lived by the river Chebar, and to where they lived; and I sat there overwhelmed among them...'

Ezekiel 3:15

Sabra is an Arab word for prickly pear cactus. It also refers to Israeli-born Jews, tough and thorny on the outside, sweet and tender on the inside. The one I was dealing with had specialized in the outside.

"Where exactly are you sending me?" I said.

"Do you like good food?" She asked.

"Of course. But where are you sending me?"

"How about a swimming pool?" She asked.

"Its January. Are you able to tell me where you're sending me?"

"Wouldn't you like a place with a library? She asked back.

"That would be wonderful. Why do you always answer my questions with another question?" She didn't even break stride.

"What, now you have something against questions?"

English Ken and I were in the Kibbutz office in Tel Aviv. I had pried him out of his bunk and his hangover the previous morning, bid shalom to Nikki and the other *Lemon Tree* huggers, and boarded Egged bus #405, for the hour trip, downhill to Tel Aviv. We found beds in the Hotel Josef annex, and devoted our afternoon to visceral pursuit. We honed the fine art of how to stuff a falafel so a dollar could last all day, and sat on a bench in Dizengoff Square, sharing impressions of passing beauty. The next morning found Ken with what I was discovering to be his usual inertia, largely because he had gone to bed only four hours earlier. Tel Aviv was known even then as 'The City That Never Sleeps,' but I had a less intoxicated appreciation for it as a cultural oasis, especially after my long sojourn in Africa. It wasn't always thus. Before it became the world's largest concentration of Bauhaus buildings, Tel Aviv, along with the rest of the Sharon coastal plain and the Jezreel and upper Jordan valleys, had been a malarial swamp. In April of 1909, sixty-six families gathered on a desolate sand dune, on what is now Rothschild Boulevard, to divide up the land. They did it by lottery, using seashells. That same year, on the Sea of Galilee, ten men and two women, from Romania, established the first kibbutz in Israel, at Degania Alef.

There had been more than enough incentive offered in Eastern Europe. In 1882, the Czarist Russian government enacted the May Laws, designed for 'one-third of the Jews to emigrate, one-third to accept baptism, and one-third to starve.' They were prohibited from living in large cities or small villages. Even fifteen years later, any Jew trying to return to Moscow had a bounty on his head, equal to that of two burglars. The more fortunate of the persecuted bought a ticket to the frontier of Socialist Zionism, to the chimera of 'land, liberty, and labor.' Instead, they got 'lean, lonely and loathed.' And typhus. And cholera. Some had partial malaria protection from the fava beans in their falafels, that caused their red blood cells to explode, but this and every other facet of their lives, was a harsh price to pay for protection. They lived in poor sanitary conditions in a difficult climate, in a choice of swamps, rocks or desert. Most of them didn't know the first thing about farming. The soil was often infertile. They were raided by nomadic Bedouins, and their crops and irrigation canals sabotaged by resentful local Arabs. The only metric of success was survival.

They had come 'to make the desert bloom.' And I had come to relive their dream- as a tanned kibbutznik with a tembel hat and khaki shorts, playing my guitar around the communal campfire, after a hard day herding goats and driving tractors.

"Your kibbutz is in the north, between Haifa and Kiryat Ata." She finally said. "Its name is Kfar HaMacabbi."

14

"Kfar HaMacabbi." I repeated, rolling it around on my tongue. It sounded Israeli-perfect, like 'Jaffa oranges' or 'Shakshooka.'

"Is that a question?" She asked.

I shook my head no. I was already playing my guitar, and herding goats on my tractor.

"Did I tell you about the good food, the swimming pool, and the library?" She asked.

I nodded my head yes. She had told me everything she thought I needed to know.

She didn't tell me about the tire factory.

*   *   *

I left Tel Aviv with English Ken, on an express bus to Haifa, and jumped on Egged #66, to our new Kibbutz.

Chaim, the ancient volunteer coordinator, and Shoshana, the camp matriarch, met us. We were soon to find out that Chaim took no notes, and Shoshana took no prisoners. They brought us first to the common dining room. The coordinator in Tel Aviv had been right. The food was amazing. Fresh kibbutz-grown tomatoes, eggs, cucumbers, peppers, olives, and radishes, home-baked bread, and biblical yogurt, in abundance. This truly was the Land of Milk and Honey. There was a promise of pizza delivery on Friday nights, when no one from the commune could work in the kitchen. I saw English Ken's eyes widen, when Chaim mentioned that the brown bottles of Goldstar beer were almost free. Noblesse cigarettes, the strongest in the country, were only a few cents a pack, and a form of local currency.

Kfar HaMacabbi was founded in 1936, by a youth movement that had migrated from Czechoslovakia and Germany. English Ken and I migrated with the rest of the new recruits, down to a porch outside an elevated bungalow, overlooking the other volunteer shacks. This was where Chaim and Shoshana delivered the commandments. Volunteers arose at four thirty in the morning, because work started at five. Breakfast was from eight until eight thirty. Don't be late for either. I saw English Ken's face fall like the Second Temple. Work was six days a week. Duties were posted on a roster in the communal dining hall. Fridays were set aside for cleaning your bungalow. All valuables, including passports, were to be given to Chaim, and locked in the kibbutz safe. I took him aside.

"Chaim, I have a lot of money with me." I said.

"How much?" He asked. I told him. His eyes grew large.

"Why did you bring such a sum?" He asked. I started to tell him about black markets and Sikhs in Tanzania, but he decided he really didn't need to know.

"It will be secure in the safe." He said. I asked him if he was sure. He nodded. I asked him for a receipt. He said it wasn't necessary. He was wrong.

I turned my head toward the new movement down and to the right, and watched my breath disappear. She had emerged onto the veranda of one of the wooden bungalows, and began to hang laundry on a clothesline. She was dressed in a diaphanous white cotton shirt and red panties. Her long blonde hair was piled on top of her head and, every time she reached up to place a clothes peg, there was a kaleidoscope of molten spheres. She must have sensed my gaze, for she looked up for just a moment, and quickly averted her eyes. My own need to look away landed me headlong into Shoshana's Old Testament glare. The local gods would show no mercy.

The attitude of the kibbutznik to romance was a work in cultural evolution. Equality governed collective living, right from the beginning of the socialist adventure. In the early days there were always more men than women. Desperate to perform physical labor equivalent to their male counterparts, females underwent an inadvertent form of self-masculinization. An early kibbutz woman would call her husband *ishi*, 'my man,' rather than the conventional Hebrew appellation *ba'ali*, 'my owner,' but no one was permitted to own anything- livestock, bank accounts, tools, clothing, or even gifts from relatives. Husbands and wives were discouraged from sitting with each other; one kibbutz refused to buy teakettles for its members, out of a fear that couples would spend more time together, rather than in the communal cafeteria. For the same reason, kibbutzim had benches, not individual chairs, in the dining hall. In a small, isolated community of ideologues, the lack of privacy, regimentation of work and leisure, and the intensity of gossip, could place severe restrictions on any opportunity for love.

This conservatism was magnified, with the arrival of subsequent generations. Because children were also viewed as communal property, they were mostly raised apart from their mothers and fathers in 'Children's Societies.' One kibbutz expressly forbade parents from putting their own children to bed at night. The determination to eradicate the natural violent instincts of competitiveness in the playpen, brought great anxiety to those early pioneers trying to create their new communist utopia. Bedwetting was endemic.

Then, there was the Westermarck effect. Despite the fact that there was no segregation of the sexes in the Children's Societies, there was also no sexual imprinting. Young kibbutzniks treated their bunkmates as ersatz siblings, and rejected them as potential partners. Without private property, there could be no private emotion.

All of this was contained in Shoshana's glare.

And yet, in her youth, I was sure there had been magic nights of campfires and dancing, and reaching out. And groans in the dark. Even with all the generations of social programming, the children of the kibbutzim were not robots. They were highly accomplished in law, medicine, music and academia. They were seventy-five percent of all the fighter pilots in the country. And that didn't happen without passion.

*   *   *

'The true love finds the light only if, like the candle,
he is his own fuel, consuming himself'
Attar of Nishapur, Light

English Ken and I settled into our old bungalow and new routines. It was a smaller adjustment for me to wake up early, but I wasn't sleeping under the Goldstars. English Ken didn't notice the geckos running on the ceiling above his head, or the demons swirling below him.

My initial assignment as a dishwasher was actually quite pleasant, and I was teased continually by some of the old hands. The first time I saw one of them come out of the soapy dishwater, with a blue numbered tattoo on her forearm, sent me a chill. The songs in that kitchen were in a dozen different languages, but the lyrics were all the same. They were about deliverance.

We got to know the other volunteers, on the long benches at mealtimes, and at the coffee bungalow after dinner. Each had taken a slightly different route to Kfar HaMacabbi. Georgie, Jochim, and Geli were Germans, trying to reconcile their own tribal history. Stanley, a pharmacist from South Africa, was wrestling with whether or not to immigrate. Irmgard from Belgium, and Madelaine from Minnesota, had taken a year off to travel. There was Alberto and Bertha and Birgita, and some odd Swiss. And a couple from Sweden, Lassa and Mimi. Lassa had chips on both his tall shoulders. There was no explaining why, by looking at Mimi. She was the vision that had danced below us, when English Ken and I first arrived. She still averted her eyes, but I noticed her cheeks flush when we were in the same room.

Less than a week after I arrived, my duties changed. Stanley and I were assigned to work in the tire factory. I was provided with power tools, and my job was to roughen up one side of the tire retreads. By the end of each day, my lungs

18

were full of rubber dust, and my muscles full of knotted pain. The fabricating plant was just getting started, so I also helped with buffing welds, and assembling parts on the extruding press. To my horror I found myself smoking Noblesse oblige with the kibbutzniks, during our coffee breaks. All the volunteer bungalows got rubber retread welcome mats.

In the evenings after work, Georgie and Jochim and I often played guitar together. Sometimes I went to the library to read. There were still three weeks before Steve's arrival but, for a little while, I was enjoying not packing Serendipity every morning and moving on.

What I wasn't enjoying very much was English Ken. He had become slovenly and bigoted, or he had always been that way. I would start each day a bit earlier, just to clean up the empty beer bottles and full ashtrays. Shoshana was starting to give him the death stare.

One afternoon our door flew open. It was Lassa, spitting bullets.

"Hey, can I move in with you guys?" He asked.

"Sure. We understand." Said Ken. "Have a Goldstar!" I wasn't really consulted.

As Ken and Lassa entered their bonding ritual, I withdrew to the library, to escape the resentment, boiling under the suds. On the return trip later that night, I stopped in at the coffee bungalow, to find Georgie and Birgita and Mimi, baking a cake for English Ken's birthday. The color was high in her cheeks. I asked if she was all right.

"Why not?" She answered with a question.

We spoke of music and books, and she invited me to her veranda to look at some of hers. I don't remember the veranda.

I awoke to candlelight, in time to shower and arrive at the tire factory by five. I brought one of her books for the coffee break. It was Hemingway. *A Movable Feast*. Indeed.

It was unfortunate for me that Lassa recognized the book, when I got back from the factory. Both chips came off his shoulder and, after the screaming finished, he cracked the doorframe with his exit from the bungalow.

"Cake?" Asked Ken, grinning.

"How old are you actually, in human years?" I said. And went back to the candlelight.

I was a little late for work next morning. At lunch, Stanley told me that English Ken had left the kibbutz, after an altercation with Chaim about his sloth and irresponsibility. When I returned to my bungalow, I found out that Lassa had left as well. With my Swiss army knife, Egyptian jeans, pocket money, and the zipper they ripped out of the Gold Kazoo. My bed had been stripped, and they had left the place in a shambles. Mimi appeared in the cracked doorframe.

"Fair trade." I thought. If I had to share, I'd take my collectivism by candlelight.

*   *   *

'The candle is not there to illuminate itself'
Nawab Jan-Fishan Khan, *The Complete Man*

The next three weeks went too fast. I worked a lot of hours, read a lot of Hemingway, and melted a lot of candles. The geckos danced in the flickering light, on the ceiling. Mimi and I adopted a cat named Hannibal. I was blue collar happy. A few mornings after English Ken and Lassa made their graceful exit, Mimi appeared in the tire factory. She was obviously upset. During the previous night, someone had broken into the kibbutz office, and burgled the safe. All my money, traveler's cheques, and papers had been taken. I immediately thought of English Ken and Lassa, and immediately dismissed them as suspects. They were missing too much, of what it would have taken, to pull this one off.

20

Chaim called an emergency meeting of the volunteers to break the news.

"You will all get your money back." He said. He was nervous, and he wasn't looking at me. Menachem Begin once attacked kibbutzniks as 'millionaires with swimming pools.' That was definitely no description of Chaim.

"All of us?" I asked.

"Do you have a receipt?" He answered with a question. That pretty much did it for me.

Fortunately, Shoshana had been there on the first day, when Chaim told me I didn't need one. His question turned out to be a problem of memory rather than morality. I had to go to Haifa to reclaim my traveler's cheques, call home to replace my papers, and meet with the kibbutz executive to negotiate how much of my cash would be returned. When the coffee and pastry came out, we had a deal. It was like the tea and biscuits that materialized during my captivity in Zimbabwe, except that this Exodus didn't threaten an eye and a life, for an eye.

Like my own ancestral Passover, the last days at Kfar HaMacabbi were bittersweet, with a little salt from her tears, and nothing to be sour about- I gave her Israeli perfume and wine. And a kiss that still lingers outside the gate of a northern kibbutz.

Travels with the Anointed

'But as for you, turn around and set out toward the desert along the route to the Red Sea.'

Deuteronomy 1:40

It had been 548 days since he had driven me across the US border into Tijuana, and I was anxious to see him again. Steve had taken two months off, to come with me on the next leg of my travels. At the airport we hugged and talked at the same time, until we were tired.

He looked a little older and had lost more hair, but he was still the same animated Steve of the Jacuzzi. California had arrived in Canaan. It was my first responsibility to show him some survival skills. Maimonides had predicted that, in the Messianic age, 'the good will be plentiful, and all delicacies available as dust.' I showed Steve how to strategically fill a falafel with eggplant, tomatoes, cucumbers, cabbage, pickles and fiery chilies, and how to use the tahini sauce as mortar. It stuck to his moustache and his glasses. He liked it. I took him to the Hotel Josef, where I demonstrated how to make his bunk and valuables secure, from more imaginative, but less scrupulous, pilgrims. We found English Ken working upstairs as a bartender, and I showed Steve how to pull me off, before my choking almost killed him. We were a team again.

It was February in Los Angeles, and Steve was hanging ten for some sun, and a little quality beach time.

The next morning, we headed south to the Red Sea. In the back of Egged bus #390, spectacular views of the Dead Sea and Negev desert, and my Sudanese chess set, entertained us for hours, all the way to the Gulf of Aqaba. When it came to seas, the consensus was that we were 'better Red than Dead.' The Negev brigade had captured Eilat from the British in 1949, so unprepared for the victory, that they had no Israeli flag with them. They hoisted one anyway, hurriedly drawn in ink. Eilat was a much smaller resort town back then.

We checked into Hostel Max (*The only Welsh and Australian hostel in Israel*), and went to the Sabra Hotel for a burger and beer, on our way to the beach. Steve was at home again. He met a young Canadian girl named René, who followed us down the Egyptian Sinai coast next afternoon.

Across from the tiny palm frond hut we slept in on the beach, the stars danced over Arabia. Here Orion was the soul of Osiris, the Egyptian god of fertility and afterlife, the '*Star of Gold*' in the Pyramid Texts. Dahab is Arabic for 'gold,' the color of the sun and the sand, and the flame of the campfires we played our guitars around. We spent two days beachcombing, riding camels, resting under the date palms, and getting lost in the barbed wire encampments of the Bedouin villages. Steve cut his foot on a piece of glass. The desert is a place without mercy or expectation. Fourteen years later, no one expected that three of these Bedouin would self-detonate in separate bomb attacks, and send two-dozen Dahab tourists to their afterlife. Osiris was kinder to us. Steve and I left our frond hut, into the golden sunrise over Arabia, with only a bandage.

The following day we had to climb over the fence at Max's Hostel, to make the six o'clock bus to Masada. The sudden realization, that Max's guard dogs were not terribly appreciative of people climbing over the fence, propelled our ambition to new heights.

Masada was the noble sacrifice epicenter of Israel. There had been innumerable instances of genocidal carnage in Jewish history, but few of them were associated with this degree of heroic resistance. It was the Hebrew equivalent of Thermopylae, the Alamo, Bastogne, and Wake Island. But those who died on the mountaintop of Masada were not entirely innocent victims. They were a radical splinter group of zealots called the *Sicarii*, or 'dagger-men.' At popular assemblies in Jerusalem, they would pull concealed blades out from under their cloaks, assassinate Roman occupiers and their sympathizers, and then quietly disappear back into the crowd. They destroyed the food supply of the city, so that people would be forced to fight against the Roman siege. Herod had constructed Masada a hundred years earlier, as a refuge from Cleopatra. In 66 AD, the Sicarii fleeing Jerusalem overwhelmed the Roman garrison that had guarded the desert fortress for the previous 70 years.

It was a seemingly impregnable redoubt. Twelve-foot thick casemate walls enclosed a palace, with vast stores of food and arms left by Herod, and cisterns full of rainwater, a quarter of a mile off the desert floor. The Governor of Judaea, Lucius Flavius Silva, brought his Tenth Legion here seven years later, and waited. Over the next four months, with Jewish slaves, he constructed eight camps, connected by a circular wall around the fortress. He built a ramp in twelve weeks, moving thousands of tons of stones and beaten earth, up the western face of the plateau. He finally attacked with ten thousand troops, siege engines, flaming torches, rock bombardments, and battering rams. On the night he set the fortress gates on fire, the 900 defenders drew pottery shard lots, and killed each other in turn, so that the last man would be the only one to have to take his own life. This communal act of self-sacrifice astounded the Romans with its audacity.

Steve and I made our way slowly up the scorching steep narrow 'snake path' to the summit. The sunlight was too bright to look up. It was eerily quiet and lonely, except for the wolf-whistles of the black and orange Tristram's starling that followed us through the ruins. In the Western palace we met Barb and Marion, two girls from Alberta, and teamed up to tour the rest of the cliff-top sights.

As impressive and iconic as it was, I wasn't entirely convinced of the unequivocal heroism of the Sicarii. Its other citizens, who had had enough of their robberies and assassinations, had actually forced them out of Jerusalem, before the Roman siege of the city. The Sicarii raided nearby Jewish villages, and were responsible for a massacre of 700 inhabitants of Ein Gedi, most of whom were women and children. Today, this might be called terrorism. There is no evidence of any real battles fought around Masada, and the entire siege lasted four months, at most. More evidence exists, therefore, that they were more besieged than that they were heroes. It took Eleazar Ben-Yair two speeches to convince them to commit suicide. Hesitation is not usually considered a valiant attribute. Moreover, suicide itself is not exactly heroic, and is strictly proscribed in Judaism, as a sin. It is also not clear that the only two choices available to the Sicarii were surrender or suicide. They could have fought to the death, created a diversion to allow some to escape, or even tried to negotiate, as other besieged communities had done. The image of the two women and five children survivors, cowering in a cistern, is a less than intrepid legacy. No one would consider the bloated of Jonestown, or the barbequed of Waco, as examples of courageous defiance. That being said, it was a different time, as much as our identities then and there were as different as they are now. Ben-Yair's last words, according to Josephus, were spoken in another world:

'Let our wives die unabused, our children without knowledge of slavery. After that, let us do each other an ungrudging kindness, preserving our freedom as a glorious winding sheet. But first, let our possessions and the whole fortress go up in flames. It will be a bitter blow to the Romans, that I know, to find our persons beyond their reach and nothing left for them to loot. One thing only let us spare - our store of food: it will bear witness when we are dead to the fact that we perished, not through want but because, as we resolved at the beginning, we chose death rather than slavery.'

It was actually that store of food that gave rise to a most worthy source of admiration. A 2,000-year-old seed, discovered during the archeological excavations in the early 1960's, sprouted successfully to become a date palm, the oldest know such germination in history. In all the inspiration that life can provide, that one is truly heroic.

There was one other detail, about Masada, that drew a crooked heroic line. The spatial relationship of Jerusalem, Masada, and Petra correspond to Mitaka, Alnilam, and Alnitak, the belt stars of Orion. *L'Chaim.*

*   *   *

'But Life will suit Itself to Sorrow's most detested fruit, Like to the apples on the Dead Sea's shore, All ashes to the taste.'

Lord Byron

The apples tasted just fine, as did the spiced beans, chicken casserole, bread, cottage cheese, and beer. Steve and I, and the Alberta girls, had caught the last bus to Ein Gedi. We found a nice free campsite on the Dead Sea, built a blazing fire, and talked into the darkness. The same stars we had over Arabia had moved to Jordan, but they were still as spectacular, a quarter of a mile below sea level. It rained during the night, but that didn't affect us much. The Gold Kazoo was still waterproof, even without the zipper, and we actually slept better because of the higher oxygen content that came with the increased barometric pressure. Dawn found us running headlong into the bromine brackishness, and rolling onto our backs. We laughed at each other, floating above the waterline in the oily brine, kicking our legs in the air and waving our hands at the same time. Steve described our mood as 'buoyant.'

We left Barb and Marion Alberta-bound at the Jericho junction, and Steve and I hitchhiked on, and into the oldest permanently inhabited city on Earth. The dark green lobby of the Arab hotel we checked into still had the original cobwebs. Nothing gets old in the Middle East without turmoil. The bedding in our room was that ancient. No one else seemed to live in Jericho, if that's what you wanted to call it, except for the desk clerk and the original bearded guy in the corner, with his white *ghutrah* and black *iqaal* cord headdress, cane, and amber worry beads. He flicked them slowly, *clack-clack-clack*, in time to the pendulum of the grandfather clock beside the staircase. The scene was all Hitchcock.

I signed the register. No one had been here for months. If there had been bedbugs, they had all long died of starvation. The hot water we had in our shower had obviously been meticulously saved over time.

Steve and I stowed our gear, and boarded a Mercedes sherut taxi to Tell es-Sultan, the site of the 'old city.'

"What are we waiting for?" Steve asked, when he figured out we weren't moving.

"For full." Said the driver. *Clack-clack-clack.*

"Will it be full soon?" He asked.

"Insha'Allah." *Clack-clack-clack.* He turned the *nya-nya* music up a notch.

"How much for not full?" I asked. He turned the *nya-nya* music down.

"Fifty shekels." He said.

"Five." I replied.

"Thirty." He countered.

"Ten." I said.

"Twenty."

"No."

"OK." He turned the *nya-nya* music up. We moved.

Judging by the pile of rubble we arrived at, Joshua's trumpets had done a hell of a job. There had been no fewer than twenty successive settlements on the site, the first dating back over ten thousand years. Alexander the Great had used it as his private estate, and Mark Anthony gave it to Cleopatra, who leased it to Herod, who named it after his mother. In the 1950s, the archeologist Kathleen Kenyon transformed Jericho into trenches. Her questionable methods and conclusions are now the subject of no small criticism. She ignored the physical work of her predecessors, and failed to properly analyze what she had uncovered, because of a bizarre obsession with the pottery types she hadn't found in Jericho IV. Kenyon seemed determined to prove that the Israelite biblical account of the fate of the city was wrong. However the subsequent findings of Bryant Wood supported the Book of Joshua's version of events. Jericho had been strongly fortified, and underwent a short siege just after the spring harvest. The inhabitants had no chance to flee with their foodstuffs, the walls were leveled (possibly by an earthquake), and the city was burned but not plundered. By the Israelites. The impressive 2000 year-old siege tower that I looked down into, must have been used for something. What was once the biblical 'City of Palm Trees,' with constant sunshine, rich alluvial soil, abundant springs and streams, wild game, sugarcane, bananas, and fragrances, had become a scene of rock and dirt devastation. I stared at the message. The story of the oldest permanently inhabited city on Earth was a parable for environmental annihilation. It was, after all is said and done, what we did, and still do best.

The next morning another sherut took us the 36 kilometers, to Jerusalem. I navigated Steve through the covered maze of the Old City, to the *Lemon Tree*. The two Arab owners warmed up the reception.

"You are most welcome, Mr. Wink, as is your friend from America."

"Do you have hot water?" Steve asked.

Their eyes looked up in unison.

"Is that a yes?" Steve asked me.

"I'll explain later." I said. And took him around to all my old haunts. We ran into Barb and Marion from the Dead Sea at Open Sesame. Sitting with them was Cecilia, a young lovely from Stockholm. They were all also staying at the *Lemon Tree*. Cecilia said there had been hot water.

"That's great news". Offered Steve.

"She's Swedish." I said.

"So?" He asked.

"I'll explain later." I said.

We spent the rest of the day socializing with some UN troops from Fiji, alternating snacks and libations at the JOC Inn and Danish Tea House, and trading travelogues, long into the evening. Before we went upstairs to our bunk beds, Cecilia took me aside to show me the little kittens she was looking after, for the owners. That night I dreamt the lyrics to her song.

Steve went off with Barb and Marion to the Israeli Museum and Yad Vashem next morning, and I had a slow omelet, pita, and yoghurt with Cecilia, on the sunlit stone roof terrace of our hostel. Branches of all three Abrahamic religions grew out of the real lemon tree, into the surrounding forest of hanging laundry and television aerials above us. We floated together on our Turkish coffee. She told me that it would be her birthday the following day.

Saint Cecilia was the Roman patron saint of music; She was the way for the blind, and provided a heaven to gaze upon. She had my vote. Music arrived at the crossroads of guitars, the friends who could play them, and the reappearance of Steve and the Albertans, on the *Lemon Tree* rooftop in the late afternoon. We played until hunger and thirst drove us back out into the cobble streets, searching for less ethereal forms of sustenance.

Returning late, Cecilia and I were disturbed by the Arab owners turning on the light in the courtyard. Hard triplets rolled out of their mouths.

"*Yaqta' 'omrak, sharmoota.*" I wasn't really sure, but it didn't sound like terms of endearment. We evaporated into our bunks.

The next morning Steve and I visited David's Tower, climbed the walls of the old city, and ended up dressing up as Bedouins in an Arab Bazaar down Al-Mujahadin Street. I'm sure they've since changed the name. The fragment of an old terracotta oil lamp, with an embossed menorah, caught my eye. For more than I should have paid, I bought the fragment, and the owner's guarantee of authenticity:

> 'This is to certify... for old oil lamp manoura qurter of the herodian oil lamp two 200 hundred B.C.E. – 40 A.D... and this certificate garanteed for it.'
>
> Ali Bedwin

Steve thought the certificate was likely worth more than the *garantee*.

In the evening, we held a well-attended birthday party for Cecilia. There was a mixture of Arab and Western music, and wine and mint tea. This was our last night in Jerusalem. As the streets outside grew silent, so did the courtyard. Cecilia turned, and asked me if I had got her anything for her birthday. I closed her eyes and placed something in her hand.

"What's this?" She asked.

"Open your eyes." I said.

"It's a key." She observed. "What does it open?"

"A door in the Al-Ahram." I answered.

"What is the Al-Ahram?" She asked.

"Come with me." I said. And she smiled as I took her other hand, and we left the *Lemon Tree* in the darkness.

> 'If I forget you Jerusalem, let my right hand lose its strength. Let my tongue cling to my palate if I fail to recall you, if I fail to elevate Jerusalem above my highest joy.'
>
> King David

*   *   *

'And the angel of God, which went before the camp of Israel, removed and went behind them... but it gave light by night to these: so that the one came not near the other all the night.'

Exodus 14:19

Steve and I left the *Lemon Tree* forever the next morning. Even the Arab owners kissed us goodbye. We boarded Egged bus #405, for the hour trip downhill to Tel Aviv, and then another to the Caesarea turnoff. It was three kilometers of almost quiet hiking to the ruins.

"It's the hat.' Said Steve, out of nowhere.

"What's the hat?" I asked, puzzled.

"The hat is the reason you're so lucky." He replied.

I had to think about this. I hadn't been exactly celibate over the previous year and a half but, since I picked up my old salt and pepper wool Ascot cap, in the mail at the Canadian embassy in Tel Aviv, I had become more distracted.

"Nonsense." I said, and continued walking.

Caesarea was originally a pagan city that Herod had rebuilt, in honor of Augustus. In 66 AD, Jewish worshippers found Greek civilians, sacrificing birds in front of the local synagogue. The Romans ignored the ensuing protest that, broadening into demonstrations against taxation, would become a widespread violent revolt in Jerusalem. After an entire legion was ambushed and destroyed in the Beth Horon pass, the Romans retaliated, with the destruction of Jerusalem and the Second Temple. Twenty five hundred Jewish captives were slaughtered in gladiatorial games in Caesarea's amphitheatre, as a celebration of its becoming the new administrative capital of the Roman province of Judea, back where it all began. That's where Steve and I spent the day. After it all ended, we walked past the viaduct into a little Arab town, to buy provisions. Steve was going into California withdrawal, and wanted to camp on the beach.

"I'm not sure this is such a good idea." I offered.

"It'll be great." He said.

We bought hummus, pita, cucumbers, tomatoes, and yoghurt, and walked back across the sand and Marram beach grass, to a depression in the dunes that offered protection from the wind. We ate, and watched the red sunset melt into the Mediterranean.

I could see that Steve was still not completely at peace with his inner California.

"Let's make a campfire." He said.

"I really don't think that's such a good idea." I replied.

"Why not? It'll be great." And he got up, to look for combustibles.

"Steve, this isn't Seal Beach. These folks are not good with surprises." But he was too far into his mission to listen.

An hour later we were lying beside a fairly formidable blaze and, even I had to admit, it was a beautiful thing. The orange light flickered off the white sand and tussock shadows, and the stars were a spray display above us. Orion stood guard, looking off towards his native Greece. Steve played with the embers, as the flames began to shorten.

The ground began to shake. Almost imperceptibly at first, it rapidly became a converging earthquake. Up and over the rise of our little dune depression, roared two Israeli halftracks, loaded to their teeth. The tremors stopped when they did, but the shouting had only begun.

They worked they way through the languages of Babel, from Arabic to Hebrew, and finally, to English.

"What are you doing here?" The biggest soldier on the bigger vehicle demanded.

"Camping." Said Steve. I could barely look.

"Camping?" Asked the Israeli captain, not sure he heard it right the first time.

"Yeah, camping." Said Steve, again. They were two continents and an Exodus apart.

"Why do need fire?" The captain asked.

"You can't have camping without a campfire." Said Steve.

We eventually came to some accommodation about our accommodation, and they left us still scratching their heads, with a word of warning about the Arab village nearby, where we had purchased our comestibles before the combustible.

"Don't go there." Said another soldier. "They won't treat you like we treat you." I didn't have the karmic energy to tell them.

It rained all night, after they left.

Steve and I managed to hitch a ride to Haifa next morning with Mahmoud, a Palestinian laborer with ten children, who worked for thirteen dollars a day. We boarded Egged #405 to Kfar HaMacabbi, where Shoshana provided us a warm welcome, an opportunity to wash ourselves and our clothes, and my old bungalow for the night. Mimi was in Egypt, and Irmgard was the only original cast member, still at the kibbutz. The extruder press in the tire factory was finished, and operational. Other than for the yoghurt tasting as good as I remember, everything else had moved on. I could only tell Steve how good it had been.

The rain fell in sheets next morning, but we managed to pack up early, on our way to Acco. It was as drenched in history, as we were with water. Acco had been captured in the First Crusade and, for almost two hundred years, provided the Crusaders with more income than the total revenues of the King of England. It was the final defense of the Kingdom of Jerusalem, falling in a bloody siege to the Egyptians, in 1291 AD. We paid a visit to the Jezzar Pasha Mosque, named after the Mamluk who walked around with a portable gallows, in case anyone displeased him. Known as the 'butcher' because of his cruelty, Jezzar had mounted the only successful defense against Napoleon, during the Egyptian campaign.

We made it back to Tel Aviv the same evening. Over the next two days, Steve and I bought our Olympic Airways tickets to Athens, visited museums, played chess, drank red vermouth, and ate our last falafel. I had forgotten about Steve's snoring, which could kick the nails right out of the roof shingles.

Adding chickpeas to the vermouth, served only to convert him to stereo. I was looking forward to Greek salad.

Across the ages, I had come to Israel not expecting, and therefore was rewarded. Unlike other coreligionists I had met on the way here, I never felt like I was 'coming home.' I was a product of the Diaspora, and would ever be thus. But Israel had moved me from the realm of prose, back to the realm of poetry. The Romans may have forced my ancestors out of Israel, but the only thing Israel forced out of me was a sigh.

At the airport I was expecting a long and complicated screening. I couldn't have been more wrong. It was simple and effective. Play the player, not the ball.

"Where did you stay in Ethiopia?" Asked the security guy.

"The Nyala Hotel." I replied.

"That's a whorehouse." He said.

I shrugged. He shrugged. Steve shrugged. We were on our way.

"Shalom." He said. Shalom. Right back at you.

In the Middle of the Wine-Dark Sea

'And when the south wind blew softly, supposing that they had obtained their purpose, loosing thence, they sailed close by Crete.'

Acts 27:13

The Jews had given the world hope. The Greeks had given it tragedy. Steve and I landed in the birthplace of democracy, unaware that the umbilical cord of democracy had slipped down around our necks. The Greek president had just issued a decree, limiting the type and number of establishments that could operate in the *Plaka*, the neighborhood at the foot of the Athenian acropolis, where impecunious travelers could usually find a place to stay. Consequently, there was no place to stay. We had coffee with Rosie, Debbie, and Louise, three Aussie girls we had met at the *Lemon Tree* in Jerusalem, and left them for a subway ride to Piraeus, the ancient port of the capital, that had supplied the Athenians, during the long Peloponnesian War with Sparta. Twelve dollars bought us tickets on the *Knossus*, the overnight boat to Crete. We waited for our vessel in a smoky seaside bar, gorging on the classic Greek triple-O slippery comestibles- octopus, olives, and ouzo. The ouzo was the most slippery. Its name came from the Italian '*uso Massalia*' - *for use in Marseille* - stamped on better grade silkworm cocoons exported from the Phallus Festival town of Tyrnavos, in the 19th century. The designation came to be a synonym for 'superior quality,' which the aniseed-flavored rocket fuel was thought to possess. Its high sugar content delayed alcohol absorption in the stomach, misleading the consumer into thinking that it was weaker than it is. The cumulative effect arrives like a higher quality freight train. In my case, it arrived just after our boat left, at the interface between the Gold Kazoo's Teflon exterior, and the tall marine oil painted cabinet it was desperately trying to remain on. As I struggled to keep the octopus in my stomach, my stomach in my sleeping bag, and my sleeping bag on the cabinet, the ship rolled further sideways than I was prepared for. This pitched me onto the deck in a most indelicate fashion, and the ouzo and I inflicted the same punishment on the octopus.

"I guess that's why they call it Greece." Said Steve, in a homophonic flourish. He was obviously inspired by the game of Scrabble he was playing, with a Scottish secretary named Cathy.

"For a man who has been through bitter experiences and travels far can enjoy even his sufferings after a time." Whimpering Homer.

I rejoined them for a chicken and bread repast, and a bottle of not-so-sneaky Demestica, revitalized by my purge. We found a twelve-string guitar, and sang long into the night.

Steve and I said goodbye to Cathy, upon arriving in Iraklion at dawn. There was fresh bread and coffee and oranges at the bus station, and a room at the Ideon Andron Hotel.

"What does it mean?" asked Steve.

"It's the cave, in the middle of the island, where Zeus was born." I said.

We checked in behind two American good ol' boys, with big voices and bigger suitcases.

'Idiot Androids." Said Steve.

We got the room next door to them. When they turned on their bathroom taps, our shower rose wilted into droplets. *Lemon Tree* Redux.

"Water, water, never touch the stuff," Said Steve, in his best W. C. Fields imitation. The showerhead eventually provided enough for two commando scrubs, and Steve and I went out to find Crete.

Its location, in Homer's 'middle of the wine-dark sea,' meant that it also stood in the middle of the forward-Asiatic and north African cultural streams, leading to the West. They flowed into harbors colliding with mountains. Four thousand years before Bonifacio the Crusader sold it to the Venetians for 100 silver marks (and his head sent to the King of Bulgaria), Crete was the centre of an advanced Bronze Age civilization that Will Durant referred to as 'the first link in the European chain.' Arthur Evans, another British archeologist, who performed to the standard of Kathleen Kenyon's amateur hour in Jericho, seriously weakened the links in that chain. He named the culture 'Minoan,' after King Minos of Minotaur and labyrinth fame, although no one really knows what they called themselves. In 1900, Arthur bought the entire site of Knossos, and set about inflicting massive excavations, before rebuilding, repainting, and recreating it, in his own image. If King Minos is still the judge of the dead in Hades, Arthur is in the seat next to him.

Steve and I visited the Archeological Museum, to gaze upon the mysteries of the Minoans. We saw the Phaistos Disc, a fired clay wheel of local hieroglyphics, whose disputed stamped symbols may have migrated all the way from Elam, in Mesopotamia. A little queasy in front of the Octopus stirrup pottery, I moved on to view the Snake Goddess, a bare-breasted brick beauty, with a long skirt and tight open bodice, holding a spiraling serpent in each outstretched hand. The snakes represented the renewal of life, presumably because of the periodic shedding of their skin.

Skin removal seemed to be a popular form of punishment in the crucibles of civilization. Marsyas was a flute player, who challenged the god Apollo to a music competition. When he lost, Apollo flayed him and nailed his skin to a pine tree, a classical Greek tragedy version of the Eurovision Song Contest; back in Israel, the Romans removed the skin of Rabbi Akiva Ben Yosef with hot combs, for refusing to give up his teachings; a ship owner named Daskalogiannis, the most revered Cretan hero of revolt against Ottoman rule in the 1770s, was skinned alive 'in dignified silence,' for his efforts.

According to the lack of evidence to the contrary, however, the Minoans actually enjoyed a fairly peaceful existence, interrupted only by the occasional eruption of the Thera volcano, the odd earthquake, and their ultimate conquest by deforestation, the Mycenaeans, and the arrival of the Iron Age.

We traveled out, to see the results of Arthur's carnage at Knossos. The site was strangely evocative, and Steve and I had it all to ourselves, in the early March sunshine. We each played Hercules for our cameras, pretending to push apart the strange blood red painted wooden columns, flanged with black and yellow stripes at their thicker tops, and planted upside down to prevent tree growth. The pillars held up the remnant palace overhangs that protected the bright colors of the frescoes underneath. Here were cavorting dolphins, and strutting pretty-boy two-dimensional wine-bearing servants with burnt sienna skin and long curled black tresses, and even more beautiful bare-breasted women with alabaster complexions. And they were shown vaulting over charging horned bulls. Steve and I agreed. It would have been a pageant worth paying for.

"There comes a time in the affairs of man when he must take the bull by the tail and face the situation." He said.

Homer wrote that Crete had held ninety cities. Roads of stone blocks, cut with bronze saws, led to multistoried houses and palaces of flagstone floors, stone and mud brick walls, and timbered ceilings with tiled roofs, all plumbed with clay pipes. The Minoans lived well on wild game, and seafood, domesticated animals, wheat, poppy seed, pomegranates, honey, wine, olives, figs, dates, and more. They traded saffron and tin, as far away as Spain and Egypt, and Israel. They had a sophisticated astronomical calendar, based on the sun and the moon, and a special constellation. For the Minoans, Orion was a double-headed axe, and an identity icon of their civilization. In the evening of the autumn equinox, the light of Betelgeuse would appear in the reflected pool in the doorway of the Central Palace Sanctuary, and set the beginning of the New Year.

The *Pax Minoica* would eventually perish, on the horns of their bulls, their serpents, and their double-headed axe. And Steve and I would almost perish, trying to hitchhike out of Iraklion, the next morning.

We discovered that the Cretans do not pick up hitchhikers.

"Start every day off with a smile and get it over with." Said Steve.

We didn't discover why we were having problems, until it was too late. It was mostly my fault. I was rusty from my Israeli inertia, and I'd forgotten that hitchhiking gestures vary with geography. Thumbs mean nothing in Crete. A ride is requested, by custom, with an outstretched hand. But this doesn't work on main roads, because the locals don't understand why you just don't take a bus, since they are so inexpensive.

We walked all day without a single ride.

"On the whole, I'd rather be in Philadelphia." Steve remarked, as his thumb sagged.

After twenty kilometers of frustration, we gave up and flagged down a Chania-bound bus, arriving just before dusk.

"Got any more of that Homer wisdom?" Steve asked, as we disembarked.

"Surely a tramp's life is the worst thing that anyone can come to." Remembering my *Odyssey*.

"What did he die of?" he asked.

"No one really knows." I replied.

"It wasn't rapid transit." He said.

*　　　*　　　*

'The people of Crete unfortunately make more history than they can consume locally.'

H. H. Munro

Our waitress was drunk. And German. She gave Steve and I the gastronomic tour of the kitchen. We were famished after our journey to the west, and we thought the Chania harbor side restaurant could lift the day. It was empty.

"Ja, und so haben wir eine kleine…" She paused. "Ja, OK, you are not German… We have here some fish eggs, a dish of pork fat, some smelly cheese pie, grilled lambs testicles, or a tripe soup."

Steve and I looked at each other. He was a fussy eater at the best of times. I had spent longer in restaurants watching Steve collect data than actually eating.

"Anything else?" He asked

"Ja. We have octopus." She slurred. I could feel the bile rising.

"Do you have Greek salad?" I asked.

"Of course." She said, almost insulted I should have to inquire.

"I'll have a Greek salad," I said. She didn't write it down.

"Und you?" She asked.

"I'll have the smelly cheese pie." Said Steve.

"Und now, für drinken?" she asked.

"What would you recommend?" Steve countered.

"Retsina. Ja, Retsina." She said. I shook my head no, at Steve.

"What's that?" Asked Steve.

"Ja, it's a local wine, very special, sehr aromatisch."

"We'll try that." Steve said.

She staggered back with some unrecognizable dishes, and the Retsina. She made a flourish of pouring large glasses of the stuff.

Steve performed a proportional swallow. It came right out of his mouth as fast as it went in.

"What the…" He tried to say.

42

"Its pine resin." I said. "Sehr aromatisch." I told him they used to seal amphorae with it two thousand years ago and, even after the Romans eliminated the need for it by inventing the barrel, the Greeks still preferred their wine to taste like conifers. This difference in Eastern and Western aesthetics had upset more than one table of negotiations between the two empires.

Brunhilda staggered back to our lone table, with no particular enthusiasm.

"Dessert?" She asked, her voice ascending in resin pitch and volume.

I told Steve about the last time the Germans met the Jews of Chania. The ones they didn't murder outright were sunk by a torpedo in the middle of the wine-dark sea, on their way to the extermination camps. We skipped dessert and made for the exit. The next morning Steve told me he had been sleeping on pine boughs in a forest. I told him he had also been using his chainsaw all night long, and Retsina was off the wine list.

We boarded a bus and played chess to the extreme southwest coast, through mountains, vineyards and orchards, and rainbows in the mist, to beautiful Paleohora. Steve and I hiked to an empty little hostel, on the expansive beach. The black-garbed elderly lady owner gave us a room with a balcony overlooking the Libyan sea, the far off snow-capped mountains, and the lone ship in the middle. It was two dollars a day. We thought of staying for a month, but paid for a week. The rest of the scenery melted into the drizzle, avgolemono soup and moussaka, a walk around the quiet town, a chat with the resident street pelican, and a late afternoon nap. Steve inquired about a nightlife experience.

"You just had it." I said.

But there was nightlife in Paleohora. It was just a day behind us. We were walking along the mostly closed beachfront cafés next afternoon, when we caught the echo.

"Hey!" It said. And there were Louise and Rosie and Debbie,

the Australian girls from the *Lemon Tree* and Athens. Chairs were produced, and the magnetic pole moved just a smidge. There are twenty-five million bottles of Demestica, produced every year in Gustav Clauss's winery in Patras, and we started to count them down. The one disco we managed to pry open later, brought Steve his Paleohora nightlife. Out of my first and last gig as a Greek DJ, came the best dance music that Crete has ever seen. Lord Acton was once quoted as saying that, 'Save for the wild force of Nature, nothing moves in this world that is not Greek in its origin.' Lord Acton never saw Steve of the Jacuzzi, moon-walking with three Australian girls, on a spring night in a small town in southern Crete.

*   *   *

'Smoulders on sea, halfway to Africa,
Stone warrior up to the waist in sea
Blue as an eye and circled by the blood
Of Minotaur and Janissary and German!'
Patrick Leigh Fermor, *Greek Archipelagoes*

The wildflowers had me surrounded. I had crossed a fast moving stream at the end of the beach, only to be overwhelmed by the purples, blues and yellows, surging on the other side. Steve and the girls had taken another route, to a distant picnic spot. Volcanic rock caves and thorny shrubs lined the path down into a dry riverbed until, finally, out onto the seashore, I caught up with them. I would have loved the now extinct wilderness of Crete.

We made our way back, along the sandy arc of the cape, to Maria's, for lunch. She had planted native flowers in large olive oil tins, and set them on the stone lintels, in front of the fading blue painted wooden shutters of her windows. Maria brought us out a large moussaka, a salad, and a bottle of local rosé. She picked a yellow inula from one of the tins, and gave it to Debbie.

"Smell." She said. Debbie smelled. And winced.

"From tears of Helena from Troy." She said, as she pulled off a pink flower from another can, and handed it to me.

"Dittany." She said.

"It doesn't smell of anything, Maria." I said.

"Not for smell, is for make you strong." She said, pinching both of us at the same time. She turned and laughed herself silly, all the way back into the kitchen.

That evening we all descended onto the beach, to a bonfire we saw at the edge of the seashore. It was a group of newly arrived Germans, with guitars and bongos, under a full moon. The two ringleaders, Volkmar and Ziggy, were very funny, and welcomed us heartily. We sang until our voices couldn't. Rosie and Debbie and I left Steve with Louise. I escorted them back to their pension on the way to my hostel. Steve arrived not long after, quiet until he fell asleep. The nails in the rafters kept time.

The remaining days in Paleohora were as idyllic as the previous ones. The bells of our donkeys jingled to their own time signature, through the mountains and olive groves, to more remote villages. On slopes, stones came to life again. We sang to the waves on the beach at night. Marias's became our headquarters and, as well as her magnificent moussakas, we discovered her dolmades and homemade yoghurt. She discovered her joy in pinching Debbie and I, and watching our averted eyes and rising cheek color.

Volkmar and Ziggy taught us a German drinking game one evening. In return, I taught them 'Thumper' and 'Colonel Puff.' No one should have won that kind of scholarship. But Debbie and I slipped away, and found a vacant room at Maria's. We filled it with yellow and pink flowers, and fell asleep.

When we awoke quietly about four-thirty in the morning, Debbie and I made our way towards where the evening began. Everyone we had left was still in their original places, except they were now still there because of paralysis. Steve was hilarious.

"It's the hat." He shouted. "It's the hat."

"Vat is the hat?" Asked Ziggy.

"It has nothing to do with the hat." I said.

"Oh Yeah? What would your buddy Homer have to say about the hat?" Steve asked.

"For it is the bold man who every time does best, at home or abroad." I said, and dragged him off to our hostel, to work on the roof nails.

It was slow the next morning, but it was finally time to leave. The girls came with us to Iraklion and, after a tour of the old Venetian fortress, we reboarded the *Knossos* for the overnight voyage back to Piraeus. We probed the first class lounge, and ordered martinis. As I was drawing a picture of an olive for the bartender, our real identities were discovered, and we received an official escort back onto the deck. And Debbie and I huddled together through the night, under the moon and Orion and the Gold Kazoo, in the middle of the wine-dark sea.

'I felt once more how simple a thing is happiness: a glass of wine, a roast chestnut, a wretched little brazier, the sound of the sea. Nothing else. And all that is required to feel that here and now is happiness is a simple, frugal heart.'

Zorba the Greek

The Air Between the Columns

At Athens, wise men propose, and fools dispose. In my wisdom, I let Debbie propose the Student Inn in the Plaka. She asked for a double room.

"You want to hold hands, eh?" Said the owner from behind the front desk. Sukros was paternally protective. He remembered Debbie from her stay here, before Crete. He turned to Steve, who could have doubled for his Greek brother.

"You look like me." He said. "What do you think about this?"

"It's the hat." He said.

I rolled my eyes, and took the keys.

"How great are the dangers I face to win a good name in Athens." I said.

"Alexander the Great." Said Sukros.

"Steve of the Jacuzzi." Said Steve, shaking his hand.

After breakfast with Rosie and Louise, we all went out to see the rudiments of Paradise and the eye of Greece, mother of arts, and eloquence. The blue and white national colors streamed across the spring sky over the city of Plato and Aristotle, and the rest of the endless proposing wise men and disposing fools of my early Classical education.

Athens was where the myth of the Heroic ideal as a Man of

Action underwent an irreversible chemical reduction to a Man of Conviction, through a jar of hemlock. It was all the fault of her first citizen. Pericles had brought Athens her Golden Age. He turned the Delian league into an Athenian empire, and built the Acropolis and Parthenon into enduring symbols of classical art and literature, and freedom and democracy. But the road up and the road down are one and the same, and Pericles drove the usual predeterminism of Greek tragedy, into a deliberate choice. He chose to start the Peloponnesian War with the Spartans. The bubonic plague, that killed him and a third of his fellow Athenians a year after it began, was a speed bump in a tailspin back into the parochial austerity of 'with your shield, or on it.' When Lysander finally sailed into Piraeus and destroyed the Athenian fleet, 27 years later, his triumphant message home to Sparta, 'Athens is taken,' received the laconic reply 'All you needed to say was 'Taken.''

In defeat, Athens would evolve, from seeking a central destiny of physical power, to a civilization of intellectual inquiry. The Homeric hero of deeds became the Socratic hero of convictions. And I too, in my own developing mythology, came off the road adventures of my South American and African odyssey, down the mellifluous streams that watered all the schools. I was arriving in Athens in synchronicity with how Athens arrived, as the cradle of Western Civilization. Unlike Socrates, however, I was downshifting from a citizen of the world, into an Athenian.

But the road up and the road down are one and the same, and Steve and the girls and I hiked the steep track to the mathematical candor of the Parthenon. The air was hewn out from between the bird skull off-white columns, in blinding light proportion. It was the exoskeleton of all that good men aspire to- grace and intelligence, with bravery and mercy. And yet, this epicenter of human dignity had suffered every inhuman indignity. The Turks had burnt fallen sculptures, to obtain lime for building material. The munitions they stored here ignited, under bombardment from the Venetians, collapsing the roof, and most of the intricate carvings. With the advent of portability came the looting. The most notorious thievery was enacted in 1806 by Thomas Bruce, the Earl of Elgin, who sold his now namesake 'moldering shrine' marbles to the British Museum, for less than the transport cost to get them there. Pollution, and the pointed metal dental cleaning methods employed by the museum staff, did the misshapen monuments no additional favor, as the Parthenon itself appeared more like a smile, with those same teeth missing. During the Greek War of Independence, the Turks melted the lead within the columns to make bullets. And there was vandalism on the Acropolis, and in the British Museum. The biggest indignity the Parthenon was destined to suffer, however, may not have been structural. Twenty-five hundred years after its creation, a self-proclaimed 'Big Aristotle' basketball player with a Bachelor of Arts, an MBA, a PhD in Education, and heir to all the adulation that Western Civilization can muster, was asked whether he had visited the Parthenon, during his trip to Greece.

"I can't remember the names of the clubs we went to." He said.

Who brings owls to Athens? Shaquille O'Neal. And who weeps for Pericles? Western Civilization.

*   *   *

'It is not everyone that can get to Corinth.'
Horace

It almost wasn't us either. We all left the Student Inn the next day on the next train, heading in two directions. The first one had already pulled away, despite the Marathon we undertook across the city to catch it. The stationmaster played the Spartan king to our Pheidippides.

"Όχι." He said. *No*.

We came to the Peloponnese, across the deep narrow trench of the Corinth canal. The afternoon sun didn't quite penetrate, all the way down the sheer white clay walls, to the blue ribbon of Aegean infinity far below. The Romans had begun the excavation with six thousand Jewish slaves, on orders from Nero. Two thousand years later, local children were collecting the flapping fish, brought up by the submersible bridges.

Debbie, Louise and Rosie were going to Italy. Steve and I got off in Corinth, late in the day. I did my best Lord Byron. *'Maid of Athens, ere we part, Give, oh give me back my heart!'* And they laughed with us through the open window, and blew backward kisses, as their train pulled away forever. We found the Acropolis Hotel, a pastitsio and salad dinner, and Hypnos. I dreamt in cinnamon and nutmeg and allspice. Steve, like Polyphemus on his back, reverberated off the roof of the Cyclops cave.

The dolomite mountain dawn pried apart the sky and the purple sea. Whitecaps reached up to their reflection in the clouds. Steve and I felt the angry liquid grasp of Poseidon, earth-shaking his golden trident in the swelling brine. What his dolphins and horses had lost to Athena's olive tree in the founding of Athens, he more than made up for, as the chief god of Corinth, and the sheer numbers of children he had by as many willing paramours. Hardly a testimony to her skill, two of his sons were accidently killed by the huntress Artemis, in separate incidents. On the limestone precipice above us sat the ancient Acorinth fortress, where Cenchrias' mother, Peirene, on hearing of Artemis's clumsiness, transformed herself into a spring, with her tears. We climbed to its white marble arches, and drank from the same open pool as the snake-haired Medusa, and winged Pegasus. The other victim of the arrows of Artemis was Orion, killed by a planned deception of her disapproving brother, Apollo. We descended to one of the oldest shrines in Greece, seven chunky Doric columns, acting as the sole support for the preeminent Temple of Apollo, shelter to a thousand sacred prostitutes. In 146 BC, the Romans put all the Corinthian men to the sword, and sold the women and children into slavery, before they torched the place. It's not everyone that can get to Corinth. Apparently, it's also not everyone that can leave.

Steve and I managed it, flagging a ride with Tasa to the illuminated Venetian castles, under the snowcapped backdrop of Nafthlion.

"My name means 'resurrection' in English." Said Tasa, too late to be of any use to the Corinthians.

We checked into the Hotel Empiricon for 400 drachmas, and then hitchhiked again down to Epidavros. We sat in the 'stone chairs for the statues of fisherman,' in the vertical amphitheatre. A tour guide, with his paying guests, struck a match at centre stage of the 15,000-seat theatre. *Whooshsh.* Steve and I heard it in the bleachers, for free. The stone seats acted as a high pass filter, and the view was incorporated into the drama.

We had come from the town of Poseidon, to the temple of Apollo, to the birthplace of Apollo's son, Asclepius, god of medicine. The most celebrated healing centre of the Classical world was the Asclepieion at Epidavros, and the afflicted traded all their possessions, to make the pilgrimage.

After a ritual purification ceremony, that included offerings to the gods of anything they had left, the supplicants would spend the night in the *abaton* dormitory hall, the holiest part of the sanctuary. Snakes slithered over the floor as they slept. The dreams they reported to the priest the next morning, formed the basis for his prescribed cure. Sacred dogs licked the more visible wounds of sick petitioners. The mentally ill would crawl in the dark through the *tholos*, a serpent-infested beehive-shaped labyrinth, cathartic screams forming their therapy. Judging by the remaining ratio of rubble to ruin, the Romans and pirates and Goths that laid waste to the place, had adopted a more naturopathic approach to disease, and the resultant screaming had been an even more holistic experience.

We returned to Nafthlion for an evening of spanakopita, salad, Demestica, and another three girls from a land down under. The geographical inspiration of 'where women glow and men plunder,' had obviously originated with the realization that the women were all away, travelling in Greece. One of the Aussies decided to hitchhike with Steve and I next morning, to the citadel of Mycenae. Diana was the Roman equivalent of Artemis, in skill as well as name. We tried to flag down vehicles for three straight hours, but the other gods were hostile, or indifferent. A local bus got us to Argos, and another to the cemetery at the ruins, where we hid our backpacks. Diana took a picture of Steve and I, leaning into the same heraldic pose as the paired stretching felines, on the Lion Gate above us. It was from under this lintel that Agamemnon left, to avenge the infidelity of his brother's wife. Both he and Menelaus had married Spartan women, in their forced exile from Mycenae. They were there because of the previous adulterous escapade involving their mother, Aerope, who had slept with their father's twin brother, Uncle Thyestes. Their father, Atreus, killed Thyestes' children and fed them to him. Thyestes went on to have a son, Aegisthus, by his own daughter. Putting the fun back into dysfunctional. Aegisthus killed Atreus and put his father on the Mycenean throne, banishing Agamemnon and Menelaus, who sought refuge at Sparta. When the dustup had settled, Menelaus had succeeded to the Spartan throne, and Agamemnon had driven out Thyestes and Aegisthus, to become king of Mycenae. And then the legend began. Menelaus's wife, Helen, ran off with a Trojan named Paris. And Agamemnon went under the Lion gate after her. After ten years of laying siege to Troy, Agamemnon's remaining Achaean troops piled into a large wooden horse, and waited until the Trojan's curiosity got the better of them. Much had been written about the annihilation of Troy, but there is no authenticated record. It was the beginning of the Greek Dark Ages. Most of Agamemnon's soldiers ended up founding their own colonies, on distant shores. Mycenae succumbed to the force of the Sea Peoples, or the Dorian migrations.

We retrieved our backpacks from the cemetery, and waved goodbye to Diana. After a sunlit picnic of bread and feta and oranges, and a couple of backgammon games, Steve and I hit hitchhiker pay dirt, when a beautiful green Mercedes eased over to pick us up. Stannis took us past breathtakingly beautiful snowcapped mountains, and roadside memorials for those that didn't make it, to a Greek coffee interlude, on the windswept terrace of an empty seaside café. Poseidon thoughtfully sent us whitecaps, to match the thick froth on our frappés.

Stannis put his hand out the window, as he left down the road to Athens. He had dropped us in Tripoli, beside the large statue of a saber-wielding helmeted man on horseback. We pronounced the phonetic sounds of the long bronze name on the granite base. Θεόδωρος Κολοκοτρώνης. Theodore Kolokotronis, hero of the Greek War of Independence against the Ottoman Empire. It was here in Tripoli, in September of 1821, however, that Theodore's heroism would be compromised by a shameful savagery. After a siege of several months, the Greek army broke through a blind spot in one of the walls and, for the next three days, its 8000 Muslim and Jewish inhabitants were tortured and killed, in the Massacre of Tripolitsa. People suspected of having concealed wealth had their limbs cut off, and were slowly roasted over fires. Pregnant women were cut open, decapitated, and dog's heads stuck between their legs. Frantic starving children were cut down and shot. Corpses poisoned the wells, and the ravines in the neighboring mountains were scenes of desperate butchery. When

Theodore entered the city, his horse's hoofs never touched the ground, from the gate to the citadel.

Once again, Steve and I faired better. Unsuccessful in a late afternoon attempt to hitchhike out of town, we checked into the Hotel Acropole, and listened to stories about the Second World War from the ancient owner. He told us of his meeting with Rommel.

"Speak English?"

"Όχι." He said. *No.*

"French?"

"Όχι." He said. *No.*

"German?"

"Όχι." He said. *No.*

"Greek?"

"Λίγο." He said. *A little.*

But those that understood him smiled at one another and shook their heads; but, for mine own part, it was Greek to me.

*   *   *

'An ancient dictum says that when Zeus wanted to destroy someone, he would first drive him mad.

Jean-Marie Le Pen

Steve and I headed out into the rolling hills early next morning. We pulled our packs out of the long shadows of tall poplars, reeling in short rides with our thumbs- Kapsia, Karkalou, and the names of a dozen other small towns of Arcadia, spun off the front of our tongues, and the back of our tires. We passed goat herders and their flocks, on the sloping hillside of Langadia, and its orange roof-topped stone houses. We stopped for the yeast smell of fresh-baked *psomi* bread in Vitina, and roasted coffee in a village where the women returned to cleaning their guns as we left. We halted briefly for a girl, crying over the crumpled form under a motorcycle. Our driver turned to look at me. I shook my head. We drove on. Finally, in Dafnia, Steve and I played chess, while we waited for the bus that would take us the last few miles to Olympia, and the poplar shadows lengthening again, outside our hostel.

The first Olympic games had emerged there, twenty-seven hundred years before Steve and I did. They were dedicated to Zeus, as was his magnificent local temple, inside of which sat one of the seven wonders of the ancient world. The sculptor Phidias had taken twelve years to complete the 43 foot-high gold and ivory statue of Zeus. If he had been able to stand, his sculpted wreath of olive sprays would have unroofed the temple. He was the most famous artistic work in Greece. His robe and his sandals were made of gold. Beyond podiatry, however, was pedastry. High above the sandals, inscribed into Zeus's little finger, was the word 'Pantarkes,' the name of the teenage boy *erômenos,* that represented the ancient Greek male ideal of perfect love. The pedophilic preference was for no hair, anywhere. Putting the fun back in dysfunctional. Steve and I were hirsutely more comfortable with the spiral inscription, in the three hundred pound block of sandstone, over at the Archeological museum, which said 'Bybon threw me over his head with one hand.' Or with the nearby statue of Hermes, his face and torso polished to a high gloss, by generations of female temple workers.

After visiting Nero's villa, the Palaestra, and other sites around the complex, we finished, standing nervously under the ruins of the limestone block arch entrance to the Stadium, trying to imagine the cheers we might have garnered, had we been allowed to cross under, and into immortality, two millennia earlier. It went quiet.

Moving on to a less Olympian contest of skill and strength, I stopped a half-ton truck with my thumb. Unfortunately, this appeared to displease Zeus, Lord of the Sky and God of Rain. Perhaps he was upset at our problem with his pedastry but, for whatever reason, he threw open the heavens, and let loose his lightning bolts. *Can't you hear, can't you hear the thunder? You better run, you better take cover.* Only slow and incremental hitching got us through the Peloponnesian precipitation, to Patras, and shelter. It was no better the next day. Poseidon's liquid plains extended over the roadbed. We walked through eight kilometers of puddles until Steve, in one of those rare moments of hitchhiking karma, flagged down a mathematician, heading all the way to Athens. Zeus turned his back on us. The sun switched on large.

Once again, in the Plaka, Sukros checked Steve and I into the Student Inn. New friends awaited. Demetrios was a large moustache from Canada, taking a year to study in Athens. His new girlfriend, Sue, was from Australia, *where women glow and men plunder*. Nick the Greek, and Alexander the Great, were Athenian companions. After souvlaki and Greek salad, we played guitar, and slow games of chess, in the spring warmth of Syntagma Square. It was a halcyon day, in the true classical Greek mythological sense of the word. Zeus was subdued, a bright interval of blue sky calm prevailed, and birds were nesting, in the air between the columns.

Alexander the Great asked me if there was anything I lacked. I gave him Diogenes.

"Yes, that I do: that you stand out of my sun a little."

"Were you a hero like Zeus, Uncle Wink?" asked Sam.

"Not at all, Sam." I said. "Zeus was a traditional superhero in Greek myth. He was like Superman. I was more like Batman."

"How is Batman different?" he asked. A shooting star streaked across the sky, above the ocean.

"There are many kinds of heroes, Sam. Most stories in real life have no hero, and real life has less meaning for it. The traditional superhero is indestructible, a paragon of ethical behavior, and easily handles any crisis, for himself and us. He is all-powerful, and totally boring.

Then there is the tragic hero, a flawed puppet of fate with inner demons who, because of their humanity, is doomed to fail. They fall headlong down the path of personal destruction, and may save our day, but not their own. They're more interesting than Superman, but nobody wakes up and wants to be one.

The comic hero is the hero of blind luck. He somehow manages to save the day, but usually only through some close slapstick coincidence. He may be a sidekick, or a catalyst for change in a more traditional hero. Again, no one wants to be this kind of hero. Luck is not a skill, or a superpower. It always runs out, and real life would kill the comic hero quickly.

There is the rogue hero, an antagonistic character, who would normally be considered a villain. He is only a hero because the evil he faces is worse than he is. He saves his own day, but not ours. He is the American hero of the next century."

"What about Batman?" asked Millie.

"The last and best kind of hero, Millie. Batman, Han Solo, and Orion, are Anti-heroes. They're the smartest, and therefore the most cynical, of champions. Society considers them to posses far less worthy qualities than traditional heroes, outlaws even, but Anti-heroes have seen the evil and corruption and naïveté that Society is capable of, and are prepared to use flexible methods to achieve honorable ends. They are the heroes of the New World and the late twentieth century. They may have the same dark gruff and moody exterior as the rogues, but inside is all sweetness and sympathy, like prickly-pear cactus. Anti-heroes have troubled histories, their behavior not just a little self-destructive, and they suffer from unrequited love. Be careful lest in casting out devils you cast out the best thing that's in you."

"Is that the kind of hero you were, Uncle Wink? She asked.

"I'm afraid so, Millie. Afraid so."

Songs of the Sirens

'The Siren waits thee, singing song for song.'
Walter Savage Landor

"Nice skirts." Said Sue. "I love the black pompoms on their red booties."

I could see Nick and Alexander wince, a few seconds before the same shiver hit Demetrios. We had all spent far too long at Peter's Pub the night before, and the stark morning light, on the Changing of the Guard in Syntagma Square, was surreal.

"Their skirts are called fustanellas." Said Alexander. "They come from the uniform of the mountain bandits, that used to fight the Ottoman Turks." He told us about the Klephts, how they always woke up in a different place from where they went to sleep, how their goats were cooked underground so that no smoke would betray them, how the Turks impaled and roasted them alive or broke their long bones with sledgehammers, and about how tough they really were.

The Evzone guards we were watching were just as valorous as their inspiration. When a Molotov cocktail set one of the guardhouses on fire, during a demonstration, the Evzone standing next to it not only didn't blink, he didn't move, until his superior officer arrived and gave him the order. One side of his scorched uniform was seen to be smoking, as he marched away.

"They're a lot more than skirts and pompoms." Added Demetrios.

The Greek War of Independence had consumed, and eventually killed, Lord Byron. In bizarre homage, this was where the Hero in the history of Western Civilization went from the Homeric, through the Socratic, to the Byronic. The hero of deeds, and then convictions, became the hero of romance. He possessed great talent and passion, distaste for society and its institutions, and a lack of respect for rank and privilege (although he had both). He had a secret past, and had been thwarted in love by social constraint. His character was flawed, arrogant, overconfident and, ultimately, self-destructive. He lived in rebellion and exile.

"Sounds like you, Wink." Said Steve. In previous days, in Peloponnese passes, he had commented that my Odyssey was an 'empty life.' And well it might have seemed. Steve was an established professional, with property and prospects, and I appeared to have become an itinerant wanderer.

"Surely a tramp's life is the worst thing that anyone can come to." He said, hoisting me with my own Homeric petard.

I countered with Socrates, who had divided humanity into lovers of wisdom, lovers of honor, and lovers of gain. I was still working on the first one. My path may have been linear, but there was a huge potential harvest, in the area under the curve.

We walked down to the National Archeological Museum, to marvel at the sophistication of the Antikythera Mechanism, a Corinthian bronze-age computer, that could accurately calculate astronomical positions, eclipses, and Olympiads. Steve bought everyone moussaka, white wine and ice cream, for betting on his confusion between Athena and Artemis. The rest of the day migrated to Demetrios's apartment, for continued good company, and a pikilia of grilled seafood.

Late evening found Steve and I in Piraeus, looking for a boat, to the islands of the Dodecanese. We found one going to Kos. It was a cool night in March. Zeus provided a light sea breeze that ran along the running lights, as we pulled out of port. Steve and I played on my Sudanese chess set. A German girl with long dark hair and a siren smile played spectator to the moves of the pieces on the board. Her Swedish friend, Lena, closed the squares on the last side of the table. There was Greek fire on the water.

"You should have ditched the hat." Steve muttered between moves.

"You might need to lash me to the mast." I mumbled back. Queen's rook to check.

Monika was from Nuremberg, and heading for trouble. Her and Lena were on vacation. When I gagged at the sight of the bottle of ouzo they produced, they brought out a bottle of orange juice, to mix it with. My octopus phobia was still an issue, but Monika's tentacles were something else again. I prevailed in chess. Monika won in enchantment. The Aegean night sky sent a perfumed breeze over a ship's blanket, and the Gold Kazoo, on the moonlit deck. Kafka had remarked that someone might escape from the sirens' singing, but never from their silence. It was quiet all the way to Kos.

> 'By the deep sea, and music in its roar: I love not man the less, but Nature more.'
>
> Lord Byron

*   *   *

> 'Hippocrates is an excellent geometer but a complete fool in everyday affairs.'
>
> Aristotle

I had come to Kos the same way Kos had come to me. Deliberate and studied, past the imposing Neratzia fortress of the Knights of St. John. Its most famous son was a bearded physician, born seven hundred years after the cult of Asclepius had arrived on the island, from Epidavros. *'Life is short, the art long.'* He had written twenty-four centuries before Steve and I got off the boat. I had perused Hippocrates as a medical student, but he hadn't been required reading. *'A physician without a knowledge of Astrology has no right to call himself a physician.'* May have been an indication of why. The art was long, but the science was now longer. Even so, he was the Father of Western Medicine, and I was one of his adopted descendents and devotees. Hippocrates had been imprisoned for twenty years, for his defiant beliefs. I had been exiled to the Canadian prairies, for throwing the Dean of Medicine into the coed swimming pool naked. The acorn doesn't fall far from the tree.

Steve and I borrowed bikes from our small pension, and rode the uphill trail through cypresses, long grass and buttercups, to the four terraces of the Asklepion. Between the remaining upright pillars of the most famous medical school in history, I demonstrated the correct technique of examination for Steve's liver and spleen, on an elevated section of the stone foundation. Monika wheeled up the path on her own bike, and we drank from the healing spring, under the bas-relief face of Pan's watchful gaze. He would have told Aristotle that I was a complete fool in everyday affairs.

Later that evening Steve and I walked into to the Snack Bar Maritina, a local taverna full of noise and smoke and fishermen.

"καλησπέρα!" Shouted the moustache, drying the glasses behind the bar. "Welcome."

"Καθίστε μαζί μας." Said the fishermen. We sat with them. A plate of pikilia arrived, brimming with calamari, salmon, tsitsiki, kalamata olives, and octopus. Big grilled fat tentacles, speckled with oregano, gripping pools of olive oil and vinegar. It was good. *'Let your food be your medicine, and your medicine be your food.'* Bottles of local Hatziemmanouil banged onto the wooden table. *'Hunger is alleviated by the drinking of neat wine.'*

"Efharisto." Said Steve.

"ευχαριστώ!" They rejoiced, thrilled that Steve and I could communicate in Greek. Which wasn't true at all, of course. Until Nick and Pete and Antonio taught us those songs, or maybe it was the ouzo, or the atmosphere, I'm not really sure. I know we were speaking what sounded like Greek, and they were nodding and slapping our backs, like we were real native sons. I still remember it all later, when an amazing tenor, with gold teeth, took over the music. The songs were about the cycle of life, mournful and lyrical Byzantine monotones, with spasms of Turkish tension pulling on bouzouki strings and Hellenic hearts. We left thanking them for democracy and freedom and octopus and ouzo and *opa!* and broken plates and napkins up into the air, and down into the serene exuberance of two more sleeping frogs around the pond.

We awoke on Independence Day, and hurried down to the seaside boulevard lined with phoenix palms, Norfolk pines, and the hard-pruned plane trees, cross-connected with lampposts, by cords of triangular blue-and-white flag pennants flapping in the breeze. We pushed into the crowd of headscarves and cub scouts, for a view of the parade. Under the flags marched Hellenic banners, stretched between garlanded young girls in snow-cotton dresses, followed by Evzones and Klephts, columns of boy knights carrying cloth shields with hand-painted crosses, red-vests and powder-blue harem pants, and a dozen other costumes I didn't recognize. Clarinets and cornets played, under blue sky and white clouds and peaked military caps too large for the puffed out cheeks under them. Steve and I followed the band to the square, in front of the blue and green grape clusters, embossed on the whitewashed curves of the 'ΔΗΜΟΤΙΚΗ ΑΓΟΡΑ' market arches. We crossed our hands, and danced in large circles with pretty girls in black dresses, not quite with the sidelined blessings of the unimpressed Orthodox priests, with their eyeglass frames as thick, and as black, as their beards. Later we shared a final Nescafe with Monika and Lena, across from their boat in the harbor. The small alabaster statue of Hippocrates I bought, still sits in my office today. We cuddled a baby lamb with our fisherman friends, in the Maratina that evening. Our own overnight boat to Rodos would leave a few hours later. The Dodecanese were islands of Byzantine churches and Venetian castles and Nazi atrocities. Kos had also brought us wine, silk, sirens and the wisdom of Hippocrates. '*You will find, as a general rule, that the constitutions and the habits of a people follow the nature of the land where they live.*' The nature of this land I liked, a lot.

Mirte: "I can grant your most secret desire."
Darios: "Which one?"
The Colossus of Rhodes (1961)

Snapped at the knees. Into the Mandraki harbor sunrise, we sailed between the two bronze fallow deer, standing on their high stone pillars, where he had been snapped at the knees. They seemed to be searching, out to the sea we had just crossed, for a reason, but the reason was simple.

In 226 BC an earthquake toppled the thirty meter high Colossus, as the Colossus had toppled his creator, fifty-six years earlier. Chares of Lindos had won the contract to build the largest bronze statue in the ancient world, because of an oversight. He was asked how much it would cost, to build a sculpture fifty feet high. When he was asked the price of one twice as tall, he answered twice as much, forgetful or ignorant of the actual eight-fold increase in materials that the doubling of height would require. The mistake drove him into bankruptcy, and suicide, snapped at the knees.

One of the Seven Wonders of the Ancient World, the Colossus of Rhodes was commissioned to commemorate the defeat of Demetrius I of Macedon. In addition to his fame as the besieger of cities, Demetrius had a reputation for besieging young boys. A particularly unfortunate youth, Democles the Handsome, found himself cornered the baths one day and, rather than submit to the charms of the Macedonian king, tore the lid off a cauldron of boiling water, and jumped in.

Two thousand years after Demetrius abandoned his siege engines, the Macedonians would exact their revenge against Rhodes. Steve and I wandered into its medieval streets, under the shadow of the castle gates. There were dead animals everywhere. On hangers. On mannikins. Dead animals from Kastoria, the world's capital of fur manufacturing, in

Macedonia. Rhodes was the place where mink came to die, leg-hold snapped at the knees.

We checked into Hotel La Luna, Tony's cozy pension in the old city, and found an open-air café around the corner that would become our regular restaurant. A Greek-American named Gus, who would take a fatherly interest in ensuring the wellbeing of two wayfaring idiot androids, owned Freshway Foods. He, and Menelaus the waiter, became our personal valets, always with a word of caution or encouragement, depending on our plan of the moment. We left to fall asleep on the beach. Sweet sun. Arms over eyes, drifting in and out, feeling the radiation. The Colossus had been a statue of Helios, the cult deity of Rhodes, and the Greek Sun god who restored sight to the blinded Orion. Streams of light penetrated through my closed fingers, serving saccades of colored halos across my retinal backcourt. I was recharging.

Steve asked me about the history of the tribe on Rhodes.

"The usual carnage." I said. "When the Arabs captured the place in 604 AD, a Jewish merchant from Homs bought and transported the bronze scrap remains of the Colossus on 900 camels, back to Syria. Good business, bad karma. After an epidemic of bubonic plague in 1498, the Knights Hospitallers expelled those who would not be baptized, only to drag them back as slaves two decades later, to build the flying buttressed fortifications of the Palace of the Grand Master of the Knights of Rhodes. In 1840 there was a nasty blood libel, resulting in a blockade of the Jewish quarter for twelve days, with the requisite torture and false confessions. The Nazis sent the rest of them to Auschwitz in 1944, snapped at the knees.

I was sure the young German girl and her mother, having dinner back at Freshway, had no idea of that history. Anthea was here for the furs and jewelry, and Petra was here for Anthea. We joined them, and local Yorgos and Katerini, at a larger table, for beans, salad, tsitsiki, bread, wine, and conversation. Gus and Menelaus kept time. After they had all left, an amorous local divorcee sent a glass of Metaxa over to my table. Behind her, Menelaus pointed, to one of his eyes. I nodded my appreciation in her general direction, finished quickly, and left.

The next three days dissolved into Aegean seawater, and Freshway frappés. Steve and I escorted Anthea and Petra around the old city on their last day, amused by the sheer volume of fur coats and jewelry, that two women could try on in an afternoon. Calamari became an intermediary metabolite. We wandered through the Acropolis, Stadium, and the Temple of Pythian, and lay on the grey-pebbled beach of Akti Miaouli, playing chess and reading. Helios was at the top of his game. Steve was smiling under his bucket hat.

"For a man who has been through bitter experiences and travels far can enjoy even his sufferings after a time." He said.

"W. C. Fields?" I asked.

"Homer." He said. "Touché."

We approached our usual table at Freshway that evening, but Gus and Menelaus ran interference, before we sat down.

"But we always sit here, Gus." I said.

"Tonight, you sit around the corner." He replied.

Then I saw why. Through the umbrellas, around the other side, was a radiance. Two sisters from Holland had Menelaus prancing like a pony. Gus seated us, at an adjacent table. The barometric pressure went so far off the dial, it looked like our shyness would sink us, into the avgolemono soup. Deadlock. But we needn't have worried.

Out of the kitchen came a Greek sheepdog puppy, followed by Menelaus, with a few kitchen scraps, for both tables. I thought she said her name was Hera, and well she could have been. Hera, Queen of Heaven, wife of Zeus, a spray of milk from her breast forming the celestial Milky Way. Her name was Ira, but her gorgeous eyes, aquiline nose, raven hair and alabaster skin, would have bested anything Hera ever brought to the prom. I was snapped at the knees.

"Hic Rhodus, hic salta." Whispered Gus. *Rhodes is here, here perform your jump.*

Steve and I patted the puppy like a basketball, as we traveled from our table to theirs. Ira was a stewardess, on holiday with her sister, Yvonna. After far too much talk about the weather, we arranged to meet them the next morning, for an excursion to Lindos. Sleep came, and went, and came again.

By the time Ira and Yvonna pulled up next morning, on the comical miniature tires of their lichen-green Suzuki rental, I had made ten drachmas busking harmonica. A cramped formality returned with their arrival, which Steve and I found initially puzzling. And then, the reason Yvonna seemed more distant than Ira, became evident. She was married, Ira divorced. Steve was in the back with Yvonna; I was in the front with Ira. Ira was wearing pearls. Pearls.

"It's the hat." Said Steve, resigned.

"What's the hat?" Asked Yvonna.

"Nothing." I said, as Ira drove the car into a river. We broke the ice pushing it out. Ira melted the rest with her eyes.

Surrounded by the sea, she maneuvered us up winding streets, through the dense white icing puddle of houses, to the fortress layer cake Acropolis, at Lindos. Later, along gravel roads and olive orchards, we crossed the mountains, to Laerma, for beer and oranges, and the Tharri monastery. Einstein's contribution of Special Relativity accompanied our journey, back to the old city. As time dilated, the space in the back seat widened, and length contracted in the front. When we met them that evening at the Taverna Kolossus, for martinis and moussaka, the electromagnetic forces of attraction and repulsion had become more assertive. Ira and I left Steve and Yvonna, to leave each other. We drove down the coast, towards exquisite voluptuousness, and arrived at our yearning. I tore the lid off a cauldron of boiling water, and jumped in.

We all met for breakfast next morning at Freshway. Gus and Menelaus had it all figured out, even before we sat down, if their massaging Steve's shoulders and patting me on the back was any indication. We drove down to the ancient Mycenean site of Kamiros, where I tripped and fell, snapped at the knees. I rolled down a hill, scraping my knuckles, bruising everything else, and losing my harmonica, equilibrium, and pride. Worst of all, I smashed Oracle II, the Olympus Xa camera I had bought in Panama, a year and a half earlier.

It was difficult saying goodbye to Ira the following day, but she and Yvonna needed to fly home, to Holland. I promised to visit her in Beverwijk. Steve and I returned to Freshway Foods, with a present for Menelaus, a priapic statuette of the Colossus, his tumescence harpooned into one of the potatoes he had served us, the previous night. Gus was on the floor.

"Wink-lah!" Boomed out behind me. I turned to find Mark, one of my interns from Woodstock Hospital in Cape Town, grinning from ear to ear. He and his wife Rosie joined us for dinner and conversation. Between his stories and Steve's, were two continents of others.

We left them to board the *Kamiros*, our overnight boat back to Piraeus. Sailing west between the two bronze fallow deer, standing on their high stone pillars, our sleep was continually disturbed, by swarms of noisy Greek teenagers. Furtive fingers removed the travelers cheques from my money belt. If Kos had been about medicine, Rhodes was all physics, chemistry, and bankruptcy. Love in the ruins, and ruination in the love.

The Isles of Greece, the Isles of Greece!' Lord Byron would have snapped at the knees.

> 'Why man, he doth bestride the narrow world
> Like a Colossus, and we petty men
> Walk under his huge legs and peep about
> To find ourselves dishonorable graves.'
> Shakespeare, *Julius Caesar*

*   *   *

'Beauty is the oracle that speaks to us all.'
Luis Barragan

It was the gas. Even the ancient Greeks had a suspicion. They attributed her predictive accuracy to the sweet-smelling vapors, coming off the rotting corpse of the Python, which Apollo killed. She was Pythia, priestess of the Oracle of Delphi and, after she brought her tripod chair to the edge of the chasm, chewing laurel leaves and gazing into her Kassotis water-imaging bowl, she got stoned. The vapors were ethylene gas, an anesthetic, capable enough of causing hallucinations, even at lower doses. In nature, when plants are stimulated, its release induces femaleness, opens flowers, and ripens fruit. Pythias' hexameter verses came from the six connected atoms, emanating out of the rock vents below her. Her response to questions of citizens, foreigners, kings, and philosophers, on issues of personal importance, political impact, war, duty, crime, and laws, was the highest authority in Ancient Greece. The supreme court of western civilization was a 'blameless older woman,' tripping on a plant hormone. There be dragons.

'The ancient oracle said that I was the wisest of all the Greeks.
It is because I alone, of all the Greeks, know that I know nothing.'
Socrates

Steve and I came off the *Kamiros,* onto a bus to Delphi. It was enroute that I realized, that some other reptile had stolen my cheques. Despite the loss, I was entranced with the Delphic panorama on Mount Parnassus, and its Athenian Treasury, the hearth of the Temple of Apollo, the Stadium and the Theatre, the quilt-patched columns of the Tholos, and, in the museum, the glass eyes of the bronze Charioteer. Outside, we brewed some coffee on my stove, and watched the Americans and French group packages, fight over seats on their tour coach, before taking our own local bus back to Athens.

Sukros welcomed us back to the Student Inn, and commiserated about my stolen travelers cheques.

"Where there is a sea, there are pirates." He said.

"I've been a pirate, Sukros." I said. "And we didn't prey on our shipmates."

Steve and I walked through the Plaka, to our sunlit square. He had borrowed my hat.

We found Demetrios, sitting with his large moustache, and a new group of travelers. I'm not sure what he was studying in his year abroad, but it didn't seem to involve actual study. There was a fellow Canadian moustache named Frank, a nice guy, who looked like Sergeant Preston of the Yukon; he was with his Kiwi girlfriend, Bev. At the extended table were also two American girls, Jo and Diedre, and Helen and Jacki, a South African mother and daughter, living on Cyprus. Jacki was all eighteen and ethylene, ripe peaches and open flowers, entranced by life's possibilities. But prediction is very difficult, especially if it's about the future.

As the afternoon flowed into the side streets, I looked around to find that Steve and Jo were missing. The rest of us went out to the Garden of Eden for dinner, and I left them early, to return to the Student Inn. Steve was quietly lying on his bed, but the grin was unmistakable.

"It's the hat." I said, falling into a deep sleep.

I dropped my camera off to be repaired next morning, and then went on to the American Express office, to report the theft of my cheques. Mrs. Lobianco was not in a generous frame of mind.

"You realize that this is the second time you have had your money stolen?" She said. It wasn't a question. I told her that, yes, I did, but that it wasn't me that cracked open the kibbutz safe, or took the replacements out of my money pouch. She told me to bring back a police report, and a healthy dose of pessimism. Steve reconfirmed his flight home for the next day. He undertook to take a bouzouki I had bought, before this latest act of piracy.

We sat together on our final evening together, in the company of friends, reminiscing and planning our next reunion, depending on where we would both emerge, in the autumn. Across the table, Jacki's eyes were transforming hexameter poems into heroic couplets. She invited me to accompany her to the temple at Sounion, the following day. No siren did ever so charm the ear of the listener, as the listening ear has charmed the soul of the siren.

Steve left before sunrise, to make his plane. We hugged each other, and he hugged the bouzouki, on the way out of the Student Inn. His previous comment, about my Odyssey being 'an empty life,' returned to stab me, and I felt a profound sadness, until the sun burnt it away. I ran up to the Acropolis and back, and then met Jacki, for our trip to Sounion.

The headlands of the ancient Temple of Poseidon are surrounded on three sides by the sea. The sea is the Aegean, named after the king of Athens, Aegeus, who threw himself off the cliff here, when he saw a black sail on his son's ship, returning from Crete. Theseus had been sent to slay the Minotaur in Knossos, and the arrangement had been that, if he was successful, he was to return with a white sail. Theseus killed the Minotaur, but forgot to change the color of the sail. Exit Aegeus. Enter Pericles, who built the temple, followed by Lord Byron, who carved his name into one of the columns. '*Where nothing, save the waves and I, May hear our mutual murmers sweep.*' Where there is a sea, there are pirates. I stole a kiss. And, in the wind and the sun and the sky and the sea, and the air between the columns, the ethylene went toxic.

We returned to Athens in the last rays of the day, and met Helen, Demetrios, Frank, and Jo and Deidre, for dinner, at the Garden of Eden. Heracles flexed his muscle on the wine label. We were enjoying honeyed yoghurt and fruit and coffee, when I heard Helen and Jacki switch into Afrikaans. Drachmas came out of mother's handbag, and Jacki came around the table, to take my hand.

"Where are we going?" I asked.

"The Eleki." She said, pulling harder.

"Banished from the Garden of Eden, Wink?" Asked Frank, with a chuckle.

"Daytime is a man." I said. "Night is a woman."

The next morning was frenetic. I was first through the door of the American Express office, when it opened. Mrs. Lobianco informed me that I would have to go to Rome, to plead my case for the return of the stolen cheques. I told her I was heading in that direction anyway, through space and time and the history of Western Civilization.

"Western Civilization?" She asked.

"Don't leave home without it." I said.

I marched with the Changing of the Guard, back to meet Jacki and Frank, for a quick breakfast, in a corner nook café in our square. Each man is a hero and an oracle to somebody. Demetrios arrived glassy-eyed, with a new friend, Manolis. When I left, they embraced me, with tight bear hugs. Jacki and I said goodbye more slowly. I would eventually reconnect with Frank in New Zealand, but I never saw Jacki again. No one could have predicted.

My thumb got me to Patras by purple dusk. I bought deck passage on the Egnatia, and staked out a spot near the warm roar of the exhaust heater, on the stern. Night fell from the sky, as we pulled out to Brindisi under a full moon.

The mountains look on Marathon- And Marathon looks on the sea. I fired up my stove. Coffee was on.

> 'When your crew have taken you past these Sirens,
> I cannot give you coherent directions...'
>
> Homer, *The Odyssey*

72

Hash as to Ashes

Dust to dust. I had left the dust of Patras, to seek the safety of Brundusium's towers. The voyage across the Adriatic was calm, punctuated by chess games and harmonica solos, raisins and *La Bonne Vache* sandwiches, and the ship hand that decided to hose down the boat deck and my towel, just before we docked in the late afternoon.

Brindisi is the harbor of the poet Virgil, limoncello, and the tarantella, the frenetic dance performed to neutralize the poisonous bite of the wolf spider. It was good that he was dancing.

I entered the port with a full sail, soon to be deflated. We disembarked into a long arrival hall, with a central raised platform. All our baggage was placed on top, and two carabinieri brought a German shepherd into the room. One of them pulled a chunk of hashish out of his pocket, to remind the dog of the scent. He pulled taut on the leash, and began a long march around the rectangle, stopping in front of selected passengers, to give the dog more nose time. As he turned the corner towards me, I inadvertently slipped my fingers into my own pockets. My left hand grazed a hard object, and my brain had a parietal lobe seizure. It was a small block of hashish but, in this particular circumstance, I doubted if size was of any major importance. I remembered the bear hugs from Demetrios and Manolis. I remembered my Virgil. *Beware of Greeks bearing gifts.* I remembered the more pleasant moments of my life. The canine and his handler were moving along, towards me. As they approached, my hand unconsciously withdrew from my pocket, clutching the object of my despair. *Mind moves matter.* I opened my hand. The dog didn't hesitate. I felt his wet tongue on my palm. His handler didn't even break stride, as they walked right by. *Fate will find a way.* They had trained him to find it. They just didn't seem to have trained him what to do, after that. I wished him well. He was going to sleep, for a very long time.

My exit from the arrival hall led to a long hike, toward the Bari autostrade. The sun was hovering on the horizon, when I got my first ride, from a well-dressed martini-aged pair of spectacles, in an Armani suit and Gucci shoes. When I looked down to find his well-manicured hand on my left thigh, I had trouble accepting it at first. When I had trouble accepting it at last, my reflex trampling of his brake pedal turned the Alfa Romeo into a death spin. It left him shaken, not stirred. My next ride got me about fifteen kilometers to just outside the white walls, vineyards, and olive orchards of Ostuni, where an elderly couple took me the final two kilometers, to an ancient stone gate, in the middle of the hilltop village. In a quiet *pensione*, I filled a bathtub, with as much hot water and me as it would hold, and cried tears of something. It might have been happiness.

My second day in Italy began with a ten-kilometer walk, before a sleepy farmer in a vintage truck, took me the same distance, to Torre di Sosta. I managed another forty-five kilometers, with a young laborer, after hiking another two hours. At the time, I was blaming my difficulty on rusty technique. But this was the terrorism era of the '*Anni di Piombo,*' the Years of Lead. The Red Brigades were dancing a tarantella of assassinations, kneecappings, robberies, and general political violence. They had just kidnapped US Army Brigadier General Dozier, and I must have looked like I was coming to get him back. For the average Italian motorist, my thumb was a middle finger. Yet for a totally different reason, my hitchhiking career in Italy was about to end.

A slovenly unshaven Sicilian stopped to give me a lift. Middle-aged jelly rolled out from under his sweat-stained singlet. Not five minutes into the ride, he lit up a cigarette and placed his matches on the same spot as the more manicured *finocchio* had, the previous day. In that identical moment the glove compartment fell open, spilling his clearly valuable collection of '*Golden Gay*' magazines into my lap. I was done. I may have broken any number of bones in his foot when I hit the brakes, but the only golden thing I was interested in, was my parachute. With my exit onto the autostrade near the Trani turnoff, I took his Fiat's rear fender off, with one last kick. He didn't wait around for it to catch up.

It was now late afternoon. I thought of sleeping in an old storage shed but, while I was pulling the Gold Kazoo out of his stuff sack, as if on cue, the rats came pouring out of the walls. I walked. Long and hard. Sunburned, and cold and tired and sore and homicidal, I walked. Arriving at a tollbooth eight kilometers later, the attendant showed me where the water was. It didn't touch the sides. He advised me to continue on to Barletta, but I didn't make it. Six kilometers later, right on darkness, I was so bone weary, I crashed on the hard concrete leeward side of a derelict farm shed. Dogs barked. Rain poured. I didn't care. Sleep, oh glorious sleep.

A cold and overcast trek brought me into Andria next morning. I walked right by the gratuitous sign at the tollbooth, more declamation than instruction. '*No Autostop.*' No hitchhiking. No kidding. A hundred lire bought me a crusty *filone*. It smelled of yeast, and life. I devoured it on the spot. The train to Barletta was late, for the ticket I had bought. Mussolini had been a long time dead. My stove made me coffee.

The bank in Barletta made me crazy. I had skipped along the Western Civilization timeline, from the Colossus of Rhodes, past the Colossus of Barletta, the five-meter high bronze statue of Theodiseus II, who had washed up on the shores here eight hundred years ago. My entrance to the bank was more like the other historical event that belongs to Barletta. Security staff cautiously pulled back in an arc as I entered, an unintentional reenactment of what had occurred here, at

Cannae, in the spring of 216 BC. I was just changing a traveler's cheque. Hannibal had changed the face of military strategy, forever. I was crossing Southern Europe with my thumb, at the tender age of twenty-nine. Hannibal, with the same number of years, crossed the Alps with 46,000 men and three-dozen elephants, half of what he started with in Spain. He used fire and vinegar to break through rock falls. *We will either find a way or make one.* He powered south, cutting off the supply depot at Cannae, and forcing a response from Rome. Gaius Terentius Varro marched onto the battlefield with over 85,000 men, twice that of Hannibal's army. Varro saw that Hannibal had the river to his rear, and all his troops were visible on the open plain. He thickened up his central infantry and placed his cavalry on their flanks, convinced that his superiority in brute force would exterminate the Carthaginians.

Hannibal viewed the river as one less flank to worry about. He personally joined his Iberians and Gauls in the middle, positioned his battle-hardened Punic African infantry on the wings, and his stronger Hispanic and Numibian light horse cavalry on the flanks. There were Balearic slingers, and mixed nationality spearmen, waiting for their own signals. Hannibal had maneuvered the Romans to face east, into the morning sun and the southeasterly winds that would blow dust into their faces, as they entered the battlefield. *With wild thyme plotted, winds along the plain.* Dust to dust.

When the battle was joined, Hannibal retreated his centre slowly, drawing in the concentrated Roman formations, creating a tightening crescent, around the bulwark of their infantry. His cavalry decimated the Roman horsemen, and swung around behind an increasingly immobilized Roman army. Those in the outer ranks, that weren't cut down, were horribly crushed to death, in the middle. The ones, that tried to excavate their way out with their heads, lost them underground in the melee. Fifty-four thousand Roman soldiers were slaughtered, in what is now considered the archetypal battle of annihilation. The two hundred gold rings, collected from the Roman knights killed that day, were poured onto the floor of the Punic Senate, to standing applause.

I got a more sedate response, to my presentation of a fifty-dollar traveler's cheque, in the Barletta bank. But I hadn't arrived with elephants.

"Attenzione in Napoli." Said the bank teller, when I told him I was heading to Pompeii. It wasn't a worry. At least if there was a hand on my thigh in Naples, I knew it was aiming for one of my pockets.

*   *   *

'I would rather be ashes than dust.'
Jack London

There is something about coffee and volcanoes. My café, on the train to Naples, was made from beans that had come from the slope of some highland tropical vent. The macchinetta in the bar car produced it with the exact same steam pressure thermodynamics, that had created the bean's birthplace, and defined my next destination. Out of an endless curtain of slum laundry lining the tracks, emerged the brooding humpbacked profile of Vesuvius. I finished the last fennel seeds of my pretzel, and switched onto a local train, to Pompeii. The Bay of Naples flickered azure in the sun, at the foot of the Gran Cono. Clouds hovered beyond the white boulder breakwaters. It was the kind of day that seemed to guarantee nothing unusual would ever happen. "Live in danger. Build your cities on the slopes of Vesuvius." Nietzsche had said. And they had. Naples is the most densely populated volcanic region in the world. Riding the Eurasian plate of Scipio, over the African plate of Hannibal, it's a magnificent geographical expression, halfway between the mafia and the pontiff. The Neapolitans sing five miles from the volcano. They need to be twenty. If you gaze for long, into an abyss, the abyss also gazes into you.

The lobby television, and the lovers next door drowned the sterility of my room at the Albergo Apollo Pompeii. 'If anyone is looking for some tender love in this town, keep in mind that here all the girls are very friendly.' Was an inscription found in the ancient Basilica here. Nothing much had changed in two thousand years, and the lack of hot water next morning was probably for the best.

In 79 AD, the macchinetta of Vesuvius blew a plume fifteen miles into the troposphere, flattening out when it reached the boundary of the stratosphere, like a 'stone pine tree.' Fine ash and pumice fell as rain, for eighteen hours. The smart ones left. The clever ones, like Pliny the Younger, continued reading, while five cities around him were buried, under nine feet of soot. The next day the abyss gazed back. The eruptive column collapsed down on itself, and a rocket engine pyroclastic surge, of 500 degrees Celsius, instantly vaporized all flesh, and boiled all blood, in the mid-swallow and mid-sentence of all stragglers. Long bones and teeth blew apart. The black discoloration, found inside their exploded skull fragments, was the last thing that went through their minds. The boathouses of Herculaneum contained no boats, only the three hundred open-mouthed skeletons, that missed them, the day before. Among them was Pliny the Elder, and Drusilla, a granddaughter of Herod.

I puzzled at why there was a battering ram on the frescoes of the Villa of the Mysteries, and stood transfixed at the endowment of Priapus on another, weighing his uncircumcised attribute on the scales of inequity. Pleasure is more precious than money. Two American girls whispered and giggled behind me. Phalluses were not only plastered all over Pompeii, after the King of Naples saw them in 1819, were all plastered over in Pompeii. Eruptive columns collapsing.

I continued on the CircumVesuvium to Heraculaneum's carbonized cartwheels, and completed my circle on the same train to Naples. My plans to stay were pulled away by gravity. All dusty roads lead, and nightfall found me 240 kilometers to the north, sitting beside the villa where the poet John Keats lived, on the Spanish Steps in Rome. Although he had tuberculosis, Keat's death was more likely caused by his physician, who bled him, and restricted his diet to an anchovy, and a piece of bread, daily. Marcus Manilius, who lived here in the First Century AD, wrote that 'When Orion rises, night feigns the brightness of day and folds its dusky wings.' Too exhausted to even finish the last swallow of my anchovy pizza, I rose, and retreated to my bunk in the Asmara.

Suckling the Wolf

'Cease to admire the smoke, wealth, and noise of prosperous Rome.'
                                                                Horace

What the Asmara lacked in smoke and wealth, it more than made up for in noise. The main source appeared to be the snoring didgeridoo below me. I spent the night half-dreaming I was still traveling with Steve.
"You poor bloody bastard." He commiserated from the bunk down under. "M'name's Peter. From Oz."
"All things atrocious and shameless flock from all parts to Rome." I said.
"Tacitus." He replied.
"You can call me Wink." I said.
Peter and I had both arrived in the Eternal city, on our respective global sojourns. We were both penurious physicians, and had been gone about the same time. Instant friends.
I fired up my stove, and made us both a coffee. He told me of another place he had heard about nearby, that had less street noise than the Asmara. I packed up the Gold Kazoo, and followed him into the streets of the Eternal city.
Into Rome. The poem pressed into service as a city, the city of the soul, the city of visible history, the hemispheric funeral procession of ancestral images and trophies from afar, the book of fables, the capital of the world, overwhelmed by its own greatness, with nodding arches and broken temples spread, the quintessential city of conquest.
The founders of Rome, according to legend, were the twin sons of Mars, the God of War. Romulus and Remus were descendents of Virgil's Trojan prince, Aeneas, and left to die by their uncle, Amulius, usurper to the throne of Alba Longa. They were found, and suckled, by a she-wolf. Shepherds discovered and raised these preeminent feral children of

ancient mythology. They grew up to restore their father to his kingdom, and argue with each other about where to build a new city. In an augury contest of omens, Romulus saw twelve vultures, and Remus only six. Romulus won the siting, and Remus lost his life. Founded on infanticide and fratricide, and war and wolves, Rome never got a whole lot more harmonious after that.

Peter and I met her on the front steps. Behind the waving hands and loud gesticulations, were the polka dot dress, apron, and leather face of a tough old Roman matron.

"Mama Germano!" She shouted, opening her big arms to hug us both at once. "Benvenuto alla Locanda Cina."

Peter and I fell in love with her simultaneously.

"Sumnabitch." Was her favorite word. No nationality was safe from imitation or ridicule. Her version of Peter and I speaking English was to stuff her mouth with grapes, and lower her Italian an octave. She brought us tea and a natural affection, and found us beds.

I left them both for the American Express office, in Piazza di Spagnia, where I picked up my reimbursed cheques.

"If you lose them again, they're gone." Came the warning. I nodded, and left to meet Peter on the Spanish Steps.

We walked up the Pincian Hill to the Villa Medici, Ferdinando's monument to Mannerism and money. And moderation. He had enacted an edict of tolerance for heretics, which allowed the Spanish Jews expelled by Ferdinand and Isabella in 1492, to move to Livorno. We moved next door to the Casina Borghese, an 'Elysium of delight with fountains of sundry inventions, groves and small rivulets of water.' Bernini's statue of Daphne, turning into a laurel tree, while Apollo's hand was still able to feel her heart beating beneath the bark, made me conscious of an inferiority, which Samuel Johnson had assured me, only existed in a man who had not been in Italy. It was solely because I was here, that I now felt it more.

Inside the echo chamber of the Basilica di Santa Maria

Maggiore was the earliest image of Mary, supposedly painted by Luke the Evangelist, on her cedar dining room table from Nazareth. Peter and I moved, from the sanctuary of the most celebrated virgin, to the most celebrated sanctuary of virgins.

The Roman Forum was the site of, among many other things, the Temple of Vesta. The complex held the priestesses of the goddess of the hearth, responsible for ensuring that the sacred flame of Rome would never go out. Vestal Virgins were recruited before puberty and sworn to chastity, free of physical and mental defects, and from two living free born Roman parents. They were committed to thirty years of celibacy, ten as novices, ten as practitioners, ten as teachers. After that, they were free to marry, but few did. In addition to taking care of the Emperor's household fire, they were tasked with taking care of wills and testaments, guarding sacred objects, and the creation of *mola salsa*, a special salted flour, sprinkled between the horns of animal victims before their sacrifice. They could free condemned prisoners by touching them, and any condemned man was pardoned, if he saw one on his way to be executed. Anyone injuring a Vestal Virgin was put to death. There were penalties for virgins as well. Allowing the sacred fire to go out, or engaging in sex, was punishable by death. They were buried alive, but left with a little food, so that the burial would not technically take place within the city, but in death's antechamber.

Here at the Forum, the Roman Senate began, Marc Anthony gave Caesar's funeral oration and, two years later, displayed Cicero's severed head and right hand. For me, on the Via Sacra to the southeast, was a more infamous memorial. It was a triumphal arch, with a south panel showing the Menorah from the Second Temple in Jerusalem, carried away in the presence of a laurel-crowned Titus. Roman Jews still refuse to walk under it. Neither did I. When in Rome.

The other triumphal monument, built from the plunder of Jerusalem, became infamous for activities that were the antithesis of the Temple those treasures were stolen from.

The iron-pierced charred walls of pallid stones, that Peter and I saw that day, were idle remnants of what the Flavian Amphitheatre became in Vespasian's Rome. It was named the 'Colosseum,' after the giant thirty-meter statue of Nero that existed nearby, and had been modeled into a likeness of Helios, based on the Colossus of Rhodes. The outer wall of the Colosseum had been constructed with a hundred thousand cubic meters of travertine stone, held together with three hundred tons of iron clamps, and no mortar. The fifty thousand spectators it held could depart in minutes, through rapid discharge passageways called *vomitoria*, from which we get our word, 'vomit.' Or maybe it was from what happened inside- the nine thousand animals killed during the building's inaugural 'games,' the private gladiatorial contests, mock sea battles, animal hunts, and executions, where the condemned were mauled by beasts or burned to death. *Let Rome in Tiber melt, and the wide arch Of the rang'd empire fall.*

We went from the ridiculous to the sublime, Michelangelo's statue of Moses. Here the face of God, on the Sistine Chapel ceiling, broke free from his rock prison and grew demonic horns. His right elbow pressed on stone commandments, articulated with a hand tangled in the Smokey river beard of coiled rope snakes. His left vein-throbbing muscled forearm tensed in righteous fury. He was an icon of wrath. The miracle was that the souvenir moneychangers, on the other side of the San Pietro in Vincoli nave, could withstand his Old Testament glare. The Jews of Rome flocked to him like starlings, every Sabbath. Freud had portrayed him as a heroic image of self-control. I saw his marbled mind, wondering why he was sitting idly on the tomb of some Christian pope, when he had been chosen, truly chosen, for an infinitely more important mission.

Rome is the city of echoes, illusions, and yearning. The mail I had picked up forced a phone call to the past. It was Lynn from Lamu. I remembered.

"Big problem or little problem?" asked Silas.

"Big problem." I replied.
"Ehh." He said in two syllables
She wanted to meet me. I wasn't sure. She suggested Madrid.
I told Mama Germano about her back at the Locanda.
"Tira più un pelo di figa che un carro di buoi." *A pussy hair can pull more weight than a bunch of oxen.*
I told her about how reliable she had been in the past.
"Fra il dire e il fare, c'è di mezzo il mare." *An ocean lies between what is said and what is done.*
That evening Peter and I went to the Capitoline Museums, to see the pieces of Constantine's giant statue, and the bronze images of Romulus and Remus, suckling the she-wolf.
"I'll bet they regretted doing that, Mate." Said Peter.
"The Romans?" I asked.
"Naw. He said. "The wolves."

*   *   *

'There is no half-way house between Rome and Reason.'
Benjamin Tucker

Mama Germano woke us with tea. She lightheartedly went through her standup imitations of the newcomer Israeli, Brazilian, and Uruguayan in our room. The Israeli made the mistake of imitating her back. Sumnabitch.
Through a throng of primavera marathoners, Peter and I edged our way to the Pantheon. Two thousand years after its construction, it was still the world's largest unreinforced concrete dome, big enough to have its own climate. The rain spray that parachuted down through the open oculus, 150 feet above us, abated into a moving sundial beam of light on the circular wall, when the sun reappeared. Via the Ara Pacis Augustus, we went to throw coins into the chalky blue water of the Trevi fountain. Convention required tossing with the

right hand over the left shoulder, two coins for a new romance, and three for a marriage or divorce. Peter and I threw one each, through a loophole in the contract. The gigantic statue of Oceanus on the back wall was unamused by our paltry contribution, to the five thousand dollars a day that normally went into his baroque bathtub. It was all supposed to go to local charities, but fishermen, trolling with magnets, made a reasonable living.

The most famous looter came after the magnets stopped working. He was an eccentric, named Roberto Cercelletta, who arrived for his early morning swim, and a thousand non-ferrous Euros a day, before most of Rome was even awake. Repeatedly arrested by the police, the courts ruled that, because the money had been thrown away, it didn't belong to anyone. The carbinieri continued to fish him out of the fountain anyway. One day he slashed his stomach repeatedly in protest, and in vain. Rome had passed a new bylaw, prohibiting swimming in the city's fountains. No more levy from the heavy 'cause the Trevi went dry.

We stopped for some slow food crostini, with chicken livers and sage, in a hole in the wall near the Spanish Steps, before the MacDonald's went in, and boarded a bus to the 'dagger in the heart of Italy,' a hundred acres that controlled the lives of 1.2 billion people. Augustus found Rome a city of bricks and left it a city of marble. The Catholics found a city of marble and left it a city of gold. For all I had been led to believe about chastity and poverty, there wasn't a hell of a lot of it to be seen in the Vatican. When Remus had been looking for vultures, he should have been looking here.

"Come on over to my basilica." Said Peter. And we gazed at the hand of God giving life to Adam, Genesis on the Sistine ceiling, and the Last Judgment on the wall, painted by a squalid man with a punched-in nose and scraggly beard, who slept in his clothes and boots. We saw his *Pieta*, sculpted at the age of twenty-four. Whatever Michelangelo Buonartti lacked in personal charm, emerged from his fingers and soul, as heartbreaking beauty and heroism. He had seen the angels in the marble, and carved until he set them free.

Time filled the Roman evening with eternity. Peter and I finally returned in the rain, to Mama Germano's, drenched and dizzy with all the material superlatives that we had set out to wholly see in the Holy See.

In March of 2008, Pope Benedict added seven new mortal sins to the list of deadly vices. Number three was the showstopper- *'The accumulation of excessive wealth.'* The city, that was weaned from the wolf, now had it back at the door, holding it by the ears and unable to let go.

I said goodbye to Saint Peter and Rome next morning, heading north to Florence. Mama Germano nearly broke my back, with her train station bear hug. A short disembarkation in Pisa brought me to the white marble leaning tower, before it was straightened in 1990. By the time I had spiraled up the three hundred stairs breathless, my head was spinning four meters off the centre, at the top. A Sicilian family shared food and good company, on the late afternoon connection to Florence. After an hour of looking, I found the Saggiarno d'Errica, for five dollars a night, *tutti I confort moderni*, except for the hot water. It did come with a young Oxford student named Mark, Raquel and João, a Brazilian couple from Ipanema, Australian Reine, and Gary the Chess master. I had traveled from Rome to the Renaissance, from the city of the wolf to the city of the fox, in just over two hundred kilometers, and a dozen centuries.

'A fox is a wolf who sends flowers'
Ruth Weston

Stendhal Syndrome

'It would be a very plausible river if they would pump some water into it.'
(The Arno)
Mark Twain, *Innocents Abroad*

I dreamt myself up through the water shaft of the Gihon Spring that night, emerging into the City of David by morning. But it was a different city, and a different David. He was an uncircumcised Greek, with too large face and hands, a homoerotic homunculus. Not an indigent Israelite Goliath killer, but a gold florin Renaissance dandy, with his sling slung like casual jewelry- adornment rather than armament, poise rather than prowess. My, my, Michelangelo, but he was magnificent.

I was eating yoghurt in the market in Florence, the Athens of the Middle Ages. Pericles had given way to Petrarch, and Lysander to Lorenzo il Magnifico. Florence was the home base of Leonardo da Vinci, Botticelli, Machiavelli, Brunelleschi, Dante, Michelangelo, Donatello, Galileo, and a thousand other Renaissance men. I wanted to see it all, way too fast. The inlaid pietra dura of the Medici Chapels had already burned the colors out of my retinal cones and, like a fool, I went directly from there to the Uffizi, without a debriefing, or a decompression stop. Nothing prepared me for the lineup at the corner of Piazza Della Signoria. Even less prepared me for what lay beyond it, inside the doors of Cosimo de Medici's old office building. Room after room of Botticelli, da Vinci, Titian, Giotto, and art junkies from all over the world. Dante was sent from here into exile. The Medicis hung the Pazzi conspirators from the windows. In 1497 the Dominican priest, Savonarola, threw all the art and books he could find into the flames of the Bonfire of the

Vanities. A decade later, the Florentines threw Savonarola in, after them. They've been hoarding art ever since.

After the quiet open spaces of the Americas and Africa, I had become averse to noise and crowds. It is still one of the most frustrating maladaptations I inherited from my Cartwheels. In the Uffizi, I was not only swimming in both but, everywhere I looked, was some new art masterpiece, demanding my attention. I felt my heartbeat compete. I became lightheaded and confused. Perspiration ran down my temples, and under my arms. The *Birth of Venus* was the death of me. I had full-blown hyperkulturemia, Stendhal syndrome, and hurriedly escaped out, past the Loggia di Lanzi, before the hallucinations arrived.

Mark and Raquel were eating pizza outside a café, and invited me to recover with them. She showed me the wool she had bought, from a street vendor.

"You like it?" She asked, knitting away. I told her I did. I wondered where João was.

"Is a scarf... for you." She said. The palpitations and dizziness returned, leaving with me a few minutes later.

I spent the rest of the afternoon reacclimating to the Renaissance, in the Bargello, making antibodies to Cellini and Botticelli. I had almost recovered, when I encountered the second iconic Florentine version of David. The symptoms of art overdose are the same as those caused by art incongruity. Here, before me, my image of the young warrior, that slew Goliath, was transformed into a naked transvestite, dressed in a garlanded French hat and riding boots. The man that sent Uriah the Hittite out to die in battle, in order to steal his wife, now had long hair flowing into languid dreamy, downcast eyes, with half closed lids. His victory visage had converted to a patrician smirk, and his soldier stance had softened, into a provocative contrapposto swagger of pubescent breasts, curved waist, and protuberant lower abdomen. Slender feminine arms lead to dainty rolled backhands, clearly too weak to lift his sword. A feather from Goliath's helmet wound its way up the inside of David's feminine thigh. Uncircumcised male genitalia seemed to have been added as an afterthought. Donatello has cast an armored Old Testament Israelite King, into a She-male Sodomite Queen.

I hadn't known that, like the ancient Greek male ideal of perfect teenage boy *erômenos* love, the Florentines had their own *fanciulli* phenomenon. The preference was for no hair, anywhere. So famous was the local practice that, in Germany, homosexual sex was known as 'florenzen', and in France was called 'the Florentine vice.'

My return to the Saggiarno d'Errica found another. I was retreating into a stalemate with Gary the Chess master, when three young American girls skipped into the salon, carrying their body weight in shopping bags.

"What're y'all doin'?" The tallest one asked.

"Playing chess." I said.

"Oh." She replied. "We're from Texas. Don't y'all just love this place?"

"Magnificent." Said Gary, blocking the advance of my rook.

"Yeah." Said the middle one. "Gucci, Prada, Cavalli..."

"Botticelli, Brunelleschi, Machiavelli..." I replied.

"Where are they?" asked the youngest.

"Dead." I said.

"Do they still have a leather outlet?" She asked.

"Checkmate." Said Gary. My king fell onto his side.

The oleander, on the walls of the Ponte Vecchio, grew crimson in the evening oil. At a wavering instant, the swallows gave way to bats, changing guard. Raquel and I stole little kisses from each other in the alcoves, along the Arno. But this is all we were able to keep. For the Ponte Vecchio is birthplace of bankruptcy. When a merchant couldn't pay his debts, the *banco* table on which he sold his wares was physically broken, *rotto*, by soldiers. Bancorotto. Without a table, one cannot make a living. Whatever Raquel and I had, we left padlocked to the bridge, with all the other lovers.

I found a scarf sitting on my pillow next morning, and João

sitting with Raquel in the salone. Her long hair flowed, into languid dreamy, downcast eyes, with half closed lids. Mark and I went to the market for sustenance. My milk was sour, the replacement only slight less so. We walked to Santa Maria del Carmine, to see Masaccio's fresco of Adam and Eve's *Expulsion from the Garden of Eden*, a day late and a dollar short. The day dissolved into the elaborate ivory of the Pitti Palace, the Palazzo Vecchio, and the Moorish Great Synagogue, where schoolchildren danced in a circle, in the courtyard outside the blue and gold-filigreed dome. Later I had my first shower since arriving in Florence. It would have been very plausible, if they had pumped some water into it.

*   *   *

'A bad smell mixed with glory, and the cold
Eyes that belie the tessellated gold.'
Louis MacNeice, *Ravenna*

The mosaics knocked me flat. I was three days out of Firenze, at the end of five central Italian architectural arias, all frozen in light. I had seen the ribbed pumpkin dome of the Duomo, Santa Maria del Fiore's crown jewel of brick and mortar. Brunelleschi had invented his own hoisting mathematics, and machines, to build it. To scaffold and form thirty-seven tons of material, and four million herringbone bricks, into the largest freestanding masonry dome in the world, would have required more timber than existed in all of Tuscany, if he had used conventional methods to construct it. Instead, he employed ribbed platforms, hanging from ascending rigid barrel-hooped internal stone, and iron chains. The dome's power rose out, from the grace of the red and green inlaid white marble facades of the Basilica, Baptistery and Giotto's bell tower. It wasn't clear to me, whether what Brunelleschi created was to worship God, or what God created was to worship Brunelleschi. Mark and I spent the afternoon on the steps, watching the freaks. They all could have dropped from the dome's interior frescos.

The Black Death of 1348 killed off half of Europe. In Santa Maria Novella, we passed Elizabeth Barrett Browning's left stair,

> 'where, at plague-time, Macchiavel
> Saw one with set fair face as in a glass,
> Dressed out against the fear of death and hell,
> Rustling her silks in pauses of the mass,
> To keep the thought off how her husband fell,
> When she left home, stark dead across her feet...'

At the top of Sienna's Torre del Mangia next day, Mark and I looked down onto the vertiginous view of the Palazzo Publico, below. The tower was finished the year the plague arrived. It felt as though the Siennese had been building skyward, to escape the coming carnage at their feet. Romulus and Remus were also the mythical founders of Sienna, but they would have been counting a different kind of vulture, from our vantage point in 1348. The *beccamorti* could become wealthy, if they survived, by digging deep trenches to the waterline, and transporting the dead, on their backs, into them at night, alternating *lasagna* layers of bodies and dirt.

The same pestilence had destroyed the political independence of our third aria, San Gimignano. We climbed patrician tower houses that rose 150 feet in the air, and wondered at the social perversity, that required their construction.

Mark had become a good companion. I made coffee for him, on my stove next morning, before boarding the train to Bologna. I arrived 630 years after the great plague, and as many days after the Bologna Massacre, that killed eighty-five people in the Central train station. I walked to the Piazza Maggiore, to see San Petronio Basilica, the still-unfinished fifth largest church on the planet. Inside, there was a late

Gothic fresco, painted by Giovanni da Modena, depicting Mohammed in Hell, being devoured by demons. Al Qaeda tried to blow it up in 2002, and again, four years later- plagues exciting religions; religions inciting massacres. The renovation black shroud, over San Petronio, made it look like a death star. Inside the darkness, organ arpeggios grated up and down my spine, like chewing on aluminum foil. The Mass baked inquisition and molestation and exorcism and stigmata and the blood and body of a crucified convict into a special cookie, which was supposed to take away the bad smell that mixed with glory. It was what you got by adding the Roman, to the Catholic.

So I arrived in Ravenna with my eyes dim and the world flat. I had lost my train ticket, and was forced to buy another. The youth hostel wouldn't open for another three hours, and there would be no hot water. Here Julius Caesar had gathered his forces, before crossing the Rubicon. Here Augustus had created his harbor. Here Byron had come alive, and Dante was buried. My soul sank into the old malarial marsh. And then I entered San Vitale, and Sant'Apollinare in Classe, the inspirations for Brunelleschi's Duomo dome, and the Hagia Sophia.

The mosaics knocked me flat. The golden golds and emerald greens mixed with air and silica and sunlight. I was breathing Byzantium. Here was a joy of earlier rapture. Here Jerusalem's towers shone from the walls. I pulled down on Raquel's scarf, to keep my feet under me.

The Most Serene Republic

'Venice is like eating an entire box of chocolate liqueurs in one go.'
Truman Capote

It had started with the stamps. I had collected their luscious postage picture panels as a boy. Images of a far philately mountaintop refuge had jumped off the pages of my album. In dreamy youthful moments I would visit, for sanctuary and inspiration.

I was covered in sweat by the time I had climbed the last cobblestones, to the three towers on Monte Titano. Postage stamps decorated the window of the *Ufficio touristico*. I entered to find the backs of a Japanese couple, screening the soft soprano accent behind the counter. As they turned to leave, I caught my first glimpse, and my last breath. Raphael had painted her, but I just couldn't place the name.

"Isabella." She offered.

"Charmed." I said. She was all High Renaissance dangerous beauty.

"What would you like to see in San Marino?" she asked. I was already there.

"What else is there to see?" I asked. She looked down, and began telling me about the oldest and smallest sovereign state in the world. I had taken a bus from Rimini that morning, up the eastern side of the Apennine Mountains, to the Most Serene Republic of San Marino. Founded in 301 AD, by a stonecutter who came up from Rimini the hard way, Marinus of Rab was fleeing the wrath of Diocletian.

Isabella convinced me. There was a lot to do- the Army Museum, the Pinoteca, the Castillo... I drifted on her voice for an hour, and awoke with a handful of brochures.

"Is there anything else I can do for you, Signore?" She asked. I asked about dinner. She told me of a place, Giuletta's. No, I said, I was asking if she would have dinner with me. Raphael threw the blush on her cheeks, and I remembered the Baronci angel.

"Si." She said. "Incontriamoci alle sette." *Meet me at seven.*

I spent the afternoon finding accommodation, seeing the sights, and trying the local delicacies of *piadina* and *torta di tre monti*.

Isabella entered Giuletta's, serenely at seven, and we ate lasagna, and drank cold Guinness, and laughed. She was from Rimini, but was studying in Paris. San Marino was a summer job for her, but she wanted to know what it was for me. I told her about sanctuary and inspiration, and how she seemed to be providing both. Raphael returned. Later, we walked around the ramparts, and I pushed her on a swing in a playground. We spoke of life and love until very late.

I slid downhill next morning to Rimini, on my way to Venice. A miscalculation left me on *Binario 10*, at the train station Bologna, with a knot of provolone and an orange, until a *locale* arrived in the late afternoon. I sat with three old men, who spent the four hours alternately spitting out the window, and calling out the names of the cow town stations. It was the last stop that I was unprepared for. Stepping onto the platform, I discovered why Venice was sinking. There was a carpet of heads, as far as the Grand Canal, and it was only the end of April, thirty years ago. Thomas Mann called Venice 'half fairy-tale and half tourist trap.' The day I arrived, they had apparently run out of fairies. Or maybe they were still all back on the autostradas. After a frantic hour of jostling, and searching for a cheap place to stay, I retreated with the last of the sun, on a vaporetto, to the island of Giudecca. The Youth Hostel was pandemonium. The front desk *Fascisti* bunked me in the middle of a forty-bed room, overflowing with a noisy horde of adolescent Italian schoolboys. My dinner was a hard-boiled egg, and a glass of milk. I had forgotten my passport, back in San Marino, and had signed in under an alias, Gustav von Aschenbach. As pillow feathers and bread rolls flew across the ceiling, in the clamor of the *cazzos*, I consoled myself with the thought that, as I smothered the little bastards in their sleep, no one would ever know the perpetrator's name. I dreamt of cholera, and Death in Venice.

'Though there are some disagreeable things in Venice there is nothing so disagreeable as the visitors.'
Henry James

*　　*　　*

'I stood in Venice, on the Bridge of Sighs,
A palace and a prison on each hand...
Above the Dogeless city's vanished sway:
Ours is a trophy which will not decay
With the Rialto, Shylock and the Moor.'
Lord Byron, *Childs Harold's Pilgrimage*

The little darlings were still fast asleep when I jumped vaporetto #5, to the marbled arches of Piazza San Marco, next morning. I remember leaving most of them alive. In the white swan of cities, Napoleon called the piazza, the 'drawing room of Europe,' before plundering the four bronze horses that presided over it, from the plundered Hippodrome of Constantinople, off to Paris. I lingered between the granite columns of San Theodore, and the winged lion chimera symbol of Venice in the Piazzetta, unaware that this was where public executions took place. It was strange that, after the carpet crowding of the previous day, no one else was waiting outside the lighter-than-air lancet arches of the Doge's Palace. When the Porta della Carta door opened, I found the missing gravitational force of the palace exterior, hiding inside. The heavy gold ceiling, inside the Senate Chamber, compressed whatever air I had left, out of my lungs. The Hall of the Philosophers pushed me into the weight of the Great Council room. Standing under the solemn tension of Tintoretto's' *Paradise*, the largest painting ever committed to canvas, I fathomed the triumph of Venice. At the head of the Adriatic, across 117 islands of a marshy lagoon, squeezed between Byzantium and Islam, the Venetians had created a trade empire of silk, salt, grain, and spices. On shifting shadow pavements, of palaces and strips of sky, they hung bridges and girandole mirrors and murano glass chandeliers and lacquer, and velvet and damask and silk drapery, and bed heads carved with flowers and angels. Vivaldi's contrapuntal concertos glided over asymmetric gondolas, guided through floating canals. With over three thousand ships, carrying thirty thousand of sailors, over three hundred years, it seemed like Venice's fortunes would never subside. But whatever goes up. Venice started falling back into the Adriatic slowly- from wars with the Turks, the Black Death, and the loss of competitive advantage. Columbus found the New World, the Portuguese found a sea route to India, and Venice's oared galleys found they couldn't keep up with either. Decades of water extraction, from the aquifers, sunk the rest.

I stood on the Bridge of Sighs, a palace and a prison on each hand. Byron had given it the name, because it was the last view of Venice that a convict saw, before his imprisonment. They went to one of two kinds of prison cells, the wells, *pozzi*, and the leads, *piombi*. Neither were vacation spots. The *pozzi* were damp, stuffy, crowded, and insect-infested. The lead-lined *piombi* heated up in summer, and conducted ice cold in winter. Casanova escaped the *piombi* through the roof; Marco Polo escaped via Spain; I escaped to the Foundry.

At least that's the name in English. In Italian, its called the *Ghetto*, and the one in Venice was the world's first. Adherents of the longest established religious faith in Italy, the Jews in Venice were compelled to live in a few island streets, surrounded by water, and controlled by two large gates. They had to pay for Christian boat patrols, to ensure they were all locked in at night. I remember the cultural sensitivity preamble the teacher gave my English class in high school, before we opened the Shakespearean gates, to the *Merchant of Venice*. For authenticity, he invited me to read the part of Shylock:

'I am a Jew. Hath not a Jew eyes? Hath not a Jew hands, organs, dimensions, senses, affections, passions; fed with the same food, hurt with the same weapons, subject to the same diseases, heal'd by the same means, warm'd and cool'd by the same winter and summer, as a Christian is? If you prick us, do we not bleed? If you tickle us, do we not laugh? If you poison us, do we not die? And if you wrong us, do we not revenge? If we are like you in the rest, we will resemble you in that.'

In that moment, I learned about hatred. The room filled with fury. Later, at recess, my classmates exacted their own pound of flesh.

It all came flooding back, watching the school kids, cats, and pigeons in the *Campo Ghetto Nuovo,* playing obliviously, under the Holocaust wall memorial. The quality of mercy is not strained.

After the Tintorettos in the Scuola di San Rocco, the Accademia, the Peggy Gugenheim, San Zaccharia, San Maggiore Giorgio, and a half dozen other attractions, I felt I had done justice to Venice. More, anyway, than Shakespeare had done to its most famous merchant.

I watched some canal dredgers, amused, until the vaporetto arrived, to return me to my island prison for the night. The *cazzos* were different, but the game was the same. I dreamt of plague.

Early next morning, I left Venice, to retrieve my passport. I was in Rimini by ten, and back in the Most Serene Republic, not much later. Raphael put the glow back on Isabella, as I entered the tourist office.

"I forgot my passport." I said.

"Is there anything else I can do for you, Signore?" She asked. I asked about dinner. She told me of a place.

When she finished work, we met at Laura's restaurant. Two friendly local policemen serenaded us with guitars, in the small space between our wine and pasta, but we didn't see them. Later, sinking like Venice into a most serene bath, we made a bridge of sighs. Vivaldi's contrapuntal concertos glided over asymmetric gondolas, guided through floating canals.

The moon sailed out from behind the cloud armada, spotlighting the liquid curvature below, in precious metal.

"Are there any other kinds of heroes, Uncle Wink?" asked Millie.

"There may well be, Mil, but more important, are the qualities and character of the main ones we know about." Said Uncle Wink.

"What do you mean?" Sam asked

"There are gung-ho heroes and reluctant heroes." Uncle Wink said. "I was willing and active, but the reluctant ones can be fascinating. The Romans used to say that the fates lead him who will; him who won't they drag. These are heroes that are thrown into their adventures, like the princely hunter of Celtic myth, or the Wandering Jew.

Then there are group-oriented heroes and loners. The group heroes are part of a society when they leave. Their journey takes them into the wilderness, and they return to rejoin their community and share what they learned. The loner hero starts separated from Society, discovers his natural habitat in the wilderness and solitude, reenters Society, and while there, has an adventure or a realization, before returning to his natural isolation."

"Which one were you, Uncle Wink." Asked Millie.

"I was a loner, but your Auntie Robbie makes sure I don't escape too far back into the wilderness."

"There must be a lot of different kinds of hero characters." Sam observed.

"As many as you can think of, Sammy. There is the Hero of Chivalry, who takes on dangerous quests to fulfill his goals, usually involving confrontation, and the Hero of Destiny, the Chosen One, a messiah, destined to save the world."

"And you, Uncle Wink?" asked Millie.

"Chivalry, if that was at all possible in an Anti-hero loner." Said Uncle Wink. "Succeeded by committees, computer algorithms, and the cult of collaboration, extinguishing forever the glory of the knight-errant."

"Was that good, Uncle Wink?" Millie asked.

"No, Mil. That was bad." He said.

Michelin Star

'There was no hitchhiking in France that I could see.'
Jack Kerouac, *Lonesome Traveler*

Our life is made by the death of others. Thereby hangs a tale. Isabella gave me her jacket for the road. Poetry is as precise as geometry, and I was aiming to leave Italy through both. My first destination was the inverted wooden cone of the dissecting anatomy theatre, at the Palazzo del Bo, in Padua. At the bottom of a tall walnut funnel, human forms were disassembled for the curious, squashed on top of each other. I peddled through Giotto's fresco cycle of the Virgin Mary, at the Cappella degli Scrovegni, before the restoration, refrigeration and requisite reservation. Beyond Donatello's giant bronze statue of the Venetian general, Gattamelata, there was force and acceleration in the moving mass in Il Santo, and in the Titians of the Scuolo di San Giorgio. I arrived at the youth hostel late in the day, for the small choice among three rotten apples I had purchased in the market, for my evening meal.

May Day in Mantua meant the same thing as in the navy.

Everything had shut down, except for Virgil's statue. The *locale* I boarded for Milan, deposited me at a peripheral station. I waited an hour before the next train took me one stop, and as many kilometers. Forty more north of me stood the three pyramids of Montevecchia. I didn't know they were there, nor did anyone else, until satellite imaging uncovered them in 2003. Like the ancient Egyptian wonder of Giza, they represented the belt stars of Orion, aligned with his passing at the sunrise of the summer solstice.

The Pensione Arnold had no shower. I washed my socks in the sink, and fell into a deep sleep. In my dream I fell further, into a deep wooden funnel. I saw my old anatomy professor, waiting to catch me at the bottom.

The next morning floated me back over the top. Shop windows, in the glass-vaulted arcades of the Galleria Vittorio Emmanuel II, tortured a hungry traveler. Smells of Gorgonzola, veal Milanese, osso buco, risottos, cassoeulas, buseccas, brasatos, and pastries, sang Verdi's *Gerusalemme,* all the way to La Scala. I emerged, under the profile of the flamboyant perpendicular sharp gables and spires, of the Gothic cathedral that had taken six centuries to build, and five minutes for a noisy tour group of *ragazzini* to dismantle.

Between the poison ring collection at Museo Poldi Pezzuoli, and the weaponized crucifix in the Castello Sforzesco, were the Palazzo di Brera's Mantegna's 'Dead Christ,' and other sacred snapshots of Rafael, Caravaggio, and Carvello. The gold and jewel-encrusted altar of Sant'Ambrosia led to my last stop in Italy. In the refectory of Santa Maria delle Grazie, I was alone, with the scaffolding and the geometry and poetry, of Leonardo's Last Supper. The square window framed the triangle of Christ, on which sat the tilted circle of his visage. Art is never finished, only abandoned.

Beyond Ventimiglia, Italy turned into France. My resurrected thumb lifted my spirit, along orchards of lemons and oranges and olives. I bought a postcard in Monte Carlo, wrote it on the Promenade des Anglais in Nice, and mailed it in St. Tropez. Brigitte Bardot had been discovered here, but not by me, and not that day. The rocky inlets, that had been my company, left me hiking the next ten kilometers, to the deserted beach of Pampelonne. Under a natural tree cave on Plage de Salins, I waited out the afternoon, drawing portraits of the pines. You get better at staring into space in the South of France. It grew overcast. My stove made soup, to ward off the chill. The rain that came later, forced itself into the Gold Kazoo, now breathing deeply after so many nights on the road. I slept fitfully, and in my near narcosis, heard a screeching cat. I looked up into the face of dog, foaming at the mouth. When I awoke at dawn, their paw prints were still there, in the sand.

'Down the road to Avignon, The long, long road to Avignon,
Across the bridge to Avignon, One morning in the spring.'
Amy Lowell, *The Road to Avignon*

The passing plane trees went *'shah-shah-shah,'* through the
open window. I was moving again, like I was meant to move.
The sun had returned, and my thumb had caught a solar
energy merchant, named Norbert, who took me all the way to
Marseille. Another few rides got me to Aix-en-Provence, site
of the Roman defeat of the Teutons at Aquae Sextiae, and the
mass suicide of all their women that followed. The highlights
of my stay were considerably more sedate, consisting of the
big squares and polka dots of the Vasarely Foundation, my
first hot shower in days, and a communal evening repast, at
the Youth Hostel.

105

I waited for an hour and a half next morning, before an elderly lady gave me a lift to the medieval ramparts of Avignon. My tour of the Palais de Papes was pursued by a group of infatuated French girls, positioning themselves to have their picture taken with me.

Later, on the road to Nimes, I met Peter and, after good fun trying to catch carp in the river, we walked across the *pont,* to spend the night on Isle Barthelasse. The evening chill had chased away the sun by the time we arrived, at an encampment of gypsies and Germans, sitting around a large fire. It was peaceful and friendly, at first. Guitars played soft melodies. I was sitting beside Christina, a Swiss girl, with a motorcycle helmet. The circle shared marzipan and road stories, and brandy and bravado. The gypsy king, with the flowered hat, became greedy with the brandy, and generous with the bravado.

"This is my natural territory." He shouted, stumbling to his feet, and kicking burning logs and embers out of the fire, onto the Germans. He then focused on the English travelers, who seemed to stare at everyone. There was blood. Christina invited me to sleep in her tent, enclosed within that sunset wreath of oleanders tall.

The night was freezing.

Christina took me, on the back of her motorcycle, to the highway next morning. I made a big sign. Thierry, a math teacher, drove me to Nimes, via the Pont du Gard. The valley filled with the shadow of a work of such profound isolation, dignity and weight, that no engineers, before or since the Romans that built it, could ever be considered as great. Here was a fifty-kilometer triple arch of enormous stones, painted with olive oil and covered with a mixture of lime, pork grease and the juice of unripe figs, and assembled without mortar or clamps. It took twenty-seven hours for a drop of water at the top, to fall seventeen meters, into a mouth in Nimes, below.

I ate bread and oranges in the amphitheatre's sunny solitude. I wandered the Musée des Beaux Arts, the Maison Cairee, and the Temple of Diana in the Jardin de la Fontaine, before stopping, just to watch and admire the old French men, playing boules there. The two medical students, at the top of the Tour Magne, shared training experiences, and the view. I made a rare phone call home, to find my parents well, and worried from care. This was always the hard part. My mother told me that Lynn had called. She was flying into Madrid in six days. I did the math, and made the long climb to the hostel, where I met a young bicyclist from Oregon, named Robert, and his English bank teller girlfriend, Sally. We ate pâté and fois gras and bread together, and I told them of gypsies and campfires, and long-distance love. There was no hot water.

I was beginning to think that Kerouac was right about the absence of hitchhiking in France. My two-hour wait, on the autoroute onramp next morning, was turning into three. Citroens and Renaults whizzed by, oblivious, and no one was even looking at the road. I looked at my right thumb and shrugged, throwing it haphazardly back where it had been. The next moment was struck by lightning. A magnificent giant silver eighteen-wheeler, with French and Arabic script on its fuselage, stopped, so hard and fast, that the back four Michelin tires came off the tarmac, for just an instant. The air brakes hissed, and oinked in pain. A pair of mirrored sunglasses reached over, to unlock the mile-high passenger door. I blew on my thumb.

"Ou allez-vous?" The driver demanded.

"Carcassonne!" I shouted, above the whine of the engine.

"D'accord." He said. I threw serendipity into a parabola, and followed it in. It took a full minute to shift through the gears, and resume cruising speed. Elvis came out of the speakers.

His name was Serge. He had just driven from Baghdad, and didn't look like he had stopped for much. He was heading to Madrid, and so was I, but I didn't need to get there as fast. Serge was decked out for planetary travel. He had a waterbed behind the cab, quadraphonic sound, fridge and coffeemaker, and kid leather driving gloves. He made me a cappuccino, to go with my croissant. I made him laugh, with tales of my hitchhiking exploits.

"Vous êtes Le Passant." He observed. *He who passes through.*

"Comme nous tous." I said. *As we all are.* He grunted.

We bid each other adieu, at the Carcassonne Est turnoff. I watched him roar off, towards Spain. Two freaks from Montpelier rolled to a stop, and then rolled a joint. I rolled out into La Cité, dazed from both morning experiences. Clearly, Kerouac had been a lesser mortal.

I thought to see fair Carcassonne — That lovely city — Carcassonne! It had been the stronghold of the Occitan Cathars, until the crusading army of Simon de Montfort set fire to them, in their cathedral. 'Tuez les tous, Dieu reconnaitra les siens.' *Kill them all, God will recognize his own.* In 1210, he burned 140 Cathars in Minerve, for refusing to give up their faith. Other prisoners, from a nearby village, had their eyes gouged out, and their ears, noses and lips cut off, before he sacked Lastours. Simon was not a nice man. But the stained glass in the Basilica was as beautiful, as he was horrible. A piper played a tune outside. And the pushbuttons in the hostel shower delivered hot water in abundance. I stayed, until fir trees replaced my fingerprints.

Carcassonne receded next morning, under an uncertain sky. A foreign legion gendarme, from Paris, offered me a *Gitanes,* and a lift just south of Narbonne. A couple from Perpignon drove me to where another couple drove me to the Pyrenees, seven kilometers from La Fronterra. I finished my cheese and bread in magnificent surroundings, and walked for what seemed like forever. It began to rain. In Spain. Gently.

Damascenery

'When therefore I have performed this, and have sealed to them this fruit, I will come by you into Spain.'

Romans 15:28

As Daddy said, life is ninety-five percent anticipation. I was four days away from a rendezvous, with one of the most volatile women I had ever met, and I was using all my hitchhiking expertise to get there. Through the Hebrew Bible, Athenian democracy, and Roman law, I had spent a lot of space and time trying to reach the essence of Western Civilization. She was a wild American and, just like her native land, I was preparing to go from barbarism to decadence, without passing through any of it. A gruff old Spaniard drove me ten kilometers south of the border. The sun was burning. They slowed down, and then the *Guardia Civil* stopped.
"No es possible aqui." They said. "Otra lado." They pointed to a parallel road. I began walking. It was lined with vineyards, and trees, and castles and churches. I got a lift on a tractor for a few hundred meters, before the sun climbed higher. I began tilting at windmills. Then came Juan, a Marine, chain-smoking *Ducados*, and singing in Catalan. We laughed in Castellano, through spectacular pine forests, to his apartment in Girona. I had a fantastic hot shower, and bread, and local *fuet* sausage. Juan returned in his military uniform.
"Vamos a Barcelona." He said. Like sudden madness burst thy grateful glee. And a hundred kilometers brought us onto La Rambla. He saluted, and drove away. Later, I found five hundred pesetas in my back pocket. It bought me a bed in the Pension Nova, and a simple supper, of chicken and chips.
La Rambla was the only street in the world Garcia Lorca wished would never end. From my vantage point next morning, it hadn't. Gaudi's alien Church of Sagrada Familia looked like it had jumped out of Christ's chest. It was started

in 1882, and they're still working on it. Gaudi had said that his client wasn't in a hurry. The residents of his Casa Mila apartment house couldn't have been either, as there were only lifts on every second floor. Horses that pulled the carriages, through the Wonderland portals of his Palau Guell, must have thought they had been fed some of Alice's cake. I went by here, the market, and the Royal Academy of Medicine, down through the old Gothic quarter and the red-light area, to wait for the Picasso museum to open.

I found a bar, and ordered an *agua tonica,* and the paella. In the eighteenth century, they used to cook the rice with marsh rats and eels. I was more fortunate.

Hitchhiking to Madrid was off the menu, for the limited time I had to get there. I bought a Herald American, lemonade, and a can of tuna, for an overnight train ride. I forgot that I had no can opener. Colonizers, three conformicrats, from the Ministry of Foreign Affairs and Cooperation, colonized my compartment. They inquired about my journey. I told them of South America.

"We are the Fathers of South America." Said one. The word for 'fathers' in Spanish, *Papas*, carried more weight, and less cooperation. I told them that some of their children weren't terribly proud of their fathers, nor their foreign affairs.

Repetitive passport checks, by the *Guardia,* disturbed my night. Perhaps they were making sure I hadn't lost it, in a fugue state, somewhere along the way. No one expects the Spanish Inquisition.

I awoke into a magnificent arid landscape at seven, seven hundred kilometers later. El Centro was five more away. I walked it. A small room in the Hostel Buenos Aires surrounded me back to sleep. I dreamt from barbarism to decadence, without passing through civilization.

But then she didn't come, did she. Her plane was delayed but, even when it landed, she didn't get off. Iberia and TWA had never heard of her. My bus back to Plaza Colon was empty. The proprietress at the hostel didn't understand. I told her that Madrid was the first European city to have been bombed by airplanes, and that civilians were specifically targeted. When I walked down to Via Gran 28 to place a Happy Mother's Day long distance, I got the news. She wasn't coming. She would explain in a letter. Death in the Afternoon.

I found a hole in the wall, in the blood-raw light, among anchovy-oiled faces with whiskey voices, Cuban rice, *cerdo y lechuga*, and too much Rioja. The beatific Christ above the bar gave me the rest of the news. Waiting for a messiah is a long business, and you get many fake ones.

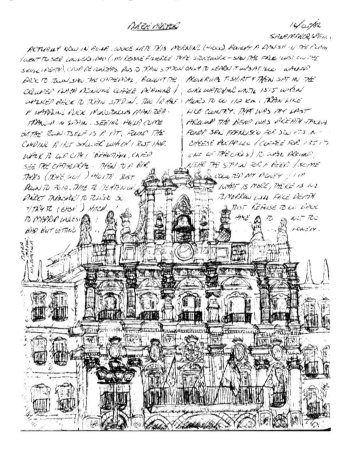

*   *   *

'We agreed to go together to the land of the Moors, begging our way
for the love of God, so that we might be beheaded there.'

Teresa of Avila

I awoke midmorning. Saturn had been eating his son. Dressing was slow. Waiting in line for pesetas at the bank, I decided to fall in love with the two Rhodesian girls ahead of me. It had to go somewhere.

We went to the Prado for Velasquez' *Las Meninas*, Goya's transition to madness, and Cano's peculiar painting of the Virgin Mary, shooting breast milk across the room, into the mouth of the *Vision of St. Bernard*. We walked up Calle del Amor y Dios, Love and God Street, for a lunch of artichokes and garlic green beans, asparagus tortilla, and delicious bread and wine. We told stories, and held each other's eyes. After a tour of the Casa Real, I left them, in the hot sun. Later, on Calle Echogary, we met for a trout dinner, and flamenco at Las Grabieles. They both kissed me goodnight, each of them earnest and different, solemn and beautiful, like the slow old tunes of Spain. Sleep followed, the first in a week.

I left Madrid next morning, for Castile. I hitchhiked into the Guadarrama Mountains, to Segovia, for the Aquaduct and the Alcazar, a fortress shaped like a fairytale stone ship, in which Isabella was proclaimed queen in 1474. Here she married Ferdinand, before expelling the Jews of Spain, in other boats, eighteen years later.

I managed a ride to Medina del Campo, and then a deadly slow *tranvia* in the rain, from the mediocre to the magical. The Plaza Mayor baroque bell tower in Salamanca was illuminated red, masonry mortared with chivalry. University students promenaded, around the shops and restaurants and carnival ice cream parlors, lining the old Iberian public square. Young girls waved to me from balconies. Christopher Columbus had lectured here. Hernando Cortes had taken his courses. Sleep

112

pulled me inside the wrought-iron grills, and simplicity, of the Fonda Las Vegas.

Late next morning, I had a coffee and *facture* pastry in the plaza. The day melted into drawings of the bell tower, and the ochre sandstone of the Casa de las Conchas, embossed with over three hundred shells. There was rumored to be an ounce of gold under one of them, and only the devil knew where. Unfortunately, he was on the railway tracks, too otherwise preoccupied to make the disclosure, further slowing my already inert *tranvia,* for the next hundred-kilometer journey. We waddled like an iron duck through the brown prairie monotony, until a rocky summit, with two kilometers of medieval walls, came around the bend, three hours later.

I had landed in Avila, the city of song and saints, although neither was much in evidence. Anselmo, one of Hemingway's characters in *For Whom the Bell Tolls*, was a lonely hunter from here. Emerging from the same guild, Orion climbed above the city walls, on darkness. I found a shower in the Fonda San Francisco, and a bar near the station, for food. There was a choice between tripe, and something called *Judías del Barco*, a Jewish 'food ship,' local white kidney beans cooked with pork sausage, chorizo, pigs ears, and anything else that oinked. Here in Avila at least, blasphemy had kept pace with the austerity of religion.

There was no linear connection to Toledo next morning, without going around all eight centuries of Avila's walls, looking for the highway. My first ride was from a Catholic teacher, who brought me twenty parochial kilometers, into a small town. An old man volunteered his son to drive me a further ten kilometers, to a castle on a lake, surrounded by bleached hills. A couple from Madrid took me to what they said was the turnoff to Toledo, but it wasn't. I hiked back into town, through red poppies, and a sea of yellow and blue flowers. I bought a cheese and ham bocadillo, on my way out the other side, where a young caballero gave me a lift, to Escalona. In the inferno of the Castillian midday, we had a beer. I walked for about two kilometers, past a ruined castle, and down across a bridge, to sit in the burning sun. The air trembled, and I fell asleep. A local bus stopped two hours later, and took me the rest of the way to Toledo.

The Alcazar fortress, and its black-capped corner towers, stood stalwart on top of the hill, surrounded on three sides by a bend in the Tagus River, manchego, marzipan, and metal. Its sword smiths had poured rich patterns, of Damascene gold and silver and oxidized black steel, into each other, to sever the Moors from Al-Andalus, during the Reconquista. But Spain itself was Damascene- African Black edges poured into the gold and silver of the Americas.

The two old Agatha Christie sisters of Casa Maria Soledes greeted me, with synchronous *'muy buenas tardes,'* hot water, soup, and tranquilo.

Before the Damascene arrived, Toledo was inlayed with tolerance. Jews, Christians and Moslems coexisted under the Caliphate of Cordoba, during the period known as *'La Convivencia.'* I began my day in the remnants of the old ghetto sinagogos, 'El Transito,' and 'San Maria la Blanca.' The first had a domesticated Mudéjar polychrome paneled ceiling, and Hebrew inscriptions of the names of God around the walls. I chose to believe that photos weren't allowed because of the embarrassing ignorance of the Spanish descriptive labeling. The second had been built in 1180 AD, but was now owned by the Catholic Church. The clue was the statue of the Virgin, where the Ark should have been. Saint Mary, the White. It was Moorishly, hauntingly empty. I went from the expelled to the expellers, through a Damascene shop, where I found a little *cajita* with an intricate black, gold, and silver Star of David on the hinged lid. As I hold it now, thirty years on, I still marvel at the incongruities of its existence.

Inside the Cathedral of San Tome were heavy Gothic vaults, of white stone and light. The floor, horizon, and sky dissolved into the swirling amniotic clouds, and tall phantasmal saints, of El Greco's greatest work, *The Burial of the Count of Orgaz.* Below, stood the sallow bruised and bearded corpse faces of his noblemen. You could smell the mortuary breath of both congregations.

I fetched Serendipity from the Agatha Christie spinsters, and walked the long march across the bridge, toward Aranjuez. Two hours, and the wooden flatbed of an old Pegaso truck, got me to Royal Palace. I heard Rodrigo's slow haunting Concierto echo off the porcelain floor, and the malachite, platinum, silk, and marble, of the Casa del Labrador.

Spanish blondes are haughtier than those of other nations. The regal straight back and pure Castellano of this one carried me out into the garden, for strawberries and cream.

"Deliciosa, no?" she asked.

"Si." And they were. As the sun departed, she directed my damascenery through the lavender and blue, to violet. I sat in the train station, watching the swallows swoop parallel arcs under the roof beams. When the locomotive pulled in, just after nine, I shared my compartment with Sadid, a Moroccan from Tetuan. We ate sardine sandwiches, and drank wine.

Córdoba arrived long before sunrise. I rolled the Gold Kazoo out onto the sidewalk. *'Bingbongbingbong'* broke the night air at intervals. *'Bongbongbingbong.'* I slept between the bongs and bings. A panhandler woke me, to ask for change, but quickly recognized the folly in his form.

In the 10th century, Córdoba was the world's most populous city, and its intellectual epicenter. Its streets shone with public lamps, when Europe went dark at sunset. It had three hundred public baths, when Europe was dirty. Its streets were paved, while Europe lay in mud. It had a library of a million volumes, when Europe's monks and nobility were still illiterate. It had arabesques, when Europe's palaces had smoke holes in their ceilings. Even a far-off Saxon nun, Hroswitha, called it the 'Jewel of the World.' Contrary to more idyllic claims, Córdoba thrived, not because the Moslems treated their Jews and Christians with that much more charity, but because the Christians, when they held the upper hand, had treated their Jews and Moslems with that much less.

The morning sun lit uneven whitewashed walls. I wandered the narrow alleyways of the Juderia ghetto, to the Mezquita, the final vanishing point of tolerance.

The Visigoth church had been converted to a mosque during Abd al-Rahman's Umayyad conquest, until bloody swords and banners of crosses on charger hoofs, trampled the turbaned dead back into the floor of the new cathedral, during the Reconquista, in 1236. I random-walked the landscape maze of double red and white candy-cane arches, inspired by those in the Dome of the Rock. The marble, jasper, onyx, and granite supporting pillars had been ripped from the original Roman temple. Eight hundred years later, a half a dozen Muslims knelt to pray during Holy Week. Security guards were injured. A knife was found. The ripping continues.

I sat in the park, until the Alcázar de los Reyes Cristianos opened next door. What the Moors had built into gardens, baths and libraries, Ferdinand and Isabella converted into torture and interrogation chambers, for the Spanish Inquisition. The screams of those confessing went on for three centuries. Isabella had the irrigation watermills destroyed, because they made too much noise.

Back in the Juderia, I bought my mother a silver filigree pendant, inspired by Golden Age artisans of Jewish culture in Spain, inlayed into the burnt charcoal of Moorish 'tolerance.' They were still *dhimmis* living under the Caliphate, paying an annual golden dinar *jizya* tribute tax, and forbidden from engaging in public demonstrations of their piety. Despite this, the Caliphate Jews prospered, and so did Andalusia as a whole. The freedom to engage in language translation and Talmudic study, led to inevitable advances in commerce and industry, poetry and philosophy, and science and medicine. Ten statues of the patron protector of Córdoba, the Archangel Raphael the Healer, are scattered throughout the city. And the living manifestation of Raphael, then and there, was Moses ben-Maimon. My own medical oath was that of Maimonides, not Hippocrates. His was just that more evocative, a larger canvas of the calling. Maimonides wrote ten medical works: three commentaries on the medical aphorisms of Moses, Hippocrates, and Galen, a drug pharmacopeia in Arabic, Greek, Syrian, Persian, Berber, and Spanish, and treatises on wellness, cohabitation, asthma, epilepsy, hemorrhoids, and poisons and their antidotes.

There was no antidote for the poison that came with the death of Abd-al-Rahman. The puritanical Almoravids, followed by the even more radical Almohades, invaded the Umayyads. The increasing burden of vowels in the conquerors, translated into an increasing burden of terror, to those in the middle of the Damascenery. Property and wives and children were confiscated, as these were all the same. The ones with heartbeats were sold as slaves. Muslim massacres against Jews occurred in Córdoba in 1011, and Granada on December 30, 1066. On that day, the mob stormed the Royal Palace, crucified the vizier, and put four thousand of his followers to death. They were lucky it wasn't the avenging Catholics who would come later, thrusting blackness through the silver of a golden age.

> 'And 'tis great pity that the noble Moor
> Should hazard such a place...'
> Shakespeare, *Othello*

*   *   *

> 'This could be heaven or this could be hell.'
> Eagles, *Hotel California*

It was both, actually. I took a late afternoon bus through narrow streets of whitewashed pueblos to the city of the pomegranate, *Gárnata al-Yahud*, Granada of the Jews. After a two-kilometer hike, I found my bit of heaven, across a sea of white clouds and red terracotta. Hotel California, just up from the Restaurant Reys Catholicos, the *Restaurant of the Catholic Kings*. The gazpacho, fried fish, bread, wine and oranges were so sabroso, I fell asleep later under the hot shower.

The real heaven was the 'Paradise on Earth' of the Alhambra, next morning. Moorish poets had described it as 'a pearl set in emeralds.' I walked into an emerald park of wildflowers, roses, orange blossoms, narcissus, camphor and myrtles, through the sounds of nightingales and running water, to open-columned arcades, reflecting pools and fountains. A palace of sun and breezes, and balsamic perfumes. Canary date palms. Sponge toffee on sticks. Its tiles and walls faded through blue, red and golden yellow, into an ethereal geometry. The fountain in the Court of the Lions was modeled after the Temple of Solomon. Here I fell entranced. I sat in the garden of the Generalife. Here I fell in awe.

In 1492 the Emirate of Granada surrendered to the Catholic Monarchs, and Heaven became Hell. Cardinal de Cisneros gave the order to 'convert or emigrate.' For those less compliant the first time round, the next order was to 'convert or die.' In Spain, the dead are more alive than the dead of any other country in the world.

The rest of the day was never going to measure up. Halfway down the hill from the Alhambra, in Cuesta de Gomerez, I came upon a one-armed instrument maker. I paid Señor Ferrer a small fraction of his asking price, for a half sized guitar. It was the least I could do.

Checking out of the Hotel California was easy. The wooden seats on the slow *tranvia* were hard, and the sweltering compartment pitched and jolted, all the way to Ronda. I remember a mouse-faced elderly priest, and a hairy Andalusian farmer traveling with his Albino son. The DNA was in Arabic script.

That I was a foreigner was not my fault. I would have rather been born there, living with a hawk in the sky, and an earthen jar of water in the dust. Ronda was quintessential Spain, where great bridges spanned bottomless canyons, where bullfighting began and Goya's funeral grin ended, where Republicans threw Nationalists off the cliffs of El Tajo, where George Eliot wrote of her Jewish roots in *Daniel Deronda*, where Hemingway wrote For *Whom the Bell Tolls*, and where I wrote my journal, and found a place to play my half-guitar, in the old bullring, and the Fonda Español. Later I lingered, over the tuna bocadilla and yoghurt, and the deepest ravines and loneliness in Spain.

But how simple it is when one knows nothing. I didn't know that the mosquito larva-laden swimming pool I would check into next day in Marbella would be called *Albergue Africa*. I wasn't sure that was where I would be going next. I was supposed to be following Benjamin of Tudela's journey in reverse, from the Holy Land, along the course of Western Civilization. But the scent grew colder, as I traveled further west, and my immune system cried out for a tonic. I knew I would definitely find that in Africa. The afternoon drizzled sand down the beach. The wind was blowing it offshore, across the Strait of Gibraltar. I didn't know what I would be returning to, at the Albergue, but it was all there, waiting.

In Barcelona I had encountered an Australian, named What-else Bruce. He invited me to join him, and his brother, at a table, around the pool. I didn't know that we would spend the evening here, eating bread and cheese and oranges, and half-playing my half guitar. I didn't know we would be joined by others, and would talk of Morocco. I didn't know that she would sit next to me, with her flowers and castanets. And I didn't know, when the last of us left the table for their beds, she would turn to me with her question.

"Will you take me to Morocco?" She asked. *This could be heaven, or this could be hell.*

I told her. I didn't know.

Gates of Paradise

'Morocco as it is a very fine place spoiled by civilization.'
Richard H. Davis

But then she did come, didn't she. Not at first, of course, and certainly not that you would have noticed. She had come to me across the patio next morning, as I was finishing my coffee and bread and jam. I told her that I was flattered, but that I was going to Morocco, and that it would be dangerous enough without a beautiful young Western woman, and that she really needed to make other arrangements. She turned, and left, without a word.

When I boarded the bus to Algeciras, I found her sitting in the back. I sat in the front. On the boat to Ceuta, I caught, and then released her, out of the corner of my eye. A Parisian named Denis struck up a conversation, and we shared a San Miguel. We caught a bus to the Centro, and another to the Moroccan border. She got on both.

We arrived into a scene of chaos and witchcraft. There were wizards with hooded djellabas. The African flies were back. Berbers with broad-brimmed red hats, hung with red pompoms, pushed us aside. Women wore bands of silver coins, on their foreheads. There was mineral water and vegetable carts and animal cruelty. The sun went into supernova hyperdrive, and hygiene went into limbo. Hustlers appeared out of the dust and disorder.

"What is your country? You are my friend. Where are you going? You are welcome. I will be your guide..."

It was Islam, and Bedlam, and every man for himself. Denis kept his hands in his pockets, but I could see the swindlers getting in through his mind. I looked back to see her in panic and pain. She was being accosted from all sides, by the menace of Moroccan manhood, pinched and cajoled, grabbed and led by the multitude of hands, on her backpack and body.

I whistled. Loud. She ran to catch up.

"My name's Astrid." She said. "I'm from South Africa."

"I know." I said.

We boarded the bus, for the last thirty-three kilometers to Tetuan. Orchards of cypress, almonds, oranges, and pomegranates lined the river road, through the Martil valley. I gave Astrid the rest of my water. She took my hand as well. Denis had struck up a conversation with a tout, and it took us forever to shake him, on arriving. We found the Pension Iberia, and agreed to meet Denis later. Our room was on the third floor. We showered and, wrapped in our towels, peered out on the glorious view of the circular plaza, with its small pool, and marble fountains, and Canary Island palms. Whitewashed houses floated all the way up the mountain. Astrid and I soared up right behind them. But Denis arrived too early. We dressed hurriedly, and unlocked the door. He entered, and smiled.

"Aren't you worried for your safety?" He asked.

"No." I replied. "Are you?"

"Not at all." He boasted, and removed a revolver from his right pocket. Astrid's eyes grew wide.

"Are you crazy?" I asked him. "You brought a gun through a border crossing, to this country?"

"Of course." He said. "It is only for protection."

"If you ever need it, you will have already lost." I said. He put it away.

We went to the Restaurant Moderno, for couscous. The food so nice, they named it twice. Astrid and I left Denis and his pistol in the psychedelic colors of the Medina, at dusk. Our ceiling in the Iberia was exquisitely carved, and painted in Hispano-Moresque designs. Nobody noticed.

Maybe it was the drone of the muezzin that woke us before dawn. *Allahu Akbar*. Maybe it was the birdsong. Maybe it was the jasmine, or the citrus blossoms, or the scent of ourselves. Whatever it may have been, we awoke before dawn. And slept again.

When Astrid finally saw the ceiling, it was already midmorning. We left the room, to allow our laundry to dry in private, and wander the Medina. There were overflowing exotic spices, beautiful antiques, robes and fabrics, fishmongers and olivemongers, and the smells of oranges and donkey shit, cardamom and incense, and mint and thyme. The view from the top of the hill was mesmerizing, the salad and orange juice at the Moderno, delicious. At the top of the stairs in the Iberia, we found What-else Bruce and his brother, Andrew. It seemed fated, and we all left for the bus station, to buy tickets to Chefchaouen.

*   *   *

'Perdition catch all the guides'
Mark Twain, Innocents Abroad

Illusion is the first of all pleasures. In Morocco, reality was always waiting outside, to beat it to death. The guides at the bus station maneuvered us like a goatherd. One dirham was paid for each bag up onto the roof and, after the two-hour journey through the Rif mountain scenery, one dirham for each bag down.

We emerged outside, under the two goat-horned mountains that had given the town its name. Jews and Moroscos, driven from Spain by the Reconquista, founded Chefchaouen. Their blue pastel stucco houses still lined the narrow alleyways, like alien sponges.

Before the prolific local hashish landed on illusion, to become the second of all pleasures, reality was waiting outside to beat the first one to death. Half a millennium later, a quarter million Jews were driven out of the country, just before our bus arrived. They fled to where Yasser Arafat had just announced that he would 'knock on the Gates of Paradise with the skulls of the sons of Zion.' *In the name of Allah, the Compassionate, the Merciful.* The spawn of the guides that had maneuvered them into that goatherd exile, were waiting outside, like reality, when the bus doors opened.

"American Kike!" Shouted the finger. And it began.

"This isn't England. This is Africa." From another. We descended into the mob. Another pushed my shoulder from behind.

"Hey Capitalist. You like gold?" It was going to be like that. I carried Serendipity's one dirham arc off the top of the bus, around to the source of the adoration. It was a backhand shot, but the goal was good.

Astrid and I moved faster than What-else Bruce and Brother Andrew, but they kept up with us. One of the guides picked up a rock.

"Your girlfriend wants to fuck us, not you." He screamed.

A man is what he fights for. My right hand crossed his face somewhere between Hollywood and the Bible. Rocks came off the ground. Knives emerged.

"Faites attention!" Came off to my right. It was Denis. His pistol was half out of his pocket. Everybody went home.

"If you ever need it, you will have already lost." He mocked.

Astrid and I were happy to take the rest of the day off. We checked into the Hotel Rif, and did room service omelets and oranges.

The flute that wailed at sunset, had tutored the Moroccan roosters at dawn. They crowed in a strange sad minor key. *Allahu Akbar.* Green hills were covered in mist. Astrid and I met up with What-else Bruce and Andrew for breakfast, and a furtive reconnoiter through the beautiful wool carpets, in the Medina. We managed to avoid a replay of the carnage of the previous day at the bus station, and set off on the road to Fez. Two Australian girls sat in front of us, gum-chewing above their see-through T-shirts and short shorts. Illusion is the first of all pleasures.

Just outside Ouzzine, we stopped at one of the many

roadblocks that seemed to punctuate road travel in the Maghreb. The soldiers were obviously having difficulty disengaging their vision from illusion, but their Captain had us all brought outside, for the offense of laughing. A lecture on the evils of disrespecting police control officers ensued, and lasted until his own eyes grew tired. Fields of wild yellow flowers and red poppies followed us the rest of the way to Fez. We were met by the usual welcome wagon of misfits. I paid one to pull down Astrid's pack, and then asked him for directions to the Hotel Jardine Publique. When he pointed, the hustlers went wild. We escaped in that direction anyway, What-else Bruce and Brother Andrew, and see-through Aussies in tow. The hotel was hung with sinuous wrought-iron balconies. Astrid and I settled into the white plaster, faded cedar, and intricate *zellij* tiles of our room. Later, in the Medina, we met Abdul, who convinced us to hire him as a guide for the following morning. After a delicious chicken couscous, we lingered in the little Souk restaurant, sucking our third tiny glass of mint tea through sugar cubes, and into each other's dreams.

> 'Le premier verre est aussi amer que la vie,
> le deuxième est aussi fort que l'amour,
> le troisième est aussi doux que la mort.'

> *'The first glass is as bitter as life,*
> *the second glass is as strong as love,*
> *the third glass is as gentle as death.'*

The sunrise blazed on our door, and seeped into the rest of the day. It was the color of the cherries we ate for breakfast, the red carpets in the Karouiyne mosque, the pigments in the honeycomb stone vessels of the Dyer's Souk, and the cornelian bark of its felt *tarboosh* hats. As the light lifted off the rose petals and rust, Adbul arrived to show us his city.
We saw where Maimonides landed at Al-Karaouine University, after being forced from Spain. He brought us to

the thirteen windows of the Dar Al-Magana water clock house, just as the first opened, and dropped a metal ball into one of the twelve brass bowls. Hides dropped into square cement vats of pigeon shit, in the tannery. The effluent steamed and streamed, down wide curved channels, into the horizon, leaving its stench behind. We lingered under the old Jewish quarter balconies. In a small alcove near the Royal Palace, our spoons glided through the saffron and ginger and pepper, of harira soup. Bubbles roared into the glasses of mint tea, poured from a great height. Little by little, the camel goes into the couscous. Little by little, Astrid and I went into each other, in the same way.

*   *   *

'Mutual forgiveness of each vice, such are the Gates of Paradise.'
William Blake

There are eight Gates of Paradise in Islam. According to Mohammed, they are all open on Mondays and Thursdays. Astrid and I arrived in Meknes, on a Thursday.
Depending on your sources, the eight Gates are the Gate of Jihad, the Gate of Fasting, the Gate of Prayer, the Gate of Charity, the Gate of Repentance, the Gate of Faith, the Gate of those who are pleased with Allah and what He has given them, and the Gate of those who suppress anger. There doesn't seem to be much of a lineup to get through the last one.
Unfortunately, the gates of Meknes are not the Gates of Paradise. The Mansour Gate was named after the Christian convert architect. It has magnificent mosaics and marble columns, from the nearby Roman ruins of Volubilis. When the Gate was finished, Sultan Moulay Ismail asked Mansour if he could have done better. Mansour felt obliged to answer

126

yes. The Sultan had him executed on the spot. In 2010 a minaret crashed into the Lalla Khenata mosque at the Berdieyinne Gate, killing 41 worshippers. There was blood at the Gates of Paradise. Fortunately, it happened on a Monday.

For twenty-five dirhams, we checked into a dark green room, on the second floor of the Moroc Hotel. House buntings flew random flight paths, from the branches of the orange grove and leaking septic air, rising from the interior courtyard. We opened the wooden shutters for the breeze.

What-else Bruce and Brother Andrew mounted the stairs, to collect us for a reconnaissance. We found the old weapons and Korans in the Museum, and new ones in the Medina. The See-through Aussies caught up to us, visibly upset about their harrowing near-rape the night before. I pointed out the frenzy of flies on the uncovered lamb. They bought shawls.

We left the Mansour Gate, for the Mercedes taxis scattered outside. Evading the guides, we found a pleasant old driver, to take us to Volubilis. The open windows were refreshing in the heat. The lush green countryside carried us, through olive groves, flowers and wheat fields, to the small town of Moulay Idriss. These were the same crops grown by the Romans. We had Volubilis to ourselves. Among the daisies and poppies, were large mosaics with elephants and sea creatures, triumphal arches, and temples. Hebrew grave markers and a menorah would be found, long after we were there.

Two Moroccan police moustaches were waiting for us, on our exit. They spoke to me in Arabic. I spoke to them in French. They forced me into the back of their vehicle, and drove back into Meknes. Moroccans were apparently not allowed to travel with tourists in taxis, and they were convinced I was a local, even with the presentation of my Canadian passport.

"Pouquoi parlez-vous Français?" They asked. *Why do you speak French.*

"Pour la meme raison que vous parlez Français." I said. *For the same reason you speak French.*

It was the source of no small amusement for the six of us later, at dinner. We ate in a small place, just around the corner from the Moroc. As it turned out, it was so small that everything we ordered took forever to arrive. What-else Bruce eventually solved the mystery. Every time we asked for something, young boys would dash out the back, towards a direction specific to what was being requested. Chicken couscous came from the south, beverages from the west, and salad from the east. We played with the compass until the boys were tired, but they were well pleased with their tip.

Our transport to Khenifra next morning departed at five. The bus attendant's left glass eye was too large for its socket. It was just as well we were all half asleep. He allowed us a stop, to purchase bread and oranges in Azrou, before we ascended into the foothills of the Mid-Atlas Berber encampments. Their black tents, faces, and goatherds, were a perfect complement to the sunrise, on the tree-dotted slopes.

Khenifra's walls were redwashed, to absorb the sun. We pulled in around noon, and checked into the fleabag Hotel Essada, across from the bus station. The welcoming warmth of the rickets-afflicted old proprietress, made up for its lack of amenities. We boarded another bus to Mrirt, for the Berber livestock market, that we had seen on the way through, earlier. It was a carnival of gravel, tents, spices, donkey saddles, and heat. Astrid told me on the way back to Khenifra. She had pain, and redwashed urine. I had aspirin, and some old ampicillin. Honeymoon cystitis in Morocco. Unfortunately, it was a Friday. And there was blood at the Gates of Paradise.

'Beware of good intentions and the passion in their eyes
For none of them can open the Gates of Paradise.'
David Byrne, *Gates of Paradise*

Atlas Shrugged

'Wouldn't you know we're riding on the Marrakesh Express,
they're taking me to Marrakesh.'
Crosby, Stills, and Nash, *Marrakesh Express*

In Berber, it meant 'the Land of God.' *Mur-Akuc*. Marrakech.
It made the same sucking sound of sudden halted breathing,
as we did when Mount Toubkal came around the corner, and
the snows on the other peaks of the high Atlas range collided
with our Bluebird. Sunlight from Heaven danced along the
pinnacles.
Astrid was feeling better, well enough to travel. The first bus
we caught to Beni Mellal that cloudy morning, stopped at
every post office on the way, through green hills and black
tents. We sat drinking mint tea, until our next bus boarded
midmorning. The young boys sat behind Astrid, nostrils
flaring. One claimed to be Italian. A few words disabused him
of the notion, and earned him an award of punches from his
fellow admirers.
There were horse-drawn carriages waiting at the station. We
hired one for six dirhams, to take us to the interior courtyard
trees, tiles, and wrought-iron balconies, of the Hotel Afriquia.
It smelled of orange blossoms and methane and sulfur. The
rooftop terrace opened to the sky.
The desk clerk was named Aziz. He was eyeing up my half-
sized guitar.
"You can play?" He asked me. I answered with some
humility.
"You can play Hotel California?" I answered with less
humility. It was my Magnum Opus.
"You are my friend forever." He said. And that was that.
Around the corner, we walked into the pure sorcery of the
Djemaa el Fna. There were children dragging chained Barbary
apes, psychedelic water sellers festooned with brass cups and

leather water bags, and turbaned men 'charming cobras in the square.' Orange juice ran through its lymphatics. The entertainment changed as the day progressed. Snakes gave way to snake oil peddlers. Storytellers competed with each other, in adjacent circular islands of myth. Magicians and musicians, and Chleuh dancing boys, enjoined the spectacle. As the sun fell, the opening food stalls merged, into one busy open-air restaurant. The air was replaced by mint and carbonized meat and couscous.

The blood had abated, and the Gates of Paradise had reopened. We spent the next morning in the labyrinth of the Medina, out of the bright light and suffocating heat. Striped shadows crossed the stalls and their owners.

"You are welcome." They said. Mint tea lubricated every offer, within the low ceilings and high prices. There were mountains of dates and almonds, red paprika and yellow turmeric, caged chameleons, incense, ostrich eggs, silver teapots, and pointed-toe yellow leather slippers. We discovered old French postcards, box cameras and Berber chests, held together by cobwebs. After a tour of the 14th century Ben Youssef Medersa, What-else Bruce and Brother Andrew joined us in the carpet souk, where Jubi, and his son, surgically extracted a critical mass of dirhams *in the name of Allah, the Compassionate, the Merciful,* in exchange for a Berber carpet and a striped djellaba, that I 'could wear at home' (if I wanted to be arrested on sight).

The waiter at Café Oriental that evening was paralyzed with fear, until an interpreter convinced him that we only wanted food. The chicken with olives, oranges, and cumin, took us through the ninth Gate of Paradise. Back on the terrace of the Afriquia, I played Hotel California for Aziz. We were friends forever. Mint tea arrived later, to Brother Andrew's room, where I discovered him prostrate, with a fever. We had planned to leave the next morning, to climb Mount Toubkal. It would have to wait.

The next morning found Aziz and I, playing guitar on the terrace again. Our chords echoed off the blue tiles and arabesque grillwork and lanterns, down into the citrus courtyard. Mint tea rose up from around the central fountain, in appreciation.

In the afternoon we visited the Koutoubia mosque, whose minaret was the model for the Giralda in Seville, and whose form was the model for most of the church towers in Spain and Eastern Europe. There were originally four golden globes at the top, one donated by the wife of the great Moorish general, Al-Mansur, for her inability to keep the Ramadan fast. From the ninth gate quality of all the food we were finding in Morocco, the punishment had been too extreme for the crime.

I fell asleep climbing Mount Toukbal, rising out of the Land of God, out of the heat, the flies, the decay and desperation, ascending to the only base of tranquility in Morocco.

*   *   *

'But it was Fauna's conviction, born out of long experience,
that most people, one, did not know what they wanted;
two, did not know how to go about getting it;
and three, didn't know when they had it.'

John Steinbeck, *Sweet Thursday*

Aziz wanted us to wait an extra day so he could come with us. We told him we couldn't. He told us it was 'no problem.' "Relax." Said the night man. "We are programmed to receive." He sang it all. You could check out any time you want, but he could never leave.

Astrid and I boarded the bus to Asni, with What-else Bruce and Brother Andrew. The views through the mountains were exquisite. We squeezed into a ten-person taxi, for the rest of our journey to the base camp hill town of Imlil, and were extruded into a dense fog, rolling between rectangular orange stone houses, with white painted window frames. Orchards of cherries, walnuts, and apples, lay just beyond. We found a room in the Café Soleil, and the owner, Hajj Mohamed, welcomed us warmly, with mint tea and extra cushions. The falling water roar of the river carried us off to sleep, after our candlelight ran out.

At over four thousand meters, Toubkal is the highest peak in North Africa. The Marquis de Segonzac made the first successful European ascent in 1923, thirty years after he was acquitted of the murder of Lieutenant Paul Quique, his explorer companion in the Ivory Coast. Segonzac said that Quique had died of a fever. The skull, that Quique's family exhumed, had bullet holes.

My head felt like it had that kind of fever next morning, but it cleared with purpose, and breakfast bread and jam. We began our hike through the irrigated valley across the river. We climbed a steep scree scramble to the east, into a high corrie, and then another sheer slope, above the snowline. I gave Astrid the encouragement she needed, until we all finally arrived at a shelter, onto a col, at thirty-nine hundred meters. The hut was locked, and no amount of ingenuity on our part could open it. The fleeing sun left us freezing. We boiled tea and soup, but the cold began to penetrate our morale, and then our marrow. Just as our shivering was shutting down, the custodian arrived, to open the refuge. We spread out our sleeping bags, and ate the last of our couscous and spicy sardines.

Unconsciousness came quickly, but it was broken through the night by the altitude. I went outside to pee, and lingered within the Milky Way. The firmament luminesced against the blackness of the High Atlas night sky. Orion sparkled.

I made coffee, and woke the others at five. After muesli and oranges, we abandoned the shack, and turned left towards the summit. I held Astrid's hand until we were almost there. Then What-else Bruce and I raced, across the curvature of the Earth, to the strange pyramidal metal frame at the top. We became elated with the terrain gained, and the oxygen lost. The views were unsurpassed. From the summit, we saw the curvature of our kismet. Everyone hugged everyone.

I destroyed my jeans sliding down the snowfield, back to the shelter. A brief respite for soup and couscous refueled our descent, through eerie mists, down slippery shale. Beautiful costumed Berber girls joined us, singing us all the way back to Imlil. The taxi to Asni, that Hajj Mohamed had arranged, broke down with a flat tire, but we still made it back to Aziz and the Hotel Afriquia by dusk. After a celebration of lemon chicken at the Café Oriental, Astrid and I withdrew, to a cold shower and warm breath.

I think it was the muscle stiffness that finally woke us next morning. Astrid and I had to help each other get dressed. We started at the Bahia Palace, an immense courtyard with a central basin, surrounded by innumerable rooms, for the Grand Vizier's four wives and forty concubines. He had been a busy man. The old codger guarding the museum wouldn't let us in without a guide. By a wonderful coincidence, his grandson, Mustafa, was available. There were marriage thrones, weapons, and rugs, but I was most enchanted by the intricacy of the hexagonal ceiling. Little Mustafa brought us to the Italian Carrara marble Saadi Tombs and gardens, rediscovered in 1917. Here was gold, stucco, finely worked cedar, and rosemary and flowers. Back at the Hotel Afriquia, Astrid and I bid adieu to What-else Bruce, Brother Andrew and Aziz, for a final lunch, at the Argana Café, in the Djemaa el Fna.

It was not far from here, several years after we ate our lemon cumin chicken and olives, that a bilingual French nun was injured, in a moped accident. The head trauma she sustained, left her with a bizarre disability. Every second day, she was able to speak French, but not Arabic. Alternate days in between, she was able to speak Arabic, but not French. God speaks Arabic, but modernity speaks French.

Djemaa el Fna is Arabic for *'Assembly of the Dead'*. Shortly before noon on April 28, 2011, a blast destroyed the Argana Café, killing at least twenty people. Among the dead were two and a half Canadians. Some Jews who were driven out of Ancient Israel by the Romans, fled to Spain. Some Jews who were driven out of Spain by the Reconquista, fled to Morocco. Some Jews who were driven out of Morocco by the Arabs in 1947, fled to Israel, thus completing the two thousand year old circle. Michal Zekry was an Israeli-Canadian visiting her Casablanca in-laws, with her Moroccan-born husband, Messod. The bag, containing an explosive device packed with nails, was waiting for them in the Argana Café, on their day trip to Marrakech. The nails missed the three-year old son they had left in Casablanca. The detonation didn't miss Michal's unborn child, floating with his parents, in the Assembly of the Dead. In Berber, it means the 'Land of God.' *Mur-Akuc*. Marrakech. It made the same sucking sound of sudden halted breathing, as we did when Mount Toubkal came around the corner. God speaks Arabic, but modernity speaks French. On that day, the nails were speaking Arabic.

*   *   *

Captain Renault: "What in heaven's name brought you to Casablanca?"
Rick: "My health. I came to Casablanca for the waters."
Captain Renault: "The waters? What waters? We're in the desert."
Rick: "I was misinformed."

Casablanca

The peddlers were flogging Vick's VapoRub, on the bus, before we left. The one with a hook where his hand should have been, told me it would cure anything. I pointed to his hook.

The Aussies would have felt right at home in the lingering eucalyptol and overheated Bluebird, but Astrid and I had left them far behind. We rode, for what seemed like forever, into dry savanna and semi desert. Cud-chewing camels turned into argan tree-climbing goats. And through the cedar forest, just before dusk, we hit the salt air of the Atlantic coastal paradise that was Essouira. *Es-saouira*, the 'beautifully-designed,' was home to pirates, and the ultimate destination of sub-Saharan caravans, from Timbuktu. Mohammed III had hired an Englishman, nicknamed Ahmed el Alj, *Ahmed the Renegade*, to recruit French and Genoese engineers, to direct Christian slaves, in the construction of his trading port for Christian European merchants and diplomats. He encouraged Moroccan Jews to settle here, to serve as commercial intermediaries. They built many synagogues, and once constituted forty percent of the population. There is still an annual pilgrimage to the grave of the seer, Rabbi Haim Pinto, but all the former inhabitants have gone. In Essouira Winston Churchill met Orson Welles filming *Othello*. We passed Orson's bust, nose busted, guano basted.

The wind blew us through narrow whitewashed walls, and white-shrouded wraith women, profiled in apricot light. The local gendarmerie guided us into the Hotel Tourisme, a fresh fish dinner, and each other again.

Essouira was now all white and yellow and blue, but its real

135

name was originally Mogodor, and its real color had been Tyrian purple. Phoenicians had originally settled the Iles Purpuraires, the islands in front of the town, in their search for the murex marine snail mucus, the pigment used to color stripes purple, in everything from Israelite priestly garments, to Imperial Roman Senatorial togas. When Jimmy Hendrix stayed in Essouira, he produced another textile of Tyrian purple,

> 'Purple haze all around
> Don't know if I'm comin' up or down
> Am I happy or in misery?
> Whatever it is, that girl put a spell on me'

The spell was complete. I was happy. Astrid and I were living in an illuminated Persian manuscript, the title page of caring and carnal perfection. We ordered freshly baked whole wheat bread and homemade apricot jam breakfasts in bed, and ripe apricots and more coffee later, in the Medina. A Muscleman sold me another carpet I didn't want. We bought intricately carved local cedar boxes, and pairs of matching new purple baggy pants. Astrid almost split hers laughing, at my close shave from a Berber barber, possessed of a straight razor and curled toe camel shoes. We ate grilled sardines on the limestone wharf. Rogue waves crashed over us. We didn't care. Beyond the seagulls hovering over long rows of canon along the seawall, we met some French travelers, who gave us the pouch containing the key to the Portuguese fortress. There was a clod of hashish inside.

"Bon voyage!" They said as they left, laughing.

> 'Purple Haze was in my brain,
> lately things don't seem the same,
> actin' funny but I don't know why
> 'scuse me while I kiss the sky.'

The sunsets on the roof of the Hotel Tourisme were fine. Our time in Essouira had stood still, for just long enough. It had been a dream, a magic haunting. Astrid quoted me in her diary the last evening there. '*Losing dreams makes one old.*' I'm old now.

We found our way to the bus station by moonlight, and our punishment was to arrive in the early dawn. With writhing abdominal cramps that only struck after we had started on the road to Casablanca, like the gunpowder tea of our destination. We held our breaths to inspire our sphincters, between the few pit stops we were allowed, en route. By the time we arrived in Casablanca mid-afternoon, we were exhausted from the jarring pain, and the jarring jarring, but our ordeal seemed to have ended.

Astrid and I found the Hotel Gallia, a nice old place for twenty-five dirhams, across from the central market. We spent the evening sampling the pastries, and finding a bus, leaving for Tangier at five the next morning. A kiss is just a kiss. A sigh is just a sigh. The fundamental things apply. As time goes by. *I'd bet they're asleep in New York. I'd bet they're asleep all over America.*

We almost missed our bus next morning, by lingering too long over our last mint tea and apricots. Our flight to Tangier, became our flight through Tangier, on arriving. The guides were back with a vengeance, but we were now well honed in our aversion skills, and managed to evade their weaselness by directing them, to slower tourist 'preferred clients,' with more obvious needs and means of support. We boarded the *Zaragoza*, to cross the narrow straits with the heron-billed pale cattle birds, and 'dawn breaking upon those mingled seas.' We ate cheese sandwiches and drank cold beer and swore in Spanish, because it felt so good.

Disembarking in Algeciras, a friendly sailor directed us to accommodation, in a small Fonda. There was a magnificent meal of roast pork and wine, waiting for us at Casa Maria. It was exactly that sort of thing one could expect to find, on the other side of the Gates of Paradise.

❋ ❋ ❋ ❋

Querencia

'The air soft as that of Seville... and so fragrant that it was delicious to breathe it'

Christopher Columbus

It came out of bullfighting. *Querencia.* It charges out hard from the back of the mouth, forward in a final sigh. There is a place in the bullring, where the bull feels most comfortable, to where he repeatedly returns because, by repeatedly returning, it becomes even more repeatedly familiar. It is this intensifying homing instinct, in the face of increasing danger, that makes him more and more predictable, more and more vulnerable. The pain of not being able to return grows faster than the incremental torment around him. His world ends in nostalgia and stasis, seductive liars that seal his fate. For everything can be killed, except nostalgia, and nostalgia, as they say, is not what it used to be.

It was in this way that I returned to Spain, *a mi querencia.* Through sinking moon and rising sun on misty hills of sunflowers, fighting bulls, tearful virgins, whitewashed walls, and the hoarse sailor, clapping flamenco in the aisle of our bus, I came back into Andalucía. Seville was like an old cigar box label.

It was so hot you couldn't sweat, too painful to breathe. 'La lluvia en Sevilla es una pura maravilla.' *The rain in Seville is a pure marvel.* But there wasn't going to be any. The city's motto was a rebus, scribbled everywhere: 'NO8DO.' The figure eight represents a skein of yarn, a 'madeja.' So 'No madeja do' sounds like 'No me ha dejado,' which means 'It (Sevilla) has not abandoned me.' You can find it scrawled on Christopher Columbus' tomb. When the Moors built their mosque, they imported Sevilla's orange trees, to provide shade and scent, and to mask the hot stink of the medieval city. The oranges, like the history, are bitter, but make excellent marmalade, as the inhabitants of the English coast discovered, when they boiled them on their beaches, in the same salt water that sank the Armada. Sevilla grew rich from the royal monopoly it held on colonial imports. The New World goods that passed through the Casa de Contratación, purchased its 'golden age.'

Astrid and I found the Pension Perez Montilla in the Juderia, and reemerged to run errands in Barrio Santa Cruz. I bought my ticket for the Novillada bullfight, to be held two days down the road, in the oldest bullring in Spain, the *Plaza de Toros de la Real Maestranza de Caballeria de Sevilla*. It was that old.

We fled the heat, into a little bar for beer and tapas. The little plates didn't cover Astrid's big cerveza fast enough. The ricochet, back to the pension, threw us into throes, and a deep siesta. I had a disturbing dream about my father, in the after burn. On returning home from the last leg of the cartwheels in China, he was leaning over a pushcart, selling bread made from multicolored strips of plastic. I awoke drenched, conflicted and confused. Freud would have had a fiesta.

We passed through the last cobalt light, profiling the iron filigree cross, in Plaza Santa Cruz, that evening. It was the kind of cross that would stab you in the heart, for not being Catholic enough, and it pointed our way to the flamenco, at Tablao Los Gallos. Astrid caught the fever. She strutted and posed, chin in the sky, all the way back to our room. The heat drove the mosquitoes crazy, and they drove us to the same querencia.

We donated our second day in Sevilla, to history. The royal palace exotic Mudéjar majesty of the Alcazar, and its walled gardens, were enchanting. The name translated as 'Courtyard of the Maidens,' a reference to the annual hundred virgins, that the Christian kingdoms, were to supply their Moorish masters. As Reconquista propaganda, it couldn't have played better. The Virgin of the Navigators hovered over embarking Spanish ships in the Casa de Contratación, where Columbus met Ferdinand and Isabella for his first debriefing.

We walked to where he was buried, in the largest Gothic cathedral in the world, the Catedral de Santa Maria de la Sede. You could float a zeppelin inside. According to the minutes of the meeting at its inception, the planners conceived of 'a church so beautiful and so great that those who see it built will think we were mad.' They weren't mad. They were batshit crazy. The dome collapsed, over a hundred years into its construction. It collapsed again in 1888, killing 'every precious object below.'

The adjacent Giralda is a twelfth century Almohad minaret, for the bottom two thirds, and a Renaissance wedding cake, for the remainder of its hundred-meter height. The tower's interior was built with ramps, rather than stairs, to allow the muezzin and others to ride to the top on horseback. Astrid and I climbed it on foot, for views of the molded cement ice tray roof, and Barber pole of Seville balustrades, of the Cathedral, and the tiled canopies and courtyards of the city beyond. The bells tolled, and were deafening. We had moved to another room, in our own interior cloister at Pension Cruces Perez-Almeida, earlier in the day, and were greeted by a flute and guitar ensemble in the quadrangle patio, upon our return. The evening flowed into tapas, and a visit to the master guitar maker Antonio Barba, followed by flamenco, until two-thirty in the morning at La Troucha. And that's how I remember the dawn of my Spanish querencia, watching the sunrise on the western wall, wondering how a trout gets to Sevilla.

I awoke to Astrid's smile, clenching a red rose from the previous night. She had foraged for pastries and coffee. We went together, to see the gardens and azuelos tiles of the Casa de Pilatos palace, and the expansive half-circle of the Plaza de España. She sat with me, for a tigernut horchata drink near the museum, before I left her for the bullfight. For a hundred pesetas I had purchased a *Sol y Sombra* seat, half sun and half shade. The shade half was right on time. I had read enough Hemingway, to be dangerous with the elemental metaphysics of bullfighting. I had been seduced by his almost religious dedication to it, as a ritualized ballet of fear and courage, and life and death.

'There are only three sports: bullfighting, motor racing, and mountaineering; all the rest are merely games... Bullfighting is the only art in which the artist is in danger of death and in which the degree of brilliance in the performance is left to the fighter's honour.'

I was in rare company, for those deaths in the afternoon. The viewing public, in this *Plaza de Toros de la Real Maestranza de Caballeria de Sevilla,* had the reputation of being the most unforgiving in Spain. Before and even during the paseíllo procession, there was an unnerving serenity. When the first bull came out, however, he shattered the calm with his raw brute energy.

In a Novillada, the toreros are amateur bullfighters that have not yet decided, whether or not to commit. The same cannot be said of the bulls. They were committed, although they weren't initially quite sure to what. The first matador gave me a sense of what Hemingway saw in it all. He was elegant, dispatching his first bull quickly, with a well-aimed *estocada* sword plunge, into an instantly ruptured aorta. I was almost converted, but the other two toreros ruined it. The second was a clumsy bastard, and a sadist. The third was a showoff. By the third matador's second appearance, I was cheering for the bull. The other patrons booed, and then cheered, when he was thrown. The sport had become a game, and the game was rigged. When they dragged the last bull out of the ring, they took Papa's metaphysics along for the ride.

I shared my disenchantment with Astrid, over a bottle of wine and paella, at El Meson. She told me she had told me.

We had membrillo and cheese for dessert, and retreated forward, to the final sigh in our querencia.

"Can anyone be a hero, Uncle Wink?" asked Sam.

"Yes, Sammy, but heroism is an individual and not a collective activity. There are some egalitarians that would accept any journey through a birth canal, as the only requirement for membership. Remember when you won the foot race at school, and I shouted out my celebration of your victory? And the tie-died furry fairness fascist next to me went vocal about how 'everyone was a winner.' And I told her that, no, they weren't, and that you were. So no, not everyone is a hero. And heroism is not the same as celebrity, nor is it the same thing as leadership. Napoleon was a leader, but few of the citizens of the countries he invaded, would have considered him a hero. Also, heroism has nothing to do with democracy. In heroism, the majority is always wrong.

"So what do you need to be a hero?" Millie asked.

"You need three things, Mil. Certain personal qualities, a quest, and a transcendent journey that includes a crisis."

"What kind of qualities, Uncle Wink?" asked Sam.

"The list of heroic values can be long." Said Uncle Wink. "Courage, decency, maturity, reliability, selfless sacrifice, and self-control are important."

"Why self-control, Uncle Wink?" said Sam. "Rambo didn't have self-control."

"Rampage may feel good, Sammy. But it's not heroism. More heroic was the Samurai who, sent to avenge the murder of his overlord, couldn't do it, because the man spat in his face. His actions would have become an act of personal revenge. There's one quality above all others that a hero must employ in his quest, and along his journey." Uncle Wink added.

"What?" they both demanded.

"Love." He said. "A hero must act with love."

Shadow on the Moon

'The church says the earth is flat, but I know that it is round, for I have
seen the shadow on the moon, and I have more faith in a shadow
than in the church'

Ferdinand Magellan

Despite our heading, the progress of Western Civilization had
not always marched in the same anointed direction. Its
pedigree did not continue into the *Al-Maghrib al-Aqṣá*
'Farthest West' of Morocco we had just returned from, or
into the sunset of the *Al-Gharb* 'West' of the Algarve. Islam
had beaten the 'civilization' out of that compass bearing, in
both Western Kingdoms. The ascendency of the West had
actually turned to advance south from Portugal, around the
coastal bulge of Africa, in the caravels of Henry the
Navigator.

It took Astrid and I two days to get to his homeport, via
Albufeira. An ancient Portuguese woman, deep-lined and
white-haired, met us in her black frock and thick shoes, at the
Lagos station. We had taken a *tranvia* to Hueva, an *omniferia* to
Ayamonte, a *ferry* to Villas, and a *bus* to here. She brought us
to a Madonna and lace-decorated room, and crossed herself,
as she left. There was swordfish waiting in a nearby café, and
a beer in Sir Harry's Bar. The second day was given over to
recharging on the beach, feeding each other melon and
peaches, and drinking vinho verde. The Madonna above us
averted her eyes. Faith hovered in the shadows.

After the travails of Morocco, and the severity of Seville,
Lagos was an oasis. Astrid and I sprawled out on our towels,
under the candy-corn cliff formations of Praia da Dona Ana,
not that long before the British invasion of the Algarve, but
long enough. We had it to ourselves. For it's history as the
oldest slave market in Europe, and the Cape Canaveral of the
Age of Discovery, the local museum's one-eyed sheep, three-

eyed dog, and eight-legged goat, were a whimper. The gold *talha dourada* carvings and polychrome cherubs in St. Anthony's church, in contrast, were in contrast. We emerged, to an equally blinding sun and sandstone, slower and slower, for sangria and sandwiches, and satiation in the Pension Carvela. We were becoming gold and slaves to each other, golden slaves to each other.

I played my half guitar and whole harmonica, for a little boy on the train platform, in the late afternoon we left Lagos. It was so hot, we couldn't get enough orangeade, on the journey across the Tagus.

Lisbon, whereon a thousand keels did ride, and Vasco da Gama unfurled his sails to India. Lisbon, of wine and salt, and fermented *garum* fish sauce, and fast horses. Lisbon, of the endless wooden staircase of the Pensão Imperial, and the large standing fan and bidet and sink in our room, overlooking the Praça dos Restauradores.

Astrid and I clip-clopped noisily down to a nearby café, for arroz con mariscos, strawberries and cream, and vinho verde. An old Lisboan at an adjacent table, proferred *Ducados* cigarettes, and treated Astrid to a chocolate cup full of *ginjinha*, the local Morello cherry liquor. Her face contorted in that way I had only seen when we were alone. It was certain trouble. In 1755, an earthquake destroyed eighty-five per cent of Lisbon. The resultant tsunami reached the level of the second floor. It was the inspiration for Voltaire's loss of optimism, in *Candide*. Back at the Imperial, Astrid produced a bottle of *ginjinha*. In sour cherry, she repainted the devastation of Lisbon with her tongue, to the level of the second floor.

The room was perfumed with erubescent musk, in the heat of the next morning. I wrote twenty-one postcards while Astrid slept. We set out later, on the path from the lost tribe, to the 'Illustrious Generation.' The first had occurred in Rossio Square. Although the Jews remaining in their Portuguese querencia, after the expulsion in 1492, had been forced into becoming 'New Christians,' these *Conversos* continued to be suspect, in times of social strain. In 1506, a plague appeared, after two years of bad weather. Light rays emanating from the glass crucible containing a crucifix and reliquary, were interpreted by a parishioner, as the 'face of Jesus.' When a Converso suggested a more optical explanation, he was dragged from the church and beaten to death, by an infuriated woman. Dominican friars stirred the populace, with cries of 'Heresy!' and a mob materialized, enjoined by Dutch and other sailors in Lisbon port. Thousands of Conversos were torn from their houses, and raped, and burned alive at two stakes. The 'Easter Massacre' lasted three days. There was a penalty to be paid by some, for having more faith in a shadow, than the church.

We came to the Castle of Sao Jorge, a Moorish fortress that was saved for the Crusaders by a knight named Martim Moniz, who had thrown his body into the crushing breach of the last open door, as it was being closed.

Two hundred years later, King João I married the English princess Philippa of Lancaster, who produced the six famous princes and princesses of the 'Illustrious Generation,' of whom Henry the Navigator was but one. She hadn't met her husband until twelve days after their wedding, having been 'bedded by proxy' on her wedding night, by an appointed stand-in bridegroom. Not that it mattered terribly. Her husband already had three children by his mistress, and ultimately did what he had to do, for the benefit of the Anglo-Portuguese alliance. King and Countries. As the Royal Palace, the castle was the setting for the reception of Vasco da Gama, when he returned from discovering a maritime route to India. *Oh salted sea, how much of your salt are Portuguese tears?* Magic leapt from the top views, onto the serene gardens below. I'd never seen swans and reindeer together before. It was a surreal Catholic postcard.

Astrid and I took a double decker bus to Belem, to see the fantastic Coach Museum, and the sumptuous limestone Mosteiro dos Jerónimos.

The hybrid Moslem and Christian ornamentation, that characterized Mudéjar construction in Spain, was paralleled by the Maritime and late Gothic elements that delivered Manueline architecture to Portugal. The birth canal was along the lucrative African and Indian spice trade that led to the Renaissance. Navigational instruments, anchors, ropes, shells and seaweed, and botanicals were born into Monastery stonework. It was a Christian cloister of complex convex conical curved and crenellated capitals, crosses and canopies. I gave it a see plus.

We went, via the Nina's anchor at the Maritime Museum, to that other paragon of Manueline construction, the Torre de Belém. The tower was built in the early 16th century, on a small island in the Tagus River, to commemorate the expedition of Vasco da Gama. This is probably the right place, to place da Gama's place. The Portuguese had a certain reputation as colonizers, and Vasco's behavior was prototypically cruel. During his second voyage to Calicut, he intercepted and looted a ship of four hundred Moslem pilgrims. Da Gama locked them in the hold, peering through the portholes, at the women bringing out their gold and jewels, and holding up their babies. He burned them to the waterline. When the Hindu leader Zamorin sent his high priest to negotiate da Gama's demand that he expel all Moslems from Calicut, Vasco cut off his lips and ears, and sewed a pair of dog's ears to his head. Faith hovered in the shadows. *Where Gama marched his death-devoted band, while Lisboa awed with horror saw him spread, the daring sails that first to India led.*

We took a yellow tram to the narrow labyrinth and small squares of the impoverished Alfama, for chicken and aguardiente. An expatriate Angolan sent us little glasses of ginjinha later, at a café in the Juderia. The national soccer team, on the flickering screen above us, was murdering the Turks. Just like in the good old days, when the Earth was still flat.

'We gave the Brazilians, the land, people and language, and we are the ones with an accent?'

Raúl Solnado

Seated across from us, in our northbound carriage, Albert Einstein was conducting his train-thought experiment. He certainly looked like Einstein. Twin brother, at least. Antonio turned out to be an organic chemistry professor, teaching in Coimbra. His university had been established in 1290 AD, and Antonio looked like he hadn't been established much later. From the beginning, he was a puzzle. He told us that he was a follower of the mystic, Meher Baba. But Baba had been dedicated to the twin goals of seclusion and silence, and Antonio wouldn't have qualified for either. He was gregarious and generous, and chatted incessantly, sometimes to us. A highly respected academician, Antonio lived alone, in two separate places- in Coimbra, and in the spiraling descent of his dementia. This was of no concern to Astrid. She thought he was 'cute.' When he invited us for dinner later that evening, she accepted with alacrity.

We checked into the Residencial Vitória, and set out to see the attractions. The sand-colored menacing fortress on the sloped hillside was actually the Romanesque Cathedral. The artists involved in its construction were from Arab territories, responsible for the absence of human representation and biblical scenes inside, and the imposing demeanor of the stone ramparts outside. We entered the remains of the Roman catacomb town, to play with the Portuguese statuary at the Museu Machata Castro, and the literature collection in the Joanina Library of Antonio's University. Somewhere under the opulence, were a quarter of a million books, but it was so magnificent I didn't care. Astrid and I finished our tour at the Monasterio Santa Cruz, and with coffee at the Café Mandarin, in Praca do Republica.

When Antonio walked by, Astrid called out. He appeared surprised to see us, but was garrulously friendly, in an instant. He walked us to his apartment. We entered a room with no electricity, or telephone. There was a threadbare sofa, an old table with three chairs, and a map of India on the wall, beside his photo of Meher Baba. We sat at the old table, and listened to him talk. Time passed. Astrid asked what he was preparing for dinner. He looked puzzled, and held his breath. I was suddenly aware of how thin he was, in the darkness. Energy, but no mass or light squared. I suggested we go out shopping. He exhaled and forced a smile. We foraged in the market, for beans and eggs and tomatoes, some kind of sliced meat, bread and cookies, and candles. We returned to his flat, and lit them. During our meal together, Antonio rambled on about the sanctity of seclusion and silence. Relativity theory. Later, we thanked him, and left. From the street below, we looked up at where we had been. In the wavering light above, Antonio's shadow was still talking.

The train 'Normal' to Oporto next morning was anything but. Our rocking and jarring only seemed to encourage the staphylococci, from the previous night's salami. Another iron horse took us through eucalyptus, rice paddies and vineyards, to the fishing village of Viana do Castelo, in full downpour. We hurried to find the Residencial Floresta and, once secured, ventured out into the deluge, towards the municipal museum. Five escudos bought us a guided tour of blue and white ceramics and unsigned Spanish paintings of dogs and lions consuming each other. Astrid and I retreated through the rain, to do the same.

Up until this point, I still had no feeling for Portugal. Spain sung Flamenco to me; I knew the sambas of Brazil, in Portuguese. But Portugal, itself, had an accent I couldn't place. Portugal was seclusion and silence, a shadow on the moon.

Until I roused Astrid for dinner, and we walked to Largo de São Domingos. A little black dog accompanied us. He curled up on the sidewalk, as we entered the Restaurant Almeida. The moment the waiter smiled and seated us, Portugal came swooping down from the heavens. Fresh baked bread and two crabs hit the table, like a moon landing. Appetizers fandango'd across the table. Piping hot caldo verde, muscular with kale and sausage and potatoes, arrived with a bottle of vinho verde. The green soup sang a mournful *fado* to the green wine. Astrid had arroz mariscos. I ordered the Codigo Portuguese. A plate the size of a soccer pitch, stacked to the posts with beef, chicken, lamb, pork, carrots, potatoes, and kale, was placed in front of me. God came onto the field, and scored the winning goal. Chocolate mousse and coffee finished off the bullfighter. I had been looking for Portugal, but it was already here. The little black dog followed us home. A spear of light and birdsong, breaking through the drizzle, woke me slowly next morning. The Faustian face in the mirror had been undergoing a transformation, from metallic to organic. I had been on the road for almost two years now, and my invincibility was trading heavily on the Dorian Gray exchange. Astrid was eighteen, going on honeymoon; I was a decade older, going on forever. We spent the day playing, with our little black dog, each other, billiards, and penitents, at the cathedral. Portugal was still waiting for us at the Almeida that evening.

We rose through the clouds on the fifty-year old *elevador* next morning. The church of Santa Luzia waited for us, like a megalithic sentry on the mountain. We climbed to the top but there was no visibility. Our little black dog was waiting at the bottom of the funicular. He followed us to the Almeida later. The waiter pointed to the wet black mass curled up outside the restaurant window.

"Amor é fogo que arde sem se ver." He said. *Love is fire that burns unseen.* Astrid took my hand.

A Whale Stranded

'Spain: A whale stranded upon the coast of Europe.'
                                          Edmund Burke

We left Portugal, still wagging his tail on the platform next morning. The scenery grew lush as we crossed into Galicia, munching cheese bocadillos. We traveled with a Swedish couple, Astrid and Ani, and a young Asturian, who produced a smile and a bottle of ginja, when I played *La Bamba* for him on my half guitar.

Two more trains finally pulled us into Santiago de Compostela. That's how we got in the 'Way of St. James,' but he likely hadn't noticed, for a number of reasons.

He had been dead for almost two millennia, and we were but two of thousands of pilgrims that followed their own personal paths, to the burial place of the 'first martyred of the disciples.' He was covered with too much ground, and had too much ground to cover. Sant Iago was born in the Galilee as Ya'akov, son of Zebedee, came to Iberia to preach, and then traveled all the way back to Jerusalem, in time for Herod to cut off his head, in 44 AD. Miraculously, his body floated back to Galicia and, despite the fact that a 'massive rock had closed around his relics,' he continued to travel after his demise, slaying Moors at the Battle of Clavijo, and putting in an appearance in the Central African kingdom of Kongo. If he had seen us, he would have detected that Astrid and I were not properly accessorized. We didn't have the requisite scallop shell, hooked staff, pilgrim's hat, badge, gourd or *credencial* passport. The French sacked the place during the Napoleonic Wars, and no one is really sure whether the apostle's remains were truly found, or not. Finally, Santiago de Campostela is one of the wettest places in Europe, receiving about seventy-five inches of rain annually. Ya'akov wouldn't have been able to see us, through the kind of cloudburst we walked out of the station into. If Spain was a stranded whale, it wasn't going to be stranded long.

The Compostela part is from the Latin '*Campus Stellae,*' for 'Field of the Stars.' The pilgrim route through Burgundy goes through L'Hôpital d'Orion.

A lovely old señora provided a cozy double room with a hot shower, and Astrid and I went off to see the cathedral. Beyond the stone forest of columns, was a baroque altar, ablaze with contorted Baroque lamps and fat angels. The statues of St. James, festooned with shells and jewels, were so gay as to be idolatrous. In 2004, there was a public outcry from Moslems, who demanded the removal of Jose Gambino's eighteenth century statue of the Moor-Slayer, portrayed as merrily chopping off, and surrounded by, heathen heads. The Church told them to suck eggs.

Astrid and I arrived in time to see the procession of the *botafumeiro*, the giant silver censer that flies through the cathedral. A procession of purple and red vestments, carrying gold and silver miters, signaled the beginning of the air show. The botafumeiro weighed eighty kilograms, and was almost two meters high. The goldsmith José Losada recreated it in 1851, after the previous thurible had been stolen by Napoleon's troops. A great hook from a pulley mechanism at the apex of the dome, was attached with long ropes, and sailors knots added for added security. The censer was shoveled full of forty kilos of combustibles, about four hundred dollars worth of charcoal and incense. The botafumeiro was ignited, and eight red-robed *tiraboleiros* gently pushed the heavy artichoke from one to another, as if playing a game of medicine ball, to start its motion. Gradually at first, the arc of the turible increased, as the tiraboleiros pulled harder and harder on the ropes. The swinging excursions and speed grew larger with each pull. Thick trailing fire clouds of fragrant incense began to spill their trajectories into the transept. The organ shattered the apse, and choirs on both sides of the altar soared into the medieval hymn of Santiago, from the Codex of Pope Calixtus, in stereo. The butafumeiro was now a flaming meteor, trailing flames and smoke, inches from the ceiling of the dome, and the gallery below. It had taken only seventeen pulls, and eighty seconds, to reach a near escape velocity of seventy kilometers per hour. I did the momentum math in my head, and shuttered, as the monster returned, for another rush at our heads.

The ritual had begun in the eleventh century, to mask the stench from hundreds of unwashed pilgrims. They thought it would prevent plague in the St. James infirmary. They were wrong. They were also wrong when the botafumeiro flew out of the cathedral through the Platerias high window, when Catherine of Aragon stopped by on her way to marry the heir to the English throne in 1499, and on three other occasions, when it spilled a trail of hot coals onto the faithful multitude. The ropes are now replaced every twenty years.

The tiraboleiros had stopped pulling, and the oscillations of the censer slowed and shortened. As it drew its final breath, and sank lifeless to the ground, it was corralled back to the library lair it had come from.

Astrid's moods were becoming like that. Her travel time and resources were coming to an end, and she would soon need to return to South Africa, to continue her studies. We both knew that, as much as we cared for each other, our pilgrimage would not become a pledge.

I took her to the checkered tablecloths and history of the Restaurant Asesino, in Plaza de Universidad, owned by three old sisters, who restored her spirit, with a delicious meal of sopa Gallego, tortilla esparagos, Ribeiro vino, and a flan as smooth and bitter as our love and destiny. She smiled at the Amenedo chocolate I had left under her pillow. It carried her off to sleep. I lay awake, under the influence of a fiery meteor, wondering at wanderers and their fate. Perhaps some day, I, too, would have pilgrims, with accessories of half guitars and Gold Kazoos, Diogenes and Serendipities, and I would need a botafumeiro, to take away their smell.

*　　　*　　　*

'Iron hand in a velvet glove.'
Charles V, Holy Roman Emperor

The day began in iron, and ended in velvet. Like the motto of the Holy Roman Emperor and Spain, Astrid and I were heading '*Plus Oultre.*' Further beyond. After a real coffee and a false start at the train station, we boarded a self-propelled *autoferro,* east. It ran us on iron rails to El Ferrol del Caudillo, the birthplace of Francisco Paulino Ermenegildo Teodulo Franco Y Bahamonde, El Caudillo de la Última Cruzada y de la Hispanidad, *Leader of the Last Crusade and of the Hispanic heritage.* Unlike Charles V, Franco ruled Spain with an iron fist in an iron glove, responsible only to God and history. His principal skill set consisted of imprisonment, 'purification,' forced labor, summary executions, hunger, and the annihilation of the small town of Guernica. His 'white terror' killed almost a quarter of million of his own countrymen. When he said 'There will be no communism', there was no communism. When Astrid and I arrived in El Ferrol, his imposing Caudillo statue in the Plaza España was still just winding down, from decades of 'crushing communists like worms.' In 2000, the worms painted it pink and, ten years after that, carted it out of his hometown on a flatbed truck.

Astrid and I rode a bus, through the weighted slate roofs and green Gallego countryside. The couple, dancing flamenco in the aisle, had consumed just enough sherry to make it believable. We pulled into Iron Age nursery of Vivero, through the Gate of Charles V, but the only iron left in the day had been beaten into curls, along the intricate balconies of the medieval houses, lining the Plaza Mayor. As was to be expected, the bus was met by little old ladies with rooms to let. The two Doñas that greeted Astrid and I were just too precious to refuse. They weren't doing this for the money. We were welcomed as family, and invited to dinner.

156

As the shadows went long in the afternoon, Astrid and I became a Renaissance scene. Charles V had spoken Spanish to God, Italian to women, French to men, and German to his horse 'In my realm the sun never sets.' He claimed. I can still see Astrid poised with her neck extended off the raised stone platform of the square, the last of the sunbeams dancing through her long hair. In parts of my realm also, the sun never sets.

Our venerable hosts had been in the kitchen all afternoon, but had dressed elegantly for dinner.

"Conoces pulpo a la Gallego, Señor?" The older one asked me. I didn't know about the Galician bit, but I remembered octopus from Greece. I feigned surprise. They were both delighted to provide our education.

Wooden plates with steaming boiled potatoes appeared. Young red wine, in old bottles, slid into the middle of the table. A picante pot of paprika tentacles, salted and drizzled with olive oil, were spooned onto the potatoes.

"Buen provecho." They said in unison. The tendrils grabbed at us, and we at each other. It was velvet.

The Doñas got long embraces next morning. Astrid and I hiked into the Galician hills towards Bravos. We had cheese and bread and strawberries, and an aching for nature. As it was for Charles V, we had become 'most greedy of peace and quiet.' After a visit to a 16th Century monastery, we ambled though oak forests and ferns, to picnic beside a stream. We fell unconscious, and woke laughing, having slept through the departure of our train to Oviedo. Back at the station, we caught a later Pullman but, after Vivero, Oviedo was a disappointment. Woody Allen now has his own bronze statue there, for referring to it as 'a fairy-tale city.' For a man who wrote that 'eighty per cent of success is showing up,' Oviedo would be as good a place as any, for a bronze statue of Woody Allen.

Astrid and I had decided to visit the Paleolithic cave paintings at Altamira, even though there was a three-year waiting list, and they were only open to selected invitees. The cave had been closed in 1977, because the carbon dioxide in the breath of visitors was destroying the artwork. It is still closed.

To get there, we had to travel to Santellana del Mar, the 'town of three lies.' There was no saint, it wasn't flat, and had no sea. To get there, we had to go through the mountains of Cantabria, to Torrelavega. Our train arrived at noon, and we sought sustenance in the Bar Munich, until our bus left for Santellana. José Antonio watched us enter, and served up complimentary chocolate milk, and conversation. His Spain was divided into loyalties that divided him back. He was stranded.

"We used to be governed by fascists; now we are governed by fascists wearing white collars." He said. "Like the anarchists, I have found my passport in my mouth."

I asked him which political philosophy best defined his beliefs.

"Catholico." He said.

Behind him, Franco's pink statue went by on a flatbed truck, speaking to his horse in German. Waving, unwavering.

*   *   *

'After Altamira, all is decadence.'
Pablo Picasso

And before and within Altamira, all was reverence. In the Cantabrian cobblestoned country town of Santillana del Mar, with its flowered balconies and heraldic shields, Astrid and I brought reverence. The Altamira cave entrance was sealed, but we stopped a departing vehicle, with '*Ministerio del Interior*' painted on the side. Inside was a government official from Madrid. Altamira was closed. We were so reverential, that I began substituting Castilian *th*'s for my *esses* and *zeds*. He invited us to come back the next morning at ten-thirty, but insisted that it would be very unlikely for us to be allowed entry.

Discouraged, Astrid and I returned through the *campo*, to view some Cantabrian dancing at the monastery. Later in the evening, we watched Ireland beat Spain, over mushroom tapas and wine, and found a little café, for a bittersweet flan.

It is an unscrupulous intellect that does not pay to antiquity its due reverence. Astrid and I were at the cave entrance on time. The Minister of the Basque Provinces arrived, with a retinue of other officials, and an army of Guardia Civil bodyguards, with enough automatic weapons to reenact the Civil War. Spitting *th*'s, I explained that I was writing a book, and quoted Erasmus. I left out the part about other destinations, and the thirty-year delay. We waited another forty minutes. Two American diplomats that were to have accompanied the Minister didn't show. A finger was raised, and we held our breath, while a phone call was made to Madrid.

"Sigame, por favor." He said. *Follow me.*

We followed. The Guardia saluted reverentially, as we entered the cold dampness. I saluted them back. We were invited to lie down on the floor, and look up. The lights hit the twenty-five thousand year old blood and charcoal herd of bison, and then my solar plexus. I lost my breath. The art was not a celebration of meat, but of meaning. The polychrome images on the ceiling were not depiction, but devotion. Not just the forms, the souls of these horses, deer, and wild boar, had been painted. Diluted pigments of ochre and hematite and graphite, were layered over natural rock contours. This gave them three dimensions. Hundreds of prehistoric Bagliones, Caravaggios, Rafaels, El Grecos and Goyas, and Rubens and Rembrandts, took thousands of years, to create the high contrast *chiaroscuro* that removed my oxygen. This gave them four dimensions. They had signed their masterpieces on the cave's rock wall, with a negative image, from pigment blown over the back of their hands.

It was a nine year-old girl who had rediscovered Altamira, in 1879. When she showed her amateur archeologist father, the scientific world accused him of fraud. They couldn't believe that prehistoric man had the intellect, to create something so artistically sublime. It is an unscrupulous intellect that does not pay to antiquity its due reverence. It took until 1902 to authenticate, and its validation changed the perception of humanity forever.

In 2001 a 'replica' cave and museum were built. There were plans to have Barack Obama reopen the real cave in 2011, as visiting Altamira had been one of his 'lifelong dreams.' Perhaps he could visit the replica cave. There is also a Spanish brand of Altamira-inspired 'Bisonte' cigarettes he could blow over the back of his hands. That might, however, have produced even more of a negative image. As Pablo said, 'After Altamira, all is decadence.'

Astrid and I caught a late bus to Santander, and hid out in the drizzle, and the Fonda Maria Luisa. I made a chickpea stew, on my butane stove. We hunted blood and carbon all night long.

Our intention was to cross back into France next day, but we stayed too long for the mass, at the cathedral in Santander.

When our train arrived in Bilbao, we found out that our next one left from the dilapidated station, on the other side of town. I played my half guitar, inside the oldest rickety wooden Pullman in Spain, until our slatted hardwood seats clack-clattered us into San Sebastion, several hours later.

We disembarked into the province of Gipuzkoa, a land of berets and too many x's and k's. We had crossed into a Basque borderland of Mata Hari and Leon Trotsky. Tapas had morphed into pintxos. The wealthy chic navigated by Michelin stars, and the little old ladies were too otherwise occupied, to meet us at the station. They sent their grandchildren to offer us accommodation. Two niños brought us from La Perla, to a private home. We couldn't afford to eat out, so we still spent too much at a self-service cafeteria. On our last night in Iberia, Astrid knew that crossing into France meant only a few days, until we got to her aunt's house in Switzerland. What had begun in velvet, would end in iron. She curled up naked on the white bedspread, digging her nails into my wet shoulder. Jesus looked down from above the headboard. There was nothing he could do. Our love grew furious through the night. Fiery meteors blazed across the bison herds on the ceiling.

Entre-deux-Mers

'It is not what France gave you but what it did not take from you that was important.'

Gertrude Stein

The train station in Hendaya was where Hitler asked Franco to enter the war. He tried to impress upon Francisco what a great opportunity this was. Hitler had two hundred divisions under his command. Franco needed wheat. The Fuhrer had his usual vegetarian meal for dinner. He was a teetotaler. El Caudillo drank wine and ate meat. Franco told Hitler he would not fight. The carnivorous wine drinker told the abstinent vegetarian, that he would remain neutral. In water one sees one's own face, but in wine one beholds the heart of another.

The two old ladies, in the carriage seats in front of us, entertained Astrid and I, all the way to Hendaya next morning. They were rattling in Basque, faster than the train was rattling to the border. Crossing into France converted our mode of transport, from public to private. Luckily, it was free. Unfortunately, it was hitchhiking. It was a first experience for Astrid. More unfortunately, was the hiking part. We walked for over three kilometers, and waited on the side of the road in the hot sun. Astrid asked why we couldn't walk to the name on the sign in front of us. I told her that *Péage* was not a town; it was a toll road. I taught her the thirteen rules of hitchhiking. She cast her thumb in an arc, and caught a semi-trailer on the first try. Roger took us all the way to Bordeaux. We had no sooner descended from his cab, and Maria came by. A friendly blonde, from an English father and Spanish mother, she invited us to her apartment, and insisted on cooking dinner. Like Hitler, she was a vegetarian. I asked her if she was a teetotaler.

"Monsieur, nous sommes a Bordeaux!" She replied.

163

We stowed Astrid's pack and Serendipity in Maria's flat and, after hot showers, went shopping for sustenance. In a boulangerie, the big bread, les baguettes, les ficelles, les croissants again captivated me. We bought these, and rice and legumes, and cheese, and Bordeaux, of course. But, of the ten thousand wine-producing chateaux in the region, we picked a wine without one. We returned to cook and chatter, and became animated with the new company, and the wine. Everything in France is a pretext for a good dinner. But sometimes it is not easy to remain neutral. As the evening progressed, it became obvious that Maria was lonely, yet another victim of unrequited love. In water one sees one's own face, but in wine one beholds the heart of another. She gave us her bed. Astrid thought she needed a smaller one.

We said goodbye next morning, and thanked her. A bus to Cours d'Alsace Lorraine took us to the beginning of a lovely promenade, through Hugo's hybrid of Versailles and Antwerp, ending with the storage of our packs at Syndicat d'Initiative. We visited the bombed-out Cathedral, but the Musée des Beaux Artes was closed.

We were Entre-deux-Mers, *between two seas*, in two ways.

Entre-deux-Mers is a wine region, between the Atlantic tide that washes into the Gironde, and the Dordogne to the south. Rivers of wine wash out the other way. Astrid and I were heading to Switzerland across the Rhone, another river of wine on the other side of France.

We walked the seven kilometers across the Dordogne, towards the remaining love and time we had in between. A punk photographer stopped, to provide a lift to Libourne. The rides were short but continuous. A young girl to Bergerac, a sailor in the wrong direction towards Agen, and an Exocet missile engineer to Lalinde. The Falklands war had just ended. I asked him how business had been.

"Good for business, bad for friends." He said.

He dropped us on a beautiful curve in the Dordogne, with a view of a church tower, and a castle. The Gendarmerie came by to check our passports, for the second time that day. Astrid flagged down a garbage truck, but I didn't like the transport, or the cut of him. He drove us to La Bugue in three separate vehicles, the last one a bulldozer. When he invited Astrid to sit beside him, I was on edge. When he pulled her onto his lap, I fell off it. She was shaken, and it took me a long time to console her. In formulating the rules of hitchhiking, there were clearly some I had missed.

It did get better. A Dutchman, with an impeccable British accent, gave us a lift in his Mercedes sedan to Les Eyzies-de-Tayac-Sireuil, the home of the discovery of the first five Cro-Magnon skeletons, and the prehistoric cave paintings of Font de Gaume.

We checked into the Hotel Perigord. The proprieteur asked us if we had come to see the Cro-Magnon. I told him he was still driving a garbage truck and a bulldozer, just down the road.

*   *   *

> 'Switzerland is a country where very few things begin, but many things end.'
>
> F. Scott Fitzgerald

Astrid and I brought back sardines and tomatoes and olives and Camembert and apples and yoghurt. I played with the bidet trajectories, until she was laughing again.

The birds woke us next morning. Water for Nescafé boiled on my butane stove. We had leftover bread and cheese, and new intimacy. There was a tour in French, waiting at the Font de Gaume. The reindeer, horses, and frieze of five bison were reminiscent of Altamira, but fading, like our memories would. We attended a local food exhibition, at the museum. Astrid and I took our first taste of Perigord truffle, and looked at each other, with full mouths and wide eyes. We switched our gaze to the provider, and she smiled and nodded. Next were samples of fois gras. There was more butter, and less pheromone.

Fois gras had come to France from Judea. The Romans had learned how to overfeed geese from the Egyptians. The Jews took this knowledge into the Roman Diaspora, after the destruction of the Second temple. Dietary laws forbade the use of lard. This was no problem around the Mediterranean, where they had olive oil, or in Babylonia, where they had sesame oil. In northern climates, however, there was only poultry fat, and more of it, with the use of gavages. Gentile gastronomes began buying goose livers in their local ghetto, and the chefs of Popes and nobles responded with dishes, and cookbook recipes. Astrid and I couldn't afford these gems. We bought a raspberry tart for the road, and hitched a ride with a young teacher to Sarlat, the fourteenth century epicenter of black truffles and fois gras. The steep streets of medieval yellow stone buildings and black slate roofs were exquisite.

We had hiked a long way out of town, before an old man and his daughter piled us into the back of his Citröen, and took us to the Brive turnoff, via an old château. A maxillofacial registrar named Serge brought us to Brive, and took us for a beer. Astrid and I toddled another three klics, to yet another junction, where a young Portuguese guy from Viana do Castelo, drove us to Tulle. In 1944, the Waffen-SS hung ninety-seven local men from lampposts, as a reprisal for local resistance activity. Good for business, bad for friends.

Astrid woke me with coffee, at dawn. We hiked up the hill, and she threw a thumb-arc into the Limousin light. An Algerian driver pulled his car transport onto the shoulder, and we climbed up into his world. Mohammed amused us with his political banality and anti-French sentiment, all the way to Clermont-Ferrand. At one point, he stopped the rig to feed dog biscuits to a stray cur on the side of the autoroute. It wasn't expected, from a man who appeared to be a devout Moslem. Three kilometers of walking transported us from Mohammed to Moses, a bearded salesman in a Peugeot 504. He drove like a madman, heading for the Promised Land so fast, that the resultant bad karma shattered our windshield, showering us with glass. Moses didn't want to stop but, with some encouragement, finally pulled over to allow us to clean off the shards. Astrid wore her kerchief as a hood over her sunglasses, and we were off again, into the wind. Moses squealed his tires, going by a confrerie of gendarmes on the side of the road. I expected return fire, or at least a chase vehicle on looking back, but they all just shrugged, and went on with their deliberations. The thirst for truth is not a French passion.

Our final ride of the day came from a shirtless camion driver, who took us to Lyon, with its Rhone barges on the other side of our two seas, and the producer of silk, and two kinds of butchery, Klaus Barbie and bouchon charcuterie. We found the Hotel Bellecombe, run by a fatherly Italian stamp collector, and foraged for bread and cervelle de canut, *silk worker's brains*.

Our march down Boulevard de Stalingrad next morning must have not appeared to differ much, from the original Wehrmacht exodus of its namesake. We were slow, tired, and the odds were unfavorable. An hour later, Astrid threw another arc light, and captured a teenage sleeveless t-shirt, who took us to within sixty kilometers of Geneva. Her next hour's efforts got us nowhere. I teased her about 'catch and release.' We reviewed the thirteen rules, and I moved us on to a slow sexy fifteen-degree curve, with a pullout at the bottom. I cast my line and hooked a Swiss insurance broker in an Audi. Astrid laughed when I blew on my thumb. He took us through vertiginous views of Mount Blanc and Neufchâtel, a beer en route, and a gentle landing at the Bahnhof Enge station, in Zürich. The swans in the river, open-air cafés, and fashion femmes, gays and hookers, flowed into the cosmopolitanism precisely. We found the one star Hotel Rössli, boiled a pouch of Knorr *jardinière de legume* soup, and finished with a flourish of Toblerone. Thinking globally, acting locally.

We awoke late morning, to do the sights. First visit was to the simple Grossmünster cathedral, centre of the Swiss Reformation. The Kusthaus was as full of works by Rembrandt, Monet, Renoir, van Gogh, Munch and Chagall, as the Schweitzerische Landsmuseum was of relics- Neolithic, old weaponry, and grandma's. I bought an Internal Medicine manual as an amulet, and a Victorinox 'Champion,' as a replacement for the one that Lassa and Ken had run off with, at Kfar Hamaccabi. Billy Connolly once remarked that he 'always wanted to go to Switzerland to see what the army does with those wee red knives.' I didn't think much. All the little gnomes in Zürich, they would have remained neutral.

We stopped for bratwurst and a roll, and followed the prostitute street action for a while. It left me cold. Chagall's blue, green and yellow windows in the Fraumünster, in contrast, left me buoyant, and deflated at the same time. The mirth I took in Moses with his glass intact, only just balanced the foreboding I felt from Zion's angel, trumpeting the end of the world.

Astrid and I knew it was coming. I had originally planned to say goodbye in Zürich, but I couldn't do it. I girded myself to face Tante Lottie, and Astrid and I boarded the last train to Zug.

Our walk uphill from the platform was lightened by the appearance of Astrid's cousin, Annette. We received warm welcomes, hot showers, and a delicious meal of melon and prosciutto, cream Camembert, chilled asparagus, toast and apfelsaft. We had just finished playing a game of touring Switzerland, when Annette's parents arrived.

Tante Lottie was a doting Germanic cautionary tale. Not that I blamed her. Her niece had just arrived with a vagabond, ten years her senior, who had delivered her to say goodbye. What wasn't to love? Her husband, Astrid's Uncle, was polite enough, but gave me the impression of feigned neutrality. He may have actually used his wee red knife. Good for business, bad for friends. He poured out the kirsch, and probed. Astrid remarked that *ginja* was better. In wine, one beholds the heart of another.

We walked down to the lake next morning to say goodbye. Our tears were quiet. There was salt in the water, and in water one sees one's own face. It had been less than six weeks since she ran to catch up with me at the Moroccan border, and I never heard from her again. She went on with her studies, and I must have gone on to forever.

Canton Ease

'In Switzerland they had brotherly love, five hundred years of
democracy and peace, and what did they produce?
The cuckoo clock!'

Graham Greene

'Switzerland is a small, steep country, much more up and down than
sideways, and is all stuck over with large brown hotels built on the
cuckoo clock style of architecture.'

Ernest Hemingway

Despite the fact that the Swiss have no official national bird,
the common cuckoo would win a Canton election, with ease.
Not because of the clocks, or the architecture, but because of
their uncommon behavior. Cuckoos engage in brood
parasitism, laying their eggs in the nests of other birds. Their
fledglings are stronger and, because they hatch earlier, are
able to nudge host eggs out of the nest, over the edge to
oblivion. During the Second World War, the Swiss took in all
the Jewish eggs, waited until the owners had been pushed
over the edge to oblivion, and ate the eggs. It was a billion
dollar omelet.

The distance of the Hotel Juge from Astrid's last kiss, was
either infinite or fifteen minutes by train, depending on
Einstein's mood that day. I played my half guitar on the
balcony, and then went out, to see the extremes of Swiss
character on display in Lucerne. The best was represented at
the *Löwendenkmal* Lion Monument, commemorating the Swiss
Guards who were massacred at the Tuleries Palace in Paris,
during the French Revolution. Mark Twain, who had
described Switzerland as 'a large, lumpy, solid rock with a thin
skin of grass stretched over it,' lauded the sculpture of the
mortally-wounded lion as 'the most mournful and moving
piece of stone in the world.' He may not have noticed, that
the profile of the nook the lion is dying in, was carved in the
shape of a pig, the artist's statement regarding the incomplete

payment of his services.

On my long walk to Wagner's house, I crossed the oldest covered bridge in Europe. Under the roof of the *Kapellbrücke* Spreuer Bridge, hung Kaspar Meglinger's 67 paintings of the Dance of Death, each skeleton scene more macabre than the last. The Tribschen lakeside villa I arrived beside, was deceptive. Heidiland. Here, Wagner had written his Ring Cycle, and entertained King Ludwig, Liszt, and Nietzsche. But he also wrote *Das Judenthum in der Musik*, 'Jewishness in Music,' an attack on Mendelssohn, Meyerbeer, and the tribe. Hitler called him 'the one legitimate predecessor to National Socialism,' and played his overtures in Dachau.

I returned, via the Weinmarket, the old town hall, and the Hirschenplatz, for rösti, at the Bristol restaurant. It was the fourth of July. Mick, Ken and Cory were whooping it up, and I joined them for the star bursting fireworks display over Lake Lucerne.

After a bowl of birchermüesli and cream, I left early next morning, to catch the rides. A wee Swiss army mechanic drove me through magnificent alpine scenery to Thun, where I hiked an idyllic trail. A ride from a driving instructor, and one from a nurse, got me to the tram station in Bern, in the afternoon.

Three types of fourbearance awaited me. The first was the pit of four bears in the Bärengraben, the heraldic symbol of the city, since the 1220s. The bears looked fairbored. I sat in the park, and climbed the cathedral. The second fourbearance was the subject of the local painter, Karl Bodmer, and the original owner of the elaborate painted bison robe, hanging in the Historiches Museum. It belonged to the legendary Dakota Sioux chief of the Mandan, Mato Topé, or 'Four Bears.' He was tough. He had killed a Cheyenne chief, in hand-to-hand combat. He was tougher. Four Bears had completed the complex Okipa ceremony, a torturous reenactment of the Mandan creation myth. It began with the denial of food, water, and sleep, for four days. The participants were then led to a hut, where they had to sit smiling, while their chest and shoulders were sliced open to receive wooden skewers, thrust between the exposed muscles. Their bodies were suspended from the lodge roof, by the skewers. Heavy weights were tied to their legs, until they fainted. Once unconscious, they were pulled down, and watched carefully. The moment they awoke, a hatchet severed the small finger of their left hand. They immediately were prodded into a last grueling race around the village, still skewered and weighed down. It was unusual to finish the ceremony. Four Bears had done it twice. As tough as he was, however, it wasn't enough for what the American Fur Company steamboat brought up the river, in 1837. Smallpox killed his wife and children, and eighty percent of his tribe, in just a few months. Then it killed Four Bears. His final lament was that his scarred face in death would be so ugly, even the wolves would turn away.

The third Bern fourbearance was actually forbearance, a process to deal with a temporary financial problem. Mine was purely preventive. Some frontiers had been difficult, because border guards were skeptical about my means. In this nation of chocolate and cheese and cuckoos and clean, I had found my solution. The Swiss had a reputation. They were not so much a people as a neat, quite solvent business:

> 'The Swiss are inspired hotel-keepers. Some centuries since, when the stranger strayed into one of their valleys, their simple forefathers would kill him and share out the little money he might have about him. Now they know better. They keep him alive and writing cheques'
> C.E. Montague, *The Swiss*

I decided to open a Swiss bank account. With the air of an international bon vivant, I floated into the Schweizerische Kreditanstalt. They treated me with a cautious deference, as though they had no idea how much money I had. And so they didn't. I was led quietly into an interior office, and introduced to Herr Betrüger. His suit was worth more than I had earned working for a month, as an emergency physician in South Africa.

"Ja, und how much would you like to invest, Herr Winkler?" He asked.

"That depends, Herr Betrüger." I said.

"On what, Herr Winkler?" He frowned.

"On what kind of interest I can expect." I said, assertively.

Herr Betrüger looked stunned.

"Herr Winkler, Vee do not pay you." He said. "You pay us." It was my turn to look stunned. Then I thought about it. These Swiss were clever. I would give them my money and, in return, I would give them more of my money. I gave Herr Betrüger seventy-five dollars, about the same amount I estimated he had just spent on lunch. He gave me a peculiar look and, when I explained that I would send the rest by courier, a new Schweizerische Kreditanstalt card with my account number. It would turn out to be a great investment. Months later, whenever I would run into Third World border shakedowns, I would simply pull out my Swiss Bank account, and the skewers and weights would be removed.

Somehow, checking into the youth hostel later was an anticlimax. As well, the Nazi desk clerk said I needed an IYHF card. *They keep him alive and writing cheques.* I bought one, and gave him my passport to gain entry.

"You cannot use your card right away." He said.

"Why not?" I asked.

"You have to go out, and come back another time." He said.

I went out, and came back.

"How's that?" I asked.

"Welcome to the Bern Hostel." He said.

I was thinking how much these people could use an official national bird.

*   *   *

'Nurse, O my love is slain, I saw him go
O'er the white Alps alone.'
John Donne, *On His Mistress*

Time is what prevents everything from happening at once. But not for the *Zytglogge*, Bern's magnificent astronomical clock of moving puppets. In the fourteenth century, it was used to imprison the *Pfaffendirnen*, 'priest whores,' women convicted of sexual relations with clerics. There was a special theory of relativity.

I lit out for the highway, after a pilgrimage to Einstein's house at Kramgasse 49, where he had lived during his Annus Mirabilis.

I had just entered my own third year of wonders, and time was not doing its job. A young man named Martin drove me to a roadside café, for a shandy and a *Globe and Mail* newspaper. Not long after, an elderly Swiss grandpa gruffly invited me to ride with him and his frau, to Interlaken. His fourbearance slowly turned to warmth and humor and proferred apricots. I was looking for Balmer's Herberge, a hostel that had become a traveler's destination in its own right. *Keeping them alive and writing cheques.* It was buzzing with activity, and full of Yanks. I was invited to return the next day, and given directions to the IYHF hostel. The girl behind me was provided the same information and, together, we set off to find it. Jill was a social work grad student from the Bay area, escaping to a first and last European tour, before returning to San Francisco to get married. We sat by the river eating apricots and playing half guitar, until the hostel opened.

There were a hundred American travelers outside the hostel at the moment of opening. We all entered a world of Swiss regimentation. To the camp guards, time was what prevented anything from happening at all. I was berated for wearing shoes, and Jill was chastised for laughing. When we returned from town with groceries, we were criticized for using the outside ping-pong table for dinner, and for our glass of wine. Regulation sleeping sheets were mandatory, *keeping them alive and writing cheques*. When Frau Hilda snapped off the lights in the dorm, all the Americans in the world began snoring in synchrony.

The lineup waiting for a shower next morning was too daunting. Jill and I contrived an escape, and commenced an escapade. A couple from Hamburg stopped their gray Mercedes, to give us a ride to Grenoble. We began hiking up to the Kleine Scheidigg pass, between the Eiger and Lauberhorn peaks, through storybook scenes of old wooden chalets with flowering geranium window boxes, belled cows, and an old pipe smoker. As we climbed higher into the warmth of the July sunshine, the snowcaps of Mönch and Jungfrau broke upon us in full grandeur, rising from the narrow gorge of the Trümmletental. An Oberland alphorn echoed off the mountains, summoning cattle. Jill and I walked on a little further and stopped in front of Heaven, for a picnic of bread and cheese, and minestrone from my breathless stove.

The view was aphrodisiac, the air rarified, and Jill was the come hither All American Sally in the field. But I had not long left Astrid on Lake Zug, Jill's engagement diamond sparkled in the alpine sun, and the hills were alive with invisible but palpable Trapp family chaperones. We smiled a lot, and ate our minestrone.

The problem was Wengen. We hadn't counted on a small Bernese village interfering with time. Caesar, Napoleon, Mendelssohn, Shelley, and Byron had each made a day in their lives for this magical place. It only seemed right for us to plan a return.

By the time we had descended to Interlaken, and despite our arrangements, the only place available at Balmer's was the baggage room, discounted for the other bodies already draped over whatever space they could find. The owner woke us at dawn to fetch backpacks, and Jill and I walked to the

Wengernalp cogwheel railway station. Our ardor rose with the sun, and the ascent of the yellow wagon to Wengen. We found the chalet perfection of the old Hotel Schweitzerheim. The owner asked if we were having trouble breathing, and checked us into number twenty-two. The only thing that is supposed to happen in a Swiss bedroom is suffocation by feather mattress, but we began to have even more trouble breathing. I stopped to ask Jill about her engagement, but she seemed to be disengaged. Time is what prevents everything from happening at once, but we had run out of time.

The day flickered in and out of coma and arousal and, finally, both awake, we ventured into meadows and mist and snowmelt. Waterfalls and pine forests cascaded down the forehead of every precipice. Back under an umbrella, on the patio of the Schweitzerheim, we watched the Gruyère melting into the wine. The owner came to our table. She remarked that we did not appear as breathless as when we arrived. "Acclimatization." I offered. The fondue was ready.

"Figugegl." She said. Swiss German was a peculiar language.

"Fondue isch guet und git e gueti Luune." She explained. *Fondue is good and creates a good mood.* We were already in a good mood. The owner went on to explain that, if a woman loses her bread in the melting pot, she must kiss her neighbors. We were the only guests. As the sun began dropping behind Jungfrau, Jill started dropping her bread in the fondue.

> 'When I am gone, dream me some happiness...
> Think it enough for me t' have had thy love.'
> John Donne, *On His Mistress*

*   *   *

I Regain'd my freedom with a sigh. After a last breakfast on our terrace next morning, Jill and I hiked down, through idyllic green forest paths, and a final embrace in Lauterbrunnen. It was the only forest I had ever seen with manhole covers in the trails.

My hitchhiking attempts were only half-hearted, and unsuccessful. I made the mistake of retreating to Balmer's, to a monoglot American graffiti of alcohol, hormones, white teeth, and noise. 'M.A.S.H.' played for the masses on the big screen, and the fact that they might not have been in their hometowns was but a small blip on their radar. 'When good Americans die,' Oscar Wilde had once remarked, 'they go to Paris.' This lot were all going home.

The two bread rolls that joined me for breakfast went into my pack, on into the autobahn tunnel, and the trunk of a car that took me to the Lausanne turnoff. I was daydreaming, in and out of coma and arousal, when a '*Hey!*' from a printer with a casted broken arm, heading to Fribourg, got my buns moving again. He let me out in time for Prescient Paul, an IBM executive, who understood my flight path. Our first stop was Château de Chillon, not because of the Counts of Savoy, who moved every season with their furniture from castle to castle, but for the son of the Seyssel Seigneur de Lunes, Byron's Bonivard, his 1816 '*Prisoner of Chillon.*' The protagonist, imprisoned for five years in the dungeons, was a typical Byronic hero- an isolated figure bringing strong will against great suffering, seeking solace in nature's beauty, a martyr to liberty, and a product of his experiences as a traveler. Prescient Paul said I had the same '*eternal spirit of the chainless mind.*'

I bought him a young very cold white wine at Yvorne, and he took me on to the Abbaye de Saint-Maurice d'Agaune, for more Swiss mythology.

The Abbey was the ancient Roman staging–post of Agaunum, and sat against a picturesque cliff. It was renowned, for two things. The first was its practice of perpetual psalmody, a three hundred year continuous chanting, by rotating choirs, that went on uninterrupted, day and night, until the ninth century. The second was the story of the martyrdom of the Theban Legion. According to Eucherius, the Bishop of Lyon, a garrison of 6666 Roman legionnaires, were ordered by Emperor Maximian to march from Egypt, against the rebels in Burgundy. When the legion converted to Christianity, and refused to attack at Agaunum, their commander Maurice was ordered to 'decimate,' or put to death, a tenth of his men. Maximian repeated the order, until none were left. The only problem, with the story, was that it was a complete myth.

Prescient Paul left me with the gift of a bottle of white wine. I ate my breakfast rolls on the side of the road. The only problem, with the hitchhiking, was that it was a complete myth. All the BMWs and Mercedes, in Middle Earth, were competing to see how fast they could fly past me. Two hours later, a hippie pulled over to give me a lift. His name was Francois, and he barely spoke. He dropped me at his walkup apartment, in Vevey. It was full of painted driftwood, an obstacle course of hanging carpets, Metro, a demented dog, at least five kittens, and disorder. I came of out the toilet, to find that Francois had left. I never saw him again.

Vevey was famous, as the place where Daniel Peter invented milk chocolate, in 1875. It was only reasonable that Vevey became the world headquarters of Nestlé, about the only reasonable thing that has been said about the food giant.

Nestlé had not been the poster boy for corporate citizenship. It had promoted its infant formula as superior to breast milk in developing countries, demanded the Ethiopian repayment of six million dollars during one of its worst famines, denied its melamine-adulterated milk powder scandal in China, took out full page color ads in Canadian newspapers, claiming that their water bottles didn't end up in landfill sites, bought milk from farms illegally seized by Robert Mugabe in Zimbabwe, deforested large tracts of Borneo rainforest, for hardwood and palm oil plantations, at the expense of orangutan and other endangered species habitat, brought E. Coli O157:H7 sickness in refrigerated cookie dough, to 69 people in 29 US states, and purchased cocoa beans from Ivory Coast plantations that used child slave labor.

I made myself a hot chocolate, and took a nap. I awoke to the door opening. Two bare-chested freaks, with long hair and loud *Schwiizertüütsch* voices, crashed into the apartment. They didn't see me at first and, when they did, went on with their conversation, as if I was simply no big deal. They said '*Ja*' a lot, as in '*Ja... Ja... Ja.*'

I thought I finally had their attention by waving, and speaking to them in English, but I was wrong.

"Is this your guitar?" The less hairy one asked. I said it was. And two more guitars were produced, and wine, and a phone cord, followed by three other friends with shirts, and music and apples and hashish. I finally got to see the real purpose of the wee red knives. Walter and Mark were the freaks without shirts. Music was played. We had coffee and cake. I slept well. As I left quietly among the debris next morning, I realized they had never asked who I was, or how I got into their apartment.

A few Swiss francs, and twenty minutes, got me to the Palais Beaulieu in Lausaune. I had heard of a museum dedicated to Art Brut, *outsider art*, art of the Insane. The prototype was Adolf Wölfli, a psychotic patient, a tiny fraction of whose work, of twenty-five thousand pages, appeared in a book by his psychiatrist, Dr. Walter Morgenthaler. The Collection de l'Art Brut at the Palais was strangely intricate, and disturbing. I meandered through the glassware of the Musée d'Art

Decoratif and the Roman Museum but, even next to Lake Geneva, the July day was a hot and sticky affair. I swam in a large glass of lemonade, and made my way through the cemeteries, to a wooden cabin single room, at Pres de Vidy. The World Cup soccer final that evening brought Italy to a 3-1 upset over Germany. I pretended to remain neutral.

The hitch to Geneva next morning took a frustrating hour to catch a ride. A black guy pulled over in a blue compact.

"Yo Bro', you are some sight for some sore eyes." I said, as I sidled into the passenger seat.

"Comment?" He said in French, nervously. He was shaking. Apparently, the Ambassador of the République de Guinée had never picked up a hitchhiker, before today. I put him at ease, en Français. He threw a West African *fatoumata* tune into the cassette player, and took me to Geneva.

The fountain in the lake was iconic enough, but Geneva also represented that same extreme contrast of Swiss character, I had seen in the history of Lucerne. In Lucerne, the moral extremities of Swiss society had fallen between Wagner and the Lion Monument; in Geneva they fell apart, between Calvin and Rousseau. John Calvin was the soul of the Swiss Reformation. He began his career as that ultimate oxymoron, the humanist lawyer. This would undoubtedly had explained his humanitarian attitude to Jews: '*I have never found common sense in any Jew... profane dogs... model evildoers who stupidly devour all the riches of the earth with their unrestrained cupidity... a rejected people... their rotten and unbending stiffneckedness deserves that they be oppressed unendingly and without measure or end, and that they die in their misery without the pity of anyone.*' Or maybe that was the lawyer bit. His most stupendous humanist act was inflicted on a Spanish *Converso,* named Michael Servetus, a physician from Benjamin's hometown of Tudela, and the first European to describe the function of the pulmonary circulation. When Servetus arrived in Geneva, Calvin denounced him as a heretic. '*If my authority is worth anything, I will never permit him to depart alive.*' The City Council burned him fully conscious, atop a pyre of his own books. It was the Geneva Convention. The only thing holier was the cheese.

I sat in a park, eating my bread and Gruyère, before a visit to the other end of Swiss humanism, the house of Jean-Jacques Rousseau. He had more faith in innate human goodness than his predecessor: *'The Jews in Dispersion have not the possibility of proclaiming their own truth to humankind; but I believe that when they once have a free Commonwealth, with schools and universities of their own where they can speak out safely, we shall be able to learn what it is that the Jewish people have to say to us.'* It was a good bet that the first thing they would have said was 'Stop burning us alive.'

After a random walk through the Museums of History and Fine Arts, I checked into the League of Nations, at the IYHF hostel.

"Vich language do you speak?" Asked the warden.

"That one." I said. Canton Ease.

I had come through Switzerland, without the snowdrift experience of a Saint Bernard bringing me brandy, but I had still found alpine affection between its extremes.

Bird chirps woke me early next morning. I hoisted my pack, and hiked past the famous chestnut tree, whose buds had begun blooming earlier and earlier, every spring. Maybe it was the carbon dioxide, escaping from the holes in the Emmental. On a quiet day in mid-July, I walked the eight kilometers across the border, into France.

Aérospéciale

'The poplars in the fields of France
Are golden ladies come to dance.'
Bryan Waller Procter, *In France*

Her cat was named *Dracula*, but I would only find out when the sun went down, tomorrow.

It was Ramadan. A starving Algerian gave me a ride, to the hot sun just outside Gex. It wasn't long, before an old metallic blue Ford Escort wagon, pulled over to ask my destination. I mentioned Dijon. They said it was on their way. Gerard was a 35 year-old psychiatric nurse, and recently separated, in favor of Nadie. She was a psychologist, half a decade older. They were clearly smitten with each other. We pulled off into a shady glen, for salami and tomato sandwiches, and a beer. Gerard played on my half guitar, and then said,

"Come to Orleans with us." I asked where Orleans was. Nadie told me it was on the other side of the country. The chemistry was better than the geography was worse. Dijon lost.

We traveled all day, with only a short break, to see the medieval Cathedral St. Lazare in Autun. Orleans appeared just before midnight, and we jammed late until it was early.

In the morning, Gerard's mother had replaced the little cups of coffee that the French normally drink for breakfast, with large tumblers of Scotch. There were many rights hard won, on the guillotines of the revolution. France is France, and a grand place for Frenchmen, but Picasso had been basically correct. Only the peasants were left. Gerard thanked her, far too happily to be driving and, in our chemical conviviality, we picked up Tony, a young Irish traveler, who also thought he was heading somewhere else. We drove to the Loire chateau

183

of Chambord, with its double helix staircase, hundreds of rooms, and a dozen kinds of multiturreted towers, designed to resemble the skyline of Constantinople. I preferred the intrigue of Chanonceau, whose previous owners included a Medici, a Cuban millionaire, a Scottish gaslight tycoon, a chocolatier, and a widow night-wandering somber black tapestries, stitched with skulls and crossbones. It was one, of only a few ways, to cross the Loire from Nazi to Vichy France, during the war.

We picked up bottles of Bière and Bordeaux and Bourgueil in Beuxes. Gerard seemed to be searching the countryside, until we pulled up through the poplars, into a farmhouse driveway, on dusk. A feminine figure held a cat, at the top of the path.

"Her name is *Dracula*." Said Gerard, opening his car door.

"The girl's name is *Dracula*?" asked Tony.

"No, the girl is my younger sister, Marie. The cat's name is *Dracula*." He said.

I didn't see the cat. *An entire lifetime would not be long enough for you to exhaust the glance of the young harvest-girl.* Nor the stare I must have returned. Marie greeted each of us with the requisite number of air kisses, and welcomed us in, to a groaning board. After coffee and liqueur, we played guitar and sang. Gerard teased Marie about me, and then me about Marie. She had long bangs, that almost covered her eyes, and the way she said '*leetle*' drove me crazy. Long after Gerard and Tony turned in, we filled the spaces between the ticks of the echoing clock, with English and French versions of ourselves. I watched how she caressed *Dracula*, and wished to be a vampire. We said goodnight, just before dawn.

Gerard woke me with coffee around eleven.

"Now we go to the aerodrome." He said.

"The what?" I asked.

"The aerodrome. You are going to fly over the Loire chateaux.' He said. He had schemed this, from the first moment of our encounter. I was thrilled, until I met Gustaf, the pilot of the stunt plane. It was a stunt plane. *'Red Robyn'* was written on the fuselage. I took Gerard aside.

"How old is this guy, Gerard?" I asked. He looked ancient.

"I don't know, exactly." He said. "He fought in Algeria."

"For Rome, or for Carthage?" I asked. Gerard said he would check.

"J'ai quatre-vingt-deux ans." Gustaf said. He was eighty-two. Gerard gave me his nonchalance pout. Gustaf was born three years before the first flight of the Wright brothers, and they had been dead for forty. It was raining buckets. What could go wrong? We retreated to the clubhouse, and watched Gustaf play ping pong with Tony. Tony lost.

When the clouds parted, I climbed into the back of the stunt plane, and Gustaf tore down the runway, like the Luftwaffe were bombing the aerodrome behind us. At one point, I thought our tilt to the left was going to turn into a barrel roll, but Gustaf managed to overcorrect it enough times to find the sky. It all changed into a miraculous experience in an instant. The views of the Loire and the chateaus we had visited yesterday, and the checkerboard fields in the clear French landscape, were as pure as a verse of Racine. I reached out and touched heaven.

After a pastis for Gustaf, on the ground, I was invited to return the following year. He's probably still flying Cuban Eights over Chambord.

Back at the farmhouse, Marie had prepared a Pâté Bretagne, and other country specialties. *Dracula* hung around the table all evening. The wine flowed. I thought we were all going to play some music after dinner, but Tony said he had to get going, and Gerard said he was taking him. I looked out the window, to see Gerard's Mick Jagger grin, flashing back at me, as he roared down the driveway, and turned to find that Marie had lit a candle, and poured me a glass of Anjou. I asked about her attachments. She told me about the long-term relationship that had ended eighteen months previously. I asked if there was anyone else.

"Moi et toi." She said. "Éteins la bougie. J'ai pas besoin de voir la couleur de mes idées." *Blow out the candle. I don't need to see what my thoughts look like.*

She blushed under her bangs, and took me into her room. We were clearly smitten with each other. I told her that Gerard was like a brother to me. She told me that he was her brother. And she kissed me like I wasn't Gerard, and caressed me like I wasn't *Dracula*. I reached out and touched heaven, for the second time that day. And I bit her neck anyway.

"What is the quest for, Uncle Wink?" asked Millie. The waves pounded the shore below.

"Depends on the hero, Mil." He said. "The object of the search is not a lost puppy. The old traditional heroes went around slaying monsters, and that was enough in our planetary prehistory, when men were shaking their world out of a dangerous unshaped wilderness. Prometheus brought fire, stole it even. But, as culture and civilization evolved, heroes did as well. The coming of age became a coming of consciousness. Orion was a hunter, but it wasn't the pure pursuit of protein that characterized his myth. He was not simply seeking some form of personal ecstasy, but the wisdom and the power to serve others. There was a moral dimension that morphed physical deeds into spiritual ones. The founders of all religions have gone on quests like that."

"Is there something special that heroes are searching for, in their quest?" Sam asked.

"There are two main kinds of spiritual quest, Sammy." Said Uncle Wink. "The first is the Father Quest, where our hero seeks his own character, derived from the notion that, while your mother supplies your mind and body, your father provides your nature, your source, your career. Your father determines your destiny."

"Was that the subject of your quest, Uncle Wink?" He asked.

"It actually was, but I didn't know it at first. I thought my father had never done anything he wanted, because he had stayed in the hometown imperfection of the human, the living, and the ordinary. All his warmth and kindness and humor derived from his love of this, and I didn't see it, because I went off on what I thought was a better quest, one which would serve a higher purpose, and bring me to a superior level of consciousness."

"What kind of quest was that?" He asked.

Rundai

'One mustn't ask apple trees for oranges, France for sun, women for love, life for happiness.'

Gustave Flaubert

The sun was already up when Marie rolled over.

"*Encore. Encore.*" She said. Encore, it was.

While she went back to her dreams, I cleaned the farmhouse kitchen, made us coffee, and had a shower. I played my half guitar until she awoke. She dropped me on the road to Tours. "Merci, Marie. Au revoir." And that was it. Sad. But, that was it.

I walked for an hour, before a jolly French farmer couple, brought me alongside two American hitchhikers.

"You won't get a ride here, man." They said. A few minutes later, I was roaring towards Chartres, in a Renault driven by a maniac legionnaire, at the speed of derision.

After savoring the last of Marie's Pâté Bretagne, on the sunny balcony of the youth hostel, I moved toward the Middle-Ages spirit world, inside the High Gothic cathedral. How high, I was about to find out. The heavy flying buttresses were aérospéciale, existing only to provide architectural structure, for the vast interior array of stained glass. Built on the same site of at least five previous churches, Chartres was constructed at the speed of mass hysteria, by the 'Cult of the Carts.' *Nobody knows the names of the men who made it. To make something as exquisite as this without wanting to smash your stupid name all over it. All you hear about nowadays is people making names, not things.*

In 1145, a crowd of more than a thousand hymn-singing penitents, began harnessing themselves to carts, like oxen, and dragging building materials to the construction site, in frenetic acts of religious piety. It was the original Bandwagon effect. When the local grain supply sprouted ergot fungus, an

LSD precursor, the fervor was furthered, by fever and the fire of St. Anthony, producing bewitchment, hallucinations, convulsions, and gangrene.

Once completed, Chartres Cathedral became a free trade zone marketplace, for meat, vegetables, textiles and fuel.

Moneychangers and wine sellers plied their trade in the naves, and the knaves negotiated a cut for the church authorities.

Chartres' state of preservation was a state of grace. According to Zola, the perfection of civilization wouldn't occur, until the last stone from the last church, fell on the last priest. If the mass of this behemoth was any indication, it was going to be awhile.

When the Revolutionary Committee starting collecting explosives, to blow it back to its inspiration, a local architect pointed out how long it would take, to unclog the streets from the rubble, that the demolition of the cathedral would produce. Instead, they took the lead roof, to make bullets. During WWII, the stained glass was removed to a safe location before the Germans arrived. Not much later, an American Army officer saved the church, by ignoring the Allied order to destroy it.

For all the surface area that the original, intricate stained glass covered, the interior was still dark. The feeling, however, was radiant, and contemplative. I reached out and touched heaven. Cathedrals had become my second favorite kind of mountain scenery, and Chartres, arising from rocks, and sand, was a perfect medieval image of eternity.

*   *   *

'Paris is a disease; sometimes it is several diseases'
Honoré de Balzac

The aerobat doing loop-de-loops above me, on the side of the N10 next morning, wasn't daring enough to have been Gustaf. Three rides took me the last fifty miles, to the City of Lights. I felt like de Gaulle, returning down the Champs-Élysées sunshine, under sail and a blue sky. My chauffeur physics teacher dropped me at Gare St. Lazare.

It had been exactly two years since I caught my first lift into the prairie buttercups, and Paris seemed a perfect place to celebrate such an *anniversaire*. It was mid-July, and sizzling.

I set out to find accommodation, and ended up homeless. Eight hours after landing in the epicenter of élan, I had lost count of all the places I had inquired about a bed. My legs were numb and unresponsive. There was one more hostel on my list, in the Quartier Pigalle, home of the Moulin Rouge cabaret, and where Picasso, van Gogh and Toulouse-Lautrec had found rooms. As I navigated the gauntlet of seedy sex shops and prostitutes, I tried to stay positive.

The stairs into the dark foyer of the hostel, took me to a booth, lit by a single bulb. There was a hole in the glass to talk through.

"Oui?" Said the skeletal moustache behind the window, without looking up from his magazine. I gave him the benefit of the doubt. His existence was clearly weighed down, by his hair grease. I asked for a bed. He hesitated.

"Pas de lit." He exhaled, again without eye contact. Perhaps he had a neurological condition. I told him that I saw him hesitate, that I knew he had a bed, and that I wanted it. He spat.

"OK." He said. "You pay, but if you leave, you still pay." I asked him what the problem was. He hesitated, again.

"There is a Japonais in this room." He said.

"And so?" I asked. He told me he had sent two other travelers, on separate occasions, the same way, earlier. They both came down the stairs, in some kind of hurry, and left. I

191

paid the thirty-five francs, heaved Serendipity and my half guitar onto my shoulder, and began to climb the staircase.

"Remember!" said La Graisse after me. "If you leave, I keep the monnaie." Whatever.

I knocked on the door of the room, and waited. Nothing. I knocked again. Less of the same. I opened the door.

Inside, sitting cross-legged in the middle of the floor, wearing a white robe, was a Japanese guy, the size of a house. He growled a low growl. I had seen smaller Sumo wrestlers, and friendlier Rottweilers. He growled again.

I had some postcards of the Eiffel tower. I handed one over, counting my digits on the way back. I pointed to my chest.

"Wink." I said. "Canada." His growl went up an octave.

"Janada!" He exploded, and pounded his own chest.

"Sora!" He said. "Nippon. Fukuoka." We had rapprochement.

There was a noise, from the balcony next door. Sora got up to investigate. The floor shook, just a little. Two German girls were enjoying the evening scene. They couldn't help but notice him.

"You vould like some chocolate?" They asked.

"Hoaaaa. I take two!" He said. He took two, and handed me one. I thanked the frauleins, who had decided to retreat to the safety of their room.

I asked Sora how long he was staying in Paris. He answered too quickly.

"Rundai!" He said. I didn't understand. I told him I didn't understand.

"Rundai!" He repeated. *One day*. Got it. It occurred to me that one day, for the City of Lights, might be a bit rushed, but I didn't know his schedule, or constraints. I asked him where he had just come from.

"Lome!" He boomed. *Rome*. I asked him how long he had spent in Rome.

"Rundai!" He said. I sensed a pattern. Who would spend just twenty-four hours in the Eternal City? I asked him where he was heading tomorrow.

"Osro!" He said.

"Rundai?" I asked.

"Rundai!" He shouted. So I probed, and found the explanation.

Sora was an engineer, with a one-week vacation. He was on his European Grand Tour. Every morning he would take a cab, to an airport, in a major European capital city, and fly to another major European capital city. He would take another cab, to an inexpensive hostel and, as they say in Japanese, 'hang out.' The next morning he would repeat the exercise, until all the boxes were ticked. Sora and I had a chat, about the philosophy of movement. I left him contemplative.

Two years later, I arrived in Fukuoka, late evening. I pulled a worn address out of Serendipity, and followed the trail. An hour later I knocked on a door. Sora opened it.

"Wink!" He chimed. "How rong you stay?" I had been waiting a long time.

"Rundai!" I said.

"Hoaaaaa. Rundai!" He laughed. For Paris is a movable feast.

*   *   *

"Paris is always a good idea."
Audrey Hepburn

Sora left early next morning, for his flight to Osro. A different surprise waited for me, in the glass booth downstairs. La Graisse had been replaced by a recurring acquaintance. I had first met Bork in Nairobi, and then in Jerusalem, leaning over the Dead Sea scrolls. And now, randomness retreating, he was working day shifts at the hostel.

"Hello, Wink." He said, like it was no big statistical event. I'd never seen him so thin and well dressed, or so depressed. Note to self. If one has nothing to return to, this is what a traveler looks like, when he stops.

It made me feel like calling my parents. After an hour in the exchange, I found only an employee on the other end. It seemed we were all out of town.

The Louvre is a morgue. Jean Cocteau went there, to identify his friends. He was in good company. It was born from the severed heads of Louis XVI and Marie Antoinette, and the rest of the confiscated property of the nobility, émigrés, and the Church. The revolutionary broom of the army swept art, from all over Europe, into its halls. There were fifteen acres of 35,000 works of art on permanent display, and I had *Rundai*. I loved the Rubens, the Italian Masters and the Egyptian collection, but I saved my moments of savory salivation, for the three works I had been waiting exactly two years to see.

The first was the Venus de Milo, the armless Aphrodite, of Alexandros of Antioch. It had been discovered by a farmer on Milos, in 1820, and sold to a French naval officer. When the officer didn't pay him quick enough, he sold it to Nicholae Mourousi, Grand Dragoman of the Ottoman fleet. After the French seized it, as it was being loaded on a Turkish ship, Sultan Mahmud executed Mourousi, in front of the arsenal in Istanbul, for failing to acquire it. In France, art was often politics conducted by other means, but in the Ottoman Empire, art was war. She was lovely.

Another Greek statue, the Winged Victory of Samothrace, was not only without her arms, but also her head. Nike had been created, to commemorate the victory of Antigonos over Ptolomy II of Egypt, in the sea battle of Cos. She is a sculpture of the space around her, where violent motion and sudden stillness meet. I could feel the wind in her garments, and the sea below her prow. Where the marble for Venus had been carved into love and beauty, the Nike was sculpted into struggle and destiny. The Rolls-Royce radiator figurine she inspired, was a cheap imitation.

My third interlude was in front of the most famous painting in the world. Leonardo's masterpiece was done in oil on a poplar panel, and famous for the enigmatic face of the portrait. Lisa Gharadini's smile had puzzled art historians for over four centuries, but I thought the explanation was obvious. Lisa had been married in her teens, to a much older cloth merchant, who became a local bureaucrat. She had six children. There is no reason why her expression would have been anything other than ambiguous. It was the same look that Rene gave me in the Petén jungle, two years earlier, after he rubbed the sleep from his eyes. Most visitors spent fifteen seconds viewing the Mona Lisa. I had a lot more sleep invested in the pilgrimage.

The exact beginning, of my third year on the road, occurred in a small Chinese restaurant, down JJ Rouseau. Thirty-two francs bought me soup, shrimp, strawberries, and steel.

I walked across the Tuileries Gardens, to the Jeu de Palme, when it was still the repository of the best Impressionist art in the world, long after it was tennis courts, and not long after Rose Vallant. Rose was a French art historian, and strawberries and steel, a member of the French resistance. When the Nazis used the place, to store looted Jewish cultural property during the war, when they were destroying 'degenerate' Picasso, Dali and other 'unworthy' art, in bonfires on the museum grounds, and when Göring came to cherry-pick the plunder, Rose was recording where it was going, and making sure that the trains, that contained this priceless treasure, were not blown to smithereens. I loved her work. Every last van Gogh, Cezanne, Dégas, Monet, Manet, Latrec, Renoir, Sisley, and Pissarro, left an impression.

Back at the hostel, Sora had been replaced by a full bunks. I entered the room, to find Gemil the Moroccan, half playing my half guitar, and a Yugoslavian, who had helped himself to my Sudanese chess set, for a game with one of the two Swiss brothers. I gave a dissertation, about what happened to the Paris Communards, who failed to show respect for private property, and then, as true Parisians, we all went out to eat for dinner. Un pour toes, toes pour UN. *One for all, all for one.*

I awoke at dawn, next to blood and a scream. A Brit named Tony had checked into our room in the dark, and sliced open his scalp, on the metal protuberances of an upper bunk. I cleaned him up, and made my way into the Latin Quarter. An impressive Senegalese guy took me on a tour of the crypts in the neoclassical Pantheon, the final resting place of Voltaire, Rousseau, Hugo, Zola, Dumas, and a host of other French luminaries. Past the Sorbonne, Musée Cluny, and ten francs worth of bread and cheese, I arrived on Ile de La Cité, to movably feast, in front of Notre Dame. During the winter of 1450, a man-eating pack of wolves entered Paris, through breaches in the outer city walls. The leader of the pack was nicknamed 'Courtaud,' or '*Bobtail.*' Over the harsh season, the Wolves of Paris killed and ate forty people. They were stoned and speared to death, where I sat. The bells rang out, as I finished my sandwich.

The days in Paris began to rundai into one another. The movable feast was becoming stationary, and there was no end in sight to the length of the buffet. It was confusing. In some of the most isolated places on the planet, in the extremes of solitude, I had felt only exhilaration. Now, in one of the most stimulating cities on Earth, surrounded by crowds and marvels, I was the loneliest I had ever been in my life. I puzzled at the performers in the Place Georges Pompidou, the drugged-out aging hippie vocalist, the African drummers, and the Highland piper, whose kilt had seen better days. Writhing in front of the giant shopping cart scaffolding of the Centre, and its Modern Art collection, they seemed to be in this place, but not of it.

I connected better with Rodin's sculptures, in his namesake museum. The Thinker, the Kiss, and the Gates of Hell, had all been way stations in my journey.

The next morning rose to the height of the Eiffel tower, two and a half million rivets, containing as many tourists. It didn't seem to be a particularly good fit, my other images of Paris. Apparently I wasn't alone in this impression. When novelist Guy de Maupassant, who was known for his hatred of the monument, was asked why he ate lunch in the tower's restaurant every day, he replied that it was the one place where he couldn't see the damn thing. Two other vignettes amused me, about the structure. The first was the story of Victor Lustig, who sold it to a scrap metal dealer in 1925. Not only did he pocket the principal, and a handsome commission, he attempted to do it a second time. The other was that of Erica 'Aya' Eiffel (née LaBrie), an American world archery champion, who married the Eiffel Tower, in a commitment ceremony in 2007. The nuptials were a little shaky. At the time she came out of her 'objectophile' closet, she already had a longstanding relationship with the Berlin Wall, and there were rumors about her involvement with her competition bow, 'Lance.' Word had it that she remained committed, but likely not within the right walls.

In Les Invalides, where Napoleon was interred, the photo of Hitler lording over him became stillstuck in my head, like a bad pop tune on the radio, corporal punishment in stereo.

I returned to the hostel, via the blue slate roofs and red brick of the Place des Voges, and half dozen lesser museums, to find two lively Irish girls, torturing Gamil. They asked him how much longer we were staying in Paris. He grinned at me, and together we enunciated the sacred word of Sora, the seer of Osaka.

Rundai.

'I haven't seen the Eiffel Tower, Notre Dame, the Louvre. I haven't seen anything. I don't really care.'

Tyra Banks

Tapestry

'How can anyone govern a nation that has 240 different kinds of cheese?'
Charles De Gaulle

Most of my last day in Paris was twenty kilometers away. If de Gaulle was unable to govern France from Paris, in the twentieth century, one can only wonder how the Bourbon kings accomplished it from Versailles, two hundred years earlier. The easy answer, of course, is that they didn't.

Louis XIV thought he was being clever by concentrating political power, in a mosquito-infested swamp, that he had gradually converted from a hunting lodge, to one of the largest palaces in the world. It took forty thousand workers to build it. The corpses were removed at night. He required nobles to spend a portion of the year in Versailles' apartments, and established a complex court etiquette, which drove them crazy and ensured their compliance. Even the simple act of the Sun King getting out of bed in the morning, was ritualized into an exacting and elaborate ceremony, the *Lever*. His meals were a mandatory spectator sport. Potential threats were neutralized by concentration, like crabs climbing over each other in a bucket. Rumors were currency in the ultimate social network. 'On dit.' *One says.*

Two thousand acres of gardens and grounds contained a thirteen-acre palace interior of 700 rooms, 1250 fireplaces, 2000 windows, 67 staircases, and 483 mirrors, all financed by Louis' personal monopoly on revenues from Quebec. Because Venice had proprietary claims on the technology of mirror manufacture, the Venetian artisans employed at Versailles came under an assassination order. The furniture was silver. As lavish as the living was, there were only nine functioning toilets, belonging only to the King, and his closest family. The other twenty thousand inhabitants had to live with the constant smell of privy-chambers clinging to their clothes, and the frequent tossing of chamber pot contents, out of the nearest window. Two centuries later, Gertrude Stein's observation that, 'In France one must adapt oneself to the fragrance of a urinal,' now seems banal.

By the time that two additional Roman numerals of Louis went by, and Louis XVI and Marie Antoinette held court, few in Versailles knew or cared, that bread was running out in the capital. The women of Paris came to warn them. The guillotine gave them a head start.

A strict elderly Gaullist matron guided my way through the Louis labyrinth. I was taken through, and with, the private chambers, the Opera, and the Galerie des Glaces. But I was just as intrigued with the profusion of decorative arts, particularly the intricacy of the tapestries. The Gobelins family was originally from Reims. To meet the demand for decorating Versailles, the factory was 'nationalized' in 1662. Gobelins tapestries were so intricate, woven with threads of spun gold and silver, that it took a year to produce a single square meter. The workers often drank, or dueled, while working, and the King often neglected to pay his bills.

Back in Paris, in the Musée du Moyen-Âge, I found six tapestries that were older. The Lady and the Unicorn series were made in Flanders in the late fifteenth century, and rediscovered, moldering in Boussac castle, in 1841. In a background of vermilion and a thousand flowers, the lady, flanked by a lion and a unicorn, was portrayed indulging in each of the senses, in five of the weavings. The sixth one was the one that hooked me. It displayed the words 'À mon seul désir,' *to my only desire*. If that was really the meaning, it was but one interpretation. I didn't know that, in transporting my own five senses from Paris to Reims, I was about to discover another.

*   *   *

> 'She maketh herself coverings of tapestry;
> her clothing is fine linen and purple.'
> Proverbs 31:22

Unlike all the characters in Rossini's last opera, '*Il viaggio a Reims*,' I actually got there. My journey had started falsely at the Gare de Lyons, only to find that my train left from the Gare de l'Est. I daydreamed the entire eighty miles, staring out on the overcast fields of Champagne. I met Roul, a young history student from Holland, on the hike up to the youth hostel.

After stowing our packs, we walked across the bridge to the Cathedral, where French kings, from Clovis to Rossini's Charles X, were crowned. German shelling in the First World War had set it ablaze, and the lead from the roofs poured through the stone gargoyles. Two of the exterior statues had their own molten history, as a medieval anti-Semitic propaganda device. The first creature was that of *Ecclesia*, a proud, erect maiden, crowned and holding the cross, the personification of a victorious, triumphant Church. The second, *Synagoga*, blindfolded to the truth of the New Testament, slumped in rags with a broken staff, shattered tablets, and a fallen crown, defeated and dejected. The contrast continued inside, with this hatred juxtaposed against the poetry and light of Chagall's stained windows, created with love and devotion, by the quintessential Jewish artist of the twentieth century.

Roul and I went on, into the universe of champagne, two surrenders, and two more tapestries. The first set of weavings was the *Life of the Virgin* chancel series, in the adjacent Palace of Tau, donated in 1530 by Robert de Lenoncourt, archbishop under François I. Across the Place Royale was the house of Mumms, where Roul and I were regaled with samples of bubbly, throughout the guided visit. Effervescent from the tour, we tripped lightly through the Salle de Guerre, the room where the Germans surrendered, at the end of WWII. The other surrender occurred back in the hostel kitchen, to the second tapestry.

Roul blamed the champagne, but that was wrong. The tapestry was fine linen and purple. It hung in flowing curves, off the convexities of her frame. She was as stunningly beautiful, as we were incoherent.

"Nice clothes." Was all I could muster. She smiled. We dissolved.

"Its my work." She said. "I'm a mode-ontwerper." I realized she was Dutch, but I didn't understand what a mode-ontwerper was.

"It's a mode designer." She clarified. I still didn't get it. The only 'mode' I could think of was 'a la mode,' like the scoops of vanilla ice cream on apple pie. Her scoops were magnificent. And she reminded me of pie. Warm deep-dish Dutch *appeltaart*, pie in the sky, the kind you wanted a finger in every, the pie-eating contest you were first in line for. Pie heaven. The room filled with cinnamon. Somehow, though, it wasn't the whole picture. It didn't explain her cat's eyes, or the brown curly mane, cascading around her brown irises and pixie nose. Or her mischief.

"My mother is Hungarian." She said. And the pie turned to strudel.

Ine was a twenty-one year old fashion designer, from The Hague. Roul and I shared our provisions and stories with her, and we sat on the grass outside, until darkness brought out the stars. If you wish to make an apple pie from scratch, you must first invent the universe.

We sat together at breakfast next morning. Roul cleared his throat.

"Listen…" He said. "You are both traveling in the same direction. Why don't you go together?" Now that would have been too good to be true.

"I'd probably slow you down." I stammered.

"Yes, you probably would." She said. And I watched my

humble pie go to mud pie. Promises and piecrust are made to be broken.

I went upstairs to get Serendipity, and prepared to leave, for the highway to Rouen. Ine was waiting outside.

"You have a sign?" She asked. I told her I didn't.

"I will make one." She said. And she did.

Once across the bridge, the hitchhiking was slow. An old lady drove us about fifteen kilometers. Ine and I waited on the roadside, exchanging buttercups, not really paying much attention to the traffic. I couldn't shift my gaze off her, even to flag down a ride. Her face was baby doll captivation. I thought if I laid her down, her eyes would close, and, if I sat her up, they would open. A medical student stopped to give us a ride anyway, and then a chain-smoking young girl, followed by the fast car guy and, finally, the blah-blah man, all the way to Rouen. Ine and I sat in the back with our buttercups. I had to hold her hands, to keep them from wandering. A very small degree of hope is sufficient to cause the birth of love.

We had arrived in the historic capital of Normandy, realm of cider and calvados, cheese, and charred Joan of Arc.

Ine and I found the Hotel Tourraine, run by a very nice Indian couple. Our room was pink, until the tapestry unraveled and the sparks came out. I laid her down, and her eyes closed. And opened. And closed.

'A wise woman never yields by appointment.
It should always be an unforeseen happiness.'
Stendhal

*   *   *

203

'The great majority of men, especially in France, both desire and possess a fashionable woman, much in the way one might own a fine horse - as a luxury befitting a young man.'

Stendhal

Jews had arrived in Rouen, half a millennium before the Vikings did. They followed behind Julius Caesar's invasion of Gaul. Those who didn't follow William the Conqueror, during his invasion of England in 1066 AD, were killed or dispersed during the First Crusade, thirty years later. They returned cautiously and, in the 12th century, not only comprised about twenty per cent of the town's population but, along the Vicus Judaerorum *Jew's Way*, established a Yeshiva of higher learning, rediscovered only in the 1970s, under the Rouen Law Courts. There is a crater on the moon, named Abenezra, after the most prominent scholar to have lived and lectured here, Abraham ben Meir Ibn Ezra. Like Benjamin and Michael Servetus, he was a wanderer from Tudela. Abenezra was known as *The Wise, The Great,* and *The Admirable Doctor.* In his *'Songs of Exile,* his tapestry was his cloak:

'I have a cloak that's a lot like a sieve
for sifting wheat and barley:
at night I stretch it taut like a tent,
and light from the stars shines on me.
Through it I see the crescent moon,
Orion and the Pleiades.'

In 1294, Phillip IV allowed the Jews of France to 'repurchase' their old liberties, in order to prosecute his war with the English. Twelve years later, he seized all their assets, and banished them, turning their neighborhood into a vegetable market. After hearing the 'clamor of the people,' the Jews were invited back again in 1315, with a guaranteed residence of twelve years. They were expelled again, after only seven. Phillip's aponym of 'the Fair' was clearly more a reference to his good looks.

Orion's light had brought me not to the moon but, in wandering back to Abenezra's Rouen, another heavenly body. I awoke to long legs, large areolas on larger breasts, and groans of pain and passion. After a foray out for sole Normande and white wine, Ine and I returned to our pink room in the Tourraine, to sleep. It was a foolish mission. The night was ferocious.

Ine and I spent the morning atoning for our sins. We floated through Monet-like impressions of the Rouen Cathedral's changing light, and the tombs of Richard the Lionheart, Normandy Viking founder Rollo, and Joan of Arc's murderer, John Plantagenet. We wandered whole-hearted, through the half-timbered old town. The flamboyant Church of Saint-Maclou stretched ropes from steeple to steeple, garlands from window to window, and golden chains from star to star. Under the rose window, we danced.

A young construction worker gave us a lift, after a long hike on the road to Caen. He complimented me on my French, and I on his. Two funny-tipsy truck drivers took us the rest of the way, in their Citroen. After an apple pastry, Ine and I walked downtown, and found the Hotel de Bolorme. We had intended to go out and buy groceries, but Ine had caprices of a marvelous unexpectedness. Alas. By the time we had awoken, and capriced and awoke again, the sun was down. Famished, we hurried to a small pizzeria to catch the last act of the only play dough in town.

Coffee was late next morning. Ine and I went out to see the Abbaye aux Dames, and the Abbaye aux Hommes, where people sought refuge, during the Battle of Normandy in 1944. Strange, that William the Conqueror had built it before invading England and, a millennium later, his descendents flattened the town around it. We visited William's Château de Caen, the high Gothic Church of Saint-Pierre, and a boulangerie, to find a friend for the Camembert de Normandie, that Ine had bought earlier.

Two rides carried us down the Bayeux highway, one via an

exhibition in a twelfth century church. Nine miles from our destination, a straw-hatted farmer in a 1943 Willys jeep, complete with white star on the hood, took us back eight hundred years, through the Normandy invasion, to the English one.

The Bayeux embroidery, over two hundred feet long and sewn in wool yarn, told the story of William's conquest, in 1066. King Harold is portrayed as either with an arrow in his eye, a spear through his chest, his legs hacked off, or all of the above. Above of all, and above all of this, was the appearance of Halley's comet, a sinister omen widely credited as the cause of the Norman victory at the Battle of Hastings. The most prolific meteor shower associated with the comet was called the *Orionids*, so named because they appeared to originate from ruddy Betelgeuse, in the Orion galaxy. William must have done a cartwheel.

Ine and I had an ice cream, and found the 'Family Home.' I remember the stone spiral staircase that took us to our room, and the ceiling beams exposed to heaven. *Les vrais paradis sont les paradis qu'on a perdus.* True paradise is the one that you have lost.

*   *   *

'France is the only place where you can make love in the afternoon without people hammering on your door.'

Barbara Cartland

Love made the thought of death a price gladly paid to have her. Our afternoon retreated from the parque pique-nique, to alternating life and death.

The other brush with death came after the other brushing in the bathroom, with the sun's return. My morning ablutions released a purge of peculiar proportions. Undulating, in the water below me, were several ribbons of rectangles, ghostly white, hitchhikers from the first book in the Cartwheels trilogy. My mind flew back to Ethiopia.

'They had prepared well for our arrival. I recognized the injera, but not what was to go with it. At first glance it looked like raw cubes of beef. Joseph brushed away the flies.

"It is *gored gored*." He said. "Raw cubes of beef." I remembered reading about the explorer James Bruce's culinary experiences in Ethiopia. The raw beef in his day was sliced off the live cow that had been maneuvered into the tent for just that purpose. I was grateful for the cuboidal separation in time and space. I wasn't going to be grateful for the other little presents that Joseph's lunch presented me in France, eight months later.'

They were identifiable but, with all the other life I was living, I chose denial. And Madame Lefevre's homemade rhubarb-strawberry jam, spread thick on my croissants, downstairs. That would kill the little bastards.

We were headed to Cherbourg. I was planning to take the ferry to Ireland, and Ine would continue her sojourn in France. But there would be more than the sea between France and Ireland. Our rides were short, but we never waited long. An older fellow took us twenty kilometers, to another, who treated us to coffee in the café next to the market.

"Les gens heureux en amour ont l'air profondément attentifs." He said. *People happy in love have an air of intensity.* I had to hold Ine's hands, under the table. An amusing old fisherman told us some stories about the invasion, and showed us the Boche cemetery. Another took us via Sainte-Mère-Église, to the church spire where American paratrooper John Steele was ensnared, on the Longest Day. Our final ride was from a young woman, who transported us to the Hotel St. Clement in Cherbourg, and into an enthusiastic welcome, from Monsieur and Madame Metayer. They brought Camembert sandwiches, a glass of wine from a vacationing old Norman, and a room, for making love and catnapping the day away. Rossel's 'Sus la mé,' *On the Sea*, played on the gramophone downstairs. No one hammered on the door.

The night, however, was full of hammers. Ine and I went out for dinner just after nine. Madame Metayer suggested *l'Assommoir,* for their fish. I asked her what the word meant. She told me it could not be translated, but it was the title of a book by Émile Zola, about poverty and alcohol. Ine and I went out to acquire more of both. The proprieteur told us that *l'Assommoir* had come from the verb, *assomer* (to stun, bludgeon, or render senseless). Hammered. It was the story of France. The Franks main weapon was a *francisca*, a heavy bladed iron hammer, thrown in volleys, before the hand to hand combat began. The unbalanced franciscas would bounce unpredictably, breaking shields, rebounding up legs and fracturing or severing limbs, and disrupting the enemy line by causing mass confusion. Charles Martel, the Frankish leader who defeated a Moslem invasion at the Battle of Tours, was known as Charles the Hammer.

Ine and I had a Dubonnet. The quinine in the recipe was designed to prevent malaria in French Foreign Legionnaires. The English Queen mother and daughter, Elizabeth, added it to gin at lunchtime, a further hammering against the disease, and sobriety.

The meal was divine, with olives and ham and asparagus, bouillabaisse, tornados with Pommery moutarde, haricots verts, pommes, cheeses, chocolate, and ice cream with whiskey. Back at the Metayers, I came out of the bath to a volley of franciscas, and shoes, and recriminations. Why was I leaving her? Why was I going to Ireland? I tried ducking, but she clipped my ear with her hairbrush, and her frustration. I asked her why she wasn't coming with me. She stopped long enough to fling one last hammer.

"Because you didn't ask." She said. So I asked. And no hollow places were left in our hammering.

France was a place where the money fell apart in your hands, but you couldn't tear the toilet paper. I was in a place where my money was falling apart anyway, and the toilet paper was useless, against the wraith wrectangles that had launched their own Normandy invasion. I couldn't tell her about the worm.

We slept until noon. Monsieur Metayer gave us two coffees for the road, and Ine and I lit out for the markets, to provision ourselves for the boat to Ireland.

Later that evening, curled up under the Gold Kazoo, we listened to the conversation of some English tourists, griping about the nasty French. We held our pain complet and Camembert with one hand, and each other with the other. In our small piece of the tapestry, nature had used her longest threads.

'I hope that throughout my life I'll sort of have the thread of my life and the thread of apple weave in and out of each other, like a tapestry.'

Steve Jobs

Guinness Record

'Two shorten the road.'
Irish proverb

We slept in the hum, between the fluorescent ceiling and the engine below. Bluegrass played over the speakers. Somewhere on board, there were slot machines, but Ine and I had finished gambling.

We disembarked in Rosslare just after lunch, and were waved through customs, into the sun. My plan was for us to hitch directly to Dublin, to exorcise the rectangular ghosts. It was one of those 'best laid' plans.

The first thing to greet us, on the motorway, was a billboard. The caption floated above a phalanx of full Guinness glasses. *Welcome to Ireland.* I had tried it before, but only as a beverage, and never inhaled. In Ireland Guinness had evolved, from nitrogen and water, to yeast to hops and burnt barley, through fish air bladder isinglass finings, beside mudskippers and toucans, out of aluminum iron lungs, and into the black stuff, a meal in a glass, the Workman's friend, a pint of plain:

'When food is scarce and your larder bare
And no rashers grease your pan,
When hunger grows as your meals are rare -
A pint of plain is your only man.'

Ine and I thought we were just hitchhikers, under a beer billboard, on a bend in the road. We were actually unsuspecting students of stout, on a hairpin learning curve.

The first instructor was Sean, a middle aged banker, driving an old blue Anglia, slowly up our hill. He barely had to brake, for us to get in the back. He wasn't going to Dublin. He asked where we were from. I told him Canada.

"Canada!" He replied, with obvious relish. "Me brother's in Canada. We're going to the pub."

He accelerated through the rocky green patchwork countryside, across the Waterford Bridge, past Jerpoint Abby, to Kilkenny. Sean dropped us at the Mena B&B, an old white stucco Tudor house, and arranged to meet us at the pub across the street 'later.' Up in our cozy room above the rose garden, Ine and I put the time and the bedside mirror to good use. *Welcome to Ireland.*

An Irishman is the only man in the world, who will step over the bodies of a dozen naked women, to get to a bottle of stout. Sean was already eleven ahead of me. Ine and I marveled, at how easily his Guinness consumption matched the ecstasy he had found in meeting a Canadian. He clearly loved his brother.

Nothing prepared me for the chill of consciousness returning. It was a black day in July. My skull felt like it contained my heart. Ine and I tread slowly downstairs, for our first Irish breakfast. Again, nothing exceeds like excess. After too many pints of the black stuff the night before, I was thinking continental. Mrs. Molloy was having none of it.

"Ireland sober is Ireland stiff." She said. And out came the liver and bacon rashers and sausages and fried eggs and black pudding and sautéed mushrooms and fried tomato and baked beans and brown soda bread. I felt bile rising, and gazed longingly into the pure clear simple cup of Bewley's breakfast tea. She poured cream into it. The ancient Greeks had them pegged:

> 'Its inhabitants are more savage than the Britons, since they are man-eaters as well as heavy eaters, and since, further, they count it an honourable thing, when their fathers die, to devour them, and openly to have intercourse, not only with other women, but also with their mothers and sisters.'
>
> Strabo, *On the Irish*

Ine and I climbed, to the endless portrait gallery, in the Norman Castle. Dame Alice, the founder of Kyteler's Inn, was born to Norman parents in 1263. Alice had been accused of witchcraft, for poisoning at least the last of her four husbands. We suffered no ill effects from her coffee, moving on to the Celtic collection of Rothe House, four centuries after Oliver Cromwell banished the last Rothe to oblivion. The dark-themed day continued, in the Dominican priory of the Black Abbey, named for the habits they wore, and the habits they bore, responsible for many Inquisition deaths, and the theft of their victims' possessions. The Black Death brought retribution to the Black Abbey in 1348. The five-panel Rosary window was almost as powerful.

Ine and I hiked out of town, via St. Mary's Cathedral. She danced a Dutch-Hungarian version of an Irish jig to my harmonica, on the side of the road. The sun blazed brighter for her performance. Our hitchhiking was unfocused and, after the black stuff diversion of the previous day, I was a little more cautious with our rides. It's a long, long way to Tipperary. I studied the young man behind the windscreen, as Ine's thumb pulled him over. He leaned across the passenger side to roll down the window.

"Where you goin'?" He asked.

"Cork." I said.

"Well, I'm headed in that direction. Hop in."

"Not so fast." I said. "I'm from Canada. That doesn't mean anything special to you, does it?"

"Not at all." He said. And we hopped in.

"You're in luck." He said, as we pulled away from the curb.

"Why's that?" I asked.

"It's my first day off in two months. I'm celebratin'. We're goin' to the pub!"

Joe was a welder. He had lied. We went to three pubs. I think it was the six pints of pain that Joe and I quaffed, over a game of billiards, in the last pub, that broke me, or maybe it was Ine's giggling at our failing skill. Joe asked if we were hungry. We told him we would likely never be again. He ordered a snack from the bar. It arrived, looking, for all the world, like someone had cut the feet off a pig, and deep-fried them in breadcrumbs.

"Do you know what they is, boy?" He asked. I told him it looked like pigs feet, deep-fried in breadcrumbs. He slapped my back.

"Good for you. Them's crubeens. Crunchy trotters, they are." I was thinking that the sixteenth century English had them pegged, as well:

'The Irish... are barbarous and most filthy in their diet. They skum the seething pot with an handful of straw, and straine their milke... through a like handful of straw, none of the cleanest... defile the pot and milke. They devoure... the intralles of beasts unwashed, they will feede on Horses dying of themselves. Neither do they any Beere... nor any Ale: but they drink... Beefe-broth mingled with milke; but when they come to any Market Towne, to sell a Cow or a Horse, they never return home, till they have drunke the price in Spanish Wine, and till they have outslept two or three days drunkenesse. It is strange and ridiculous... when they found Sope and Starch, carried for the use of our Laundresses, they thinking them to be some dainty meates, did eat them greedily, and when the stuck in their teeth, cursed bitterly...'

Fynes Moryson, *An Uncomplimentary View of the Irish, c. 1605*

For all his lunacy, Joe was motivated by pure generosity. His only valuable possessions were his joy and happiness. And a quiet, clumsy infatuation with Ine.

He drove us all the way to the Rock of Cashel, the traditional seat of the kings of Munster for hundreds of years before the Norman invasion. When St Patrick pulled Satan from his cave in the Devil's Bit Mountain, the Rock landed here, and converted the first Southern king. Joe bought us a book of Irish Fairy tales, and said goodbye, without so much as an address exchange. Sometimes, you only hear the greatness of men in their echoes.

Ine and I checked into Rockville house for five pounds, a terrific bath, and a late afternoon rest. The gray and green Cashel dusk we reemerged into, was the essence of Ireland- quiet lanes and strollers, and a thousand ravens in the trees above us. I bought an ice cream for Ine, and an orange juice for my head. We retreated to fairy tales and dreams.

The Irish breakfast next morning used the rest of the pig that hadn't escaped on Joe's crubeens. Unlike the croissants on offer in Paris, it was an immovable feast. Back out on the road, I was at my most guarded. Ine and I were into our third day in Ireland, and had only broken a hundred kilometers, and a Guinness record in Guinness. At this rate, we would die of cirrhosis, before we ever got to Dublin. I needed to exercise caution.

We waited on the roadside, with hidden thumbs. I let the cars go by, sizing up the vehicles, the hubcaps, the drivers. Waiting for Mr. Right. Finally, I spotted him, traveling the speed limit, ticking all the boxes, in a sedate silver-blue Volvo station wagon, exuding sobriety. The driver was wearing a three-piece suit and tie, short hair, and a solemn expression. Business class. My thumb threw an arc. He pulled over, pressed a button, and the automatic window, on the passenger side, migrated south.

"Would you like a lift?" He asked.

"Where are you going?" I inquired.

"Cork." He said.

"Are you going directly to Cork?" I asked. He replied in the affirmative.

"I'm from Canada. That doesn't mean anything special to you, does it?"

"No. Not at all." He said.

"You're not celebrating anything, are you?" I asked.

"No. Listen, would you like a lift or not?" He finally said. Ine and I got in. We pulled away from the shoulder. My window migrated north. I exhaled. Slumped.

"So," I said. "What brings you to Cork?" I asked.

"Me brother owns a pub there." He said.

*   *   *

215

'You can listen to traditional Irish music anywhere, anytime. But the very best place is sitting in the west of Ireland, downing your third pint of Guinness and knowing its great to be Irish.'

Conor Cunneen

Terry was a sound equipment shop owner from Dublin. We had coffee at the Cahir Inn, where Charlie Bianconi's stagecoaches used to stop, before exploring the Butler family Castle. It seemed that everything made of stone in Ireland had been constructed before 1200 AD, and then they built the pubs.

We eventually arrived at the one owned by Terry's brother. *'Tis the bells of Shandon that sound so grand on, the pleasant waters of the river Lee.* 'Welcome to the Republic of Cork,' said the sign.

"Now what sort of gligeen would you find in this bockety cowluck?" Terry said, as we entered.

"H.L.I! ya' noodenaw. I'll get moreran me own back, boy." Said his brother.

I think Terry made the introductions, but we didn't understand a word. There is a special dialect, spoken only in Cork but, from what I could discern, most of it had to do with gambling, sex, money or alcohol. Mostly alcohol. A party was a *guzzle*, a drinking session a *batter* or *skite*, the purpose of which was to get *moylow, hanging, rotto* or *paralatic*, drunk. The next morning you'd be *craw-sick*, especially if you had eaten *packet 'n tripe*, a tansy-flavored *drisheen* pig's blood sausage, and tripe. France was a galactic parsec away.

After playing darts with Ine, and a half pint *meejum* of Guinness, we jammed with my *fine half* on my half guitar, with the local rebels upstairs. Terry eventually pointed us towards Mrs. Spillane's house on South Douglas Road, and made us promise to call him when we arrived in Dublin.

In 1577 Cork was described as *'so encumbered with evil neighbours, the Irish outlaws, that they are fayne to watch their gates hourly... they trust not the country adjoining [and only marry within the town] so that the whole city is linked to each other in affinity.'* Mrs. Spillane greeted us in affinity, with tea and scones inside the gate.

The day was still young enough for a foray. Ine and I walked back into town, and took a bus to Blarney Castle. We arrived to a beautiful long path through green, and up a spiral stone spiral staircase, into an eerie, hauntingly fantastic tower. A spooky shaft of light fell strategic, in the throne room below. The 'murder hole,' inside the first portcullis, allowed boiling liquids to be poured on invaders. Blarney, like other medieval castles, was no Disney dream-come-true fairy tale. It was a booby-trapped donjon of defense, desperation, and death.

Our destination was the most unhygienic tourist attraction in the world, a block of bluestone from Scotland, set into the battlements, in 1446. To kiss the Blarney stone required the assistance of an old gent and his son, who held us by the ankles, as we arched backwards, dangling to reach the target. Courage finds its own eloquence.

> 'A noble spouter he'll sure turn out, or
> An out and outer to be let alone;
> Don't try to hinder him, or to bewilder him,
> For he is a pilgrim from the Blarney stone.'
> Francis Sylvester Mahony

Back at Mrs. Spillane's, Ine and I made some pasta and salad and tea, and some earth and wind and fire. I finished the Irish fairy tales, while she slept.

The two middle-aged Americans and the Vancouver teacher at the breakfast table next morning shared entitled lives, and angry resentment. They jabbered from topic to topic, complaining about anyone, and everything, they weren't. Eloquence is saying all that is necessary, and nothing but what is necessary. Our stone kisses had taught us to eat efficiently, in polite silence. The final romp upstairs was a celebration of our diversity.

We thanked Mrs. Spillane, and hiked out of Cork, picking blackberries, and a short ride of four miles, from a chubby local man. Several tons of heavy metal holiday traffic drove straight by us for the next two hours, until a high school teacher, named David, brought us through packed Killarney, to Muckross House.

It was the grandly beautiful estate of the Hebert family who, because they had spent so much improving it, in preparation for Queen Victoria's visit, lost it, in the financial consequences. I was impressed with the wide span of the extinct Irish elk antlers, discovered in a local peat bog. I was more impressed, however, with the short span, in which environmental degradation can change our idealized image of a place's natural beauty. The 'Emerald Isle' was emerald because of rain and grass, and without so much as a tip of a cap to the loss of all the ancient forests and wildlife, that had formed the original ecology of the place. I would be just as horrified with the pastoral rhapsodies, sung about New Zealand's green ovine countryside, and the now extinct kauri forests and songbird dawn choruses, conveniently omitted in its glorification. The ancient trees, that had served as the inspiration, for Ireland's eloquent songs and poems, had eroded to rocks and landmarks. St. Columba's hymn to his oak forest was prophetic, *'Though there is fear in me of death and of hell, I will not hide it that I have more fear of the sound of an ax over in Doire.'* The English armies consigned the forests of Ireland to oblivion, in less than two hundred years. A judge, Sir Jonah Barrington best exemplified the attitude, *'Trees are an excrescence provided by nature for the payment of debts.'* Jonah was born at Versailles. Another knight, Sir Valentine Brown, was given 91,000 acres of Killarney in 1620, the year the Pilgrims landed at Plymouth Rock. His domestication of the landscape domesticated the Irish, converting them from semi-nomadic pastoralists, to peasants, tied to a very local landscape.

And with the trees, went the wildlife. Wild boars vanished for lack of acorns, and even squirrels became extinct. Squirrels thrive in Manhattan; that they disappeared in Ireland, speaks to the thoroughness of the devastation. The last wolf had been shot two centuries before, not far from where the Heberts of Muckross House further contributed to this devastation, with their introduction of rhododendrons and Asian deer. I had kissed the Blarney Stone, but I still have no words.

David took us on to Tralee, for a pint of plain. He told us we wouldn't have seen Ireland, without experiencing the Dingle peninsula. I told David, that traveling through Ireland was like swimming upstream, against a river of Guinness. He ordered us all another, so as to give himself more time to convince us.

By the time he dropped Ine and I at the Dingle turnoff, I was almost converted. David had promised that Dingle would be a quiet diversion into a bucolic Irish rusticity, a tonic for the soul. After all that Guinness, we needed a tonic.

After almost two hours of bucolic rusticity, there was a scream, from the petrol station.

"Hey! You wanna ride?" Said the driver of an old Bedford camper van. We jumped in the back.

Fats and Gam, and Tom and Jerry, were four lads from Tralee, off to Dingle, for the weekend. They were eighteen, going on seventeen. Fats lit up a joint. Tom and Jerry handed us open bottles of wine and whiskey, at the same time. Not the tonic I thought David was talking about.

We drove directly to O'Flaherty's pub, a barn of posters and news clippings, and a crowded chamber of wonderful traditional Irish music, reverberating into the wee hours. Ine and I crashed in the back of the van, just after midnight.

The boys brought us coffee next morning, and Ine and I were invited to have a shower in the solicitor's house. We rode the van back to Fat's in Tralee, for fish sticks and beans on toast, and tea. I had forgotten my money belt at the solicitor's, but it was just an excuse for us to return, when Tom and Jerry came around later. Deep in county Kerry, we camped near Ashe's pub, at a party already in progress. Accordions and guitars, mandolins and banjos, and drums and pennywhistles kept each other in time, to the clapping and the dancing. A picnic of bread and corn beef, tomatoes and cheese, and *Aero*

219

chocolate bars, in a green patchwork field, led us back to Old World tunes, and pints of the black stuff. A Scottish medical student lectured me about the poverty in Canada, like I should be back home fixing it. I was eloquently quiet. When the pub finally closed, Ine and I once again took refuge in the van, but some of the bucolic rusticity came to visit. The first was Tom, with a German girl in tow, in a dying attempt at romance. She left him asleep in the passenger seat, unconscious before he had started. An hour later Gam collapsed comatose, beside us. The snoring began, even before his head hit the spare tire.

I was beginning to see the Irish as similar to, and totally unlike, the Jews. They had been oppressed, exiled, and knew how to cry for the dirty polluted blood of the world. They both had an abiding sense of tragedy, which sustained them, through temporary periods of joy. Other people had a nationality. The Irish and the Jews had a psychosis. But, in their hardship, the Jews turned to their religion. So did the Irish. But, in the hardship of their religion, they turned to drink. It was a Guinness record.

'This is one race of people for whom psychoanalysis is of no use whatsoever.'

Sigmund Freud (speaking about the Irish)

Óst na nOileán

'Rain is also very difficult to film, particularly in Ireland because it's quite fine, so fine that the Irish don't even acknowledge that it exists."
Alan Parker

When Noah's ark sailed by Mt. Brandon, in the Dingle peninsula, a Kerryman, sitting above the floodwaters, waved him down.

"How about a ride?" He asked. Noah told him that he was prohibited from taking anyone else onboard.

"Never mind, 'tis only a bit of a sprinkle." He said.

It was that kind of fine rain that accompanied Ine and I, on our long walk out of Tralee. We had whispered our goodbyes, and thanks, to Fats and Gam and Tom and Jerry, still half asleep on various sofas. I had promised Ine that we would find the bucolic rusticity that David told us about. Our first ride promised nothing back. It was from three crazy drunks, who sang to us for seven miles, begging us to join them, 'for just one pint.' We escaped to the roadside, beside six beautiful horses, until a Wicklow mother, with her two children, took us to another turnoff. Another lift, from a lawyer and his girlfriend, brought us to the Shannon ferry. It was here that Ine threw a tantrum, about my kissing a dog. I told her that I had always kissed dogs, and hadn't always kissed Ine. She told me that, if I ever wanted to kiss Ine again, there would be no more kissing dogs. I ate my apple and biscuits, eloquently.

On the other side of the river, two guys gave us a ride, from Galway to Ennis, where a young chap, on the other side of town, drove us to Doulin, and the search for a boat to the Aran Islands.

We were trying for Inis Oírr, the smallest of the three, but there was only an old blue fishing tug that was willing to go. Engine trouble on the way over, forced us to turn back. Our injured returning ran with the wind, and against a magical backdrop. Thousands of puffins, and other birds, animated the shale and sandstone Cliffs of Moher, rising four hundred feet straight above.

My promise to Ine, about finding our bucolic Irish rusticity, was sure to be delivered on the Arans. The islands had been decoupled from the rest of the country by the raw climate and geography. Galway Bay weather was savage and unpredictable. Once every hundred years, giant storm waves would toss huge boulders, up to eighty feet above the sea. Anyone living here had to be, by necessity, absolutely self-sufficient. Instead of soil, nature had provided wind. The islanders mixed layers of sand and seaweed, to create a growing medium, for grazing grass, potatoes and other vegetables. They built a lacework of stone walls, over a thousand miles, to act as windbreaks and enclosures, for sheep and cattle. This provided meat and wool and yarn for clothing, and their famous sweaters. Their *currach* boats were made of flimsy tarred canvas, stretched over thin laths. Fisherman wore soft calfskin moccasins, called *pampooties,* so as not to puncture the hull. They deliberately refused to learn how to swim, knowing that any sea that swamped a currach would guarantee drowning. They considered it preferable to have that done with quickly. Other contributions to Aran culture were political. Most of the inhabitants arrived in response to Cromwell's conquest, and the choice of going 'to hell or Connacht.' There were no luxuries. The language was *Gaeltacht* Irish, and the only entertainment was oral tradition. A few hours later, Ine and I were back on the water, *Riders to the Sea*, sailing towards a time capsule.

A cap and crusty beard, named John, tied our tug in Inis Oírr. The place he recommended to stay was closed, and Ine and I worked our way over half the island, before finding a little white house, with a religious reliquarium spare bedroom. Our hostess pointed us in the direction for a meal of fried cod, peas, and boiled potato. We returned to the large print of the Virgin above our bed, and turned her face to the wall. *No man at all can be living forever, and we must be satisfied.*

The richness of our Irish breakfast, next morning, had caught up with the oral tradition on the mainland. Ine and I set off on the Climb, up to the 14th century O'Brien's Castle, over views of the network of rock fences, enclosing the occasional cow or sheep. A farmer tried to sell us some twig baskets and a sweater, on our way down limestone pavements, past the graveyard, where we found some local boys, swimming in a small marsh at the bottom. Lost in the maze, Ine and I spent the rest of the morning clambering over rock walls, finally emerging to collect our bags, for the boat ride back to Doulin.

Onshore again, we spent a little time, jamming with a local banjo player, in Gus O'Connor's Pub, over some bread and cheese. An elderly couple gave us a ride to a field of cows, outside Lisdoonvarna. Ine and I had just about given up, when Father Constantine, a Greek, Latin and Irish scholar, filled our day with distance, and description. He took us on a guided tour of the 12th century Cistercian Abbeyknockmoy, before letting us off in Galway. We arrived half a millennium after Christopher Columbus, and three hundred years after it's rule by the 'tribes,' fourteen merchant families who monopolized the international trade that came through the city:

"Before France knew how to make wine,' said he, 'we made it here.' 'What,' said I, 'I never heard that you grew grapes at Galway.' 'Oh, we never did,' he replied, 'but in France the wine was simply the juice of the grape, and we brought it to Galway to make it drinkable. Unfortunately the Bordeaux merchants can prepare it now as well as we did, and that has cut the feet out from under us."

Jacques Louis de Bougrennet, *Surprises in Galway*

Ine and I found a six quid B&B, ham and pea soup, and each other, before calling it a day.

I ran out of Irish pounds next morning. We dropped into Lynch's Castle, the finest medieval town house in the country, to get more. After a purchase of some Irish songbooks at O'Gormons, Ine and I walked the three miles to Salt Hill, over Salmon Weir Bridge, past the hideous new cathedral, in the rain. Ine had almost flagged down a ride, but he bolted, after seeing me. Four more cars did stop, through the clouds, silver sea, and green mountains dotted with white sheep, until the local doctor finally took us from a small church to Lettermullen, and Óst na nOileán, *Hotel of the Isles,* a small bed and breakfast run by Billy and Mauve, but mostly by their two children, Daniel and Simon.

Here was our bucolic Irish rusticity. We were feted with brown soda bread and butter, covered with crab, and toasted cheese and chutney.

"There are four basic food groups," Said Billy. "Alcohol, caffeine, sugar, and fat."

"And only in this country can you get them all in one glass." Added Mauve, pouring out the Irish coffees. Ine and I played with Daniel and Simon until our room was ready, and then with each other in the wrought iron Celtic bed, and again, where the mattress had landed on the floor.

We emerged into an enchanting walk through the evening stillness, light in the west over the ocean, breeze rustling through the grasses, and a lilting Irish concertina, bouncing its magic off the Connemara hills.

*   *   *

'There once was a demographic survey done to determine if money was connected to happiness and Ireland was the only place where this did not turn out to be true.'

Fiona Shaw

The spell was broken at breakfast next morning. Daniel jumped on our mattress to announce that its preparation was complete. Ine and I surfaced out of our duvet to... muesli.
"A venomous porridge, unknown to toxicologists." Said Billy. "But it's better than plugged arteries." I told him the blood alcohol level in all the rides we'd been getting was driving way too fast to worry about cholesterol.
Simon and Daniel hugged us goodbye on the steps, and Mauve shouted after. "May the road rise to meet you, and the wind be always at your back."
We waved them goodbye, and set off over the Rockybog Road, picking blackberries, and thumbing rides. Three lifts got us to the Clifden turnoff, past boats, and inlets, and more blackberries. A middle-aged audiologist, named Annette, took us into town, for a coffee at the Celtic Inn, across to Connemara Tweed for a browse, and out along Westport Road, to Kylemore Abbey. Ten years later I would find myself living on a lake beside Benedictine nuns, but they wouldn't be living quite like these Benedictines-on-a-lake, in a seventy-room castle that included a ballroom, billiard hall, smoking room, gunroom, and twenty-one heated greenhouses. It was a magnificent setting.
Annette took us through green and gray desolation and peat stacks, all the way to Westport, at the foot of Croagh Patrick. We checked into Mrs. Muldoon's Asumpta B&B, and wandered out, along the stone bridges, tree-lined promenades, and alleys that led down to the Carrowbeg River. Potato cake boxtys and a Swithwicks was dinner. The only thing Ine didn't like was the wallpaper, but we struggled

to ensure that she didn't see much of it.

Annette said goodbye, next morning after breakfast, and we caught an instant hitch with a young truck driver, hauling a load of potted plants to Castlebar. It began to rain one of those Noah rains, as we walked to the Sligo road. A dump truck driver, who even I couldn't understand, hauled us along to Foxford. He loved his words, and used as many of them in every sentence as possible. We got a lift to Balyn, from a priest who knew Father Constantine. Ine and I were stranded here for over two hours, until the sun finally came out, and Liam, a psychiatrist from Dublin, brought us through views of Benbulben and Knocknarea, to Ardara, in Donegal. We waited over fish and chips, a pint of plain, and the fiddle music at the Nancy Pub, until the Burren B&B called back to invite us over. I thought we were all done in Donegal. But, in the bog of the Burren, my white rectangular ghosts returned. I had been having cramps for weeks. In Ireland the inevitable never happens, and the unexpected occurs constantly. But unless I got to Dublin's Fair City soon, I expected the inevitable was coming, and Saint Patrick, himself, would have been unable to banish this particular slow worm from Ireland. *Alive, alive, oh.*

The Tinker's Tapeworm

'I'm Irish. I think about death all the time.'
Jack Nicholson

My cramps awoke, somewhere between the porridge and the blood pudding, next morning. The monster growing inside me had been draining my energy and mass, at the light speed squared of the Irish midsummer. I felt cold.

Ina and I remembered passing a woolen shop, on our way into Ardara, the day before. We entered the door on Main Street in Donegal. I chose the hand knitted Aran jumper with the thickest stitched pattern. It had the honeycomb weave of the worker bee, the cables of safety and good luck fishing, the diamond pattern of wealth and treasure, and the basket symbol of a plentiful catch. The shop owner told me that dead fisherman could be identified, from their sweater pattern. I told her they would know me, by looking further inside.

Ine and I sat on a stone wall in the sun, until the local vet started us on our long trip to Dublin, and our short education through Northern Ireland, and its nuances.

"Everyone hates the other in the name of Jesus." He said. "Even atheists are required to indicate whether it's the God of the Catholics, or the God of the Protestants, they don't believe in. The viruses of violence and irrationality have infected their hearts with a fanatical misery, and preoccupied them more with their enemy's pain, than their own pleasure. In the North, the Protestants pray on one leg, and the Catholics on two. Because the English never learned how to speak, and the Irish never learned how to listen."

He dropped us where we could feast on blackberries. A Kennybegs fisherman brought us to Letterkenny. I thought I had forgotten my new jumper but, after we turned around, Ine found it under my seat. Once again we found ourselves in brambles, and for a while, it didn't seem like we were going to go any further. Ine made a sign that said '*Dublin.*' I asked her where she thought we would get to with that. The moment she held it up, a social welfare investigator, named Tony, screeched to a halt.

"How far are you going?" I asked.

"Dublin." He said. With the size of Ine's smirk, there wasn't any room for me in the back seat. And he drove us through the blockhouses and machine guns and vests and camouflage, to Carrickmacross, past the three Loughcrew cairn peaks, constructed to represent Orion's belt, and then across the whole country, all the way to Dublin.

Everyone we had met, that had asked us to call them, was out of town, so Ine and I ended up at the Castle Hotel, an old Georgian gem on Great Denmark Street. It was less than seven pounds. In the city of Yeats and Shaw, Beckett and Swift, and Joyce and Wilde, we had beans and cheese, and apples, and love.

There was a fish breakfast downstairs next morning. Ine and I had the plaice to ourselves. Even with the daily worsening of my cramps, I had no courage to tell her about my Ethiopian passenger, or my dire need for treatment. My ablutions were becoming more rectangular, and more ghostly, with each day. Tomorrow, I thought. I'll tell her tomorrow.

Instead, we went off to meet Harry Clarke's stained glass masterpiece, in the Hugh Lane Gallery. His '*Eve of St. Agnes*' was an Irish fairy tale, in rich deep blues of integrated finesse. Harry's artistic inspiration had come from the windows in Chartres Cathedral. I remembered the feeling... '*radiant and contemplative. I reached out and touched heaven.*'

In the National Gallery, Ine and I studied two treasures of early Irish art, the Ardaugh Chalice and the Cross of Cong. The chalice was a magnificent silver, bronze and gold 8th century metalwork drinking vessel, cast, cloisonnéd, filigreed, enameled, and engraved with the names of the Apostles, in a sea of stippling. Men looking for potatoes found it, although no one ever explained why they were digging inside a fort. The Cross of Cong was an oak reliquary, supposedly containing a piece of the true cross, ornamented with gold, silver, niello, copper, bronze, brass, enamel, and colored glass, in a hybrid Insular, Viking and Romanesque style. The inscription was a challenge to my high school Latin, 'Hac cruce crux tegitur qua passus conditor orbis.' *In this cross is preserved the cross on which the Founder of the world suffered.*

Suffering was something the Irish also had a talent for. The most status in any room full of Hibernians we had been in, went to the person who had the worst thing happen to them most recently. Bright beguilers of old anguish, they suffered more for the British indifference of our next destination.

Ine and I took bus 78a, to Kilmainham Gaol. Inside the public hangings out front, each cell received a candle for light and heat, every two weeks. In the dark and cold and damp, men slept on iron bedsteads, and women on floor straw, in unsegregated noisome dungeons.

Back at our own Castle, we called Terry, and found him home. He told us to meet him at the Salmon Leap Inn in Leixlip, around ten that night. We arrived to find him in good form, with his partner, Jenny, and the first of several jokes, and pints of plain. We ended up at their place, with neighbor Ed, sandwiches, and a tremendous jam session.

Terry took us back to the Castle, through an encampment of Tinkers, Irish nomads or 'Travelers,' originally made homeless by Oliver Cromwell's military campaign, and the 1840's potato famine. We drove through trailers, and car wrecks, and yelling, in Shelta. There were bonfires, shadow casting horses, and shadow boxing drunken brawls. The only antidote to mental suffering is physical pain, and the Travelers refused to suffer in silence. I thought I had escaped suffering by becoming a real traveler, a spectator of my own life. But a man who fears suffering, is already suffering from what he fears. And when the monster awakes, and the cramps begin, the physical pain and fear is no antidote to anything.

*   *   *

> 'Ethiopia didn't just blow my mind; it opened my mind. Anyway, on our last day at this orphanage a man handed me his baby and said, 'Would you take my son with you?' He knew, in Ireland, that his son would live, and that in Ethiopia, his son would die.'
>
> Bono

Ethiopia didn't need loud mythomaniac preachers, with Barbara Streisand sunglasses, and cowboy hats. It needed them to stay home and to shut the hell up.

The Ethiopian I had brought to Dublin was thriving. It had a ready supply of Irish breakfasts and Guinness, and was growing into a big boy. His scolex head was already the size of a cricket ball, hanging on to my guts for dear life, with four powerful suckers. I'd had enough.

Ine wished me luck next morning. I had scooped up a tailor's measure of rectangular ghosts, and placed it in a plastic film canister. We took a bus, up to Mater Misericordiae *Mother of Mercy* Hospital Casualty, where I was ushered behind a cubicle curtain, and asked to wait for a house officer. She was young, no question.

"What brings you to Casualty today?" She lilted. I asked her if she'd ever seen one of these, and poured the long ghost, out onto the tray table. She fainted.

As I was holding her legs up, in an attempt to get some venous blood back into her head, the Senior House Officer came looking for her. I explained to him, twice, that I wasn't holding her legs in the air, for the purpose of looking up her skirt. Luckily, she came to, and corroborated my story.

I collected Casper, and asked them where the Micro Lab was. We climbed stairs, until I found a door that led into a room with long benches, Petri dishes and microscopes. Atop one of them was a white coat, sitting. I figured it was safe enough, and poured Casper out, beside him.

"That's a worm." He said. I was clearly in a place of higher learning. He didn't know what kind, specifically, but pointed me in the direction of books that could tell me. I found the right page, and winced. *Taenia saginata*, beef tapeworm. Bono should have brought them fire.

I asked him where the dispensary was. He pointed, without looking up from his microscope. I thanked him, and took to the stairs once more.

The pharmacist in the dispensary actually made eye contact, and inquired after my mission. I asked if they had any niclosamide.

"That's for tapeworms." She said. Exactly. She pointed to the back, and allowed me around the counter.

The niclosamide I found had expired, but not by much.

"Take it." She said. "We'll never use it." I took it, and thanked her.

Making a point of checking on my intern's wellbeing in Casualty, on the way out, I was heading further down the stairs, when I heard someone calling after me.

"Excuse me." He said. A well-dressed young man. Tie. Jacket. Ambition.

"Yes?" I asked.

"I beg your pardon, Sir." He said. "But you haven't paid."

"Hmm." I said. "Let me see. I resuscitated my doctor, did my own micro, and got my own expired drugs. How much would you charge for that?" I hadn't kissed the Blarney stone for no reason. He excused himself again, backwards this time.

Second only to Bono, a book was Ireland's finest national treasure. After I took my first dose of worm killer, Ine and I walked over to Trinity College to see it. Columban monks had created the Book of Kells, around 800 AD. There was no other way to describe it, other than an 'Illumination.' Three Hundred and forty calfskin folios, of intricate interlacing knot patterns and mythical beasts, enlivened the four Gospels portrayal, in red and yellow ochre, green copper verdigris, indigo, and lapis lazuli from Afghanistan. How it survived the countless Viking raids on the Abbey is anyone's guess.

We continued the day at Dublin Castle and St. Patrick's Cathedral, site of Oliver Cromwell's stable, the first performance of Handel's Messiah, and its most famous Dean, Jonathan Swift. I had always loved his irreverence. *Imitate him if you dare, world-besotted traveller.* Towards the end he suffered a stroke, as I likely will, and lost his ability to speak. 'I shall be like that tree,' He once said, 'I shall die at the top.'

Even the meager soup supper I managed, with my medication nausea, was almost too much for Casper. I could feel him twisting in my wind, pulling for all he was worth. The cramps grew even more unbearable. I was locked in a life and death struggle with an alien interloper. If my suffering went on forever, as long as it resulted in the ultimate death of the monster that had invaded me, I wouldn't give a Tinker's damn. It was a distinctly Irish feeling.

'They have nothing in their whole imperial arsenal that can break the spirit of one Irishman who doesn't want to be broken.'

Bobby Sands

"I was on a Vision Quest." Said Uncle Wink. "I was on the ultimate spiritual search for the meaning of life."

"Did you find it?" Millie asked.

"Oh, yes." Uncle Wink answered.

"What was it?" She asked.

"What?"

"The meaning of life." Said Millie.

"The quest." Said Uncle Wink.

"The quest was the meaning of life?" She asked.

"Yes, Mil. The quest for the meaning was the meaning. The longing was the return message. I was hunting for the quest, itself. And the quest would provide consciousness, and consciousness would provide quality, and quality was the meaning of life."

Skye Lark

'West of these out to seas colder than the Hebrides I must go,
Where the fleet of stars is anchored and the young star-captains
glow.'

James Elroy Flecker

I went into a long labor next morning. There was a clamoring in my midsection. My solar plexus went supernova. Ine was on the other side of the bathroom door asking questions, but I knew she really didn't want to see the answer. Casper's arrival was precipitous, and the noise he made, when he hit the water, rippled up my spine. A pull on the chains cast off my own, as I consigned him to the Liffey, and oblivion.

His demise brought out the faithful. A Jesus freak picked us up, on our way north out of Dublin, and plugged in a tape about salvation. I told him about Casper. We left him with a weakened conviction. Just past Swords, a wind scattered old churchman transported us, to where we could walk across the border, back into Northern Ireland. Hitchhiking was still a spectator sport notion here and, after a short period of suspended air thumbing, it required no further deliberation to realize, that the only way we would get to the ferry terminal in Larne, would be to take the train. Ticket in hand, sprawled on a bench in the station, I was approached by an elderly lady, with a smile and a clipboard.

"Excuse me." She began. "May I ask you a few questions?" Why, sure.

"I'm from the Northern Ireland Tourist Board. Is this your first trip to Northern Ireland?" Why, yes.

"How long have you been in the country?" She continued. An hour.

"How have you enjoyed your stay?" Marvelous.

"Do you think you might ever come back?" Rundai.

"Thank you for your cooperation, and have a safe journey." She finished, with a flourish. In the previous four months, the

235

Provisional Irish Republican Army had exploded bombs in Derry, Armagh, Ballymen, Bessbrook, Magherafelt, Hyde Park and Regent's Park, killing thirteen people and seven horses, and injuring dozens of others. The safest part of our journey would be getting on the boat.

Stranraer came into view at dusk. Scotland. *Alion. Caledonia.* A ferry on the same route had killed 133 people, twenty years earlier, decks swamped by heavy seas. Our seas were calm, and we were given directions to Mrs. Lawson's. She charged us five quid, with asparagus soup and mince pie thrown in. Ine and I held on overnight, for the separation at dawn.

It was a long kiss that waited outside next morning. I promised to see her in Den Haag, in just a few weeks time. Mr. College picked me up on the outskirts of Stanraer, and drove to me Glasgow, via Rock Island, Burn's birthplace, and beans and mince pie. I got to Balloch all by myself, and then out along the beautiful bonnie, bonnie banks of Loch Lomond, with its surface islands of green tangled jewels. There was a high road, but I took the low road, so the fairies would protect my soul on its way home. There were bison and deer along the low road, and a sign. *No room for boys.* I was older than that, and curious. I hoisted Seredipity, and my half guitar, up the steep gravel drive along the rock wall and evergreens, rising onto the site of Robert the Bruce's hunting lodge, and the old turreted castle of Archendennan House.

It had been constructed in 1865, from the proceeds of West Indies slave labor, by a tobacco baron named George Martin. A pseudo-Ivanhoe manor of arches, buttresses, stained glass and slippery staircases, it was actually a youth hostel, and I managed to convince the warden that I was not a boy. I ascended to the second floor ballroom, to six chandeliers providing dim light onto the highly polished sepia wooden floor tiles twenty feet below, spinach-colored wallpaper, fireplace, and mandatory stag head. There were echoes of dead slaves, and voices of travelers. Here was Waverly, a friendly teenage cyclist, Sue, an English social worker tending alcoholic women in Glasgow, and Margaret, a thirty-year old Aussie, fresh from, and for, quitting her job as a teacher. We had tea, and later, mince and peas and fruit cocktail and chocolate. The evening and ballroom filled with spontaneous folk offerings from various countries, and I slept, reinspired by the goodness of our planetary youth.

The weather changed, while I was shaving next morning. There are two seasons in Scotland: June and winter. June was over. My path downhill dropped into storm-tossed views of the loch. A chemistry teacher and his daughter, in a yellow Renault, scooped me up before the downpour. We drove through thunderful bogs and waterfalls and mountains and lakes, to Fort William, where I left them, for soup and a scone, in the town centre. The man beside me at the counter asked me for money, to buy his own soup. I offered to buy him a bowl, but he told me he didn't want soup. I asked him what he did want. He said he just wanted the money. Back out in the rain, beyond the High Street shops, and out along the old railway line road, I found a hitching post, without a hope in hell of a ride.

First Rule of Hitchhiking: *It's not up to you.*

She stopped two minutes later. Marion. She didn't say much at first, not even where she was going. Sweater and jeans, tussled brown hair, an English beauty of twenty-nine years. We started haltingly, speaking of the psychology of hitching, stopping for photos of misted mountains and lochs. Marion was a zoologist, on vacation and, unbeknownst to me, I was undergoing a process of natural selection. I asked her where she was going. Her blush lit up the cockpit of the Cortina. She apologized for not asking me, but I waved it away. The journey is the goal. The interruptions are the journey. Marion was headed over the sea to Skye and, after studying each other *in the highlands, in the country places, where the old plain men have rosy faces, and the young fair maidens quiet eyes*, so was I.

$$*\qquad*\qquad*$$

'Come with me to the Winged Isle
Northern father's western child.
Where the dance of ages is playing still
Through far marches of acres wild.'
                                        Jethro Tull

To travel hopefully, is a better thing than to arrive. Marion and I stopped for fish and chips in Kyle, and rejoined the road to the largest island in the Inner Hebrides. Here, where Bonnie Prince Charlie escaped from Culloden, where lay the Cuillin hills and crofters, Talisker malt and salmon, red deer and golden eagles, the Battle of the Spoiling Dyke and the Battle of the Braes, here we arrived at Dunvegan Castle, seat of the chief of Clan MacLeod, and his Fairy flag. But it was closed, so we drove to a B&B, owned by clan rival, Mrs. MacDonald, and a green bedspreaded monster of a king-size mattress, overlooking the white sea, snapping outside. Maid Marion and I had baths, and carried on down to the Misty Isle hotel, for a Grouse and McEwan's, curry, and the echoes of Gaelic in the smoke and peat-reek. *Och aye the noo.*
Tipsy, we drove back to the green monster, and it engulfed us, in salt air and warm musk, storm seas breaking outside and within. *Loud the winds howl, loud the waves roar, thunderclaps rend the air... Though the waves leap, soft shall ye sleep... Over the sea to Skye.*
We awoke for the last time, midmorning. After breakfast, and a lingering pot of coffee at the Misty Isle, Marion drove me to the ferry, for a final hug. I noticed a lorry, with an Inverness sign on the back, and asked the driver for a ride. Bill was most accommodating. I helped him load some trolleys in Kyle, and he took me all the way along the famous loch, to the Highlands capital. A long hike brought me to a bed at Mrs. Woods, for four pounds a night, and another took me

for liver and onions, at the Castle Café. From lean to rich and back again.

I had booked a 'tour' with Gordon's bus on the morrow. Mrs. Woods woke me at seven thirty, for a full Scottish breakfast. The colors and portions were similar to the Irish species, with absent plant life, and animals remodeled into variations of cone geometry. In the land where most cuisine was based on a dare, Mrs. Woods' brave heart produced the quintessential start to my Highland day.

> 'The Table being more than halfe furnished with great platters of porredge, each having a little peece of sodden meate; And I observed no Art of Cookery, or furniture of Household stuffe, but rather rude neglect of both… They vulgarly eat harth Cakes of Oates…'
> Fynes Moryson (1566-1617), *On the Diet of the Scots*

There was enough to feed 'the pooch and puss' around my ankles.

Gordon arrived at the riverside in his blue bus around nine thirty and, over the pink-blue purple heather and white noise of the choppy waves, gave a fine lecture about the Loch, and its most famous mythical inhabitant. *But something in its depths doth glow too strange, too restless, too untamed.* Against the impressive background of Urquart Castle's ramparts, Gordon postulated five possible explanations to account for the various sightings of Nessie through the years: misidentification of common animals, misidentification of inanimate objects or effects, reinterpretation of traditional Scottish folklore, exotic species of large animals, and hoaxes. Pleiosaurs had died out long before Loch Ness was even created. I voted hoaxes.

Two South Africans, Charles and Robin, were part of my group. Charles had worked for the *Argus,* in Cape Town. He remembered the article about my hospital admission of the little black dog. We clambered down to the loch through the heather, to pee and pick blueberries, until Gordon called after us to return. He had sausage rolls and haggis, an animal made 'from bits and barley,' who could only walk counterclockwise, because its left legs were shorter. Fui Li, a Chinese traveler, added this to his notes, without smiling.

Gordon provided an experience of quality, expostulating on Scottish and World history, marine biology, deep-fried Mars bars, and the meaning of life in Brogueland.

Charles, Robin, Fui Li and I spent the rest of the afternoon together, drinking McEwans on a pier, watching a tug o' war with some fellows pitching eggs and being doused with custard, and crunching honeycomb on our walk back into town. Fui Li ordered for us at a local Chinese restaurant later, and I left them all for a hot bath back at Mrs. Woods, after a last cup of green tea. Many miles away, I slept like the shadow on the door of a cottage, on the shore of a dark Scottish lake.

*   *   *

'The noblest prospect which a Scotchman ever sees is the high-road
   that leads him to England.'

Samuel Johnson

There was no high road south to Perth next day. The first indication was the graffiti, on the back of the sign at the turnoff. 'I've come to the conclusion that hitching is an inefficient form of transportation.' It said. Voltaire claimed that we looked to Scotland for all our ideas of civilization. He had never tried thumbing out of Inverness.

I had waited about three and a half hours, watching the traffic file by all my professional attempts at interruption. Finally, at last, a middle-aged Scot, in full-blown regalia, pulled over on the curb. He was a stocky lad, a farm wholesaler off to the

Highland games in Perth. Unbeknownst to me, he had other sport in mind. The car pulled away fast.

"Are you liberal?" He asked.

"Huh?" Was my reply.

"Are you liberal?" He repeated. I didn't think I was liberal.

"Cause if you're liberal, we could screw each other in the bushes over there, and no one would ever know." I decided I wasn't liberal. Not broad-minded, enlightened, flexible, free, indulgent, latitudinarian, lenient, loose, permissive, progressive, receptive, tolerant, unbiased, unbigoted, unconventional, unorthodox, nor unprejudiced. What I was, was angry. *I wonder did na turn thy stomach.*

"I would know." I said, my right foot stomping on his brake, way too fast. Perhaps it could have been expected from the manicured monkeys or Sicilian sewer rats in Italy. But from a Scottish farm implement salesman, in the Highlands, it was a wee bit much. *To soothe me with fair scenes, and fancies rude, when I pursue my path in solitude.*

Ten minutes after Tam O'Shanter skulked off, down the lowlife high road, a talkative teacher, named Tom, gave me a ride to Perth. It was here they found the tomb of a four thousand year old Pictish Bronze Age ruler, layed out on white quartz pebbles and birch bark, and surrounded by flowers. I emerged to bagpipes, across the park, the lost connection between noise and music. Yeats believed that distance added enchantment to the bagpipes, and Wilde gave thanks to God there was no smell. The best way to play bagpipes was with a chainsaw. You could, admittedly, tune the chainsaw. Even the Scots had an old proverb: 'If thy neighbor offend thee, give each of his children bagpipes.'

For me, in the setting of a fantastic overcast day of Highland games, with step dancing girls and hammer throwers, caber tossers, pipe band competitions, and cheeseburgers, coffee and ice cream, they were perfect.

A friendly constable directed me to a hitching post, near the Tesco supermarket, where I waited two more hours, for an

Oxford journalist, who took me a further fifteen miles down the road. I got out of his car, directly into a green van with Jordie and Michael, two amusing tipsy students, who drove me all the way to Haymarket, in Edinburgh.

I found a hostel with a vacancy, and claimed a lower bunk with Serendipity's belt clips. Beef stew and cabbage salad mortared in the gaps, between the charcoal and auburn sandstone, and the rest of my day. *One pound forty, please.* I returned to repose and dream further out, along the southern coast of the Firth of Forth, and the islands of Fidra, Lamb, and Craigleith, lying in linear proportion, to the Orion belt stars of Alnitak, Alnilam, and Mintaka. To the northeast, the Isle of May correlated with Bellatrix. Northwest of May was Betelgeuse, and the lost stone Dunino Circle. A line drawn between May and Dunino came to rest on Shakespeare's castle of 'MacBeth,' at Dunsinane. Another from May, through Fidra, led to Rosslyn Chapel, and a third from May, through the Lamb, led to Tara in Ireland. A fourth drawn from May, through Craigleith, led to Scotland's earliest headquarters of the Templar Knights. Due south was the Castle of Yester, representing Rigel. A final line drawn through Yester intersected Melrose Abbey and Glastonbury Tor. In this knuckle-end of England, this land of Calvin, shortbread tins, oatcakes and sulphur, I dreamt of stars and skylarks, and the long road yet to come. *The rainy Pleiads wester, Orion plunges prone, the stroke of midnight ceases, and I lie down alone.* I awoke in the Athens of the North next morning, did my hostel dishwashing duty, said goodbye to Syphilitic Said from Ceuta, and hiked down cloudy Princess Street, for a coffee at Woodward's. The painting I was seeking, hung in the National Gallery of Scotland, on the mound between two sections of the Princes Street Gardens. It wasn't Rafael's *Madonna,* but Goya's *Medico,* I had come to see, the doctor warming his hands over a dish of coals, accompanied by his books and two students. I went on up to the Castle for views of Scott's Monument, Edinburgh's Folly, and the Firth of

Forth, and down past Gladstone Terrace, to Lady Alice's tenement, and memorabilia of Scott and Burns.

It was time to bid farewell to each retiring hill, and take my leave of Scotland. I boarded a bus to a hitching post, near Terant. An hour's wait got me thirty miles with a self-employed engineer. And then came Simon, a twenty-two year old antique refurbisher.

"Where are you going?" I asked.

"I'm not sure." He said.

"Good enough." I replied, and got in. We stopped in Berwick-upon-Tweed for a steak and kidney pie, and a coffee. And then we said goodbye.

Twenty minutes later, Simon stopped again.

"Where are you going this time, Simon?" I asked.

"England." He said.

"We are in England." I told him.

"Oh." He said. And he took me to Thornborough, with its three Neolithic henges, built to represent the belt stars of Orion. And then he took me to York.

Drifter

'No one ever travels so high as he who knows not where he is going.'
Oliver Cromwell

Of all his reputed characteristics, Cromwell was not commonly considered a drifter. Yet Oliver traveled high enough to lay siege to York in 1644, and where his roundheaded Parliamentarians defeated Prince Rupert's Royalists, under a harvest moon, at the Battle of Marston Moor.

I found a nice quiet hostel near the gate. Here I met Peter, who had worked in my hometown, in Northwestern Ontario. We shared chicken and salad and stories, until late.

Random beams of sunlight penetrated the clouds over Church Street next morning. For 50p, I climbed Clifford's Tower, without any idea as to what had occurred here, eight hundred years earlier.

On the night of March 16, 1190, the small Jewish community of York huddled together for protection, inside the tower. Their ancestors had come over, just over a hundred years before, with the man who built the tower, William the Conqueror. They were precluded from working in almost all occupations, except money lending, so that's what they did. Their lives were a constant balancing act, between having just enough, and having it all taxed away and confiscated, in the next impulsive need for greed, that came from their governing 'protectors.' Payment was exacted through imprisonment, property confiscation, the seizing of women and children, and even gouging out eyes.

When Abraham of Bristol refused to pay an arbitrary penalty, the King ordered seven of this teeth extracted, one a day, until he relented. And every demand for more gold resulted in more suffering for the general populace, and more resentment towards the Jews. When the Crusades began, the noble knights sharpened their ethnic cleansing skills on the local Jewish population, en route to the Holy Land, and local mobs exploded into genocidal pogroms of their own. They shouted 'HEP... HEP... HEP,' on their way to the massacres. 'Hierosolyma Est Perdita.' *Jerusalem is lost.* The one last missing word, was the one King David mentioned in Psalms 137, predicting what the Roman Children of Edom would shout, as they destroyed Jerusalem. *'Arruh.'* As in, 'for he's a jolly good fellow.' *'HEP HEP, Arruh.'* Hip hip hooray.

Rather than perish, at the hands of the violent mob that awaited them outside, the Jews of York, like those of Masada, took their own lives; some threw themselves onto the interior stone courtyard sixty feet below, some died in the flames they had lit, and the remaining, who finally surrendered, were butchered. The fate, of those few who escaped, wasn't determined until construction of the Chapelfield Shopping Centre began in Norwich in 2004. A medieval well was found, containing seventeen skeletons. DNA analysis identified them as all from a single Jewish family. They were thrown down the well, head first. Children last. Those at the bottom had fractured skulls.

The sun lit a pizza slice, of the stone courtyard below. I timed a falling tear.

In 1290, Edward the First went for a windfall. He expropriated all the property of the Jews, and expelled them from England. They weren't kissed goodbye. One captain, contracted with a full ship, convinced his cargo to take a walk on the shore of the Thames, during an outgoing tide. He made it back before the tide returned, and left them all to drown.

It wasn't until Oliver Cromwell drifted to York, three hundred years later, that the Jews were allowed back into England. A physician named Manoel Dias Soeiro, a Portuguese Rabbi living in Amsterdam, petitioned the Lord Protector to allow their return. In 1656 Cromwell stated that the ban would no longer be enforced. It was as much as any

Puritan was willing to do. Two hundred years later, a Quaker, named Henry Isaac Rowntree, founded a confectionary company in York. I bought one of his products in the Castle shop, on my way out. I still have the wrapper from the chocolate-covered caramel-covered wafer. Underlined, in big red letters, it says '*Drifter.*'

*   *   *

'The British do not expect happiness. I had the impression, all the time that I lived there, that they do not want to be happy; they want to be right.'

Quentin Crisp

I bought some green grapes, to cleanse the *Drifter* from my palate, and left York via its restored Cathedral, City Art Gallery, Bootham Bar Gate, King's Manor, and a *Vikings in England* exhibit at the Yorkshire Museum.

After three and a half miles of walking, I snagged a lift with a chubby office supplies salesman, to the A1 turnoff. A young computer game serviceman took me fifteen more miles, to the M66. At the top of the ramp, Bass, a marine engineer from Blackpool, slowed down fast enough for me to hop in. He got me through enough farmland monotony, to Stamford, where I spent the next two hours, trying to catch a ride near a petrol station. A blue Bedford van sputtered to a wheeze beside me, the driver gesturing for me to get in. I got in. He told me his name was Spud, and that he was an English Traveler, like the Tinkers in Ireland. He told me that he was a 'Drifter.' Spud spoke of his 78 year-old mother, who could still swing hundred pound weights from her pigtails, of selling a farmer his own sheep, and of being hired to demolish an old building, and renovating it instead. Spud dropped me on the Cambridge Road, and waved. In East Anglia now, I had just made my way down the onramp, when a big rig pulled over so hard, his back wheels jumped. I flashed back to Serge and Southern France, three months earlier, and my reflection of that much metallic momentum, cold-stopped dead with just one thumb. The same thrill went up my spine. The longhaired, bearded driver had just broken up with his girlfriend of eight years. He told me his story. I told him mine. On the other side of dusk, a quiet businessman drove me to the railroad station in town. I found the youth hostel, and beans and chips. For that kind of money, they got to turn the lights off. And I slept.

I ran out in the morning, when the air was clean and new, to where the men go to lecture, with the wind in their gowns. Before he became a Drifter, Oliver Cromwell studied here. So did Isaac Newton, with his prism and silent face, and James Clerk Maxwell, Lord Kelvin, Francis Bacon, Ernest Rutherford, J. J. Thomson, Henry Cavendish, Crick and Watson, and Charles Darwin. A goodly number of my minor deities had lived and worked in these dusky groves, under turrets and pinnacles in answering files. After perusing the Fitzwilliam Museum, I walked silently on hallowed ground. The rain came down.

Soaked, I made four miles through the deluge, and the turnoff south. A Cockney cabbie, and his charming twelve year-old daughter, stopped their station wagon to take me *blah blah blah,* all the way to Grimsby East tube station. A quid took me to Canada House, where I picked up a treasure trove of mail, and allowed a call home. I also called Keith from Rio, but he was back in Brazil. Instead, I found the Astor youth hostel, for a hot bath, a stuffed marrow, and stuffy bunkroom.

I had come to London for two reasons- my mail, and the British Museum. I love the British Museum, the way a chemist loves the Periodic Table. It has all the essential elements of historical acquaintance and acquisition. Heavy on the acquisition. It is the history of history. The reading room was the hangout of Conan Doyle, Bram Stoker, Lenin and his inspiration. Gorbachev remarked that if people didn't like Marxism, they should blame the British Museum. It had a collection of seven million objects, and I had a few hours. After a concentrated attempt at concentration, in the Assyrian and Sumerian sections, I had saved enough time to spend with the Rosetta stone. Unlike Plymouth Rock, which was made out of the same granodiorite material, the Rosetta stone was not a celebration of arrival, but a key to origin. For the first time, Ancient Egyptian hieroglyphs could be deciphered, with the help of the deotic script and Ancient Greek, sitting below them.

I was heading back to the torso of mainland Europe. One final train brought me to Dover, and an overnight boat to Ostend. I sat on the bench, repairing my map, and thinking about the seasons. It was approaching the end of August. I was planning on finding a medical post in Scandinavia, for the winter. The days and money were getting shorter, and there wasn't much room for miscalculation.

A down and out Drifter approached me with a supplicant stare. I asked him what he wanted.

"An end to World Hunger." He said. I asked him what his second choice was.

"Cup of tea." He said.

In my hometown Paramount movie theatre, when I was very young, I had a crush on Hayley Mills. I drank tea with my grandmother, pinkie in the air. One Saturday matinee, Marilyn Monroe came to town. Next morning I asked her for coffee, black, no sugar. Been a Drifter ever since.

Schotel of Mosselen

"Belgium' is the rudest word in the universe, <u>which</u> is completely banned in all parts of the Galaxy, except in one part, <u>where</u> they could not possibly know what it means.'

Douglas Adams, *The Hitchhiker's Guide to the Galaxy*

The rude awakening that greeted me, in Belgium at two in the morning, was met with words he could not have known the meaning of. There were rows of unconscious freaks, in sleeping bags, under the Art Nouveau iron roof. I dropped the Gold Kazoo into one of the slots, and disappeared, until a station guard found me again, around seven. The smartness of the waiters in the coffee shop shook me out, and back onto the continent, like all that cheek kissing they did. I took a long, flat, clean, strange walk to the highway. An electrical engineer drove me directly to Ghent. Until the 13th century, Ghent was the second largest city in Europe, after Paris. It was still pretty big. Sitting in the square, I asked a passerby where the tourist office was. It soon became obvious that I wouldn't need it. His name was Jeff, a Chicago lawyer with a passion for Flemish painting. He asked if I spoke French, and then invited me to accompany him, on a whirlwind two-day art history trip through Belgium. *Bien sûr.*

Our first stop was to St. Bavo's Cathedral, to see Van Eyck's *Adoration of the Mystic Lamb.* The twelve translucent painted polyptych panels, the focal point of which was a lamb bleeding from his neck, were considered 'the final conquest of reality in the North.' However more real, than the Early Renaissance Italian classical idealization it replaced in 1432, it was still a long way from Mother Nature. Nonetheless, it was spectacular, not least because of its turbulent history. The Lamb of God had survived 16th-century iconoclastic riots, the French Revolution, and the Nazi looting, which sunk it down a salt mine.

After a coffee, a castle, and a collection of fine art, Jeff and I drove to Bruges. One hand on the wheel, he reached into his shirt pocket, and fired up a joint. I hadn't expected a dope-smoking Chicago lawyer. I didn't know how far that could take us, still thirty years before it would become a qualification, for President of the United States. Jeff and I continued on up, to the top of the belfry in Bruges, '*Old and brown; thrice consumed and thrice rebuilted, still it watches o'er the town.*' I dropped a coin into the instrument case, of a flautist playing far below, an impressive feat I should have otherwise been arrested for, but for the sheer magnificence of its accomplishment. Jeff attributed my feat to 'a keen eye and a steady hand.' Bruges was the 'Venice of the North' or, at least, one of the many. At one time, it was the chief commercial city on the planet, trading its woven and spun textiles for Normand grain, Gascon wines, Scottish wool, and dozens of other products. The Bourse was the first stock exchange in the world, opening in 1309. Jeff and I visited the museums and medieval hospital, had lunch at a little macrobiotic place, and bought lace, before motoring on, to look for a place to stay. Hier, in Lier, we found the Café Hotel 'Handelshof.' Jeff lit up another joint, and we descended, to a seemingly reluctant waiter. We asked him for a menu.

"Ve haf Schotel of Mosselen." He said. Jeff and I looked at each other. My turn.

"Parlez-vous Français?" I ventured.

"Non." He offered. "Ve haf Schotel or Mussels." Jeff and I looked at each other. I knew what mussels were, but I had no clue what a Schotel was, and, if it tasted anything like the noise it made, I wasn't interested.

"What's Schotel?" Jeff asked.

"You know." He said. "It's a plate."

"A plate of what?" I pursued.

"You know. A plate." He said. Jeff and I looked at each other.

"I hear the mussels are very good here in Belgium." He said.

"Twee mussels." Said the waiter. And was gone.

We drove to Brussels next morning. The mussels had been good. Neither of us had ever had mayonnaise with fries before. Jeff was a Chicago ketchup boy, and I had come from a tradition of Northern Ontario white vinegar. The mayo was the reason we were traveling. In the big capital of Belgium, we had three goal destinations. The first was the 'white sepulcher' of the Grote Markt, or Grand Place, epicenter of the medieval meat, bread and cloth trade. Standing in the guildhall-lined central square of Brussels, was like being surrounded by giant wedding cakes. The second was Musée d'Art Ancien, which suffered a breakdown, in the hygrometrical system seventeen years after Jeff and I visited its collections. The drop in humidity went undetected for three weeks, in the middle of a cold spell. Our final Brussel sprout was a bronze statue of a small boy peeing, the *Manneken Pis*, a little like Copenhagen's Little Mermaid, but with more plumbing, and less aplomb.

If Brussels tide had risen on meat, bread and cloth, Antwerp was a seaquence of pepper, silver, and textiles, earning the Spanish Crown seven times what it was pulling out of the Americas. By the beginning of the 16th century, Antwerp accounted for forty per cent of world trade. Hundreds of ships, and thousands of carts, would enter and leave the city, daily. Unpaid Tercio soldiers, afflicted with the Spanish Fury, destroyed that, killing seven thousand citizens, and destroying eight hundred houses, in three days. Almost four hundred years later, the Nazis fired more V-2 missiles into Antwerp, than all other targets combined. But even through all these calamities, Antwerp still had brilliant pickled herring, coffee, *Antwerpse Handjes* biscuits, and some of the best beer in the world. And Jeff and I were driving to Antwerp in search of the Holy Grail, a Trappist brew called ID (*'eeday'*). We were not slaves to instant gratification, however. We recognized that there were intellectual and cultural responsibilities to discharge in Antwerp as well and, after a toke or two, we set out to see the Cathedral, Rubens' House, and the Musée des Beaux Arts. I was taken with one particular van Eyck, on loan from a private collection, whose theme was madness.

By now Jeff was madly desperate, to find the object of his desire. We hurried to the Mecca of Belgian beer establishments, Kulminator, an old café storefront, with bright yellow blinds. Inside, we asked for ID, and a smile came over the ancient visage behind the counter. Last one. Two Jews sat in a darkened temple, quietly sipping liquid light. *'And in the sky The larks, still bravely singing, fly.'* And that was the other Hebrew Antwerp icon. Diamonds. It turned out that ID wasn't just a Trappist beer. It was, and is, a US state. Turns out, that one of the cheapest places to buy a diamond is Idaho, and that, for her fiftieth birthday, and because she had never worn one, I had a carat stone shipped to Antwerp, in advance of our visit. But she's not here yet, and doesn't arrive until the next book.

Jeff and I said goodbye, in the rundown foyer of a hostel. I checked in, and did part of the Herald crossword, before heading out to eat, in a small café near the Cathedral.

I asked for a menu.

"Ve haf Schotel of Mosselen." He said. "Schotel or Mussels."

I couldn't face another bowl of mussels. And I just finally needed to know.

"What the hell is Schotel?" I asked, choking on what it did to the back of my throat.

"You know." He said. "It's a plate."

"A plate of what?" I pursued.

"You know. A plate." He said.

"But a plate of what?" I was almost hysterical.

"It's Dagschotel. In French, its called *'Plat du jour.'* In English you call it 'Plate of the day.'" He said it, like he couldn't possibly believe he was speaking to someone so stupid. I felt the key in the door, the lifting of tension, and the wave of relief.

"What's the Schotel today?" I asked.

"Paardenvlees tartare." He said.

"What's that?" I asked.

"Raw horsemeat." He said.

I had the mussels.

Stroopwafel

'Holland is a dream, Monsieur, a dream of gold and smoke — smokier by day, more gilded by night. And night and day that dream is peopled with Lohengrins like these, dreamily riding their black bicycles with high handle- bars, funereal swans constantly drifting throughout the whole country, around the seas, along the canals.'

Albert Camus

A waffle is the action, or inaction, of making up your mind. In Holland, when you slice a round one in half, and glue fill it back whole again, with warm caramel, it becomes a vice. And clamped Between the Cartwheels of the *stroopwafel*, I was the syrup, holding them together, and apart.

A gender-challenged Mohican, with transdermal metal and subdermal ink, sat across from me at breakfast, stealing my appetite. In my attempt to escape, on the outskirts of Antwerp, I discovered that the hitchhiking out of Belgium wasn't bad because the locals wouldn't pick you up; it was bad because they had no idea where the exit was. My Styrofoam sign first caught a steamfitter and his family, who drove me to the only road not going to Holland. An hour and twenty kilometers later, a couple rescued me from the rain, but not the direction. The Belgian army officer, who dropped me in the centre of a horrendous traffic circle, convinced me how lucky the Germans had been, to have their own transport. A station wagon decelerated and sped up again, leaving me close to the heather and clouds and tears. Finally, a young midwifery instructor, reading my sign and desperation, took me to Den Haag. I had arrived *'in a land that rides at anchor, and is moored in which they do not live, but go aboard.'*

I stepped off Tram number eight, near the Promenade Hotel. There was a loud

"Hey!" It came out of Ine. She dropped her bike, and threw her arms around my head. We walked to visit her friend Erna, a naturopathy student, whose curriculum poured out onto dinner plates in the form of spinach, squash, potatoes, and biodynamic wine. We laughed long after the fruit torte, and Ine and I left for each other, and the Peer Gynt on her stereo. She woke me, with white lightning and black bread. And cheese, and coffee, and a Herald Tribune. We went out for a tour in Dutch, of the Ridderzaal Knights' Hall, and Binnenhof Inner Court. I liked the English stepping in from the ceiling, by Ruben's sons, but not as much as I enjoyed Rembrandt's *The Anatomy Lesson of Dr. Nicolaes Tulp,* in the Mauritshuis Royal Picture Gallery.

It wasn't Dr. Tulp's once a year dainty dissection that captivated my attention, nor the various physicians, who had paid commissions for the privilege of having their poses painted into the scene. It was the subject of the dissection, which fascinated. On the morning of 16 January 1632, an armed robber, named Aris Kindt, was strangled for his violent crimes. That afternoon, he appeared in the *umbra mortis* shadow of death, under Dr. Tulp, who would have had trouble explaining why the exposed flexor muscles of Kindt's forearm originated in the lateral, rather than the medial, epicondyle. Ine took less delight in Rembrandt's anatomical error than I did.

We walked through the Gemeente, for its collection of Mondrians, although I thought the old instrument collection was just as remarkable. Erna joined us for a macrobiotic lunch. She probed my intentions, the same way she stabbed her fork on the carrot salad. Why was I planning to work in Scandinavia, when Ine lived in Den Haag? I looked at Ine. It was an interrogation by proxy. I waffled. Fleeing Dutchman.

We all left, to race down the long sandy beach in Schevenigen. They laughed at my perserverated pronunciation as I ran *Scheveningeningeningeningen...* Flying Dutchman. The Resistance caught Nazi spies, with their misspoken initial 'Sch' shibboleth. We ate neiuw herring and ice cream, and drank cassis lemonade. Our remaining time and space were scaled to the miniature models in Madurodam. Rather than fallingeningen further for me, Ine was leaningeningen more on Erna. On our last night, we went out alone, for gado gado. So nice they named it twice. The syrup in the stroopwafel, she placed on top of my coffee cup, began to soften.

Sometimes, the road seems to go on forever. The empty tram was full of sadness. I kissed her eyes, and took my share with me. The passing windmills slowly drained my Wagon-lits coffee into canals and clouds. The cows all pointed the same way. To Amsterdam, and the other sweet battered cartwheel.

*   *   *

'People, houses, streets, animals, flowers-everything in Holland looks as if it were washed and ironed each night in order to glisten immaculately and newly starched the next morning.'

Felix Marti-Ibanez

I hadn't seen Ira since Rhodes. She talked away her tears, as we drove to her flat in Beverwijk. Eyes glistened. I hadn't ever planned for cereal monogomy. This confers a small measure of innocence. But I hadn't avoided it either. This confers a larger measure of guilt. My purpose had been to set out around the world, and allow fate to carry me, to be open for any and all experiences, out of a naïve belief that I would learn, in proportion to my dedication to the entropy. What I was learning, was that this New Age mantra was capable of causing unintended pain, to people whose priorities had a more social dimension. It wasn't fair to enter lives, with a prerequisite of leaving. There were consequences to every encounter. There were even more with every reencounter.

'Advice for good love: Don't love those from far away. Take yourself one from nearby. The way a sensible house will take local stones for its building, stones which have suffered in the same cold and were scorched by the same sun. Take the one with the golden wreath around her dark eye's pupil. She who has a certain knowledge about your death. Love also inside a ruin, like taking honey out of the lion's carcass that Samson killed.

And advice for bad love: With the love left over from the previous one make a new woman for yourself, then what is left with that woman make again a new love, and go on like that until nothing remains.'

Yehuda Amichai, Advice for Good Love

Beverwijk's original name was Bedevaartswijk, *pilgrimage neighborhood*. The Germans pilgrimmed here in 1944, in a house-to-house raid, taking five hundred hostages, to force the murderers of three collaborators to surrender. Sixty-three never returned. In 1997, two football mobs clashed in the Battle of Beverwijk. One pilgrim was beaten to death.

Ira made us a Canadian breakfast, with Dutch ingredients. We showered and let the afternoon slip away. Her sister, Yvonne, came over for dinner. It was an interrogation by proxy. I waffled. Fleeing Dutchman. I made a horrible chicken dish, with a jar of marmalade. It didn't go with the champagne.

We awoke in Nethernetherland. I set out my laundry to dry on the heater. Ira and I drove to Haarlem, city of beer and tulips. In the hunger winter of German occupation, the citizens of Haarlem ate their tulip bulbs, three hundred years after Black tulip mania ate Haarlem. The Black Death killed half the population in 1381. The Black uniformed Nazis deported the city's Jews, demolishing the synagogue, and any remnant of their hospital, yet the shape of the old city had been constructed in the shape of ancient Jerusalem.

We took in the classical collection of the Frans Hals Museum, originally an old men's almshouse founded in 1609. Qualified residents had to be honest single elderly men over 60, with household goods consisting of a bed, chair with cushion, tin chamber pot, three blankets, six good shirts and six nightcaps. They were required to make a weekly collection with a poor box, and were locked in every evening.

I locked myself in Ira's flat next morning. She was called to steward a flight to Spain, and returned at two am.

It was almost noon when we drove to Volendam, where the broad ocean leans against the land, and its old fishing boats and traditional pointed-hat women.

The one in Marken, who showed us children's clothes she had for sale, looked like Mae West would have, if she had lived to ninety. In the evening, we had a magnificent Indonesian ristafel at a friend of Ira's, with good wine and conversation.

Yvonne joined us on our trip to Amsterdam Sunday morning, for a day of canals and cobblestones and sunshine and diamonds, on the Mirror of the Sea.

Our first visit was to Anne Frank House. The floor of the 17th century Portuguese Synagogue was covered with fine sand, to absorb dust, moisture and dirt from shoes, and to muffle the noise. The inscription over the entrance was from Psalms. *'In the abundance of Thy loving kindness will I come into Thy house.'* It was no abundance of loving kindness that came into Anne Frank's House two hundred years later, turning her, and a hundred thousand other Dutch Jews, into fine sand. Nothing could muffle the noise of the silenced echoes within. In that same interval, Amsterdam went from the richest city in the world to a foraging mob. Most of the trees, and all of the wood, from the apartments of the departed deported, were cut down and out, for fuel. Dogs, cats, raw sugar beets, and tulip bulbs were pulped and eaten, for food. To survive.

We emerged from the savage tragedy, into the high aesthetic of the Rijksmuseum. Out of a million pieces in the permanent collection, we spent most of our time there under Rembrandt. Through my Western Civilization pilgrimage, I had already stopped to study the three most famous paintings in the world, the Mona Lisa, the Last Supper, and the Sistine Chapel Ceiling. The Night Watch, *The Shooting Company of Frans Banning Cocq,* was the fourth. I felt its massive size, the chiaroscuro light and shadow on the arquebusiers and dead chickens, and Rembrandt's accomplishment of '*de meeste en de natuurlijkste beweegelijkheid'*, the greatest and most natural movement, in what otherwise could have been a static military portrait. It turns out that the dim darkness of the painting had been misnamed, defaced by time. When the Night Watch was cleaned in the 18th century, the broad day was discovered, a party of musketeers stepping from a gloomy courtyard, into blinding sunlight.

In the same year he received the Night Watch commission, Rembrandt bought a house on Jodenbreestraat, in what was becoming the Jewish quarter. It was here he frequently sought out his new neighbors, to model for his Old Testament scenes. We wandered under its triangular corniced pediment, through rooms of his stereo blindness.

Descending from Amsterdam's Golden Age to its decadent decline, we landed in a maze of cannabis cafes, and alleyways with tiny one-room cabins, rented by prostitutes, behind their plate glass window undressings. De Wallen, the red-light district was promoted as a showcase of cheery liberalism, and liberation. I thought it was a slave market cesspit.

Yvonne left Ira and I in a restaurant called Thessaloniki, for moussaka and glasses of Demestica, and a rekindling of Greek fire, from the middle of the Wine-Dark Sea.

We returned to Amsterdam next morning, to see the other icon of Dutch artistry. The largest collection of Van Gogh's works was displayed in his namesake museum. A penniless preacher whose diet of bread, tobacco, absinthe, and bad love, had led to scurvy, gonorrhea, syphilis and suicide, stunned me. The Potato Eaters, Bedroom in Arles, The Yellow House, Vase with Twelve Sunflowers, and a panoply of Self-Portraits, each better than the last. The impact was draped in vivid yellow, mauve and ultramarine. He wrapped his left severed ear in newspaper and, handing it to a prostitute named Rachel, asked her to 'keep this object carefully.' His last words were 'La tristesse durera toujours.' *The sadness will last forever.* Starry night.

My second last day with Ira involved more sightseeing. After Hoorn and the cheese market in Alkamaar, we sat together on the grass, watching windmills turning their sails in the sun. Neither of us slept that night. Next morning went quickly. I remember driving fast in the rain and the flatness, past the Long Dam, stopping for coffee along the way. Inside, Ira gave me a Droste 'W' chocolate letter, and an embrace.

The syrup in the stroopwafel, she placed on top of my coffee cup, began to soften.

A waffle is the action, or inaction, of making up your mind. In Holland, when you slice a round one in half, and glue fill it back whole again, with warm caramel, it becomes a vice. And clamped Between the Cartwheels of the *stroopwafel*, I was the syrup, holding them together, and apart.

Die Sündige Meile

'West Germans are tall, pink, pert and orthodontically corrected, with hands, teeth and hair as clean as their clothes and clothes as sharp as their looks. Except for the fact that they all speak English pretty well, they're indistinguishable from Americans.'

P. J. O'Rourke

A squadron of NATO Starfighters whooshed over the autobahn.

It was becoming a long day. The oil rigger, named Cody, two drove me to Oldenburg, was followed by a social worker specializing in alcoholism, a cute nurse to an impossible Bremen turnoff, and a concerned elderly couple, who wondered why I was out in such pouring rain. They made me a Hamburger helper 'HH' sign, which flagged down a teenage girl, who dropped me at a gas station, where I met Olaf, a 20 year old freshwater snail biologist, who took me to Hamburg, for his parents to look after. It was the First of September 1982, and life was still linear. Olaf's mother and father eased my hunger and slaked my thirst, with bread, salami, eel, and wine. The Jewish Day of Atonement played on their television. On Yom Kippur, one is not allowed to eat or drink anything, until nightfall. I came in just under the wire.

Salami is, to a German breakfast, what croissants are to a French one. Olaf and I ate hearty. We went to the Schimmermann castle for the bedroom slipper tour. His mother chased us on her bicycle with my toiletries. Off the train into the Centrum, we carried on into the Kunsthalle. One of the paintings by Friedrich was stolen, a decade later. The thief returned it, for a reward. When the museum refused to pay him, he sued, and won.

I said goodbye to Olaf in the Hauptbahnhof, and called Petra and Anthea, the mother and daughter that Steve and I shopped for furs and jewelry with, on Rhodes. Petra gave me directions to Menkerstrasse station, where Anthea's blue eyes and blond hair and white stockings waited. I wasn't prepared for the homecoming. After a brief welcome hug and air kisses from Petra, Anthea pulled me up the stairs, down the hall, and into a drawn bath. The demure well-dressed schoolgirl was magnificent less dressed, and a tsunami in bathwater. She pulled me out of the tub, the same way she put me in. We spent the afternoon in her room, exploring each other's stamina. Mine was outmatched, and overwhelmed.

I awoke in a support group of stuffed animals. Mr. Winterbottom was her clear favorite. He was sitting on my chest, before Anthea replaced him. When we finally rejoined the main floor, Anthea's father was home. In North America, if the man of the house returned to find a vagabond sleeping with his teenage daughter, the judge would dismiss any charges. In parts of Northern Europe, and less primitive aboriginal cultures, this was apparently not only not a big deal, but also something accepted, as part of growing up. Projected nonchalance was the expected reaction. When Anthea's father spoke to her in German, however, he dove into sentences so long and convoluted, it took awhile for him to emerge on the other side with an actual verb in his mouth. I still believe that, if he hadn't found one, I'd have been killed on the spot.

We all had plum torte and coffee. Anthea and I went downtown to sightsee. The summit of a long elevator ride produced nighttime three-dimensional city lights, to the horizon. We giggled through the Reeperbahn red-light district, grateful at how conventional our own intimacy still was.

In German, it was also called the Die Sündige Meile, *the sinful mile*. My own road journey was beginning to appear less about the search for absolute truth, and more about acquiescence to visceral pleasure. It certainly took far less energy. If you leave yourself open to every experience, what you get depends, in large measure, on how you are perceived by whom. Chaos and Natural Selection are recipe ingredients too volatile, to be used in baking cakes of higher consciousness. Europe's largest brothel lived in the Reeperbahn. The Eros Center was six stories of unimaginable chaos and natural selection. This was about to change. When I was an ICU resident, before I left on my Cartwheels, I had a Haitian patient, on a ventilator for weeks, before he died a mysterious death. The Critical Care Attending was on my case, as intensely as I was on the Haitian's, all the way down, but the truth was that nobody knew what was killing him. The Eros Center was closed when they found out. Six floors of an AIDS palace could no longer survive in downtown anywhere. In Hamburg especially, it was mincemeat.

After whispers and wine, under a full moon over the waterfront, Anthea and I returned to Mr. Winterbottom, and his friends. She made sure that none of us got any sleep.

I awoke to an old German song on an older Victrola, '*Winke-winke*.' Anthea smiled and drew closer, in a long languid cat stretch beside me. That shot the morning.

> 'Of all the maids on earth that be,
> The German maid's the maid for me;
> A beauteous violet seeming;
> With sweetest fragrance to the sense,
> With not a thorn to give offence,
> Through many a summer beaming.'
> Aloys Wilhelm Schreiber, *The German the Dearest*

Anthea had planned for us to attend a party in the country. I kissed Petra goodbye, and shook hands with father, counting my fingers on the way out. We drove to a beautiful barn, on an estate near Grosse Gosburg, in time for a fairly subdued gathering of bad music and worse weed, Indonesian food and Flensburg, plums and pastry, and a little girl with a battery-powered dog. It was just toward dawn when I told Anthea I had no more in me, and that I was heading north to

Scandinavia that morning, in a search for the job that would carry me over the winter. She was stoically Teutonic about my decision, less so about our farewell.

Her friends, Birthe and Anna, drove me back to just north of Hamburg. I made a sign that said Århus, thinking the little circle above the first letter to be wonderfully exotic. I held it up against the onramp traffic. An hour later, two friendly lawyers, Harmut and Andy, stopped to give me a ride. They were heading to the Århus Festuge festival that was starting on the weekend, and took me into Denmark. I asked him how he was perceived by his countrymen.

"The young think I'm a capitalist." He said. "The old think I'm a Nazi."

They dropped me near the cathedral, and I made a phone call, back into Khartoum time.

"Where did you come from?" she asked.
"Today, the sky." I said, channeling Mohammed from the inside.
"Welcome." She said, and I just knew she meant it. Her name was Birgit, from Aarhus in Jutland. I made a mental note to visit... The megatruck roared into life but, for a moment, it was strangely reluctant to turn off into the southern desert. It did a large complete circle in the sand, coming around one more time to where I was standing at the Fort. Birgit jumped off the top for a last kiss, and a promise. And then there was dust.
"They don't make many like that one." Said Jerry the Dragon.

Birgit was away for the weekend, but her father came down to fetch me. Christian was a delightful sixty-eight year old retired policeman, who took me home to meet his wife, Gerda. They were both inveterate cigarette chain smokers, of the roll-your-own variety. I remember them as hand puppeteers, performing continuous manual manufacturing maneuvers, in clouds of shredded tobacco, even as they puffed on their last creation. We took a break to see the Carnival downtown in the frozen evening, along candlelit paths to fireworks, and fantastic calliope music from a German circus organ. I was starting to feel the cold and see the dark looming in front of me, on the other side of my breath. I would need to find work and shelter, soon.

Christian and Greta and I returned home, for coffee and cake and guests. I asked one of them if he spoke English.

"Only in bitter need." He said.

"But didn't you want to be an astronaut, Uncle Wink?" Asked Sam.

"Sure did." He responded.

"So wouldn't you have also been a hero as an astronaut? And wouldn't you also have had a quest?"

"Too right, Sammy." Said Uncle Wink.

"Was it the quest of the astronaut, that made you want to be one?"

"Very much. Astronaut deeds were supposed to be physical. He was the embodiment of science, the gladiator in the iconic suit, the chosen one, from so many, to cross into the final frontier. You know the rest of his five-year mission: *'to explore strange new worlds, to seek out new life and new civilizations, to boldly go where no man has gone before.'* Crisis and the opportunity are the same symbol in Chinese, and you just can't gaze into the dark glass, without dark myth taking shape. Somewhere between the pure vacuum and the extreme pressure of existence, is extruded a spiritual quest, our classic search for order and harmony in emptiness and chaos, rekindled with solid boosters. The final frontier is both outer and inner space, physics and metaphysics, cybernetics and utopianism, rationalism and God. And where else could you physically look for him?"

"Would you have been looking for him, or running from him?" Millie asked.

"You are your uncle's niece, Millie. Escaping the gravity of Earth might release you from the limitations of a mundane existence, but the exercise is not just the flight of a deserter, or a prisoner. It takes an extraordinary individual, whose sense of isolation and unavoidable destiny forces them to reject the everyday rituals, to embark upon their own quest for identity and reality. The astronaut is the lens through which the myths we created, from what we thought we saw in the ancient night sky, are reapplied back onto the universe. His journey is to advance human consciousness, up the ladder of enlightenment, further along the path to wholeness."

"And your journey, Uncle Wink?" Sam asked.

"More modest, Sammy. No less heroic."

Smørrebrød

'I had crossed over to Denmark with the most exalted plans'
Humbert Wolfe, *Denmark*

She wasn't the same cheese and raspberry–filled Danish I knew in Khartoum. Her British-accented reactions, on the phone next morning, ran from confused passivity to frenzied enthusiasm. There would be instability waiting, I thought. Christian drove his red Skoda, via the racetrack, to Birgit's flat. He drove slowly and deliberately, out of concern for my protection. From what I remembered of her in the Sudan, he was prescient.

Århus has several monikers, known variously as the 'Capital of Jutland,' 'The World's Smallest Big City,' or the 'City of Smiles.' I arrived at the 'Capital of the World's Smallest Big Smile.' Birgit seemed delighted to see me, but there was something not quite here. In the Sudan, her passion had been as relentlessly torrid, as the baked sand swirling around us. I had seen a similar disinhibition in Canadians, and other denizens of cold intemperate climates, who found themselves under the sun for the first time. Birgit was back on the reservation. It had been ten months since our confluence of the Nile. We went shopping for food and rekindling. I made some slow chili on the stove, while she phoned friends. Some of them came for chili. Birgit introduced me as her 'lover.' I remember being irritated by this although, when they had all left, the evidence was incontestable.

The next few days were mist. I remember old Viking relics at the Moesgaard, a rock concert, and buying Birgit a Mulcha Nouveau art book, at the Kunstmeuseet. There was a taco dinner for Bob and Lizzy and Nadia, swimming at the pool, and the street bands and puppet shows of the Festival. We washed down hot dogs and honey cake with Tuborgs, and strolled among the half-timbered houses of the Old Town.

I remember reading voraciously, in the too dark front room. I remember catering to her master-slave fantasy. I remember sitting up nights, confused. Heralds and oracles were written in Danish slogans on the bathroom wall and, with a dictionary, I began to understand.

I told her it was bread and butter stuff. I needed to find work for the winter, to save for the next Cartwheel. She asked me why it couldn't be here. Denmark was a land of butter and bread, she said. *Smørrebrød.*

I left the next morning. Two little old ladies gave me my first ride, to Harson. A couple of sweet German freaks were next, but their van broke down on the Nyborg off ramp. Some carmakers have a client base that is more disinclined to support hitchhiking. Two minutes later, an Audi pulled over to give me a lift, like the rare sighting of a spirit bear. The driver, Danny, was a married, ex-military, conservative knitwear factory owner, with a telephone in his vehicle, unusual for the time. He was also gay, and cheating on his wife, although happily duplicitous, and without any potential Italian or Scottish intentions. He was going to the city of Forkbeard, and I with him.

Birgit had arranged for me to stay at Lena's. I remember her from Khartoum as well. There were instructions on her door about how to get in, and word that she would be back after dark. She arrived with bread and cheese and cucumber and gin, most of which we shared with the upstairs neighbors.

My first stop next morning was the two-headed mermaid at the Canadian embassy, who initially didn't want to expend the effort to retrieve my mail. I left to visit Thoralsen's statuary, the National Museum of Housewares, the Babylonian Ishtar Gate panels at the Glypothek, and Tivoli Gardens. In the afternoon Lena and I went shopping, for the ingredients we cooked into sukiyaki for dinner. I played guitar, and she drank ouzo, until late.

I left Lena sleeping, and walked to the motorway, early next morning. The police shooed me away, until they left. My polystyrene sign eventually secured me a ride, for about thirty kilometers. I waited, until the sun rose over flat fields and flowers, and the elderly woman who took me to Helsingør, site of Hamlet's castle, and madness. The feeling was distinctly Shakespearean.

For the vessel heading northward, t'was there and hence I fled,
'Crossed o'er the strait to Sweden, in my quest for smørre and bread.

Itty Bitty Pity

'The North will at least preserve your flesh for you; Northerners are
pale for good and all. There's very little difference between a dead
Swede and a young man who's had a bad night. But the Colonial is full
of maggots the day after he gets off the boat.'

Louis-Ferdinand Celine

I was looking forward to picking myself out of the Danish
guttural, and into a Swedish lilt. The ferry across to
Helsinborg was almost empty. I was daydreaming at the
sunlight on the salt water, when the carriage door behind me
closed loudly. Two Swedish border officers made their way
down the aisle.

"Kan du pratta Svenska?" Asked the thin one. My vacant
stare convinced them I couldn't. Their faces told their
thoughts. And they thought I was a swarthy foreign
interloper, looking for trouble. Turkish delight, for them, was
no confection. It was an oxymoron.

"Passport, please." Said the even thinner one. I handed it
over. And the interrogation began.

"Why are you coming to Sweden?" Thin one. I used the
beautiful country answer.

"Are you sure you are not looking for work, or to get
married?" Thinner one. I told them I was sure about the
work part, and explained that the Danes had the same word
for marriage and poison. Their sense of humor was Swedish.

"Do you have any proof that you have enough money to visit
Sweden? Thin one. I pulled out my Swiss bank account card.

"Welkommen til Sverige." They said, already halfway through
the next set of doors.

I hiked to the motorway north, outside Helsingborg. Three
hours, and hundreds of cars went by, without a lift. Finally, a
red haired punk rocker pulled over hard.

"I was beginning to think that Swedes don't pick up hitchhikers." I said, relieved to get into a vehicle.

"They don't." He said. "I'm Finnish."

Panu was one of those instant friends for life. Erudite, young, and smart, he was into books, classical music, and mushroom cultivation. My journey enthralled him. We had a long fish lunch in Vaxjo, sharing traveler's tales. He invited me to stay with him when I got to Helsinki, and dropped me off highway 23 onto 30, amid the pines, the lakes, and the setting sun.

The wind picked up, waving slender branches of white birch, gusting to Swedish hitching despair. It was an hour later when a big truck stopped. Two dogmatic leftists, feeding the world's armed struggles, with clothes and flea markets, occupied the cab. Folk til Folk. *People helping people.* The scenery was from the Canadian Shield of my hometown, but I was half a world, and a quarter of a decade, away. The last forty kilometers were provided a witty middle-aged economist, named Sven. His ebullience faded a bit, with the last rays of light, and my questions about the Swedish welfare state. Sven told me that the marginal tax rate was over eighty percent, that the government was spending well over half the country's GDP, and that a fiscal crisis was looming large on the horizon.

My horizon was Jönköping, at the southern end of lake Vättern. Before the 16th century, the Danes had plundered and burnt the place, repeatedly. After 1845, Jönköping became know for its matchstick industry. Collectivism by Candlelight. I had given her some Israeli perfume and wine. *And a kiss that still lingers, outside the gate of a northern kibbutz.* This was Mimi's hometown.

Her father told me that she was in Göteborg until the next day, but that he would pick me up. I went home with his just adequate English, a little bread and cheese and tea, and my first night's sleep in mythical, magical Sweden. She was in the black and white photo on my bedside table, singing in a choir, holding up a candle against the winter darkness.

I awoke concerned, that Mimi might be upset with my appearance. Like Birgit, she had been back in the deep freeze for seven months, and I was no prodigal Norse god. Something urgent would need to be done about my cracked shoes, torn socks, dirty clothes, ailing toiletries, distraught mind, degenerated body, unemployment, and linguistic ineptitude. I needn't have worried. She was even more tender, and the same kaleidoscope of molten spheres. Orbital dynamics ruled the night.

Our first stop next morning was the employment office, and promising news. There were jobs advertised for doctors. All I had to do was get a work permit from the Police. Mimi and I went to the station, and spoke to the Chief. He couldn't issue a work permit to anyone applying within the country. I asked him if there were any exceptions. He suggested we ask at the Immigration Ministry. I asked him where that was. He told me Norrköping. I asked where that was. He told me Östergötland. I thanked him, and made a mental note, to get a map.

We went down to the supermarket to see Mimi's father. He was a grocer, and seemed to be doing well, better than his marginal tax rate would indicate.

"Under the table." He said. Even in this paradise paragon of state strong-armed socialist security, nature abhorred a vacuum. White witches, black panties.

I bought a Swedish language book, and Mimi took me through my first few lessons. We made spaghetti, and love by candlelight.

I was still uncomfortable with Mimi's curious parents bringing us morning coffee in bed. We dressed, and went to see the large wooden sculptures of Carl Ornemark, at Riddersberg manor. The mobile *Bounty* resembled a ship, but the 103 meter-high Indiska reptricker, *Indian Rope Trick*, was breathtaking. They were both dismantled in 2007, after their condition had deteriorated. We went for a picnic in Husquvarna, overlooking Jönköping's reflection in the lake. Mimi's parents had been to vote, and the Social Demokrats had saved the day, again.

The weather was changing. Morning light was coming later, bringing visibility to our breath, in the colder air. Mimi and I woke early, to hitchhike. Mimi's father drove us about twenty klics, to a popular embarkation point. We waited two hours, finally pulling over a big rig from Zürich. I was still amazed to have found out that, in the most egalitarian society on the planet, only foreigners picked up the hitchhikers. The driver agreed to take Mimi all the way to Stockholm, and dropped me in Norrköping, to plead my cause. Once famous for its textile industry and sugar refineries, Norrköping was increasing known for its cactus plantation and *Tropicariet* aquarium, with thriving populations of snakes and crocodiles and sharks. It was also the seat of the Statensinvandruerk, with similar colonies of bureaucrats. After a long wait, I got to speak to a government lawyer, who told me that: (1) not only did I have to apply for a work permit from outside Sweden, I would have to apply from my home country (2) I needed a job offer to get a work permit (3) I needed to be in Sweden six months to get a job offer (4) I couldn't stay in Sweden six months without a job.

"We call that Catch 22." I said.

"So do we." He replied.

I walked off the frustration over five kilometers, to the Stockholm motorway. I had just finished making a sign when Lena, two of her six children, and two dogs, pulled across three lanes of traffic, to pick me up. She dropped me at T-Centralen, where I bought a map, and trekked to the Canadian embassy. They told me there was nothing they could do to help, with my search for bread and butter. A letter from Birgit had arrived, wondering if I would return to Denmark.

I found Mimi at her friend's apartment. Eva made a fish dinner, as I related the events of the day. We went out to *Stumpen* for a beer. I was paralyzed, not by the beverage, but the bar tab. Mimi and I retired to the Gold Kazoo, and uncertainty.

After strawberry jam and cream at Kungstragarden next morning, I took Mimi down to the Jönköping train.

"Don't worry." She said. "I'm stubborn."

It wasn't enough. I never saw her again.

.   *   *   *

> 'I tell ya, I could have got some more jobs if I'd tried,
> but I went to Sweden instead.'
>
> Lee Hazlewood

The Stockholm Bloodbath of 1520 broke up the Kalmar Union. The Plague of 1710 killed forty per cent of the city's population. In this Venice of the North, I was looking for the Doge who could prevent another catastrophe. Somewhere, between the Socialstyrelsen and the Sveriges Läkarförbund, in the Medical Board office on Villagatan, was an apparatchik with the consummate power to bring closure to my ordeal. I was ushered in to a large pale perimenopausal pair of horn-rimmed glasses on a chain. I told her of my dilemma, and the Catch 22.

"Are you a refugee?" She asked. I shook my head no.

"An itty bitty pity." She said. "Because if you were a refugee, you could work in Sweden as a doctor. I told her that, unfortunately, I was not a refugee.

"Are you handicapped?" She asked. I shook my head no.

"That's an itty bitty pity." She said. "Because if you were handicapped, you could work in Sweden as a doctor. I told her that, unfortunately, I was not handicapped.

"Are you an oppressed minority?" She asked. I was puzzled. "For example, are you a homosexual?" I shook my head no.

"Its an itty bitty pity..." Continuing with her mantra.

It was a buffet of bureaucratic buffoonery.

"Let me see if I understand this." I offered. "If I was a one-armed Peruvian lesbian, I could work as a physician in Sweden. But because I'm a straight healthy Canadian, I get the Catch 22." She shook her head yes. From across her desk came a lecture, about Swedish ideals of perfect tolerance, secularism, egalitarianism, and social justice. On my way out, I may have mentioned Nazis, and ABBA.

The Karolinska was my last chance. I was partial to research anyway, and it would look good on my resume.

To my pleasant surprise, I was ushered in, to meet one of the Directors. He was enthusiastic, and inquired after my scientific interests. After much probing on both sides, we agreed that I could start as soon as possible. It was going so well, I asked about payment. He looked confused, like the Customs official I waited for, on my entry to Colombia.

"I don't understand, Dr. Winkler. I thought you were bringing resources to us."

Dejected, I left for a final rekindling. *"Where is the Al-Ahram?" she asked. "Come with me." I said. And she smiled as I took her other hand, and we left the Lemon Tree in the darkness.*

I took the train to Röninge, and Cecilia. She made big eyes and dinner, and later asked me if I wanted more. I told her it was more than enough. If the day could be measured in meatballs, I had eaten a smörgåsbord.

Cecilia woke me a second time, with a gift of film for my camera. Ethel Merman was singing happy songs on her stereo. I took her to lunch, at a Danish restaurant in Gamla Stan, and we spent part of an afternoon in the Moderna Museet, gazing at fifty million dollars worth of Picassos, that would be stolen eleven years later. The thieves came through the roof at night, copying the method used in the 1955 French movie, *Rififi*. Cecilia took me to a veterinary hospital. I had never seen a turtle receive a barium enema, but I felt his pain. I was traveling that slowly, and they were giving it to me the same way. High, hot, and a hell of a lot.

It was an itty bitty pity.

'Those who want to learn will learn.
Those who don't want to learn will lead enterprises.
Those incapable of wither learning or leading will regulate scholarship and enterprise to death.'
Ellard's Laws

The Scream

'I want to travel. Maybe I'll end up living in Norway, making cakes.'
Eva Green

In the Arctic, it is believed that, if you holler at the northern lights, they will dance. If the flag of Sweden wouldn't provide my butter and bread, I reasoned, the Norwegian wood. Cecilia gave me a kiss and a packed lunch, and I set off to hitchhike to Oslo. My first ride was a Finnish entrepreneur, named Harry, whose business card was printed on teak veneer. He dropped me in Orebro with a packet of Marlboros. Two hours later, I was still waiting for social justice, or another Finn. A jazz ballet teacher stretched my route, to just past Karlstad. The rain came down, reminding me of how much my shoes leaked. Another two hours later, out of terminal frustration, I danced my thumb to the engine timing in a brown Camaro, the back tires jacked high. The chain-smoking Norwegian cowboy, who stopped and shared his stash of soda with me, could have driven off the same road in Northern Ontario, except for his lack of English. At least I think that's why he never said a word, all the way to Oslo.

The only thing I knew about the place was that it gave out Nobel prizes, and took the one for the world's most expensive city. I wasn't on the short list for a Nobel. The youth hostel cost me fifty-five kroner, and the greasy meal that the Norwegians had discovered crude oil in, half as much again. They turned the clocks back, to make it look like I was getting a deal.

Processed cheese, and stale bread, greeted the wet bleak day. I had arrived on the weekend, so there was time to fill with sightseeing, before I could look for a job on the Monday. I took a tram and boat to the museums in Bygdøy, and mailed a postcard, for the price of a small car. Sailboats with colorful spinnakers tacked and reached around us, on the way over. The Viking Ship Museum was worth it. Three beautiful wrecks were preserved within. I thought the Gokstad and Tune ships were splendid, but most of my admiration sailed with the third. The seventy foot oaken Oseberg, complex-carved in the 'gripping beast' style, dated from 800 AD, and had a top speed of ten knots. Two female skeletons had been found in its burial site. The older women, dressed in a luxurious lozenge twill red wool dress and white gauze linen veil, had arthritis and cancer, and something called Morgagni's syndrome, a masculinizing disorder that gave her a beard. The younger one modeled a plain blue wool dress, and mitochondrial DNA from Iran.

The pointed roof projections on the four-storied Gol Stave Church, in the grounds of the Norsk Folkemuseum, looked liked spikes on a deck of cards.

Thor Heyerdahl's *Kon Tiki* and *Ra 2* were on display in his museum. I wasn't a fan of the man. His theories about Polynesian migration (and most everything else) were sloppy and wrong, and he had gone through three wives, and as many ocean voyages, to demonstrate his flawed judgment. In 1938, Heyerdahl presented a Marquesan skull to Professor Hans Günther, a Nazi race researcher, in Berlin. After the meeting, he sent his mother a letter, describing Günther as 'one of the leading men of the new Reich.' Heyerdahl was no Quisling. In fact, his views were unexceptional for his space and time. Norwegians considered themselves ardent supporters of human rights, but this indulgence was more selective than they let on. I was in Oslo, when it was still a city of Fjordmen. Anti-Semitism, like their other trolls, was still mainly subterranean, and the gang rapes and Moslem demographic, and Herr Breibart's response, had yet to arrive.

Before floating back to the mainland, I paid a visit to the Fram, a museum dedicated to the story of Norwegian Polar exploration. I was there before Roald Amundsen's ship, *Gjøa*, joined the exhibits, but after he described adventure as 'just bad planning.'

My primary destinations on the other side were two *Frieze of Life* versions of the same expressionist painting by Edvard Münch, one in the National Gallery, and one in his namesake museum. Münch was a little like van Gogh. He was a drinker and a brawler. He hallucinated, and functioned on the border of madness. His father was a little like me- impecunious physician, moved around a lot.

Münch painted themes, of love, fear, death, and melancholia. His most famous, *The Scream*, portrayed a garbed skull in the throes of an emotional crisis, a fixed posture pantomime of the single psychological dimension of agony. It had become an icon of expression, for loneliness and separation. The one I saw in the National Gallery was stolen in 1994, and recovered a few months later. The one in the Münch Museum was stolen in 2004, in broad daylight by masked gunmen. It was recovered, in a damaged state, in 2006. The masked gunmen got off on a technicality. The British agents involved in the sting operation, had entered Norway under false identities.

Whatever was floating, in my 30-kroner nursing home dinner, had entered the country the same way. On my way back to the hostel, I was accosted by a group of young girls, demanding money. I held my hands to my head, and opened my mouth wide. They got it.

.   *   *   *

'I really enjoy myself in Norway. Because I had started losing confidence in my ability of what I do. But sometimes, man, you just get tired of fighting and trying to prove yourself.'

Ike Turner

Monday morning came a day late. The last sinews, holding my shoes together, had resolved to stay together, only long enough to get me to a new pair, and not in this country.

I took the tram down to the Sunderstyrelsen-somethingorother and, after trying all the doors and floors, found the bureaucrat, who told me it could be done. He handed me a copy of the infinite loop algorithm of how to get there, and suggested that my first step should be to find Dr. Enger, at the main teaching hospital. Dr. Enger was the arbiter of *arbeiter*, the Dean of dispensation, the one who would decide my worthiness. My thumb got me here. The direction of his, would determine if I got to stay.

I met him outside his office, at the big house. He was what you would have expected. Portly, poised, white-haired and wire-rim glasses, no nonsense. He grilled me like a sardine, and then pronounced me possible.

"You will need to take a crash course in Norwegian." He said.

"OK." I said back.

"There will be an examination, in a month, to see if you qualify." He added.

"OK." I added back.

"You will need to accompany me on rounds, for another month, to see if you are really as good as you seem to be." He said.

"OK." I said back.

"Then you will need to work north of the Arctic Circle for a year." He was finished. Me too.

I thanked him for his time and trouble, and buried myself in the weekend Herald crossword, back at the hostel.

I was running out of everything. Time, money, shoe leather, patience, self-esteem, and Scandinavian countries. I needed a

Plan C, desperately. Over my dinner, of Marabou frukt & mandel chocolate, I considered my remaining options carefully. Giving up was out. There was no more going north, or east, or west, for that matter.

'Suddenly a mist fell from my eyes and I knew the way I had to take.'
Edvard Grieg

My new course heading, was south. I would either have to find work in Denmark or, failing that, England, if that was even possible.

I discussed this with Gary, a rabbinical student from London. He agreed. I was hooped. We played a game of chess, and went out to roam the streets of Oslo, looking for havoc. But they had run out of havoc, and there was only mayhem left. We settled for mayhem, and arrived back late, to find that the German warden had locked us out. Gary said we were lucky. Forty years earlier, he would have locked us in.

A tram took me to bus 73 next morning, and it dropped me in the rain, on the E6. A marine engineer pulled over, and talked all the way, to just outside Frederikshaven. Ten minutes later, a friendly marine cable factory worker drove me about fifty klics, and left me thirteen kilometers short of Stromstad. Where I ran out of Norwegians. I was back in the land of social justice, and no hitchhiking.

I waited across from a church, until the sun went down. Finally, breathing frost and curses, I gave one last thumb heave, and stopped Jonathan, a Swedish American, driving to his parents' cottage, on one of the Stromstad Islands. His father had been in the merchant marine, and met his New York mother, while traveling the world. Jonathan's sister arrived, and we all told stories, over dinner and music. I was warm and safe and somewhere, and that was good. But sometimes, even today, when I think about how close I came to running out of resources, in the most expensive city on

Earth, I feel like holding my head with both hands, and opening my mouth wide.

'Litter
    is
       turning
          brown
            and
              the
                road
                  above
                 is
              filled
            with
         hitch
       hikers
    heading
south'

Roger McGough, *In the Glass Room*

Shelter from the Storm

'I was in another lifetime, one of toil and blood,
When blackness was a virtue, and the road was full of mud,
I came in from the wilderness, a creature void of form,
'Come in.' she said. 'I'll give you Shelter from the Storm."
                            Bob Dylan, *Shelter from the Storm*

Jonathan gave me a lift to the gas station, in the morning. It was my last experiment on the effect of the burden of Swedish social engineering on Good Samaritanism. My thumb carved an arc. The British sales engineer on his way to Göteborg put it to its final rest. The ferry to Frederickshaven rolled in the wind and horizontal rain, pulled along by the one-armed bandit slot machines ringing inside. I disembarked into a dark Danish downpour, and walked three kilometers with my head down, in a tired attempt to get away from it. I was back in the happiest and least corrupt country in the world, but I couldn't see it in front of me. The Norse gods were angry, and their wolves were howling a gale. The force of it blew all time and space sideways. After about an hour, a young garage mechanic offered me a ride to the Altborg train station.

I knew I was done. It was pitch black cold, my reserve tank was empty, and the soles of my shoes were flapping off my chilblained feet. I waited an hour and a half, under the fluorescence. The late evening train was quiet and almost empty, except for a pilot from Oklahoma. We arrived in Århus just before ten. The pilot didn't have phone change, so I paid for his call with the last of mine. He put out his hand. It held an American dollar.

"What's that?" I asked.

"Tip." He said. I shook my head.

It was another long walk to Birgit's apartment. She opened the door. I put out my hand. It held perfume.

"What's that?" she asked.

"Duty Free." I said. She shook her head. And fixed my pain.

> 'Not a word was spoke between us, there was little risk involved,
> Everything up to that point, had been left unresolved,
> Try imagining a place, where it's always safe and warm,
> 'Come in.' she said. 'I'll give you Shelter from the Storm."

It was exactly a year since I had left South Africa. I had traveled all of it, used it up. Birgit and I burned up the next day as well, in reacquaintance, but the following morning saw the quest for smørrebrød, relentlessly reengaged. I went down to the physician employment office *Lægersiningenbureau*, where a young clerk called Grønstad, about an advertised posting.

"Can you speak Danish?" She asked, handset held to her shoulder.

"Nye." I replied, trying at least. The response on the other end was predictable. She put down the phone.

"How can you expect to work in a country where you don't speak the language?" She asked. Good point. I was beginning to think that this might be more than a minor detail. A handicap, perhaps. She photocopied my credentials, and told me to return the next day.

I received a list of current medical job postings next morning, but each lead was euthanized by my lack of language. And every hour was colder than the last. The days shortened in mechanical contempt. Growth had been arrested, and its fallen leaves incarcerated, in frosted fields. The last of my resources dissolved into bus tokens, phone calls, Brrugsson checkout lines, licorice, and through the holes in the 25-øre coins. My mind began to time-travel, through unfulfilled promises in other lives. I began looking for an exit toward dignity.

In the last refrain of my autumn sonata, as I was telling Birgit I would be leaving for England the next day, her phone rang.

It was Michael, an anesthetist I had met, before my northern excursion. He offered me a registrar's position as a pathologist. A pathologist. That would solve the language barrier. *Dead men tell no tales*. To be, or not to be- that is the question.

I asked him where the job was.

"Esbjerg." He said. I asked him where that was.

"Esbjerg." He said again. I turned to ask Birgit where it was. She was beaming. It was close, anyway. I thanked him, and made a mental note to get a map. Oh yes.

I told him yes.

But I needed to get my head around this. I had committed to six months as a Pathology trainee, in a cold, dark, and wet west coast fishing town, speaking in a tongue that sounded like a wild turkey caught in a carousel.

I spent a couple of days brushing up on histology, and grunting through a DYI Danish book. I bought some grey socks, two shirts, a tie, and a new pair of old sneakers, for a few kroner. On my last night in Århus, I took Birgit out for Chinese food at the Restaurant Shanghai, in celebration. Dylan played on the radio.

$$* \qquad * \qquad *$$

'Something is rotten in the state of Denmark'
William Shakespeare, *Hamlet*

The flat train ride back from vagabond to veneration took three hours. I had become a resident Resident Registrar *Reservelaeger* in the promised land of pigs, pornography and pilsner. Esbjerg was Denmark's biggest fishing harbor, and the main centre for its oil and offshore activity. I walked past the Halliburton office, to the Centralsyghuset.

Until 1890, Esbjerg's had no hospital. The year after it opened, there was still no doctor. The first permanent physician arrived ten years later. His name was Dr. Cold. Really. He could have partnered with Drs. Lonely and Desolate. A decade after that, the Sisters of St. Joseph added a disinfection plant, coach house, a TB Sanatorium, and a morgue. This is where I came in. Seven years before I got off the train, they built the Chapel and Pathology Institute together, along Frihedsvej. Practical, these Danes.

The hospital was big, modern, and a little bit scary. I introduced myself in Emergency, and they directed me to the on call administrator. She gave me a key, and a map to get me to what would become my new home for the next six months- *Niels Lambersonsvej 14, Værelse 17, 6700 Esbjerg, Danmark.*

Room 17 was Spartan modern, with a bed, desk, bookcase, and private bath. My view included a dormant tree, power lines, and a traffic sign. The Danes have a word '*hyggelig,*' which means cozy, in a Danish way. This wasn't it. I went for a run, and a trip into town, to buy some bread and cheese and milk, and a Mars bar. Birgit called. I was a stranger in a strange land, due north of Cape Town, and half a world away. The next morning, I met Metro-Goldwyn Meyer, the hospital's Chief and Comptroller, whose job it was to take my earnings, and put them towards a greater social purpose. I met Astrid, the pathology department manager, who introduced me to my boss, *Overlæger* Herr Mønster, a quiet cellist. He introduced me to Herr Unders, who specialized in female pathology, and Imtof, who looked like she was next. They handed me over to the Quasimodo corpse cutter dever, Messen, a crusty old Dane with a lethal sense of humor, as he should have had, for what he did. When he opened up my first assignment, I felt my knees weaken. If he noticed, he didn't let on, and covered the rest of the dissection with jokes about the English.

I gradually developed an intellectual interest in the details of Messen's dismemberments. I would dictate my findings in English, and these would be translated into a report by the Drop-dead Gorgeous transcriptionist, in the Pathology office. Herr Mønster invited me to his home, for an excellent dinner, later in the week. He was studying me like he studied his other subjects, looking for pathology, and missing the vital signs.

I had signed up for Danish lessons two evenings a week. An excellent teacher provided them. Greta refused to speak English during class. My group was small. There was a German named Helmut, an arrogant Brit named James, a nicer one named Morris, and an acne-afflicted Texan, who didn't stand a chance. There is a commonly held opinion, that Danish is an intelligible language. It is not. It is a speech impediment, and difficult to learn. There was also no weather to speak of. It was raining and dark, all the time. Birgit came down for the weekends, and we drank wine and ate curry.

Black and early Monday, Messen joked, that he only had half a patient for me that morning. He wasn't kidding. Each autopsy was a sensory saga. I had never seen some of the things I was seeing. The cold rubber texture of death crept through my latex gloves, and the razor slices I made, with my pathology knife, threw voltage and current across my spine. *The undiscover'd country, from whose bourn no traveller returns.* The symphonic roaring grindsound of the bone saw cutting through a sternum, or around a skull, was accompanied by the smell of that bone burning. Through my own nasal cribriform plate, the formaldehyde penetrated into my brain. I can still smell it today. Underneath its icy hydrocarbonic sharpness, was the other smell, the one the formaldehyde was there to displace. Liquifactive necrosis, decay, rotting flesh, disease. I can still smell that, as well. Finally, there was something industrial in the odor of the sheets I slept under, in a state of half arousal, in the state of Denmark.

After a year of continuous change, the sudden lack of motion and momentous momentum, was a shock. It would have been enervating anywhere, but in the dreary downspout deluge of daily dissections, it was deadly. Life lay immobile, on an anvil.

There were still moments of pleasure, of course. Birgit threw a party for me in Århus, for my 29th birthday. Michael and Jorgen gave me a gift of marzipan, and Esther bought me a coconut. We played charades, and got happy on Tuborg. Back in Esbjerg, I raided and pillaged the English section of the public library, like Birgit's ancestors had done to the English coastline. I threw myself into my Danish lessons, and was beginning to handle simple conversations. In the evenings, I would play my half guitar, and write to friends. During the day, I would try to do the best job I could, although it was abundantly clear that, both to Herr Mønster and me, pathology was not my chosen calling.

I suppose it was only natural, that distance would defeat devotion. Birgit and I were passionate about, and for, each other, in the moment. But we were both too hesitant to think or feel, beyond. The weekend I went up to Århus, for Birgit's long-awaited video of her African trip, was our last. She had gathered a large group for the premiere, including her parents, Esther, Karen, Michael and Jorgen, and Lizzie and Nadia. As she started her presentation, she began cutting up her pizza, and then me. She talked incessantly, first in English, and then only Danish, without inhaling, until the last guest departed. And then she went silent. I understood enough, to understand.

> 'Now there's a wall between us, something there's been lost,
> I took too much for granted, got my signals crossed,
> Just to think that it all began, on a long-forgotten morn,
> 'Come in.' she said. 'I'll give you Shelter from the Storm."

I tried to talk to her before I left for my train back to Esbjerg, but there was nothing to say.

'Birgit and I fell asleep on a mattress under a giant date palm. Orion peeked over the fronds of our desert night.
"I've got something better than this." I said.
"Not much better than this." she replied... She tried to talk me into going south with her; I tried to talk her into going north with me. We spent long languid afternoons at the Lido. I watched her extend her neck, open her mouth, clench her eyes and breathe, and we both secretly hoped that the new parts for her megatruck were faulty. But they weren't and, finally, we had one night left...'

And then there was dust.

Rødgrød med Fløde

'He who does not understand a joke, he does not understand Danish.'
Georg Brandes

I was discovering that many Danish delicacies were delicious, but impossible to pronounce. My hunger for smørrebrød was adequately satisfied in the hospital cafeteria at *frokost*, the lunchtime meal.

Trays of sourdough rye bread dominos, blanketed with diverse luxury *pålæger* toppings, formed mouthwatering matrices, along the buffet runway. At the bottom of the food chain were smørrebrød of sliced cold smoked salmon *gravid laks,* with shrimp, lemon and fresh dill, smoked eel, with scrambled eggs and sliced radishes, a 'Shooting Star' *Stjerneskud* of steamed white fish, and battered plaice with shrimp and red caviar, or a 'Sun over God's Home' *Sol over Gudhjem* of smoked herring, and chives with a raw egg yolk on top. Moving on up, were open sandwiches of thin-sliced roast beef with remoulade, shredded horseradish and toasted onion, warm rough-chopped liver paste *Leverpostej,* topped with bacon and sautéed mushrooms, and the 'Veterinarian's Midnight Snack,' *Dyrlægens natmad* of liver paté, corned veal, sliced onions, meat aspic, and garden cress.

It was customary to have one or two beers with your meal, before returning to the sharp knives of the operating room, or the autopsy suite. Malpractice was unheard of.

Dessert was even tastier, and harder on the pronunciation. My favorite became ever more available, as Christmas approached. It was the same color as the flag, red berries with cream, *rødgrød med fløde*. As I was to discover about my own circumstances, the longer it settled, the more fruit floated up through the cream. My December was buoyant, with all manner of sweetness breaking the surface.

I was beginning to think that I would succumb to hypothermia, exposed as I was to working on, and with, the dearly and nearly departed, linguistic and geographical isolation, and the molecular slowing of a Danish winter.

Herr Mønster was becoming more demanding, turning thumbscrews on appendages I would need for the Final Cartwheels. He had stopped smiling at anyone, and now insisted that I dictate all my reports in Danish. I could still barely get through the checkout line at the supermarket, and I was suddenly, and magically, expected to produce fluent and grammatically-correct medical documents, in a language I only started learning two months earlier. I tried to point out that was also unfair to the Drop-dead Gorgeous transcriptionist, but he didn't care, and began to implement even greater demands, and tighter deadlines. I took extra lessons from Gerta, in a mad race to comply, but I was already plotting mutiny. I coped, in the same way that I had survived the Winnipeg winter preceding my initial departure, two and a half years earlier. Planning. I was heading east to the Soviet Union, after ice melt in the spring, and there was much preparation, and dreaming, to do in advance.

There was also one more piece of unfinished business from Africa, waiting for me here on the west coast of Jylland. Esbjerg was the hometown of the flatbed truck driver, who had tried to help me near the Mozambique border, just over a year before. His efforts got me kidnapped by Nkomo's guerillas, more thanks to the lesbian duo running the *Folk til Folk* Jonestown debacle, masquerading as foreign aid, than anything deliberate Jimmy had done. I called him, and we met for a beer. He was still sorry about his inadvertent role in my near tragedy, and had traded in his old Nordic 'activist' politics, for something more sensible. We were glad to see each other, and for the closure.

Other than for my Danish lessons and groceries, I hadn't been out for weeks. Across from us were two young Danish girls, hands gesticulating, between sips of their Tuborgs. One was even more Drop-dead Voluptuous than my transcriptionist. Jimmy invited them to join us. Birthe and Bente worked as drafting technicians, for Maersk. Bente was the captivating one. When all the glottal stops stopped, I was speaking low and slow, to Bente. She was from Viborg, twenty-three years old, and shy. Her caution came out of the pain she was still feeling, from a broken involvement with an American oilman. I asked if she would like to go out with me sometime. She said she would think about it. Jimmy and I said farewell under the streetlights, on the downtown cobbles. I whistled home walking.

I had made friends in my dormitory accommodation. One of the inhabitants of Niels Lambersonsvej 14 was Dorte, a homesick Polish Reservelæger, with a big Jewish heart, and self-declared phone monitor, who would answer all calls, so as not to miss her own. The price she paid, beyond the lonely loss of most of her family in the Shoah, was the responsibility to knock on all doors to who calls had been made, that did not belong to Dorte. She began to knock on my door, more and more.

"I thought you were alone, Wink." She said.

"So did I, Dorte." I replied, apparently incorrect, like trying to achieve oneness in a cloning lab.

I had just returned from meeting Bente, when Dorte tapped on my door. I thanked her and floated out into the common room, to collect my call. The voice was vaguely familiar.

"I'm coming to see you, Wink." She said. I asked who it was.

"It's Lynn." She said. I thought we had already tried this, and asked if she was serious this time.

"I'll be there in a week." She said. Oh Joy.

At least this time I didn't have to try to get somewhere. If she didn't come, she didn't come. If she came, well, I'd worry about that if she came.

"Big problem or little problem?" asked Silas.

"Big problem." I replied.

301

"Ehh." He said in two syllables.

*   *   *

'Slings and arrows of outrageous fortune.'
William Shakespeare, *Hamlet*

Fortune's arrival was obscured by the size of the volley of slings and arrows that accompanied it. Lynn flew off the train, like it was an aircraft carrier. I'd forgotten how shy she wasn't. There was no room for respiration. We had just finished her unpacking, when Dorte knocked on the door. It was Bente. She had changed her mind from maybe. I told her the truth, and asked if I could take her out once Lynn had left. She said she would think about it. I had just returned to Lynn's unpacking when Dorte knocked on the door again. I opened it a hair. It was a telegram. From Ira. She was driving from Holland, arriving that night, as a surprise. Surprise.

It was an impossible situation. I regret my actions to this day. But I hadn't intended to hurt anyone, nor had I deliberately set this thing in motion. My most immediate concern was how to minimize the injustice I was about to dispense. There was no way to do this. If I stayed and waited for Ira, she would walk right into it. I had no resources to send Lynn somewhere else, and she had just flown halfway around the world. There was only one unacceptable option left, and that was flight. *I must be cruel, only to be kind: Thus bad begins and worse remains behind.*

I left an explanation for Ira, as much as there could ever have been. She eventually wrote me back, with all of her grief enclosed. I took it all as my own, and have never forgiven myself.

Lynn repacked, and we boarded a train to Ribe, the oldest town in Denmark. We spent the weekend hiding down cobblestones, among ancient whitewashed houses with sharply sloped tiled roofs, at the four hundred year-old Weiss Stue Inn. *Shelter from the Storm.* Steam from our bath crystallized on the small cold windows. The fireplace flickered rays of gold over every slow curve. I was unsettled at the biblical subjects on the panel walls, watching our movement. Lynn, less unnerved, saw more of the decorated ceiling, when her eyes were open. We took the long way back to Niels Lambersonsvej 14, via Fanø, to secure our tryst. The rest of the week we read books and each other's minds during the day, and held on frantically at night. Both of us knew that what started in Lamu would end in Esbjerg. Pat would finally be a lucky man, in two syllables. *Ehh.*

Lynn left me strangely reinvigorated. I was getting my reports done in reasonable Danish, and in reasonable time. My Herr Mønster mutiny was proceeding apace. I had asked myself what other specialties I could apprentice in, that didn't require complete fluency in Danish, and would more materially contribute more to my ultimate goal of becoming an Internist. The Head of Anaesthesia was named Thor. I knocked on his door. Together, we conspired to have me join his *Narcoseafdeling* department, at the end of January. When I dropped Thor's hammer on the toes of my pathology Overlæger, it was the Mønster mash. He did the Mønster mash.

My language lessons were going well. I had found a sweet spot in the back of my throat to communicate with. The English section in the public library was taking a beating, and my plans for the Soviet Union in the spring were on fire.

And there was Bente. I let a week go by, and called. She had changed her mind from maybe. That was the last maybe. I fell head over heels for her blue eyes, long legs and soft curves, quick humor and slow tears. I took her out to some of the Esbjerg eateries in our evenings- Løven og Lammet, Gjesing bistro, and Munkestuen- and she taught me Danish in our nights. We began spending all our free time together and, because she preferred her own apartment to my dorm room, I ended up sleeping there. We would wake up early, and then wake up early again, so she could drive me to work. She began making dinners for two. She stretched out lithe, beyond the winter equinox. She was dazzling. I called her '*Scattebugge.*' She called me all kinds of things, most in Old Danish. Her hair grew longer and shinier, with the increasing daylight. I did the weekend Herald crossword, while she worked at her drafting table. We had Christmas lunch *Julefrokost* together, and Christmas dinner with friends. Our circle widened wide. Bente's workplace contributed Barbara and Birthe, Ude and Jytte, Ellen and Holgar, and Joe and Herman and Roger. Ingalise, an Americanized divorcee, seemed to pop up everywhere. I had just started putting people to sleep in the anesthesia department, and had bonded immediately with Mads, a cautious but very kind mentor, and brother. We played guitar together, and his wife, Marianne, made us pizza. With short plump Lars, kindred spirits from the pathology department, and other troglodyte registrars from Niels Lambersonsvej 14, there was always a small village congregated, for our frequent winter celebrations. I discovered this, as the reason that the Danes are so happy. It obviously had nothing to do with the climate or the scenery. It was their national version of cheerfulness, the Danish glee. And Bente was the last sweetness to break the surface of the cream.

I would find out later how little I was earning, to put toward the next leg of my journey. However little is turned out to be, with all its slings and arrows, we were still on the receiving end, of a Viking share of outrageous fortune.

VIEW FROM A WINDOW
BASUTELE.

"What's the difference between the quest and the journey?" Millie asked. She held a stick insect in her palm.

"The quest was what the hero was seeking, Mil. The journey was the adventure he went on to find it." Uncle Wink said.

"Are there different kinds of journeys?" She asked. The insect was crawling up her arm.

"As many as you can imagine. But all heroic journeys follow the same motif, a play in three acts."

"What's the first act, Uncle Wink?" Asked Sam.

"Departure, Sammy. Departure. It begins with the hero in his ordinary world, until he realizes that everything familiar is going to change, a call to adventure. His first reaction is to refuse the call, from a sense of obligation, fear, insecurity, or any number of reasons that work to hold him in his current circumstances. This is where he usually encounters a mentor, or guide, some magical helper who crystallizes the commitment, and prepares the hero for what is to come. The crossing of the first threshold is the point of no return, and the hero leaves familiar comfort for the unknown. Into the belly of the whale, is the point of separation between his old and new self, and he faces the first test of whatever is waiting in the darkness." Millie pulled the stick insect back down her arm.

"Was that how you departed, Uncle Wink?" She asked.

"No, Millie. My call to adventure occurred a lot earlier, and I planned it without a mentor. I still remember crossing the first threshold, though?"

"Was that the man in the red car who gave you your first ride?" She asked.

"Uh huh."

"How did you feel, Uncle Wink?" Asked Sam.

"Alive."

Gammel Dansk

'Beer is the Danish national drink, and the Danish national weakness is another beer.'

Clementine Paddleford

The wall mural on the side of the house I passed, on my way to work every day, pulled me in. It was a pastel painting of some portly old man, holding a walking stick, coat draped over his left arm, leaning on the gatepost, at the foot of a path winding into infinity. He was tired. The caption at the bottom said '*Tuborg-øl.*' The earlier sunrises and gentler breezes of the waning Danish winter grew kinder to the old man, on every successive passing. He was waiting for springtime, to restart his journey.

Together we had spent the colder seasons navigating, through Tuborg Black, Tuborg Christmas, and waiting for Tuborg Green *grøn* and Gold. Every opening and closing of my mailbox, and Operating Room locker, brought me a day nearer to my own departure. The relief that was coming would be paid for in tension at home. We traded whispers and whimpers on overcast days, gazing out over the monotony of Esbjerg apartment rooftops, ingesting sweet morning Spandau and bitter coffee, and evening salty licorice and sour Tuborg. Bente was a Great Dane, and shared everything but her apprehensions. I guess that's why she never introduced me to her parents.

Dorte knocked on my door one evening, when Bente was in Viborg. It was Steve of the Jacuzzi calling, with three days notice, to inform me of his imminent arrival. It had been almost a year since I had left him in Athens. There was much to catch up on. He would bring good cheer, and film for my camera, and leave with memories and my one-armed guitar. Bente's expression didn't express anything when I told her. I should have recognized that as a sign.

Steve arrived to a warm welcome and Tuborg, at my increasingly vacant room, on Niels Lambersonsvej 14. He was tanned and fit, the result of his move from California to Texas. Bente picked us up later, and we reminisced, while she made dinner around the corner in the kitchen. Steve asked me to take him to Copenhagen for a couple of days. I remember uttering the word-

"Sure." A split second before the kitchen exploded. Steve just about jumped out of his sneakers.

"What the hell was that?" He asked.

"Plates." I said, wincing at the crescendo crash cacophony in the next room.

"Is she alright?" He asked, out of genuine concern.

"Nope." I said. She had started on the serving dishes.

"Shouldn't you go and see?" He asked.

"Nope." I said. "Look Steve, Bente is Danish. Just beneath her modern veneer of quintessential Scandinavian control, is a raging Viking queen. I just said I was going to Copenhagen with you for the weekend. She knows we're probably not going to spend all our time on the wooden roller coaster at Tivoli. Hence the crashing crockery. Let it burn itself out. Another Tuborg?"

"Sure." He said. And Bente started in on the serial bowls.

I wouldn't get to the capital directly. A call from work came in, requiring me to aero evacuate a patient back to London. I managed to pick up a return SAS flight to Copenhagen, in time to meet Steve at the Hotel Triton. We went down to Nyhavn for a schnapps, and beer. He began coughing violently, clutching his throat.

"Too slow on the beer." I said.

"What the hell was that?" He asked.

"Gammel Dansk." I said. "Old Danish. It's a stomach bitters made in Dalby, down the road in southeast Sjælland. There are twenty-nine herbs, spices and flowers in it, including angelica, laurel, and gentian. It'll preserve a corpse."

"Tastes horrible." He said.

"It is." I agreed.

The next morning I went back to the Glypotek to show Steve the Babylonian panels from the Ishtar Gate, before we ended up at the Tuborg Brewery *Bryggerier Besøgs Afdeling,* for a tasting tour. It turned out more tasting than tour. I warned Steve about the Tuborg 'grøn fog,' but I knew it was too late when the 'Skål!' toasting started up behind me. He had met Vogn and Jens, two unemployed hippies, who took us on a walking tour of the mud and dogs of Christiana. If there was ever a post-apocalyptic version of a hyperindulgent socialist Valhalla, this was the place. The *Monocle* journalist, who voted Copenhagen the most livable city in the world, had stayed in another part of town. Steve and I went back to the Triton for a nap, and met Vogn and Jens at the Three Musketeers later on, after a Danish Chinese food fest. We finished in another grøn fog, at a nightclub called Exlon, which finished us back.

Saturday morning, we made our pilgrimage to the Little Mermaid, *Den Lille Havfrue,* based on the tale by Hans Christian Anderson, sitting on a rock in the harbor. Vandals kept sawing off her head but, because she wasn't the original creation, she reemerged like a Medusa on demand. I bought Bente a glass vase, and took Steve for mediocre Mexican food. We ended up at Exlon again. Steve was fully grøn fogged when he left about four am. I followed in an early morning cab, back to the Triton for a shower, and took him out to the Louisiana Museum of Modern Art in Humlebæk, impressive for its Chagall collection, and the large bronze thumb that seemed to be waiting just for me. The museum had been named after the owner's three wives, every one called Louise. Back in the city, I bid Steve farewell, on his way to the airport, and took the long train trip back to Esbjerg, and Bente's pick-me-up at the station. She didn't crack a smile, but she didn't break the vase either.

*　　*　　*

I was starting to feel Old Danish. Work was beginning to get seriously demanding. I was being drafted for most of Thor's spinals and neuroleptics, and a lot of his general anesthetics. Every morning was a marathon, of reaching over to take blood pressures, every five minutes. My back was aching. The timing of the surgical slate ruled, and woe befell you if you couldn't keep up with maintaining unconsciousness, or waking them up fast enough. One crazy Greek dentist went so quickly, I had trouble keeping up with the gases and infusions. I looked after a colleague's case of halothane hepatitis, before they were both removed from use. Each intervention had its own unique landmines and goalposts, and every few hundred, something bad would try to happen. An imperfect epidural resulted in one of my patients tipped upside down in Trendelenberg, to recover her blood pressure. Another hiccoughed, as the surgeon was about to make his initial abdominal incision. I still remember the Dansk macabre glare. Metro-Goldwyn Meyer called me to translate from French to Danish, for a Parisienne with a urinary tract infection. I was now doing call every fourth night, and falling into my own coma between inductions. *To sleep, perchance to dream: — ay, there's the rub.* My anaesthetic skills were still well ahead of my linguistic ability. Patients who got more nitrous than conversation lived longer.

Outside the hospital, the weather began to improve, out of proportion to Astrid's theory of prophetic fallacy. The ice melted, the trees budded, and the spring began to unwind, into warmth and light, and the promise of motion. Molecular activity accelerated.

Two weeks before my last day, Bente and I drove up to a DSB bank in Herning. There had been a spike in the number of Russian émigrés coming to Denmark. I had heard they had amassed a large stash of Soviet rubles, and were wholesaling them at a deep discount, to discreet patrons. We walked in, and approached the foreign teller, discreetly. She looked up.

"Jeg vil gerne købe nogle rubler." I said. *I would like to buy some rubles.*

"Russiske rubler?" She asked. *Russian rubles.* I didn't know of any other kind. She pressed a button under her counter.

A few minutes later a man in a suit came down the stairs, and invited us up to another man's office. His suit was more expensive, the wire rims on his glasses thinner. The conversation switched into English.

"You realize what you're doing is illegal?" The thin-rimmed expensive suit said.

"You realize what you're doing is illegal." I parroted.

"How much do you need?" He countered. I asked him what kind of exchange rate he was offering. It was astonishing. I told him how much.

He counted it out personally. It was a big pile of rubles. I wondered how I was going to smuggle it into the country.

The foreign currency cost of my trip to the USSR had also been discounted. Intourist officials had categorized me as a Danish student, and part of the international struggle to create world Communism. During the cold war, that was worth brownie points. Even with the air miles, however, the price of admission for a month behind the Iron Curtain was still going to set me back 13,000 Kr, almost nineteen hundred dollars, more than I had spent in all of South America. It included breakfast.

The next day I called my parents, to a frosted moodiness.

"How much longer will you be?" Asked my mother.

"As long as it takes." I said. "Another two and half years, perhaps." It was a guess.

"Don't lose your training." Said my father. I had just come off a brutal night shift, but I conceded the point.

"Take care." I said. Take care. *This above all- to thine own self be true.*

I cooked dinner for Mads and Marianne that evening. We played some guitar, and watched a movie about the Russian revolution. Bente reentered the room, just as the heroine returned in the final scene. *Now cracks a noble heart.*

*   *   *

There were festivities to commemorate my imminent departure. Jytte hosted an *aftenmad* party for Bente and I one evening, with luxury smørrebrød, Gammel Dansk and Tuborg grøn, good village company, and Danish glee mixed with sadness. My anaesthesia colleagues held a more formal farewell feast at Café Denmark, with a groaning board of herring, shrimp, lax, frikadella, cutlets, rødkol, cheese, and ever flowing Tuborg and schnapps. Odo told Norse sagas, Mads tetanized diaphragms with a Swedish U-boat story, and Thor delivered a two-edged testimonial that attempted to connect Eric the Rød with my own odyssey. They gave me a bottle of Gammel Dansk, and a Danish-Russian dictionary. I looked inside at the verbs- Past imperfect, Present indicative, Future conditional.

"Are you up to your Destiny?" Thor asked. *Hamlet.* It would be prophetic.

On my final day of work, I went to see Metro-Goldwyn Meyer, for the last time. I looked at the balance sheet of my earnings and deductions. They were almost the same amount.

"Where's all my money, Meyer?" I asked him.

"You spent it." He replied.

"On what?" I asked

"On benefits." He said.

"What benefits?" I pursued.

"Social benefits." He said.

"What social benefits?" I cornered him. "I never received any social benefits!"

"Ahh." He said. "But if you had needed to, they would have been there for you. That's the Danish system."

"Beggar that I am, I am even poor in thanks." I ended. *How weary, stale, flat, and unprofitable, seem to me all the uses of this world.*

What little was left in my hospital locker and room, was mailed in a large package back to Canada. I restored the Gold Kazoo and Diogenes, into their natural curved spaces, inside Serendipity.

The same occurred with Bente. I took her to lunch at Follet, and dinner at Monkestuen. She unwrapped a watch, the only gift of more time I could provide. The card was addressed to '*Scattebugge.*' We made love desperately before midnight, before she drove me to the train station in the mist.

Tight embraces pulled hard on the shadows. She had held on, and off, for so long, but it came- tears in waves, waves in anguish, and anguish in a language only viscera could speak. My one, lasting, and final, impression was of her expressionless terror and agony, under the platform lights. *But break, my heart, for I must hold my tongue.* I boarded the train, and the fog rolled in, filling the space between us.

The rest is silence.

'Doubt thou the stars are fire;
Doubt that the sun doth move;
Doubt truth to be a liar;
But never doubt I love.'
 William Shakespeare, *Hamlet*

Café Metropol

The ferry across to Helsingborg was almost empty. I was
daydreaming at the sunlight on the salt water, when the
carriage door behind me closed loudly. The same two
Swedish border officers, who had interrogated me on my last
Nordic excursion, made their way down the aisle towards me.
"Kan du pratta Svenska?" Asked the thin one.
"Nej, men jeg kan godt forstar lidt Dansk." I said.
"Welkommen til Sverige." They said, already halfway through
the next set of doors.
Drunken fishermen had hijacked the night train to
Copenhagen. There was no sleep to be had. Cecilia waited for
me at T-Centralen, and put me to bed. She had just become
engaged; I had just become disengaged. We slept. The next
day we went to see the Wasa museum in Gamla Stan, for
kebobs and coffee, and to a movie, *Gandhi*. She kissed me
goodbye, on the gangplank of my overnight boat to Finland,
and I glided out into the Baltic.
The vectors flowed under me. Valkommen ombord, *Silja
Line*. The seal's head logo, towing me towards Mother Russia,
was keelhauling me through currents of remorse and ecstasy.
I woke around five am, to catch the sunrise on the
archipelago. I had forgotten my soap in Cecilia's apartment,
but I remembered the pâté and cucumber smørrebrød she
had placed in my pack, with the blood orange. The ferry
docked in Turku, and I sailed on, through Finnish
immigration. A proselytizing pamphleteer wanted to know if

315

I was looking for God. I asked if he had gone missing, and boarded the train to Helsinki.

All I knew about the Finns came from the button-down *Suomi* postage stamps I collected as a child. They gave no real clue to their identity. Tacitus had described them in rather unflattering terms, in his *Germania*:

> 'The Fenni live in astonishing barbarism and disgusting misery: no arms, no horses, no household; wild plants for their food, skins for their clothing, the ground for their beds...'

But there are great mistakes to be made in generalizing a national character, especially if you're Roman. There were three acknowledged Finnish attributes, which I found to be fairly reliably representative. Like any culture, they were a product of their geography and climate. Their settlements had chased the receding ice sheet out of the last ice age. Pushkin described them as 'Nature's unhappy stepson' but, despite the severe winters, toil, and famine, they also felt an intense kinship with the wilder variety of their nature- virgin forests and wolves and bears, and the midnight sun.

Second, the Finns loved their liquids. They were masters of the sea. As early as 1555, Olaus Magnus had commented that they built vessels 'better than those which I have seen built by the Venetians.' Herman Melville remarked on their 'great influence among sailors.' They loved their baths and saunas, *steeping their bodies right down to their most secret selves*. And they loved their drink. Voltaire noted that the Finns 'live to a good old age when they do not undermine their constitutions by the abuse of strong drink.' From what I was about to encounter, there weren't going to be many of them.

Third, the Finns were ferociously protective of their independence, especially from the Russians:

'The Finns are accustomed to skiing as fast as they wish, so that it is said that now they are close by and soon again they are far away. As soon as they have inflicted damage on the enemy, they rush away as swiftly as they came.'

Saxo Grammaticus Gesta Danorum, 13th century

'The Finnons have continual warres wyth the Muscovites in the arm or bosome of the sea Finnonicus: using in Summer the ayde of Shyppes, and in Wynther they combat upon Ice...'

George North, 1561

They had fought the Russians in the 18th century wars of the Greater Wrath and the Lesser Wrath, the Bolsheviks in 1918, and the Soviets in the Winter War of 1939 and the Continuation War of 1941. Even Stalin acknowledged that the Finns had fought valiantly, and 'deserved respect.' Respect, yes. Independence, not so much.

The rocking motion of the train, the sun on my face, the strange little railroad town signs, the squared-off red slatted farmhouses, among their freshly surfaced furrowed fields and conifers- all worked beautifully to put me to sleep. I awoke in time to see Finlandia, Sarenin's train station, and the massive green Russian caterpillar that would swallow me whole, the day after.

I left the terminus, to see the neoclassical Helsinki that Czar Alexander I had dragged 300 kilometers from St. Petersburg in 1809, to replace the original Swedish settlement of poverty and plague. Carl Engel's burnt orange Georgian architecture surrounded me in Senate Square, with 'the good Czar' statue of Alexander II in the epicenter. The steps to the Cathedral on the north side were so steep, my head started to spin. I needed food, and headed through the swooping seagulls and old American cars, to Market Square. I surfaced among tall-masted wooden ships, trapped in floating harbor ice, and an accordion playing in a sad minor key, confined in the same manner, by buoyant drunken drifters. Drab small old Finnish ladies, with ornamented round brim hats and long coats, occupied scattered tangerine tents, selling everything from fish to fox pelts. The market colors of the day, were blue and white and orange and gray. I approached one of the tents, where the smell was particularly inviting.

"Lihapiirakka?" Said the drab little old lady. "Lihataytteinen? Lappeenranta? Grilleillä? Mäkeläinen? Lenkkisämpyläksi?" Which brought me to the fourth Finnish singularity. John Story overwhelmingly understated it, in 1632. 'They have a peculiar language of their own.'

One of the inebriated offered to help me.

"You can have atomic or hydrogen." He said of the lappeenranta. It seemed elemental. The exothermic end reaction was a lihapiirakka, a delicious meat pastry. It makes me hungry now to remember.

Reenergized, I walked to the *Kolmeseppa* statute of the three blacksmiths, said to ring out on the anvil, whenever a virgin passed. The day I was there, it was quiet. And there wasn't enough room for them to bring their hammers down together. Within the inexorable nature of nature, the game was rigged against the virgins from the beginning.

My visit to the National Museum was an enlightened experience, but not quite as much as the methane leak into a broom cupboard, which blew apart the silver collection, a dozen years later. I managed to contact Panu in the late afternoon, and he dished out smoked herring, cheese, bread, Earl Grey and Finnish music, until my need for sleep won out over his hard floor, around midnight.

I regained my Baltic bearings in the filtered sun and wood smoke of his living room next morning. After coffee and yoghurt, he dropped me in the rain, at the organ pipe stalactites of Sibelius' monument. I walked to the rock temple of the Temppeliaukio church as it opened, and sat, listening to a Bach cantata wash over me, under the glazed and slatted dome's natural light. The acoustical serenity was stunning. I filled in time, and the squares of a Herald crossword, over a lihapiirakka at Kaupahalli Kauppatori, and shopped the Academia bookstore. It was there I discovered a neurology text, written by one of my former Residents in Boston, likely department head by now. He used to badmouth anything from outside of New York. I remember asking him what the Big Apple had, that the rest of the world was missing.

"The Metropolitan Opera." He said. I asked him the last time he attended a performance.

"That isn't the point." He said. "The point is, I can."

"So can I." I had remarked. And in a week, I'd be sitting in the Bolshoi.

The kiosk by the guarded synagogue sold me a *kaukoliikenneliput* ticket, for the bus back to Panu's. We chopped firewood, and I drove his little red car behind his truck, for a drink at his parent's place, further into the country. Panu's father asked me why I was going to the Soviet Union. The metallic aftertaste of raisins and vodka filled my mouth.

"To see where the Finns go on the weekend." I said.

It was the first smile I'd seen since I arrived.

'The Finns also have a bent for drink, even though there is no wine here whatsoever, except for illicit tavern keeping, which is harshly suppressed. But, all the way to St. Petersburg, the Finn will drink himself into forgetfulness, lose his money, horse, bridle, and return home poorer than a church rat.'
Mikhail Saltykov-Shchedrin, *Life's Little Things* 1886

*   *   *

'Leningrad sits astride the Neva, frozen in time, a haunting mélange of pale hues, glorious façades and teeming ghosts.'
Serge Schmemann

I was walking on air. That was about what they cost me. I had paid almost as much for my new footwear, as the thousand rubles I had wrapped in plastic, and hidden beneath the insoles of each shoe. Whether you referred to them as 'sneakers,' or 'runners,' would depend on whether their contents were discovered.

Panu loaded me up with hard-boiled eggs and bread and Emmental, and drove me down to my train. I returned his salute, as he made his turn. The enormous pea green train with the single yellow stripe sat all by itself way out on platform 6. Every carriage had a red and gold hammer and sickle shield on the side, emblazed with 'CCCP.'

The squat little conductress, with the Khrushchev mole, squealed with delight, as she examined my tickets and itinerary.

"Ooh, Tashkent!" She bubbled. Must be special, I thought. She led me into a compartment with an old Finnish man, who decided we should speak German. The windows were sealed shut.

Exactly on time, a shudder rippled through the metal monster, and back again. We started to pull out of the station. I realized then, that there was no going back. Evil empire, here I come.

We rocked and then rolled through the Finnish countryside, as though we were on an excursion, to any other place that a train would go. I saw us cross the border without stopping. Peculiar perhaps but, if you're the biggest kid on the block, there might be nothing much to stop for. Then, a few kilometers later, in the middle of a birch forest nowhere, we came to a sudden standstill. Nothing more happened for a good quarter of an hour, and then they came out of the taiga, like smoke. Dozens of them, with gray trench coats and too large military capped visors, boarded us, pirates on an open sea. I heard heavy boots and deep voices drawing closer, and the dissonant slam of compartment doors closing, locked from the outside corridor. It grew warm. Nothing more happened for a good quarter of an hour, and then our own compartment door slid open.

"Доброе утро, господа. Паспорта, пожалуйста." *Gvidye, Tvariche. Pasport, pozhalsta.* He said, swift and polite. We handed him our passports. He looked under our seats, and over the ceiling with a stepladder. Then he locked us back in. It grew warmer. I looked across to the old Finn. He shrugged, and looked away sheepishly. We had left Kansas.

Captain Soviet returned in fifteen minutes, with our passports stamped. He started asking me questions in Russian, before he realized he was wasting time. He asked to see my money. I handed him my traveler's cheques. American Express.

"No more?" He asked.

"No more." I said.

"Do you have rubles?" He asked. I almost jumped out of my shoes.

"Rubles?" I coughed. My feet grew unbearably hot.

"Da. Rubles." He repeated. "Or diamonds, religious articles, propaganda, contraband?" I was grateful for the diversification of his interest. Captain Soviet motioned for me to open Serendipity. He went through it meticulously, scrutinizing everything,

"Here, you open." He said, handing me one of my film canisters. I opened it.

"Take off your shoes." He said. My world ended.

Meanwhile the old Finn, mindful of his prostate, and possibly my predicament, began berating Captain Soviet for all the small talk, and demanded access to a toilet, or someone would have to clean it up.

Captain Soviet shrugged, and let him out.

"Okay, finished." He muttered, and went on to the next car. I mentally recounted my toes.

There was a celebration of sorts going on in the next car. They invited me in. They were all Finnish, and drunk. They told me they were going to Leningrad, for women and cheap vodka. Kari threw me a can of Carlsberg. We stopped at a Berioshka shop in Wiborg. A large painting of Lenin supervised their purchases.

"Six months ago, that was a picture of Brezhnev." Said Kari. Back on board, they looked at my itinerary, and told me that no one would meet me at the station. I told them that would be highly unlikely.

Our train pulled in to the most western city of Russia, the most northerly metropolis of over a million people, and the home of the Hermitage, the largest art museum in the world. No one was there to meet me.

I wandered aimlessly around the soldiers and the babushkas, until a sweet young thing looked at my papers. She found two very KGB-looking hoods, who dropped me into the back of a black 1960's vintage Chekha limousine. It looked like the push-button Valiant I had bought for a buck from my cousin, but it was black, and chauffeured. They drove me to the Astoria Hotel. I left them with the bell staff, and approached the registration desk.

I had read about the Astoria. When it was built in 1911, it had innovations, like central heating, in-suite running hot and cold running water, Art Nouveau facades, splendid salons, a classic ballroom and glass ceiling winter garden restaurant, and dumbwaiters and custom-built refrigerator in the kitchen. Hitler had planned to hold his victory party here. He was a bit premature, but I arrived right on time. They ushered me upstairs, to a palatial prerevolutionary gold brocade suite. I climbed into the closet, and withdrew two thousand rubles from my sneakers, worth about three thousand dollars on the official Soviet exchange rate. I went back downstairs to make a dinner reservation. I approached the Intourist desk in the lobby. She knew who I was.

"Yes, Mr. Winkler, what can I help you with?" She said. I already knew the answer.

"I'd like to go to the Café Metropol." I said. The blood drained from her face.

"We generally discourage going to this restaurant." She offered.

"That is one of the reasons I would like to have dinner

there." I replied. I had heard about the Café Metropol. It had everything I wanted.

"It is not a good idea." She insisted. I inquired as to why.

"There are certain... undesirable influences, that may be sometimes found in such a place." Her brow furrowed. I insisted. She picked up the phone. I caught a flurry of formality, and then some.

"Da. Udeen tourist. Weenkler. Da... da... da... Nyet." It was done. I thanked her, and got up to leave.

"Excuse me Dr. Winkler." She said. But do you have rubles?" My head turned back, smiling.

I marched down Nevsky Prospekt, like Napoleon had wanted to. Dostoevsky would have been proud. In those days, there was almost no vehicular traffic.

You would have been forgiven for missing it. There was no sign on the door, but when I put my hand to it, I could feel the heat and vibrations, of the inferno on the other side. A slat slid back.

"Da?" Said the eye on the other side.

"Udyeen tourist. Hotel Astoria. Weenkler." I said. *Open Sesame.*

And it did, unleashing the tension of the evil spirits within. The wave of noise and smoke and hormones bowled me over. My first view was of two waiters, in a fistfight. It took seven Marlboros for me to get to my table. The band was playing 'Rock around the Clock,' better than Bill Haley ever did. No sooner was I seated, than company arrived. Natasha and Nikita dropped in by parachute, their two chairs pulled out in unison by chivalrous penguins. Two bottles of champagne, at 10 rubles a magnum, hit the table running. The meal was splendid. Lamb appetizer with prunes, carrots, sauerkraut and pickles, chicken Kiev, a nice dry white, ice cream and coffee. After cognac was poured, and consumed, more was poured.

It was becoming clear that, whatever Natasha and Nikita wanted, Natasha and Nikita got. Natasha and Nikita wanted 'dencing.' We denced 'til the end of time, and that came immediately after we sat down to catch our breaths. Two Mongolian black marketers with sunglasses, with almost identical mouths of gleaming gold teeth, rolled up their arms, to show us the Rolexes for sale. We made room for them, and their friends. They lit up strange cigarettes, more cardboard tube than tobacco. The vodka and music and musk kept coming, until I just had to go. There were kisses and hugs for my generous hospitality, and heartfelt sad animation at my departure.

I held up two fingers on Nevsky. Some moonlighter drove me back to the Astoria. The desk clerk asked me where I had been.

"Café Metropol." I offered. His eyes widened.

"What did it cost you?" He asked.

"'Bout three dollars." I said. "And change."

*   *   *

> 'The duality of St Petersburg and Leningrad remains.
> They are not even on speaking terms.'
> Joseph Wechsberg

I hadn't come to Leningrad to see Leningrad. I had come to Leningrad to see St. Petersburg, despite the fact that it had been locked away, and wouldn't be available for another couple of decades. I had always been fascinated with the dimensions of the place, physical and human. It played on the big historical screen.

In founding the city in 1703, Peter the Great had conscripted peasants from all over Russia, and Swedish prisoners of war. Over the first twenty years, two hundred thousand people

324

would die, trying to turn a swamp into the Petrine Baroque metropolis of his vision. Even after its completion, bands of discontented serfs rebelled, and wolves still roamed the squares at night. There was so little light, that only turnips and cabbages could be grown.

As if to compensate for my shady black market depravity of the night before, I was handed a plate of white things for breakfast- bulki, blini, riazhinka, pale cheese, and a hardboiled egg. I asked for black coffee, and was given 'just tea,' with some kind of white stuff in it.

My first stop outside the Astoria was the Bronze Horseman, Étienne Falconet's statue of Peter the Great, and the symbol of St. Petersburg. Catherine the Great had commissioned it, the former Sophie of Anhalt-Zerbst. Similar to Marie Antoinette, who flung herself into the extravagances of the former swamp of Versailles, Catherine confirmed the notion that nothing exceeds like excess, particularly that of former Germanic princesses inhabiting former bogs. The statue of Peter was impressive enough, taking twelve years to cast, the mould breaking at one point, and releasing enough molten bronze to start several fires. But I was more taken with its pedestal.

The Thunder Stone, weighing in at 1500 tons, was the largest rock ever moved by man. Men only, actually, no animals or machines. It was originally found half-submerged, and embedded in another marsh. It took 400 men nine months to move the stone six kilometers over frozen ground, on a metallic sledge that slid over 6 inch bronze ball bearings, on a track. There were only 100 meters of track available, which had to be constantly disassembled and re-laid. The large capstans took 32 men at once to turn, which just barely moved the gigantic boulder. Once at the Gulf of Finland, an enormous barge was constructed, for its transport up the Neva. It, in turn, had to be supported on either side by two full-size warships.

Catherine went on to line the Neva with granite

embankments. I went on, to her most lavish indulgence. The Hermitage was founded in 1764, inspired, if you can believe it, in the spirit of the natural primitivism advocacy of Jean Jacques Rousseau, as an austere simple retreat, designed to contrast with the Winter Palace. She didn't quite achieve it.

The Hermitage was actually another large palace, in and of itself, connected to the main Winter Palace by covered walkways and heated courtyards, and the rare exotic birds that flew among them. Catherine acquired six major art collections in seventeen years, including for the Gotzkowsky assemblage. She delighted in beating out Fredrick the less Great, who could no longer afford to complete, because of his wars with Catherine. By the time I arrived, there were over three million items, including the largest collections of paintings in the world. I was swamped. There were 2 DaVincis, 7 Titians, 26 Rembrandts, 42 Rubens, and the incidental Veroneses, Raphaels, Tiepolos, Tintorettos, El Grecos, Velasquez', van Dycks, Brughels, Renoirs, Monets, Pissaros, Degas', Rodins, Picassos, Gaugins, and more. It was ridiculous.

The eight foot high jasper Kolyvan Vase, weighing in at 19 tons, had to be installed before the walls were erected. I extended my reach through the 1786 doors, 1500 rooms, and 117 staircases of the green and white Elizabethan Baroque Winter Palace. From here, by the end of the 19th century, the Czar ruled over a sixth of the Earth's landmass, and over 125 million subjects. There had actually been four successive Winter Palaces. The last, and the most ostentatious, had been the creation of the wife of an admiral, Tsaritsa Anna Apaksin. From her solid gold dressing table and ruby-encrusted silver stool, to the first ball decorated as an orange grove in the middle of an Arctic blizzard, Anna was the embodiment of gilded squalor. The dining table sat 1000 guests, but no chairs were provided for up to 10,000 other patrons, standing in the staterooms. Below the metal framework in the attics lived so many servants that, undiscovered by the palace authorities, a former retainer and his family moved in under the roof with his family, and his cow. They were only 'unearthed' by the smell of manure. When a fire nearly destroyed the palace in 1837, Czar Nicholas I, who slept in a Spartan room, on a camp bed with a straw mattress, ordered it rebuilt with a year. Any workers, who died from the great frosts, in the resultant frenzy, were replaced the same day. A peculiar man, Nicholas required his visitors to wear evening dress, even in the morning, except for grey top hats, which he declared 'too Jewish.'

In 1880, an attempt was made on the life of Czar Alexander II. A great quantity of dynamite was stockpiled beneath the dining room, by one of the carpenters. For the first time in years, a guest and the dinner were delayed. Eleven members of the Finnish Guard were atomized, but the Romanovs escaped the devastation. They got him twice the same day, in the next year, riding in his carriage. Only shaken by the first anarchist's bomb, he got out of his conveyance, to remonstrate with the culprit. A second conspirator then took the opportunity to explode another, killing himself and, after bleeding to death back at the Winter Palace, the Czar. The section of the cobblestoned street where he was assassinated, now garnished with topaz and lazerite, is part of the Church of the Savior on Spilled Blood, the Cathedral of the Resurrection. It contains over eighty thousand square feet of mosaics. They used it to store corpses, during the siege of the city in the Second World War.

I was shaken by the stupendous opulence of the Winter Palace, especially the green malachite gazebo in the green malachite room, Peter's throne room, and Nevsky's silver tomb. Back out in the wide arc of Palace Square, five hundred tons of red granite Alexander column, rose 150 feet over Napoleon's failure.

Overwhelmed, I went back to the Astoria for a late afternoon nap. My walk, down Nevsky later, was to a more sedate destination than the previous evening. I arrived at Kavkazky, for excellent Tbilisi food, served in portions so prodigious, I didn't make the main course. The smoked salmon and lemon, beef with scallions and a spicy sauce, fresh beans with paprika and almonds, Georgian wine, and dessert, costing pennies in running shoe rubles, lifted me up, and back to my prerevolutionary room at the Astoria. It was still furnished in 1911. The bathwater was brown, and smelled like sweet medicinal beer. For some never discovered reason, my phone kept ringing. I tried to watch a Soviet paratrooper trainee-meets-girl epic on my *Record* television, but the plot was too diabolic dialectic. A few chapters of *Crime and Punishment* sentenced me to sleep. The theme from *Exodus* played in the next room.

*   *   *

'Old St Petersburg remains a beautiful stage set but to the Russians it is not what Rome is to the Italians or Paris to the French. The decisions are made in the Kremlin. The city of Peter remains a museum, open from 8:00 am to 5:00 pm.'

Joseph Wechsberg

I was up long before 8:00 a.m., to get to all I wanted to see, on my last day in Leningrad. Olga handed me the usual white metallic breakfast, and 'just tea.' The riazhinka tasted like it sounded, sour cold molten zinc. I had already learned to give a wide berth to the tinato red muck in the thick glasses. At the double oxymoronic 'special service' desk, I was seeking some historical information about my self-guided planned excursion of the day. No matter what my question was there appeared to be only one answer.
"Five rubles." She said.
"Foreign currency only." said her sidekick.
Extracting a smile would have demanded expensive surgery.
I walked to the Peter and Paul Fortress, the original citadel

founded by Peter the Great in 1703. It was strange that the two patron saints of St. Petersburg, were mirrored in the names of the first two Czars assassinated, Catherine the Great's husband and son. She was probably responsible for the first. Paul I was justifiably paranoid. He started by positioning sentries at the Winter Palace every few meters but, recognizing the futility of establishing any effective form of security there, built St Michael's Castle as his residence in 1801, on an artificial island accessible only by drawbridges. He was murdered three weeks after moving in.

Two rubles got me a cab across the Neva, to Mathilda Kshesinskaya's mansion. She had been the prima ballerina of the Imperial Russian ballet, and the mistress of Czar Nicholas II. She didn't get the house for her dancing skills. I rambled through the mosque next door, and then through the rain, from St. Petersburg to Leningrad. I boarded the Aurora, the 1900 Russian cruiser, still possessing its Eisenstein mystique, whose forecastle gun had set off the 1917 Revolution. Finished with simply glaring through the large windows of the Winter Palace, frustrated mobs ripped priceless paintings from their frames with bayonets, smashed rare crystal and china back to atoms, ransacked the libraries, and piped the finest vintages, of the largest wine cellar in history, straight out into the waiting mouths of those clustered around the palace drains on the Neva. At the time of the Revolution, dogs howled day and night, all over Russia.

Vladamir Lenin had turned Dostoyevsky's 'most abstract and intentional city in the world,' into the most feared manifestation of class warfare reprisal since Paris, after the French Revolution. There were multistoried red murals of him all over town. They had built him a monument at Finland Station, and 230 more places named after his life and former activities, if I had possessed the stamina to see them.

I didn't. Instead I walked past the entire shirtless jogging Red Army, down long avenues, to experience the chromosomal memory of a man for who Peter the Great built a monastery in 1710. Nevsky Prospect was named after Aleksandr Yaroslavish Nevsky, and he, in turn, after the Neva River. Grandson of Vsevold the Big Nest, Nevsky was the Prince of Novgorod, of the medieval Rus. At the age of nineteen, in 1240, he defeated the Swedes, and the Teutonic Knights during the Battle of the Ice, two years later. He paid tribute to the Khan of the Mongol Horde, estimating that Catholicism was likely a greater threat to Russian national identity. Entering his monastery, I followed the wrong crowd into the cathedral. In session was the most moving heavy mass imaginable. Hundreds of wailing, singing little babushkas, took kerchief kommunion with their mouths from an insect-headed bishop, while a baritone cantor and background choir, among the countless candles and icons, filled the smoky space with opium. Outside, past Dostoevsky's granite slab, I found four musical stones, along a neat row in the graveyard-Rimsky-Korsakoff, Moussoursky, Borodin and Tchaikovsky. I put my hand on them, and felt the heat and vibrations, of the inferno on the other side.

I returned up Nevsky Prospekt, via the glass globe-crowned tower on the old Singer House at the intersection of the Griboyev Canal, and arrived at the department store. A swish little fairy, with an otherwise uncanny resemblance to Lenin, stood in his high heels, next to the industrial brassiere counter. Even with the Russian dressing, it still wasn't Macy's. I checked out of the Astoria, in more than enough time to catch my evening train to Novgorod. Intourist's failure to greet me in Leningrad was offset by the company they provided on my departure. My byebye buddy at the Moscow station was surprisingly candid, given his vocation. Eric told me that, not withstanding the fact that he was, himself, an ethnic German, he hated the Germans. His parents had been on the wrong side of both sides during World War II. They had survived the 872 days of the lethal Nazi siege, and the deaths of a million of Leningrad's citizenry, of starvation and worse. If it hadn't been for those few supplies, that made it down the *Road of Life* across Lake Ladoga, they would have perished as well. He hated the Finns as well.

"They come here to drink and fuck." He said. He also hated his living arrangements, stuck as he was in a *kommunalka* apartment with two other families. I asked him if he had any aspirations.

"My dream is to become an ambassador." He offered. I told him I though he was a bit too frisky for the position.

He got defensive then, and closed down. I felt the love.

"I know a lot about you." He said. "A lot."

I told Eric that he was actually from Potsdam, lived near Smolny, desperately wanted to emigrate to the West and, at the ripe old age of twenty-two, didn't know shit from shinola. He asked me what shinola was. I told him that shinola was what Nicolas II had said to the dignitaries, when he left for warmer climes.

'I am only sorry for you who have to remain in this bog.' Life under communism sucked. The train whistle blew. I told him you can't suck and blow at the same time.

Failing Marx

'There are several reasons why Russians view the oppressive state positively. First, in the Russian Orthodox religion, there is an understanding of authority as something sent by God.'

Ryszard Kapuscinski

The first evidence of the impending demise of Soviet communism came strutting alongside, as I left the Intourist Hotel next morning at dawn. He couldn't have been more than six years old.

My train the previous evening had rattled the life out of forever, through flat swampy countryside, along 20th-century smokestacks that turned into 19th-century small wooden shacks that turned into dirt roads. At one point we passed an unending stream of military vehicles, going the other way through history. A mischievous Georgian sent me back in the wrong direction, away from my carriage.

I engaged a Russian soldier on the platform just before midnight, in the presumption that no one had sent a welcome committee. He backed off with relief when a sweet middle-aged woman of girth intervened.

"I was expecting a big tall man." She said. I told her I was sorry to have disappointed. Back at the monstrous multicolored mosaic matron mural of the hotel façade, laundry and mosquitoes delayed any idea of sleep.

Novgorod the Great could have been a far-flung realm in a Tolkien trilogy. Under the rule of Yaroslav the Wise, it rose to become the founding city of the Kievan Rus in the 10th century, and one of the largest states in medieval Europe. Surrounded by the marshland that protected it from being conquered by the Mongol Golden Horde, Novgorod controlled everything that moved, from the Baltic to the Ural Mountains. I found an open-air museum of monasteries, exotic wooden buildings, and a frontier of fifty ancient

Orthodox domed churches. Here, along the Volkhov River, was the oldest palace, and the oldest bell and clock tower in Russia. Novgorod's strength, however, was also its weakness. The swampland setting meant an inability to feed a growing population, and famine arrived for the first time in the 1560's. Ivan the Terrible sacked the city, slaughtering thousands of inhabitants. The final straw was broken by an event that happened half a world away, in 1600.

The Huaynaputina volcano erupted in Peru, resulting in below freezing temperatures through the entire summer, and the coldest year in six centuries. It caused the death of a third of the population of the country, Swedish and Polish invasions, massacres and Cossack atrocities, and enough conspiracy and political unrest to kill off the Rurik Dynasty, establishing the Romanovs as the new absolute rulers, for the next three hundred years. It was called, in true understated Russian nomenclature, the *Time of Troubles*.

It wasn't as much trouble as they were going to have with this six year-old. I had just finished my first decent breakfast in days- poached eggs in oil, meats, cheeses, bread, and sour kefir so good, you could taste the goat leather it had been fermented in. 'Just tea' had turned into coffee. I headed out the door, towards the Novgorod Kremlin, and there he was, matching me stride for stride. Straw cowlick hair, blue eyes with a touch of Tatar, navy and white polo jacket, and attitude. I looked down. We both stopped.

"They have strawberries all year in America?" He asked, looking around furtively.

"What?" I replied.

In an instant, he had ripped open the metal snaps of his jacket and spread the wings wide, pushing his chest towards me. Inside, organized in rows and columns, was a formidable collection of medals, commemorative pins, lighters, coins, and war memorabilia.

"Jeans, cassettes, Marlboros, American dollars?" he said. My, oh my, I thought. What have we here?

"Coins, stamps, foreign currency. Monyey." The 'y' and the why were in the wrong place. He gave me a pin. I gave him a Marlboro. He helped himself to three more, produced a box of Soviet matches, and fired one up.

"It'll stunt your growth." I said. But he wasn't buying it. Everything else, he would buy. The short stuff, he had no time for. I owe my Order of Lenin, and my faith in the free market, to Vlittle Vladamir. He would turn the Evil Empire into condos.

Inside the nine capped stone towers and rose-orange walls of the 15th century *Detinets* Kremlin, a mile in circumference, was an eternal flame, paying homage to the sacrifice of the soldiers who fought and died, in the Great Patriotic War. When the Red Army liberated Novgorod in the midwinter of 1944, fewer than forty out of over 2500 original stone buildings were still standing. At the base of the 1862 bronze monument to the Millennium of Russia, I understood two of the three Cyrillic words on the broad crimson banner-'CCCP' and мир. *Peace*. The third one likely didn't matter. I slipped inside mute, with a Soviet tour group, to see the delicate birch bark letters in the museum, the treasures of the Chamber of the Facets, and St. Sophia's austere 11th century rock walls, helmet cupolas, bronze gates and belfry.

There were so many churches and cathedrals and monasteries to visit, I lost track of who founded what, and which frescoes and domes were dedicated back to whom. In the two days I searched through the Orthodoxy on both sides of the Volkhov, exploring the Holy Wisdom, the Antoniev, the Annunciation, the Assumption, the five blue domes and gold stars of the Yuriev, the Stratilat, the Zerinov, the five Saviours, the Peryn, the Exhaltation of the Cross, Christ's Nativity, the Vyachizhy the Mother of God of the Sign, the Twelve Apostles, the Myrrh-bearing Women, and all the Saints- St. Nicholas, St. Peter and Pavel, St. Peter and Paul, St. Olaf, St. Anthony, St. Paraskeva-Piatnitsa, St. Theodor, St. Simeon, St. Demetrios, St. John the Apostles, Sts. Boris and

Gleb, I found no sign of the most important essence, of why I had come. I found no sign of faith. There was plenty of proof for principled positioning. The babushka sweeping Proletarskaya *serf row,* along the path to the graveyard, with the broom twice her height, under a statue of a mounted rider with a sword, believed in civic cleanliness. The machine-gunned Soviet soldiers believed in defending their homeland from Nazis invaders, who in their turn, believed in their Aryan superiority. Marx believed in communist revolution. Vlittle Vladamir had a dollar doctrine. And I believed that what I was doing would somehow raise my consciousness. But nothing of what I saw in all those religious ruins, conveyed any affirmation for the value of enduring faith. It was consciousness-raising.

I hopped onto an empty derelict bus, droning back towards the Detinets. The driver was somewhere else, and ignored my attempts to pay.

I jumped down in front of the first queue I'd seen in Novgorod. A dozen old men were lined up in front of what looked like a galvanized oil tank, balanced on two rubber tires far too large for the logo. The Cyrillic said 'kvass,' and the white capped and coated attendant was handing out large mugs of dark liquid, for a few kopeks each. I got in line. At the Russian front, it tasted like pungent liquid black bread. It was a beer made out of black bread. Napoleon's soldiers had called it 'pig lemonade.' It was definitely down the breadline food chain of refreshing beverages but, for a poor Russian with little hope, faithfully fulfilling.

There was a restaurant inside the Detinets, called the 'Detinets Restaurant.' Around six, past the *'No! Nein! Nyet!'* antinuclear posters on the way, I arrived through the elms to the tower, for a more erudite evening than I expected, after the Orthodox overdose of the previous hours. The classical music was soothing. I was seated in the enjoyable company of a very friendly and sincere math professor, named Serge. We conversed in French over a meal that was simple, but well prepared. We had cognac, Russian salad, meat and cheese stew, and long discussions about everything. After a final stroll inside the Kremlin, we exchanged addresses. It was a silly thing to do, back then and there, but it somehow served to restore our faith.

My blisters ached next morning. Vlittle Vladamir was waiting outside the hotel.

"Jeans, jackets, tapes." He ripped open his polo jacket, to show me new merchandise. I gave him an American nickel, and picked out two Novgorod pins. He took one back.

"Inflation." He said. Goodnight, Mr. Brezhnev. He pocketed a Marlboro.

"Merci." He said.

I limped past an old Tupelov biplane, to the enthralling wooden architecture of old churches, houses, windmills and other folk buildings, collected from the region. An old babushka crossed herself and cursed me spitless, when I tried to photograph the remains of St. Phillips church. I decided she could keep it, and resumed my *Marche Slave* along the riverbank, overgrown with weeds. My thirst was slaked out of an old hand pump, in a 19th century neighborhood. I got back to the hotel just before my transport left for the train station.

"You will read our paper while you're waiting?" Asked the Intourist apparatchik.

"I'd rather put pins in my eyes." I said.

> 'Don't you forget what's divine in the Russian soul and that's resignation.'
>
> Joseph Conrad

*   *   *

> 'Moscow is the only city where, if Marilyn Monroe walked down the street with nothing on but a pair of shoes, people would stare at her feet first.'
>
> John Gunther

I hadn't even stepped off the train.

"Mr. Winkler?" he asked. He was staring at my sneakers. I answered positively.

"Follow me." The service was improving. My carriage compartment company had been convivial. Dmitri, a 37 year-old photographer from Kiev, shared his bulkas, taught me some Russian, and showed off his command of the Queen's English to the other bunkmates, Valoiev and Ivan. I had tried to explain the difference between 'still born' and 'stillborn,' but it was stillborn. Like our attempts to stop Valoiev's snoring. The relationship between a Russian and a bottle of vodka is mystical.

I arrived at the National Hotel, another prerevolutionary gem that the Bolsheviks had quickly proclaimed as the *First House of the Soviets* government residence, in 1917. They filled it up with priceless furniture and objets d'art, from the estates of the tsars and more unfortunate aristocrats. Judging by the embalming fluid that came out of the taps, I had been given Lenin's room.

He was first on the list of people that I planned to look up while in Moscow.

A surreal view of the Kremlin woke me next morning. I was so transfixed by the latent afterimages on my retinas, it was difficult to accommodate the New York accent of Lonesome Charlie, a businessman from Long Island, down in the breakfast stadium a little later. I bolted and unbolted the white metal quickly, and found myself in Red Square, before my last swallow.

Red Square was not Red Square because it was red. The Russian word красный ('krasnaya') can also mean 'beautiful' and this, according to my sources at the time, was the real inspiration for its name. Red square was not Red Square because it was beautiful. St. Basil's Cathedral was beautiful. I thought Red Square was Red Square because of the rust of Soviet military parades, and the rusting leaders on the dais. The Kazan Cathedral and the Iverskaya Chapel, with its Resurrection Gates, had been demolished to create a cobbled parade ground to the horizon. St. Basil's had been next, but was saved by Stalin who, seeing it come off the architectural grand plan, apparently objected.

"Put it back!" He said. Perhaps.

Through the heavy haze and oppressive austerity of the space, I could begin to make out the red granite hybrid step pyramid of Cyrus the Great, and the line to see the eternal lighting of Lenin's bones. I waited over an hour in the procession, teased mercilessly by the Finns, for the frequency with which the 'Number One Sentries' checked my anorak. What they thought I was capable of conjuring up, between searches, was bewildering, but they were taking no chances. Nothing other than quiet breathing was allowed- no photography, talking, smoking, eating, hats on heads, or hidden hands. I finally got a short 'move-along' ghoulish glimpse, of waxed fruit and ginger-dyed gilded hair, a 16 °C and 90 percent humidity low lit absurdity, bordering on insanity. I had spent more time with Christ in the Holy Sepulcher in Jerusalem, and there weren't as many chemicals involved. They had been keeping Lenin 'alive' with moisturizing, and the injection of preservatives under his clothes, daily for the previous sixty years. Every eighteen months he got a special glass bath of alcohol, glycerol, distilled water, potassium acetate, and quinine. If he hadn't been in it, you could have drank it down, to prevent malaria. They were in a constant battle against dampness, discoloration, dark spots and skin wrinkling, for which they had an arsenal of hydrogen peroxide, acetic acid, and phenol. Even a decade before I got there, more than ten million people had already visited the cleanest Russian in the country. I made a break for the GUM department store, on the eastern side of the square, but it had as nothing in it, as its namesake in Leningrad. I hiked across the wide Moskva River, to the fairy tale façade and interior of the Tretykov, to marvel at the Repins. I loved the Repins. A few kopeks and fewer words of Russian fed me standing up and undetected at a little *stolivnai*, on a lunch of pierogies, meat with kasha, and a thin drink drained from a tank of floating rotten apples.

On my way to the Pushkin Museum, I was amazed how few vehicles there were in the broad boulevards. The largest collection of European art in Moscow held Heinrich Schliemann's fabulous gold loot from Troy, and an impressive enough collection of French classicists and impressionists. But the rooms choked with plaster casts of the rest of the world's great art were rather more proletarian. It didn't hold a candle to the Hermitage.

I trudged back to the National for a nap in the Kremlin shadow. A couple of hours later, I made my way to Tverskaya 6, to the Aragvi Restaurant, fabled for its Georgian cuisine, and its most famous patron, Ioseb Besarionis dze Jughashvili. He had other names as well. At various times during his career, he was known as Koba, Soselo, Ivanov, Uncle Joe, Kremlin Highlander, Dear father, Vozhd, Coryphaeus of Science, Father of Nations, Brilliant Genius of Humanity, Great Architect of Communism, and the Gardener of Human Happiness. Harry Truman had called him 'a little squirt.' Harry was wrong. He may have started with bank robberies, ransom kidnappings, and extortion, and sent to Siberia seven times, but he was responsible for many of the great events of his century- the Great Famine, the Great Terror, the Great Purge, and the Great Patriotic War. In 1930 he exterminated the Kulaks and defiantly exported large grain reserves, in the face of bitter need, shaping the Great Famine that would take the lives of up to ten million people. In the same decade he passed a new law, requiring that 'terrorist organizations and terrorist acts' be investigated for no more than ten days, with no prosecution, defense attorneys or appeals, followed by a 'quickly' executed sentence, ranging from banishment to the Gulag labor camps, to execution after trials held by NKVD troikas. Nearly 700,000 people were executed in the course of the Great Terror, most of whom were interred in mass graves. He had honed his talents for the Great Purge just after the revolution, in Tsaritsyn, where he had ordered the extermination of counter-revolutionaries and former Tsarist officers, and burned villages into submission. In 1940 he set out to 'solve the Baltic problem,' merging Lithuania, Latvia and Estonia into the Soviet Union, at a cost in lives of 160,000 of their citizens. He made the loyal Nikolai Yezhov head of the NKVD secret police, and had him purge it of Bolshevik veterans. He then executed Yezhov for 'excesses.' He rigged new show trials for old enemies. He had Leon Trotsky assassinated in Mexico. Between 1941 and 1949 nearly three and a half million people were deported to Siberia and the Central Asian republics. Almost fifty per cent died of disease and malnutrition.

The little pipsqueak had no love left for the Jews. In 1952 he concocted the 'Doctors' Plot,' accusing Jewish physicians of conspiring to murder Soviet officials, and ordered even those acquitted to be tortured to death. 'Among doctors, there are many Jewish nationals... every Jew is a potential spy.' He announced. 'Good workers at the factory should be given clubs, so they can beat the hell out of those Jews.'

He razed synagogues, and planned to send millions of Jews to four large newly built labor camps in Western Russia, using a 'Deportation Commission,' that would purportedly act to save them from an enraged Soviet population, after the trials. It was hardly original.

When his son botched an attempted suicide, the Georgian father lamented, that his boy couldn't 'even shoot straight.' He is also known for having said that 'Death solves all problems - no man, no problem'... 'I trust no one, not even myself'... 'Ideas are more powerful than guns. We would not let our enemies have guns, why should we let them have ideas'... 'In the Soviet army it takes more courage to retreat than advance'... and... 'The people who cast the votes decide nothing. The people who count the votes decide everything.'

He decided to collect estates and dachas and luxury villas and mountain retreats in Zuvalova, Kuntsevo, Lipki, Semyonovskaya, Gagri, Abkhazia, Novy Alon, Lake Mitsa, and Zelyony Myss on the Black Sea, and would never travel or arrive by air. During World War II, his name was included in the new Soviet national anthem. The 20 million people who died by his hand would probably think that Joseph Stalin was not a nice man. But they would have never called him a pipsqueak.

*   *   *

'Gaiety is the most outstanding feature of the Soviet Union.'
Joseph Stalin

Stalin had a private tunnel, from his office in the Kremlin, to the basement of the Aragvi Restaurant. I walked right in the front door. Unlike the direct assault I had experienced at the Metropol, the Muscovites at least allowed me to get to my table. Remembering that Uncle Joe loved the Georgian *Tsinandali* white wines, I ordered a bottle. It landed on the table, a split second before they landed in the other two seats. Sasha was a chubby Mafioso who, when he figured out he wasn't going to change money, sell me a watch, or score a pair of spare jeans, flipped up his sunglasses and began looking around for the waiter. His sidekick, Valery, was an alcoholic motorcycle racer, and a former MIG pilot in Syria. Life insurance would have just been in the way. When I looked back down at the table, the wine was finished, and a bottle of vodka had taken its place. The waiter had returned, and Sasha was ordering off the menu. Actually, that isn't quite correct. Sasha was ordering the menu. It started coming in a

342

continuous line- karcho soup, fish in walnut sauce, and a spiced meat stew, each course matched with its own libation. Actually, that isn't quite correct either. Every libation was a new bottle of vodka. While Sasha was talking *biznez*, Valery was canvassing the crowd, on a mission to find me a female companion. By the time he had found the right redheaded princess, however, Sasha had decided that we absolutely must go back to his apartment, to listen to his collection of American rock music. We left the Aragvi in a hail of a hurry. What I found outside, gave me pause. It wasn't that that Sasha and Valery had already consumed the better part of the annual production of Stolichnaya, and were approaching a vehicle with the intention of making it move somewhere. It wasn't that the vehicle they were approaching looked nothing like anything I had seen in the Soviet Union. It was that the vehicle they were approaching looked nothing like anything I had seen anywhere. It had started life as a Lada, like Stalin had started life as a choirboy. It was the child of a former MIG pilot alcoholic motorcycle racer. To say it had been modified was immoderate. It had been reincarnated. With muscle and pilfered titanium aircraft parts and hormones, Valery had reconstructed this Lada in his own image, from the collective to the consecrated. He told me it wasn't painted bright yellow for our protection, but for theirs. The back was that much higher than the front, to hold the engine in. When Valery turned the key in the ignition, the sound was otherworldly. The hundred and twenty kilometers an hour past the Kremlin, blew over the traffic cop that blew his whistle a split second too late. We stopped to pick up Sasha's girlfriend, Marina, who treated the intrusion like it was an everyday occurrence. Then I made a mistake.

"Here, you drive." Said Valery, handing me the keys. I admit that I did think about this for a minute but not, as posterity would eventually confirm, carefully enough. Would it be better for someone like me, who didn't know the vehicle, the city, or the language, to drive? Or someone with a blood poison level approaching grain alcohol? Silly me. The correct answer was actually (c) neither. But, like most momentous decisions in Russian history, I had been given only two choices. Valery and Sasha settled into the back, and Marina sidled into the passenger seat. *Vroom vroom.*

In Moscow they had these cute multiple intersections of countless street spokes, converging on central hub kiosks, manned by an army of traffic cops waving multicolored light sabers, to help guide the flow. I exploded through the first one at a hundred, and it looked like a battle of Jedi knights in my rear view mirror, if I would have had one. Valery and Sasha loved it, and provided encouragement. In retrospect, this was wrong. I roared through the second cartwheel nuclear core at a hundred and twenty. The baton action looked like a congress of epileptic symphony conductors, and the other noise from between Marina's knees let us know that there was now radio traffic as well. Blinking lights and sirens seemed to come out of nowhere, if you count four different directions as nowhere.

"Faster." Shouted Valery. "Faster." This sentiment was echoed by Sasha but not, if her white-knuckled silence was any indication, by Marina. I went faster. The blinking lights and sirens receded into the horizon. I looked up ahead. Between the Cartwheels, we were entering along another spoke, into another large intersection. I glanced at the speedometer. It said a hundred and forty. I figured that was enough. Unfortunately, so did the half dozen converging police cars that cut us off, and to pieces. As they say at the end of the adventure, 'everything happened so fast.' Two rather uncivil police officers, with hats too big for their heads, pulled me out of the driver's seat and indelicately deposited me in the back of a cruiser. How they got the handcuffs on so fast, without my knowledge, was a riddle wrapped in a mystery inside an enigma. I watched as Sasha and Valery ended up the same way, each in his own individualized transport. Practice, I decided. It was practice. Marina was parked, unencumbered and unshackled, in the seat beside me. Another agent of the Evil Empire slid behind the wheel of the Yellow Lada. In his eyes you could see the virus replicating. We all drove away down the yellow-bricked road. The Yellow Lada blasted past us at light saber speed. We drove for what seemed to be hours, finally coming to rest in front of a suburban police station.

They took us in, one at a time. Sasha went first. I didn't particularly like the appearance of him, when they brought him back, and drove him somewhere else. He looked better without the new black-eyed shiner. Valery was next. He didn't come out. When they came for Marina and I, I was still thinking of an alibi. Then I realized I would need two. There were still rubles in my shoes.

Marina and I were escorted in together, but I got to go first. The room was well lit, I'll give them that. Someone with authority, likely the captain rolled in, resembling a tank at the Kursk offensive. Quite offensive, actually. He was screaming at me in Russian. Luckily for him, I had no idea what he was saying. Unluckily for him, I had no idea what he was saying. He looked puzzled for just that split second before the blood drained back out of his face.

"Разве ты не говорят на русском языке?" He asked. *Ya ponimayu po-Russki?* I knew what that meant, and shook my head no. Small beads of sweat formed on his brow.

"Sprechen Sie Deutsch?" He offered. I knew what that meant too. I lied. There was no way I was embarking on a German conversation, in a room full of Russian paramilitaries, most of whom had unpleasant family stories about the native speakers. The small beads formed rivulets.

"Tourist?" He asked, sweating through his shirt.

"Da." I replied. The cuffs came off.

"Паспорт, пожалуйста." He asked. *Pasport, pozhalsta.* Nicely. I gave him my passport.

"Canada?" He asked. I nodded. From behind him, I heard the sacred words. *Wayne Gretsky.*

"Your girl?" He asked, motioning to Marina. I looked over, and saw the right answer.

"Yes." I said.

"You go, OK?" He said, pleading.

"OK." I said.

They gave Marina and I a lift back to the National and, once they had driven off, I gave her three rubles for a taxi home.

Back in the sanctity of my room overlooking the Kremlin, I exhaled. There was a knock at the door. It was my old Long Island buddy, Lonesome Charlie.

"I was just going out to get a vodka and something." He said. I told him I was thinking of having a quiet night.

"Maybe tomorrow." I said. He looked in at the book on my night table.

"What are you reading?" He asked.

"Crime and Punishment." I said. "Dostoevsky."

"Any good." He asked.

"Dunno. I'm just getting to the exciting part." I said. And closed the door.

*   *   *

'Moscow has changed. I was here in 1982, during the Brezhnev twilight, and things are better now. For instance, they've got litter. In 1982 there was nothing to litter with.'

P.J O'Rourke

I had arrived in Moscow just after the Brezhnev twilight, in the Andropov twilight.

"Yes, Samantha, we in the Soviet Union are trying to do everything so that there will not be war on Earth. This is what every Soviet man wants." Yuri had said. The soldier manhandling me out of the way of Yuri's limo, as it entered the Kremlin next morning, clearly hadn't heard the news.

The day had started at breakfast in the Superdome with Mead, an obnoxious young anti-American American hot and cold, cold war journalist. As he left, he threw me the address of his hotel in Warsaw, 'where all the press hangs out.' I spike it three feet further, on the way down of the stadium. Touchdown.

Outside, St. Basils was a 17th century allegorical rendition of temple of Jerusalem, a bonfire of nine kaleidoscope-dipped soft ice cream-topped Byzantine erections, revolving around the central Trinity starship cathedral. In 1933, Pyotr Baranovsky, the designated architect of its destruction, rebelled. Stalin sent him to Siberia. By 1937 even hard-line Bolshevik planners were clamoring for its preservation, and St Basil's was given a full pardon. Baranovsky, on the other hand, stayed in the Gulag.

Five kopeks dropped me 250 grandiose feet down near vertical escalators, which never seemed to reach the distant vanishing point of their victory torch chandeliers, and the spilled light of the Revolution reflected onto the marble bowels of the Moscow Metro. Stalin had it designed so you had to look up to the radiant ceiling shotgun starburst future of Social Realism, and the Sun God's own solar beneficence. He brought in Volga cement, northern timber, Siberian iron, Baku bitumen and marble and granite from everywhere. Miners were recruited from Ukrainian and Siberian coalfields, and skilled construction workers from the steel mills of Magnitogorsk, the Dnieper hydroelectric station, and the Trans-Siberian railway. The daily 'Metrostroi shock worker,' and 700 other newsletters were printed, to attract thousands of unskilled laborers, shouting *Songs of the Joyous Metro Conquerors* from a single Soviet solar plexus. The technology served the aesthetic, which served the ideology. The technology of this ideology could withstand direct nuclear external explosions, but another ideology was coming at the end of the Cold War. Subterranean Islamist terrorism would expose the Metro's design vulnerability to direct internal explosions. For all its opulent grandeur, the Moscow subway operated at an average of 16 miles an hour. The stink of the New York subway carried its passengers an average of 25 miles an hour. When Khrushchev remarked that he would 'bury us,' it wouldn't have been with productivity.

The Metro was also a series of underground cartwheels. As you travel away from a hub, the stations along the spokes were proclaimed with female voices; the stops that a train made journeying towards the hub were announced by male voices. I surfaced at the Kolomenskaya monastery, to the strains of a Soviet soprano and, reenergized with pierogies and spring rolls from another stolivnai, migrated along the Bolshevik bridleway to the heroic armed workers of the Ploshdid, the V. I. Lenin, and the Marx and Engels Museums. My serfing continued in the waves of the state *Dom Knigni* House of Books, but there was nothing there for me. Most of what was on offer was in the genre of the usual 'revolting peasants' stuff, and I was beginning to crave some evidence of intrepid individualism. I began a protest march of sorts, walking past Lenin's sports complex, across a railway bridge over the Moskva River, to the monument for a man that I truly had respect for, yea, verily idolized.

I remember an eight year-old boy, sitting outside in the snow and the subzero darkness, looking up at Orion, the night that Yuri Gagarin became the first human in space. When American astronauts came along, I gave up wanting to be a cosmonaut. I remember emphasizing the ideological difference to my friends. But I knew there was no difference. Both were disciplined dreamers, skilled in higher mathematics and aerobic training, emotionally mature and intellectually expansive, loyal to their comrades and families. They possessed the finest instincts and attributes of the species. A Soviet Air Force doctor had characterized Gagarin as:

'Modest; embarrasses when his humor gets a little too racy; high degree of intellectual development evident in Yuriy; fantastic memory; distinguishes

348

himself from his colleagues by his sharp and far-ranging sense of attention to his surroundings; a well-developed imagination; quick reactions; persevering, prepares himself painstakingly for his activities and training exercises, handles celestial mechanics and mathematical formulae with ease as well as excels in higher mathematics; does not feel constrained when he has to defend his point of view if he considers himself right; appears that he understands life better than a lot of his friends.'

Yuri played hockey goalie and coached basketball. He baptized his eldest daughter, Elena, in the Orthodox Church in Star City. His short stature was likely a deciding factor, in the choice of who would first fly in the cramped cockpit of Vostok I. In 1951 Shostakovich wrote the patriotic song, Opus 86. During reentry, Gagarin whistled it. *'The Motherland hears, the Motherland knows, where her son flies in the sky.'* Khrushchev cried. Yuri was five foot two, eyes of blue, and had a smile that lit up the Cold War. He was awarded the title of Hero of the Revolution but, to an eight year-old boy in Northern Ontario, he was just a hero. Starman.

I actually went to Gagarin's monument to pay tribute to a very different hero in the same saga of cosmic exploration. Gagarin had been the backup pilot for his friend, Vladimir Komarov, in the flight of Soyuz I. He had protested that the craft had over two hundred structural problems, was inherently dangerous, and that additional safety precautions were needed. Komarov was married with two children, and knew he would die. But he refused to back out of the mission, because he didn't want to be responsible for the death of his friend. No one dared to tell Soviet leader Brezhnev about the faults of the spacecraft, and the mission went ahead. A month before launch, Komarov told another friend that he was not going to make it back and that he had to take care of Gagarin, before bursting into tears. Soyuz I blasted off on its launch day of April 23, 1967. Antennas failed to open, power and navigation systems faltered. The parachutes became entangled during reentry, and Komarov hurtled towards Earth, and certain death. His wife, Valentina, was brought into mission control to say goodbye to him. U.S. intelligence picked up Komarov's conversations with ground control, and his screaming and cursing cries of rage, at the country that had placed him in inside a 'botched spaceship,' as he plunged to a horrific fiery incineration. He smashed in the ground like a meteorite. The capsule was flattened, and buffer rockets blew up on impact. A heel bone was found among the ashes.

A year later Gagarin died in a suspicious MIG-15 accident. He was 34 years old.

I returned to the National to recharge. Later than evening, there was a knock on my door. It was Lonesome Charlie. We went out to the Hotel Intourist for a three-ruble vodka and bad music. Charlie was more interested in the hookers, and talking about Ronald Reagan, mostly the hookers. I asked him what line of work he was in.

"Intelligence." He said. I remained unconvinced. Sorry, Charlie.

*   *   *

'A people passing rude, to vices vile inclined,
  Folke fit to be of Bacchus traine, so quaffing is their kinde.
  Drinke is theor whole desire, the pot is all their pride,
  The sobrest head doth once a day stand needful of a guide.'
  George Turbeville (1540-1610), *Among the Russes*

It was the day before May Day. This was Christmas to a communist, and I awoke to find a crane, placing a three story carmine mural, featuring the profiled heads of Lenin, Marx and Engels, over the entire façade of my hotel. There were other red banners everywhere else you looked as well. Serious stuff, this Orthodox iconography.

My final day in Moscow was destined to be like Komarov's final spaceflight. The launch occurred without fanfare.

Breakfast with Lonesome Charlie just wouldn't have felt right, accompanied by a brass section. My first destination was a stone's throw from the front door of the National, the sixty-eight stone acres of the Kremlin. Outside its twenty-foot thick walls, I paused to absorb the flame, polished red granite plates, and stiff-kneed guard change at the Tomb of the Unknown Soldier. Inside, I paused to reflect under the Ivan the Great Bell Tower, surrounded by the magical exteriors, and the iconostases and frescoes in the Archangelsky and Bucharevsky Cathedrals. I saw the two hundred ton Tsar bell, the largest in the world, cast over two years in the 1730s. The piece that broke off during a fire, four years later, was still three times bigger than the next largest bell ever made. On Judgment Day the Tsar bell is supposed to be miraculously repaired, and lifted to heaven. I couldn't wait. Next to the bell was the equally monstrous Tsar Cannon, weighing in at only thirty-nine tons. Each of the cannonballs in front weighed in at a ton and, manufactured in rival St. Petersburg, were deliberately made too large for the barrel.

I took the Metro to the Novodevichy Convent, an onion-bulb Ivan the Terrible cloister with another elaborate interior, and famous sons interred in the graveyard outside. Here, I found the resting places of Chekov and Gogol, but couldn't locate Khrushchev. They must have buried him as deep as my next subway stop, at the Rubylev Ancient Art museum.

I had reserved the evening for a quiet cultural indulgence. I had tickets to the ballet, *Macbeth*, at the Bolshoi. The theatre was magnificent, but I almost missed finding my seat among the six gilded tiers, in the last minute consumption of two smoked salmon sandwiches, in the lobby. The staging and performance were magic, and the witches particularly brilliant, although I didn't think that anyone involved had actually read the last act of the original play. I left ecstatic, and ran back to the National in the pouring rain. The floor lady informed me that my friend, Alexander, had called. I told her I didn't know any Alexander. She shrugged.

What I had forgotten was the Russian nickname for 'Alexander.' A few minutes later, there was a knock at my door. A black eye grinned at me, on the other side.

"Change money? I give you a good price." Said Sasha, with Valery and Marina in tow. He had been released from custody, with a fifty-ruble fine, a pledge not to drink, and a one am curfew. The authorities should have counted themselves lucky, to have collected the fifty rubles. I told Sasha I had an early flight the next morning to Tashkent, in central Asia.

"We have time." He said. This was about where the power and navigation was disabled.

Our first stop was the Hotel M, where Sasha dealt out a wad of rubles to get us a table. It quickly filled with champagne, vodka and limonaya, followed by delicious cold sliced sturgeon, veal tongue, beef dishes, assorted Russian salads and coleslaw, beetroot-colored horseradish, and wild country mushrooms in a deliriously sensual sauce. We dined and danced and drank. This was about where the parachutes failed to deploy.

Valery drove us to Sasha's apartment to listen to his American music collection. We all dropped into various sofas and cushions, and Sasha cranked up the volume. A little while later he and Valery went out, to get more food and drink. I remember Boney M's *'Rasputin,'* playing on the tape deck. Marina got up and locked the door. *But to Moscow chicks he was such a lovely dear.*

She turned and came toward me. *She believed he was a holy healer.* In an instant, she had ripped open the buttons of her shirt and spread the wings wide, pushing her chest towards me. Inside, organized in rows and columns, was a formidable collection of medals, commemorative pins, lighters, coins, and war memorabilia. Actually, that's not true. But the soft magnificence of what she had instead, was the reason they all fought so hard for all those medals and pins and war memorabilia. *But he also was the kind of teacher women would desire.*

Marina put her arms around my head, and her warmth and perfume enfolded and enveloped me. *But he was real great when he had a girl to squeeze.*

I remember going sideways, and her going south. *Though he was a brute they just fell into his arms.*

I looked up into blue eyes and blond hair, and undulation. *Ra-ra-rasputeen, lover of the Russian queen.*

Through the curvature of Marina, I saw the curvature of the Earth. *Ra-ra-rasputeen, Russia's greatest love machine.*

There were footsteps on the stairwell. Our eyes opened wide in unison. This was the 'hurtled towards Earth, and certain death' part. The locked door lock rattled. I saw my heel bone among the ashes.

Oh, those Russians.

'In America you can always find a party.
In Russia the party always finds you.'
Yakov Smirnoff

Ice Cream

'From the window of a flying vehicle, the scene below is just a scene. Under your own two feet it becomes real. A few steps through a country establish its scale and proportion. Its slow life becomes sensible through the soles of your boots. You begin to read the geology correctly, feeling the old uplift and the past movement of the glaciers.'

Kenneth Brower, *The Starship and the Canoe*

If you're reading this chapter, I must have survived the last one. But only just. It was long after midnight, May Day in the USSR. Marina made it to the door, fully dressed and ravishing, inside five seconds. As my belt slid through the last loop, a split second later, it captured a quizzical look from Valery although, thankfully, not from Sasha. We ate and drank some more. When I looked at my watch, it was five thirty. My plane to Tashkent would leave at eight. We were thirty minutes and half a world away from, and to, the National. Valery drove. Marina and I sat in the back, palms down. I kissed them all 'Dasvidanya,' and strolled into a crisis, in the hotel lobby.

"Mr. Winkler, we must go now!" Screamed the Intourist representative behind the counter. He accompanied me to my room, and assisted in my repacking. Back downstairs, I shook the wrists of the rest of the staff, and was ushered into a waiting Chekha limo, for the dash to the airport.

"This is from your friend." Said the driver, as we pulled away. I opened the package that Lonesome Charlie had left. Dostoyevsky. *The Idiot.*

My French got me through Security more quickly. The Russians imitate French ways, but always at a distance of fifty years. There was nothing French about their X-ray machines, as my camera film would discover.

In the waiting lounge, I met Helen, an Aussie research assistant, who kept telling me how religious she was. Judging

355

by how she talked my ear off in the departure lounge, that hadn't included a vow of silence. The noise that the Tupolev TU-134 made on takeoff provided a brief reprieve. We found ourselves squashed back in our seats, pulling multiple gravities, as the airplane took off almost vertical. A fine mist sprayed along the entire aisle above us. Holy Helen looked at me with concern.

"Don't worry." I shouted. The avionics run on direct current. It can take off from and land on unpaved airfields. They can turn it into a troop carrier in half an hour. NATO's codename for it is 'Crusty.' She looked at me suspiciously.

"I'm an aerospace engineer." I said. In the seat pockets were complimentary packs of TU-134 cigarettes. Everyone lit up on takeoff, except for Holy Helen, me, and the uniformed man beside her, with 'CA' emblazoned on his chevrons.

"Are you a chartered accountant?" She asked. He stared back. "Soviet Army." I said. "The 'C' is an 'S' in Cyrillic."

Everyone at cruising altitude was served some kind of paltry poultry, dried out rice, black bread, jam, red caviar, tea, an almond cookie, and another pack of TU-134s. We eventually landed three time zones later, in the same world. The root beer disinfectant smell from Leningrad had taken an earlier flight to Ташкент. Our chekha took us through the 'stone city,' to chekh in.

"Ooh, Tashkent!" I remembered the squat little conductress with the Khrushchev mole, squealing with delight back in Helsinki. But I can't say I understood immediately. It was pretty enough, with wide tree-lined shady streets, pleasant parks, and numerous fountains. It was also a 'model Soviet city,' with acres of apartment blocks, immense plazas for military parades, and monuments, including the largest statue of Lenin ever erected.

Life had not been easy in Tashkent. Despite its historical prominence as a trading point on the historic Silk Road, at the foothills of the western Tian Shan mountains, very little of its material ancient greatness was left to see. In 1219, it was completely destroyed by Genghis Khan. Rebuilt, it came under sequential attack by Uzbeks, Kazakhs, Persians, Mongols, Oirats, and Kalmyks. In 1865, an Orthodox priest, armed only with a crucifix, led Cherniaev's Russian force on a daring night assault, against Tashkent's sixteen mile of walls, eleven gates and thirty thousand defenders. Their army was outnumbered fifteen to one, and acting against the direct orders of the Czar. They won. A huge earthquake, measuring 7.5 on the Richter scale, had flattened the city and left three hundred thousand people homeless, sixteen years before I arrived.

Perhaps my conductress was *oohing* about the climate. It felt like California. Tashkent looked a lot like Los Angeles would have, if Los Angeles had been destroyed by Genghis Khan, obliterated by a humongous earthquake, and then invaded by the Soviet Union. By every possible measure, Tashkent was still better than Los Angeles.

In preparation for May Day, my hotel window had been covered with a small part of a gigantic landscape of Lenin. I was in the goatee section.

Holy Helen accompanied me, to where the riddle wrapped in the mystery inside the enigma, of my squat little conductress, was finally solved. Our shashlik and samsa appetizers, chicken Kiev, Hungarian champagne and cognac, and music and dancing under the grape arbor terrace of the Restaurant Zefrashan, was not only absolutely marvelous, it ultimately came compliments of the Uzbek families around us. *Ooh, Tashkent.*

Last minute May Day band practice and parade preparations, and an infernal Intourist chiming clock in the hallway, prevented any possibility of sleep. I washed groggy, in the largest city, and capital, of Uzbekistan. An obnoxious American tour group, obsessed with their own *Gee-I-wouldn't-want-to-end-up-in-jail* importance, was the loudest distraction at breakfast. I asked the concierge for directions to Chempiona Street.

357

"Why do you want to visit the synagogue?" He asked.

"What do you care?" I answered. It was a sawoff. I met Holy Helen in the lobby. She seemed confused by her choices, and asked if she could tag along. We walked down to the children's shop where we finally found a cab driver. He took us through the squalor and goats of more authentic neighborhoods, to the geometric precision of the Barak Khan Medresseh.

"Salaam aleichem." I called inside.

"Aleichem salaam." Echoed back. We followed the convoluted curves of Kanasaiakaya, until we emerged into a park enclave of street vendors and exotic Uzbek costumed musicians, blowing enormous sky-held copper *dzharchi* long horns. *'Graah, graah, graah, graaah.'* They said, deeply. Shades of Tamerlane.

We came to the market, behind the remains of the Kukeldash Medresseh, and I was home again, among spices, matriarchal cross-legged vendors, dirt, chaos and that magnificent *meatshitcrushedonionparsley* miasma of near extinct soul food.

Helen spotted an old man in a turban and a caftan, selling bad knives to a fat Russian, for fifteen rubles. After the transaction left, another knife materialized, from under the caftan. Oh, how I missed the beauty of Arab deceit. It was all here. Strolling through rose and grape arbor-lined lanes of old courtyards, Helen and I were greeted by three men. The first was dressed in a dark suit, with a Lenin badge and gold smile; the second was shorter, stubby and gregarious; and the third was gigantic, quiet, and so calm, his pulse never rose above forty beats per minute. We were invited in for *chai*. The first showed us his new Lada, his beautiful courtyard, his gold-toothed Uzbek beauty of a wife, and a table, resplendent with thick pizza, honey, peanut sauce, and halwa. The conversation was broken in Russian, Uzbek and English, but united in hospitality and humor. We produced our coins and maps, in exchange for their raisins, sun, climate, ages, wrists for pulse taking, and smiles.

"What kind of work do you?" asked Helen. And he wrote КГВ, KGB in Cyrillic, and grinned a mouth of gold. She didn't get it, but I fell off my chair, howling. Lunch over, they sent us in three different compass directions, back to the bazaar. We took the fourth, and found it again, for tea. Continuing along both sides of Novai, we wandered past the ruins of the Sheik Zein-ad-din and An-takhur mosques. Just beyond the park and into amazement, was the best part of the day- an Uzbek circus, with spinning high wire acrobats, tightrope walkers balancing May Day parade floats, and family toddlers, on their heads, clowns, games of word wit, and Genghis Khan's ghost, all laughing. A Samarkand Samson lifted four large weights with his teeth, and bench-pressed two more with his hands, lying on broken glass, while eight men jumped on the door on top of him. Afterwards, we retraced ourselves back into the market, for dinner and green *chai*. The comrade next to me at the counter was showing off his English. I asked him what we were eating.

"Manatee." He said, between bites. Here endeth the lesson. I said goodbye to Holy Helen back at the Hilton, showered, and settled in, to finish the last pages of *The Idiot*. Exploding fireworks woke me up just before midnight. It was May Day in L.A. I read *Brothers Karamazov* until four.

Because I was late for breakfast, the Daughters of the Revolution resisted most of my attempts to obtain nourishment. I got a Leningrad 'white special.'

There was one more thing I wanted to see in Tashkent. It wasn't on any itinerary, and I only thought about it among the Karamazov brothers. I asked the Intourist warden for directions to the Metro station.

"You cannot go out. You don't have time." She said. I jogged past the cumulus bearded statue of Karl Marx in the park facing the hotel, dropped into the tunnels to Chamsa station, and went one more, rising into rural rusticity. There was a mosque and a teahouse and, past lanes of arbors and roses and goats and sunshine, an expansive field of red poppies.

Among them, hundreds of black and white photos had been developed, directly onto memorial headstones, each surrounded by fresh flowers and candles, some still lit. There was something very wrong with this necropolis. The photos were all of young men. The distance between their birthdates and demise was short, recent, and nearly identical. I could only guess at what had produced this poppy puppy graveyard, and my hourglass was running out of sand. Outside the mosque, a bone-fingered old Uzbek handed me a cold white coneful.

"Мороженое" He said. *Morozhenya*. Ice cream.

Inside, it was empty and green and pillared, and lit by incandescence, but its otherwise uniform antiquity did not extend to the floor, covered as it was with new carpets. I lifted the edge of the one I was pretending to pray on. The English words on the label told the story.

'*Made in Afghanistan.*' It said.

*   *   *

'Then shall my native city, Samarcanda...
Be famous through the furthest continents,
For there my palace-royal shall be placed,
Whose shining turrets shall dismay the heavens,
And cast the fame of lion's tower to hell.'
Christophe Marlowe, *Tamburlaine*

The second piece of evidence for the impending demise of Soviet communism came, as our turboprop began its descent. Once again, I had only made it back to my hotel for my next flight, further into Uzbekistan. They asked me where I had been.

"The Great Silk Road." I said.

The views of the irrigated Central Asian desert plateaus were unexpected. It looked like one big collective farm, and made me thirsty just to look down. The stewardess, as if in synchrony, handed out cups of mineral water. The Hassar Mountains loomed up large, with their Afghan snowcaps and Persian promise. As the pilot backed off the throttle, it came out of the speakers.

'*You picked a fine time to leave me, Lucille.*' Flooded the cabin. I think my 'WTF' came out just as loud, thirty years before it was an acronym.

"Music." Explained my adjacent seatmate.

We landed in the legendary Maracanda of Alexander the Great, Timurlane's capital of Transoxiana, sacked by Ghengis Khan, visited by Marco Polo, and one of the oldest inhabited cities in the world, Самарканд. *Samarkand*.

"Good afternoon." Said the taximan, but that was all he had prepared. The splendid sunshine made up the difference. I dropped off Serendipity at Hotel Samarkand, and made for the market. There was old goat, and something else more moribund, in the noodle soup I ate in one of the canopied stalls. The Мороженое ice cream chaser was no palate cleanser. The old goat lingered for the rest of the afternoon.

I found myself standing in the heart of the ancient city, the 'sandy place' of the Registan. It's vast central square was a place of public execution and royal proclamation, heralded by sky-held copper dzharchi '*Graah, graah, graah, graaah,*' spoken deeply. The courtyard was flanked on three sides by porcelain mosaic panels and the minarets of as many imposing madrasahs, the 'Sher-dor' *Having Tiger*, the 'Tilya-kori' *Gilded*, and the 'Ulugh Beg', grandson of Tamerlane, descended from Genghis Khan. I wandered here, under the ancient Chomsu trading dome and through the Shaybanid mausoleum, until the *Son et Lumiere* sound and light show began. Normally, I'm not a huge fan of Disney historical revisionist musical productions, and I was even more abnormally unimpressed with this one. Loud Soviet marching music, and bad lighting, entertained the mainly French horde that had congregated for the occasion. I wasn't sure what the narrator was saying in

Russian, but I knew it didn't have much to do with what had actually happened here.

Back at the hotel, the lack of hot water and manners was embellished by the sterility, bad taste and bubblegum music in the bar. Marco Polo would have turned back at this point. But then again, he went with a group.

The group in the bar was a mixture of American lawyers and vodka. Marco would have bailed. Their minder from Moscow, Alla, started to tell me about her heart defect. I asked her why.

"You're the Danish doctor that was asking directions to the synagogue." She said. We spoke about the difference between reputation and character, and closed and open minds. I let her win.

The sunrise was quiet next morning. I left the dead lawyers for a mausoleum. My gaze migrated up terracotta walls of inlaid cobalt, sky blue, and white-tiled diamonds and Arabic script, and hit the crown of an azure fluted deep-ribbed dome. Forty feet high and fifty wide, ornamented with rosettes and white spots, the turquoise cupola rose against a solemn desert. The Gur-e Amir, a roaring venous-engorged Mohammedan phallus, was the definitive *Tomb of the King*, and not the Man that Would Be. It was the inspiration and model for Timur's Mughal descendants, Humayun's tomb in Delhi, and Shah Jahan's Agra Taj Mahal.

Inside, looking up from the intricately painted onyx panels to marble stalactite cornices, and then painted plaster, my eyes hit papier-mâché cartouches and an elaborately gilded ceiling. In the middle of the floor was the solid block tombstone of dark green jade, originally from the palace of a Chinese emperor. It was inscribed. *When I rise from the dead, the world shall tremble.* In 1740, an Afshar warlord inadvertently broke the nephrite monolith in two, trying to carry it away. It was a bad omen. In 1941, Soviet archeologists opened the crypt, and found an additional inscription. *Who ever opens my tomb, shall unleash an invader more terrible than I.* Two days later, Hitler launched 'Operation Barbarossa.'

Tamerlane was an inconstant contradiction. He was exceedingly strong, and truly lame, the result of a hip injury in battle. He was a military genius, planning his campaigns so far in advance, that barley was planted for the horses to be involved in the next one, two years down the Silk Road. But he lacked political common sense, failing to leave behind governance in lands he had conquered, and needing to return to put down the inevitable rebellions. He was a patron of the arts, sponsoring the creation of a Koran that required a wheelbarrow to move it, and another so small it fit tightly on a signet ring. But he also destroyed uncountable artistic treasure in his conquests. Tamerlane never paid his soldiers; loot was their principal incentive. He portrayed himself as an emissary of peace:

'I am not a man of blood; and God is my witness that in all my wars I have never been the aggressor, and that my enemies have always been the authors of their own calamity.'

Tell it to Damascus, whose inhabitants were massacred, after he defeated the Mamluk army. Tell it to Isfahan, where one eyewitness counted more than 28 pyramids, each of over fifteen hundred heads. Tell it to the people of Delhi, where a hundred thousand Hindu captives became *'food for the sword.'* Sultan Mahmud Khan had 120 chain-mailed elephants, with poison-tipped tusks, readied for Tamerlane's attack. He hadn't counted on Timur's understanding of how easily frightened elephants were. All of his camels were stacked high with tinder and firewood, set ablaze, and prodded with iron rods. A solid flaming line of howling pain charged the Indian defenders, and their elephants rampaged in retreat, stampeding their own lines. Tell it to Bagdad, where Timur had ordered every soldier to return with at least two severed human heads; some of his men killed previously captured prisoners to meet their quota. And tell it to the three ambassadors and 1500 guards from the Ming emperor,

363

Hongwu, who were executed for daring to address Timur as a vassal.

It was during the Ming campaign, that Timur was attacked, and finally beaten, by fever and plague. He was embalmed with rose water and musk, wrapped in linen, placed in an ebony coffin, and sent to Samarkand. Where I found him. In an echo chamber sepulcher, the man who conquered an empire that extended from Turkey to western China, and had caused the deaths of seventeen million people, ended up alone, with me.

*   *   *

> "'I've tried to think", said Doc. "I want to take everything I've seen and thought and learned and reduce them and relate them and refine them until I have something of meaning, something of use. And I can't seem to do it." "Maybe you aren't ready. And maybe you need help." "What kind of help?" "There are some things a man can't do alone. I wouldn't try to do anything so big without- "Without what?" Doc asked. "Without love," said the Seer.'"
>
> John Steinbeck, *Sweet Thursday*

When Tamerlane returned from his Indian campaign in 1399, it took ninety of the original poisoned-tipped elephants, just to carry back all the precious stones. He spent them on the five-year plan construction of the Bibi Khanym mosque although, other for the large marble Koran in the middle, and the tethered rabid dog behind it, there was nothing much left of the original ambience. Back in the market, an ice cream vendor issued me another free Мороженое, when he found out I was from Canada. Down dirt roads and open sewers parallel to Kozhevennava, I came into the Necropolis of Shah-i-Zinda. Mohammed's cousin, Kusam, beheaded for his faith, allegedly took his head and went home from here, to the deep well in the Garden of Paradise. If it had been a basketball, he might have been considered a poor sport. Up on the plateau of Maracanda, I found a short plump laughing Uzbek waitress, who lured me into the Ooh-Rackmat restaurant for delicious soup, quark, and bread, and salad. Reinvigorated, I trekked to the reconstruction of Ulugh Beg's observatory. His statue looked like it had been poured out of a Hero of the Revolution cement mixer. His original sextant had been accurately calibrated along its thirty-six feet length, and kept underground to protect it from earthquakes. Religious fanatics destroyed it, in 1449. Plus ça change.

Samarkand had been the home of the first paper factory outside China. The secret of papermaking was pressed from two Chinese prisoners in the mid seven hundreds. From here it spread to the rest of the Islamic world, and on into Europe. An old Bukharan Jew greeted me on my way back down Chudzimskaya. *Shalom.* Cut off from the rest of the Hebrew world for more than 2500 years, exiled during the Assyrian captivity in the 7th century BC, the *Binai Israel* traced their ancestry to the Issachar, one of the Lost Tribes of Israel. Fifteen hundred years later, after the Arab Muslim conquest, they were considered dhimmis, and forced to wear distinctive black and yellow dress. During the annual *jizya* head tax collection, the men of every household were required to be slapped in the face, by Muslims. Alla wasn't the only one with a heart defect.

I was tiptoeing on blisters by the time I made it back to the hotel. I fell asleep. It was late when I awoke, too late for dinner. In the bar I met Christian and his wife, Ute, from Karlsruhe. He was an organic chemist, she a teacher. An acquaintance they had met earlier in the day entered a little later. Sandy was a twenty-year old blue-eyed blonde bank teller from California. In every possible way. I became disoriented, by the geographical dislocation, my missed supper, the vodka we kept pouring into each other's glasses, and her smile. Omar Khayyam had lived in Samarkand. It may have been the disinhibition, but I eventually asked her why, of all the gin joints, in all the towns, in all the world, she walked this one, in Soviet Central Asia. She told me she was trying to get as far away from a broken long-term relationship as she could. I congratulated her on her success. It may have been the disinhibition, but she told me she wasn't quite where she wanted to be yet. She asked if I had a map of my journey. I told her I would get it. She told me not to bother. She told me she would come up to see it. Some things I have trouble remembering. Some things I don't. She was like ice cream.

*   *   *

'Ice-cream is exquisite - what a pity it isn't illegal.'
Voltaire

I was too late for breakfast the next morning. At the rate I was missing meals, Mother Russia would starve me, before she had a chance to kill me any other way. In the hotel lobby, I waited for my plane to Bukhara, reading Brothers Karamazov. An old Englishman regaled me with tales of the Raj, and his travels through China and Mesopotamia, a half century earlier.

The turboprop droned through the rain, and onto the 35 degrees, of a sunlit strip of tarmac. I counted forty military helicopters, with that five-rotor Soviet overkill, as we landed in the Soghian *Place of Good Fortune,* the city Fitzroy Maclean, in a surreptitious visit to Bukhara in 1938, called 'enchanted.' Fitzroy, a young diplomat in the Moscow British Embassy, wrote that its buildings 'rivaled the finest architecture of the Italian Renaissance.' He was sleeping in its parks.

Judging by the amenities in my hotel, Fitzroy may have been onto something. They still had me listed as Danish, and puzzled themselves about where my Canadian passport had come from. I was the trout in their milk. I stowed

Serendipity, and bought some bad shashlik and worse noodle fried eggs, from a large Uzbek woman wearing a yellow Mother Hubbard, in a bazaar on the other side of town. The jars on the counter, full of swimming leeches, should have been a warning.

The next morning made the fifth consecutive day without hot water. Breakfast was dried white starch and sugar bricks. Reception was still not sure who I was, and intensified the interrogation. I left them to figure it out. Down Sovietskaya stood one of the most famous minarets in the world.

The Po-i *Grand Foundation*, a circular brick pillar, 150 feet high, was also known as the 'Tower of Death.' For centuries, criminals were casually tossed off the top. It looked like God's drill bit, overshadowing the Kalân mosque below it. Nearby was Job's spring, the Chashma-Ayub, (with a conical shaped dome, that would pierce my memory when I reached Konya, in Turkey), and the Lab-i Hauz, one of the last remaining pond ensembles, and the principle source of cooling, and water-born disease. I came to the square domed baked brick jewel box of the ninth century Ismail Samani mausoleum, preserved over the centuries by being buried in sand. The threat of destruction came not from the elements. It came from Genghis Khan, who totally razed Bukhara in 1220 AD. Genghis made Timur look like a couch potato. He was born with a blood clot grasped in his fist, an auspicious sign of great leadership, according to the prevailing nomadic portents of his time. He grew up immersed in Mongolian influences of tribal warfare, corruption, raids and perpetual acts of revenge. He executed his first rival by pouring molten silver into his ears and eyes. During his lifetime, he was responsible for wholesale massacres of civilian populations, up to forty million by some reckonings. His most vicious campaign was against the people of Khwarezmia. He diverted a river through the emperor's birthplace, erasing it from the map. He attacked Samarkand, using prisoners as human shields. When the fortress fell, Genghis reneged on his surrender terms, killing everyone, and piling their heads into pyramids, outside the city walls. The same fate met Bukhara, where Genghis told the assembled population that he had come as the 'Flail of God.' Nobles were given bloodless deaths, by being crushed under wooden platforms, while the Mongols looked on, eating their dinner. When Genghis finally met his death, by a castration administered by a Tangut princess, his funeral escort killed anyone and anything across their path, to conceal the site where he was finally buried.

I was somewhat sympathetic to the sentiment. Since my departure from Moscow, I had the increasingly distinct sensation of being observed, and finally some proof of being followed. From the morning's white starch and sugar bricks, I had been tailed by at least one, and sometimes two, moustaches, each with gold teeth and big shirt collars, hanging over the lapels of their checked sports coats. The one who looked like he would never be able to get the rings back over his knuckles, followed me into the market. I ran around four corners in the maze, and came upon a young ice cream vendor. I bought two cones, lickety-split, and continued down progressively narrower alleyways, until I didn't.

Knuckleboy came around the last hairpin turn, in a sweat. I held out an ice cream.

"Мороженое?" I offered. *Morozhenya*. He took it.

"Спасибо." He said. *Spasibo*. Thank you.

"пожалуйста." I replied. *Pozhaluysta*. Don't mention it.

"Now, fuck off." отвяжись. *Otvyazhis*. And he did.

The rest of the afternoon proceeded with more dignity. I discovered the four azure-tipped mini-minarets of the Chahar-Minar. One of the small phalluses was stacked with a stork nest. The teahouse provided sanctuary from the million children whose 'timurity' I captured on film at the Taq-i Sarrafbn. And I finally found my first Bukharan synagogue, by asking a weathered old Jew. Its thick wooden doors, painted peeling powder blue, were padlocked. I gave up, and returned to the hotel. I tried to find out why I couldn't get into the Ark, but the service desk was more interested in trying to buy my watch. I gave up, and climbed onto the roof for an eagle-eyed view of blue monuments, under the metallic sky. Storms were coming. Lighting streaks and angry grey clouds destroyed the sunset, pouring molten silver into his ears and eyes. I gave up, and retired to finish off the Brothers Karamazov. The blisters on my feet were red.

I climbed the long ramp to the Ark next morning, through the winch-raised portal, and through the Dzhuma mosque. The ten-acre redoubt had come from the legend of Siyavusha, who fell in love with the daughter of the local ruler of Afrosiaba. The girl's father agreed to permit the marriage, only if Siyavusha could build a palace, in an area bounded by a bull skin. When Siyavusha cut the hide into narrow strips, and connected all the ends, he got his girl. He also got it destroyed innumerable times, and rebuilt once by Omar Khayyam himself. Avicenna was a patron if its library. I was impressed with the old Islamic and Russian vassal state memorabilia, with its double-headed eagle crest, and single-minded regal paraphernalia.

Inside the Chai house in Registan Square sat a hundred exotic mullahs, with spirited stares, praises to Allah before sipping, hand-covered hearts and sweeping bows, *Salaam* welcomes, and their fierce collective individualism. There was no safer place in town, to have a cup of tea.

I went to the Synagogue for the third and last time. The padlock was unlocked, and the heavy peeling powder blue door was ajar. I entered a courtyard to make the acquaintance of Miriam and Istvan, an old couple from Budapest, and an older Uzbek Jew, who would have looked like my Uncle Morley, if Morley had disappeared for two and a half millennia. Everyone was surprised to see everyone. Shaloms turned into introductions, and a communal reading in Hebrew, from ancient yellowed pages. There was simplicity and poverty, and an immediate acceptance of a wandering Jew, living the Diaspora of two tribes, cut off and united in suffering, through space and time. Inside was a different ark, and another word under the Shalom sign on the wall. мир. *Peace.* Unfortunately, my time was too short and too long there and, once again, my plane almost left without me.

I watched a little girl playing with her puppy at the airport. The plane and my forgotten passport arrived on the tarmac at the same time. Gordon Lightfoot's *Sundown* played on the hotel muzac system, back in Tashkent. I almost fell asleep in the root beer disinfectant in my bathtub.

I spent the last day in Soviet Central Asia in the market, among the lines of crowds, and crowded lines. Yuri Andropov's motorcade drove by with police bullhorns, and an East German delegation. They were waving out the window at the rows of people. But the people weren't queuing to see the communist parade go by. They were lining up for ice cream.

Hungry Butterfly

'You risked your life, but what else have you ever risked? Have you ever risked disapproval? Have you ever risked economic security? Have you ever risked a belief? I see nothing particularly courageous in risking one's life. So you lose it, you go to your hero's heaven and everything is milk and honey til the end of time. Right? You get your reward and suffer no earthly consequences. That's not courage. Real courage is risking something that might force you to rethink our thoughts and suffer change and stretch consciousness. Real courage is risking one's clichés.'

Tom Robbins, *Another Roadside Attraction*

You wouldn't have expected his laugh. It came out of him, too lusty and powerful for the size of his lungs. '*Ho, ha! Ha! Ha! ha!*'

I first found him in my cab, on the way to catch my plane to Kiev. He didn't laugh then, because he was sleeping. Hard to wake up, almost drugged he seemed. His T-shirt was a sailboat emblazoned with 'Okinawa.' He looked like a shipwrecked Japanese version of Yoda, decades before Yoda existed. Short, he was, and bearded, with long wild black hair. He stumbled out of the taxi, and random walked to the Aeroflot counter. I followed him, bemused, trying to figure out what a Nipponese gnome was doing, wandering around in a Tashkent transit trance.

I sat beside two Intourist guides, Helena and Yalena, on the flight. We shared paprika-sprinkled cucumbers, and mutual interest and mistrust. An IL-62 almost clipped us, as we landed on the tarmac in Kiev. A hundred raw Uzbek army recruits boarded our bus to the terminal. Yalena asked me if I thought they were prisoners. I mentioned Afghan carpets and ice cream. My Volga limo took me to check-in, at the concrete hotel cylinder they had booked me into.

'Purpose of visit?' Asked the form. I crossed off 'business' and wrote 'pleasure.' My first night of celebration in Kiev was in a hot bath. Tipping my head back, in the steaming phenolic warmth, I could hear it, three floors down at Reception. '*Ho, ha! Ha! Ha! ha!*'

I confess some ambivalence about visiting Ukraine. My hometown had a large population of émigrés, and many of my classmates were third generation. They had brilliant gardens, and I remember friendly rose-cheeked babas, loading us up with gigantic purple beets. I was fascinated with the history of the Kieven Rus, the Cossacks, and the *Holodomor* famine that killed millions of Ukrainians in the 1930s. The ambivalence came from the other part of its history. My grandmother was from Ukraine. It was difficult for her to speak about the place or the people, and I could sense her antipathy, on those rare occasions when she did.

There was a commemoration of some kind, outside my hotel next morning. Old military men in too big hats, and little girls with too big white rose pompoms pasted on each temple, joined in a mutual marshal march, in the round square below. As unobtrusively as possible, I threaded through them down Shevchenko, to an Orthodox mass at Volodymyr's Cathedral. Inside the million bricks were almost as many babushkas, with as many candles, flickering by Venetian mosaics, colorful frescoes, and richly garbed Orthodox priests, dispensing bodies and bloods. The power of the operatic choir behind them was spinal.

I emerged into a downpour, the light still so much brighter outside the Cathedral that my eyes needed some time to adjust. Twenty kopeks bought just about as much erudition in the Museums of Russian and Eastern Art, and Western Art. I wandered through the Bessarabia covered market, to the Monastery of the Caves. One of those monuments that require a lifetime of study to fully appreciate, I didn't have another one.

In the early 11th century, a monk named Anthony, from Mount Athos in Greece, settled in an old cave, on the slopes outside Kiev. Half a millennium later, foreign travelers wrote that the *Lavra* catacombs extended underground for hundreds of kilometers, as far as Moscow and Novgorod. Painted saints with solid gilt reflector halos, in white Rococo frames on a powder blue façade, stood on top of each other under two gold cupolas, to welcome and warn, like a large birthday cake for Jesus. I left its towering belfry for an even larger secular monument, on the right bank of the Dnieper. You could see the metallic massiveness of the two hundred foot high mother of all Motherland statues for miles, still defiantly resisting the Nazi aggression that required her construction. Her sword alone weighed in at nine tons. Meandering around the 25-acre complex of World War II tanks and planes, and the giant bowled 'Flame of Glory,' I was approached by two black marketers, in a stealthy attempt to change money. I pointed to my sneakers, and snucked off.

Back in the uterine lobby of the Cement Cylinder, I reencountered Yelena. She told me to meet her in the bar, but she didn't turn up. Someone else did.

He was trying to order food from the bartender in English, but it was too broken for either of them. I ended up mediating. When he realized that it was only a drinking establishment, it exploded out of him, a simultaneous exhalation and inspiration. '*Ho, ha! Ha! Ha! ha!*' I had my man. The bar crowd winced.

"Wink." I said, extending a hand.

"Hungry Butterfly." He countered. He had a grip like his laugh.

Forgetting about the relative alcohol dehydrogenase deficiency common in Asians, I bought Hungry Butterfly a vodka tonic. He opened like a lotus.

Hungry was a 22 year-old second son. His family owned a chicken and pork factory, in Kitakyushu. Hungry's father expected him to join his older brother at the plant, as soon as he graduated from economics in Tokyo. The good news was that Hungry successfully obtained his degree. The bad news was that Hungry successfully obtained his degree. Hungry told his father that he didn't want to work in a meat processing plant. His father was unimpressed. He asked Hungry what work he wanted to do. Hungry told his father that he didn't want to work, at all. His father was unhappy. He asked Hungry what he wanted to do, instead of work. Hungry told his father that he wanted to travel around the world. His father was furious.

Hungry had saved about five thousand dollars, over many years. He filled his knapsack, grew a beard (as much as possible, anyway), and left without telling a soul. Speaking no English and less Russian, Hungry spent half his money for a ticket on the Trans-Siberian railroad, and snucked off around the world backwards. '*Ho, ha! Ha! Ha! ha!*'

Hungry didn't expect anything. He certainly didn't expect to meet me. I told Hungry I liked his name, especially the 'butterfly' part. I asked him about how he was travelling. It turns out he had a lot in common with Sora, the 'Seer of Fukuoka,' whom I had met in Paris. Whenever Hungry would get off the train, he would check into his hotel and sleep, until it was time to board the next one. We had a chat. As the tonic took hold, so did his wonderment at what he had done, and what he was doing.

"*Ho, ha! Ha! Ha! ha!*" Boomed across the darkened room. The bar crowd winced. A man in a checkered sports coat came over to our table. He asked if there was anything wrong.

"With what?" I asked.

"With your friend." He said. I told him that Hungry had an incurable condition called TER, 'Terminal Revelational Epiphany,' and it would be inadvisable to provoke an exacerbation. The checkered sports coat snucked off.

Hungry showed me his passport. It had one stamp in it, so far. I told him he looked like his passport photo. And that meant he needed the journey.

"*Ho, ha! Ha! Ha! ha!*" He roared.

The bar crowd winced.

*   *   *

'No monument stands over Babi Yar. A steep cliff only, like the rudest headstone... surrounded and trapped... blood spills, and runs upon the floors, the chiefs of bar and pub rage... and reek of vodka and of onion... Wild grasses rustle over Babi Yar... like one long soundless scream... I'm every old man executed here... every child murdered... '
Yevgeni Yevtushenko , Babi Yar

Hungry Butterfly was likely still sleeping when I found Yalena, waiting for me at breakfast. We agreed to meet back at the Concrete Cylinder for lunch, and I set off to see St. Sophia, and the grave of Yaraslav the Wise. His monument was a rocky imitation of Peter the Great's Bronze Horseman in Leningrad, without any of the effort that had gone into moving the Thunder Stone.

I climbed the steep hill of Andriyivsky Descent, the site of the Castle of Richard the Lionheart; and St. Andrew's church, the place above the Dnieper where he is alleged to have erected a cross. Five gilded jade green rocket spires perched on their Corinthian column boosters, above a powder blue and white and gilt baroque basilica. More than a thousand slabs of gold were used, above the iron floor slabs that came from Moscow. Cracks in the foundation grew larger every year.

Over a lunch of soup and cold cuts, Yelena asked me what my plans were for the afternoon. I told her I was going to the Historical Museum. I didn't tell her I was going somewhere else first.

My cab arrived at a beautiful dandelion-carpeted couloir. Yellow undulations danced with green waves, in a soft breeze. It was dead quiet.

In the early autumn of 1941, a notice was posted in Kiev, in Russian and Ukrainian:

'Kikes of the city of Kiev and vicinity! On Monday, September 29, you

375

are to appear by 08:00 a.m. with your possessions, money, documents, valuables, and warm clothing at Dorogozhitskaya Street, next to the Jewish cemetery. Failure to appear is punishable by death.'

On the eve of the Nazi invasion of the Soviet Union, Kiev had a Jewish population of 175,000. The Nazis expected 5,000 to comply with the order. Instead, more than 30,000 arrived beside the cemetery, at the appointed hour. Ukrainian neighbors participated in the festivities. The Jews thought they were being sent for resettlement. When they were lined up and through a series of checkpoints, they moved slowly towards what they thought was a train. When they were ordered to relinquish their luggage and other possessions, they believed it would be sent in a baggage car, later. When they gave up their coats, they were reassured that the coaches were heated. Then they were told to take off their shoes. The sound of machine gun fire became audible nearby. When the ones, who realized what was happening, asked to leave, their papers were checked. If the person was Jewish, they were forced to remain in line. At subsequent stations, enclosed with barbed wire and guarded by Ukrainian collaborators, they were asked to remove additional articles of clothing and place them in a designated pile. Then, emerging into an area, overgrown with grass, they were asked to remove their underwear. When some hesitated, they were pushed, then kicked, then beaten, then helpless. The Nazis took advantage of the fact that no naked human is capable of resistance. Only submission. They were counted out and driven forward, in groups of ten, down a corridor about four feet wide, lined by laughing soldiers wielding clubs and knuckledusters and shouting '*Schnell! Schnell!*,' as if it were some circus act. Brutal blows descended on heads, backs and shoulders from two sides, drawing blood. Drunk in a fury of sadistic rage, the soldiers beat men women and children in the most vulnerable places, ribs, belly and groin. Screaming and crying, the Jews exited the gauntlet, into a gully about 150 meters long and 30 meters wide, and 15 meters deep. The ravine was an enormous, almost majestic, deep wide chasm, like a mountain gorge. Sounds made on one side could be only scarcely heard on the other. They looked down and their heads swam, they were so high up. Beneath them was a sea of bodies covered in blood. At the bottom of the chasm they were handed off to members of the *Schutzpolizei* and forced to lie down on their stomachs, on top of increasing layers of corpses. A police marksman walked across the bodies to the next victim's neck. Then he shot the next ten, and the next ten. For two days. According to the *Einsatzgruppe Operational Situation Report No. 101*, on the 29th and 30th of September, 33,771 Jews were killed at Babi Yar. Their money, valuables, underwear, and clothing were given to local ethnic Germans.

What happened two years later was pure salinity. Before the Nazis retreated from Kiev, they made a concerted effort to conceal their atrocities. More than three hundred chained prisoners were forced to exhume and burn the corpses, in '*Sonderaktion 1005*.' Some had to dig into the graves. Others were given hooks to pull out the tangled corpses, from under the chin. Sometimes the heads came off. Sometimes two or three bodies came out at once. Sometimes axes were needed. The lower layers had to be dynamited. The Nazis drank vodka to drown out the smell and the visuals; the prisoners weren't even permitted to wash their hands. A few were tasked with pulling gold-filled teeth and conducting final cavity searches, looking for valuables. Funeral pyres were constructed for thermal efficiency. Tombstones from the Jewish cemetery were laid flat on the ground, and piled with wood. The first layer of bodies was placed on top of the wood, with their heads on the outside. The second layer of bodies was positioned with their heads extending out the other side. The layering was repeated several times, resulting in approximately two thousand bodies in each pile. The hair of the projecting heads was soaked in gasoline, and set alight. German engineering. Prisoners used other larger tombstones from the cemetery to crush the bones that came out of the ashes, and the ashes were sieved one more time, to ensure that no gold had escaped. The ashes were scattered, on nearby farms. To this day, some Ukrainians refuse to eat the cabbages grown there.

The *Sonderaktion* had taken six weeks. The prisoners knew they were next. Shackled, starved, and covered in filth, gated in at night with a large padlock, covered by a machine gun in a wooden tower, and infiltrated by at least one informer, death made a final turn in their rearview mirror. They often found small items from the victims, and began to collect scissors, tools, and especially keys. They were looking for the one that would open the padlock. The day before they learned they were all to be executed, they found it. Only fifteen succeeded in escaping. Only ten percent of the original Jewish ethnically cleansed have been identified. The memorial I saw there commemorated the 'Fascist victims' and, it is true that other lives were taken at Babi Yar. But to find no recognition of the single largest massacre and pure genocide that had occurred among those dandelions in that abyss, was abyssmal.

I walked in stunned silence to the Historical Museum four kilometers away. It was accurate to within a hundred years. I arrived back at the Cement Cylinder, too late for my designated drive to the train station. Intourist had their usual spasm, and squeezed me into a minibus full of Swiss for the short haul. They hurried me onto the Odessa-bound train, and into a compartment with two passengers.

"*Ho, ha! Ha! Ha! ha!*" Bellowed out of the short one. It was Hungry Butterfly, who had slept the entire two days in Kiev, was headed to Odessa to sleep another, and would return on the night train to Kiev, likely for another great wink of eternity.

The second passenger was Erica, a twenty-year old dentistry student from Odessa, whose beauty was causing Hungry a considerable amount of feverishness. He wrote her name in Japanese, and asked if she could read it. She wrote down his name in Cyrillic, and asked if he could read that.

'*Ho, ha! Ha! Ha! ha!*' A mile-long touché bonsai, right on cue. I wrote my name in English. They could both read it.

"My team wins." I said. A samovar came down the corridor, and we shared cups of chai, and life's impressions. At a more remote rural station, an old Ukrainian babushka was added to our compartment. She stared at me. I settled into my bunk, hoping that the rocking of the rails would carry me to sleep. But the train wasn't carrying me to sleep. It was carrying me to Odessa. My grandmother was from Odessa. It was difficult for her to speak about the place or the people, and I could sense her antipathy, on those rare occasions when she did. The ambivalence came from the other part of its history.

I looked across at the old babushka. She was wearing a silver object around her neck. I looked more closely. It was an antique silver mezuzah, from the entrance of a Jewish home. It wasn't hers. She stared. There was no ambivalence.

Hungry was difficult to wake when we pulled into the terminal in Odessa. I finally got him out of his bunk. Brave girl that she was, Erica agreed to meet us at the Krasnaya restaurant, later that evening. Hungry and I were whisked off to Hotel Chornoye More, where he had difficulty understanding why they wouldn't give him a room to sleep in, even if he was taking the night train back to Kiev. After a bliny and sour cream breakfast, and draining the black backpacker bathtub water off my laundry, I gave him mine. There was a message, to report to the Intourist Inservice Insouciance downstairs. I left Hungry, already slumbering.

The reprehensible was clearly agitated.

"How did you enter the Soviet Union without a booked flight?" She asked.

"You let me in, overland." I said. "I thought you would just let me out, overland." She told me there had clearly been a mistake. I would have to fly out of Moscow. I told her I didn't want to fly out of Moscow. I wanted to take the train to Romania. She told me there were no trains to Romania. I paid two rubles for a call to the Canadian Embassy in Moscow.

"It just might be their bureaucracy." They said. Your tax dollars at work.

I told her I was happy to stay in Odessa. She went quiet. No one had probably ever told her that they were more than happy not to leave the USSR. She issued me a train ticket to Bucharest.

Hungry and I met Erica at seven o'clock. We had an evening of magnificent détente, courtesy of two bottles of champagne, cold mushrooms and onions, chicken salad, beef stroganoff, and chicken Kiev. Hungry ate a steak while we weren't looking. The band played brilliant jazz, and we all danced all over my black market rubles, until it was time for Hungry to leave for his night train back to Kiev. We bowed, me a smidge lower. Then we hugged and he left. I took Erica to a cab, and walked the random walk back to the hotel, and my diary.

'This is the beginning of your story, Hungry. May your bed be eternally soft, your stomach hard, your horizon long, and your baptism short. May you find your Zen, and forgiveness greet you on your return to the Rising Sun. And when your beard grows white, may you still remember.'

'You may have a Japanese elf named 'Hungry Butterfly' drop in to say hello sometime in early autumn. He's going around the world backwards.'

Postcard to Parents, May 1983

"What's the second act of the hero's journey, Uncle Wink?" Asked Sam.

"The adventure, Sammy. The adventure." Uncle Wink looked wistful.

"What kind of adventure? He asked.

"The adventure that the hero is ready for is the one he gets. I was ready for many, so that's what I got. The classic hero's adventure begins with a road of trials, a series of tests, which begins his transformation, often occurring in threes. Sometimes he fails. He undergoes an internal union of the opposites inside himself, resulting in an unconditional love, or 'hieros gamos.' He encounters the physical temptations of life, intending to lure the hero to stray from his quest. It is usually a woman who acts as the temptress, along the approach to the inmost cave. The centre point of the journey is the crisis, the ordeal, the confrontation with, and reinitiation by, what had been the ultimate power in the hero's life. The result is the apotheosis of the hero, and his death and rebirth in the bliss of his divine knowledge. His reward is the ultimate boon, his fulfillment, his achievement of the goal of the quest."

"Was the adventure dangerous, Uncle Wink?" Sam asked.

"Like the edge of a razor, Sam."

The Buried Dreams of Baba Rhea

'This Government has found occasion to express, in a friendly spirit, but with much earnestness, to the Government of the Czar, its serious concern because of the harsh measures now being enforced against the Hebrews in Russia.'

Benjamin Harrison

A long time ago in a far away place, lived a pretty four-year old girl. The town was pretty too, with tree-lined cobbled streets, sun-reflected Baroque townhouses, and a crystalline atmosphere, that always reminded her that the sea was at the bottom of the hill. Something horrible came off that sea, however, that bleached the colors from her childhood memories. A ship of the King mutinied, in support of an unsuccessful peasant revolt. The King crushed the uprising mercilessly, for he understood its potential. The townspeople roamed the streets in frustrated anger. They looted, raped and killed neighbors who had lived with them for centuries. People who believed they had finally found a haven after 2000 years of forced migrations. Frightened by the violence, the parents of our four-year-old girl decided to leave their home, for a land across the sea. They sold their possessions to buy steamship passage, and carried what they could. The salt of the sea dispersed the salt of their tears. But their souls were still there, a long time ago in a far away place. The pretty four-year-old girl grew up in an alien land, in a language without soft curves. Her parents had traded cold-blooded neighbors for a cold-blooded climate. She married a young man of her tribe, a butcher, bore him two children, and worked hard to give him what had been taken from her when she was young. Her husband died early, slowly and in pain, leaving her to raise their daughters alone and in poverty. She lived to see a grandson, the first child of her youngest daughter, walk and talk and do well in school. She loved to make tea, teach him card games, and buy him toys she could ill afford. When she died in quiet dignity, she had perhaps forgotten that town, with the tree-lined cobbled streets, sun-reflected Baroque townhouses, and a crystalline atmosphere, that always reminded her that the sea was at the bottom of the hill. But her grandson had not. Seventy-seven years later he arrived on a morning train. He walked her cobbled streets, silently admired her townhouses, breathed her air, and came to understand the soul of a pretty four-year old girl, now buried in a distant land. And he was very happy, and very sad. The salt of the sea had dispersed the salt of her tears. But her soul was still there, a long time ago in a far away place.

It was the tuberculosis. The reason she used so much face powder. The tuberculosis had affected her cheeks. Baba Rhea looked like a kabuki doll. The card game we played was called kaluki. She would make tea, and we would settle in for another long tournament of kabuki kaluki. She chained smoked *duMaurier*. You could tell when she was cheating by how hard she inhaled, and the pattern of her exhaust. If her vapor trail came out long and straight, she was worried. If it billowed in clouds, she had a good hand. I used to ask myself what kind of grandmother would cheat her own grandson playing cards. The answer wasn't in the old sepia photograph of her before she got the tuberculosis. She was a stunning Venus of baroque Romanoff Russian elegance, with round cheeks and cats eyes, and the jewelry that would eventually disappear, into other parts of the family. She wouldn't have cheated at cards. Then came the Potemkin uprising and the pogroms and the starvation and the tuberculosis. All of her university professor uncles were shot.

She crossed the Atlantic from a cosmopolitan city in a Mediterranean climate, to a Canadian prairie conurbation forty below zero, the point at which Celsius and Fahrenheit were the same temperature. All the joys of life were frozen there, and she found herself, after all that distance and time and energy, once again surrounded by Ukrainians. My grandmother was from Ukraine. It was difficult for her to speak about the place or the people, and I could sense her antipathy, on those rare occasions when she did. The ambivalence came from the other part of its history. It took her 34 year-old husband six months to die of his colon cancer. My own mother told me she could never forget the smell. My father's mother was cold to Baba Rhea, colder than the climate. When I was born, Baba Rhea tied a red ribbon around my little finger, to ward off the evil spirits that she thought were still chasing us. Six years later, she bought me a space gun when I asked her to. It took as many of those big batteries, just to make the noise and sparks that came out of it. My parents were horrified at what she paid. She said it didn't matter. And that's when I started to let her win. So she would billow clouds instead of inhaling hard. So she wouldn't have to cheat.

'I have reflected many times upon our rigid search. It has shown me that everything is illuminated in the light of the past. It is always along the side of us, on the inside, looking out.'

Jonathan Safran Foer, *Everything is Illuminated*

*   *   *

'In the same proportion Russia is the misfortune of Europe and the Israelites.'

Isaac Mayer Wise

It was just the way she had described it. I started at the bottom of the stairs. Originally the Boulevard steps, the Giant Staircase, or the Richelieu steps, they're now called the Primorsky Stairs. When I climbed them, they were still the Potemkin Stairs. Like the Mediterranean architecture, the staircase is an optical illusion. From the bottom you can see only stairs; from the top, only landings. They seem longer looking up because they're wider at the bottom. An English criminal fugitive, John Upton, constructed them. The Trieste green sandstone that Baba Rhea walked on, had been replaced by rose-grey granite, and the landings covered in asphalt, but the harbor view expanded in the same way as I climbed into the sunshine.

"You must be from ship. Change money?" Came from over my shoulder.

At the top of the stairs was the bronze statue of Armand Emmanuel Sophie Septimanie de Vignerot du Plessis, 5ᵗʰ Duc de Richelieu. Richelieu had been on the wrong side of the French Revolution. One of Marie Antoinette's dragoons, he became the *Premier Gentilhomme de la Chambre,* for the daily *lever* and *coucher* rituals of Louis XVI. When it all went sideways in France, Richelieu went to work for Catherine the Great, who had taken the Ottoman fortress of Khadzhibei, in the Russo-Turkish War of 1792, and founded Odessa on the site two years later. She made Richelieu Governor, before he eventually became Prime Minister of France. He was Baba Rhea's connection to Catherine the Great and Marie Antoinette. And mine.

Maybe I just wanted to see it through Baba Rhea's eyes, but I did. There were influences of French and Italian Art Nouveau, Renaissance, and Classicist, in Odessa's mélange of streets and arcades. I inhaled the cosmopolitan air that Pushkin described as 'filled with all of Europe,' and exhaled it in billowing clouds. Lenin with love songs. Russian Riviera. I wandered the most romantic place in the USSR.

Old painted English letters sat fading, on the ground level red-trimmed windows of a white brick building I passed.

'O. S. Brown Steamship Agents.' I wondered if they had brought her.

Down Primorsky Boulevard were the Naval and Archeological Museums, with a nice Egyptian collection in the latter. I came to the Italian Baroque Opera house, with a large arched red, white and black mural of Lenin in its upper colonnade, facing the sea. Lenin and I would both be gone the next day.

The Opera house had been managed by the medical inspector, who would announce fictitious epidemics, and quarantine newly arrived passengers at their own cost, whenever ticket sales were low. The luxurious rococo hall acoustics could deliver a whisper to any part of the theatre. The Edison Company had supplied the novel electric illumination and, during the hot summers, wagonloads of ice and straw would be dropped down a 35-foot shaft, to subterranean vents beneath the seats.

In 1819 Odessa had been made a free port and, despite the Soviet stranglehold, the shops up and down Beribasovskaya were still well provisioned.

As I strolled around Odessa at dusk, I tried to imagine how anyone who lived in this kind of light, could raise a voice or a hand in hatred. But for that, I could have been born and still living here, now all buried dreams.

My last breakfast in the USSR was a rerun of my first. It was as if they knew they could just stop trying. I was back in the land of white bricks and nyet. No matter what I asked Olga for, she didn't have any. Judging by the size of her, I may have been just too late. I left a kopek tip. After confirming my late afternoon departure with the disservice desk, I went up to my room to find the very same kopek on my bureau. You would be forgiven for thinking that an organization operating at this level of efficiency, couldn't come up with an egg and a cup of coffee.

The day before I had walked down Yevreyskaya, *Jewish Street*. Today I was determined to see Baba Rhea's synagogue. Odessa had an important Jewish community during the 19th century, and by 1897 Jews comprised almost forty per cent of the city population. It became a hotbed of intellectual activity, and one of the birthplaces of the Zionist movement. The reason for that was fairly simple. There were pogroms in 1821, 1859, 1871, 1881 and 1905. The Tsarist police would disarm Jewish self-defense units, to clear the path for Ukrainian murderers.

Despite this, in Russian culture, the Jews of Odessa were viewed as sharp-witted, street-wise, and eternally optimistic. They undoubtedly cheated at cards. They had their own dialect, of wise and subtle dissension, and opportunism, that unwittingly pointed out the flaws and absurdities of the Soviet regime. The Jew in the jokes was an endearing character, and always prevailed against adverse circumstance. During the first six months of Nazi occupation, eighty percent of the 210,000 Jews in the region were killed, along with the folklore. The blackness of the Black Sea overflowed into the city.

I walked a few blocks, before asking a taxi driver to take me to the Synagogue. He pulled up beside an iron-spiked metal fence, behind which stood a nondescript Gothic gray building. There was no one at the powder blue guard post booth. I walked in through the open gate. It seemed deserted. Then I caught a whisper of mournfulness, on the wind. Every so often, with a change in breeze direction, I would catch a few notes of liturgical Yiddish music. I followed it, around corners and passageways, expecting to emerge, at any moment, onto a plain of piety. Instead, I tripped right into a 1920's backroom Chicago mob scene. I had to rub my eyes, to make sure they weren't lying to me. Seated, around a big rectangular table, were eight gangsters with peaked hats and pin stripes, chain-smoking Marlboros. At the head of the boardroom, was the boss, with the Sanyo tape player and the pinkie ring. No one looked up. The pinkie finger went up, a sign for me to wait. I waited.

When the song ended, the pinkie pressed the stop button on the tape player, and everyone turned his gaze to me.

"Shalom aleichem." I said.

"Aleichem shalom." I got back. I was in the right place, after all.

In the ultimate historical irony, we only had German in common. The boss was the de facto leader of the synagogue, but he was not an ordained rabbi. He told me that, despite still having a population of 100,000 coreligionists, Odessa still had no *rebbe*. I asked him how he resolved religious issues. He told me he had a telephone. He called Moscow. His hero was Meyer Lansky. We were clearly in trouble. They took me into the main part of the synagogue. It was beautiful. In this room Aleichem's fictional character, Mendel, came to plague God with unanswerable questions. In this room Moussorgsky and Rimsky-Korsakov were influenced by the music they heard. In this room was the only voice of hope, during the chaos of the Soviet Civil War, from 1918 to 1921. The painted sun over the ark had come a long way. I left a donation. They left me with the same word they had left me with in every synagogue I had visited in the Soviet Union. Мир. *Peace*. It was just 'Shalom,' in Russian. Hard to come by.

I returned to the Intourist desk at Hotel Chornoye More, to reconfirm my émigré status for that evening.

"What were your impressions of the synagogue?" She asked. You can't play Russian roulette if all the chambers are loaded. The young peach who accompanied me to the train station was new on the job. She asked me not to make her nervous. I told her she would have to stop being so beautiful, and bought her a citron. My compartment contained the Chernovtsky party commissar and his entourage, so I elected to spend my time in the restaurant car. It was here I met the waiter, Alex, ex-boxer, ex-soldier, ex-ponent of humor and outrage. He was graphic in his description of his exploits with the blushing waitress. He brought me a large bowl of almost inedible goat noodle soup. Even more unfortunately, he opened a bottle of Stolichnaya, and brought two glasses. I asked him if he was allowed to drink on the job. There was nothing I could do to make him understand the question. We laughed through the sunny richness of Moldova.

I arrived in Kishinev, and spent four hours watching the tanks go by. Inside the station was a carnival freak show, a geneticist's dream. My last twenty kopeks procured an amazing meal of smoked salmon, beef stroganoff, and coffee. What I hadn't known about Kishinev was that, two years before Baba Rhea's family experienced the Potemkin pogrom, the Russian anti-Semitic newspaper, *Bessarabian*, published a blood libel incitement. The day following Russian

Easter, local priests led a mob on a well laid out plan of riot and murder. 'Kill the Jews!' echoed through the streets. The Jews were taken unaware, and slaughtered like sheep. Babies were literally torn to pieces. By sunset the streets were piled with corpses. The massacre went on for three days, and no authority interfered with the brutality. The Nazis shot surviving relatives, and the next generation, thirty-five years later.

I couldn't believe the sumptuousness of my compartment, on the train to Romania. Everything that protruded was baroque gold ornate; everything that didn't was regal red. They clearly wanted me out of the country, and were willing to escort me out with bourgeois accoutrements. The bed was pure marshmallow, but I wasn't going to use it much. At midnight, Natasha brought me forms to fill in, and told me to dress for the party. An hour later the Moldovan GoodCopBadCop duo rapped on the door. While the GoodCop expressed geysers of peace and friendship, BadCop went through everything I owned. He searched the cabin so thoroughly, I couldn't have hidden a doubt. GoodCop left, only to return with a guestbook for me to write impressions of my trip. While Badcop took apart and reassembled one of the light fixtures, Goodcop regaled me with his Cuban friendship missions, and the guiding light of Communism in world history. Meanwhile, Badcop had found Sasha's Moscow address. I never did find out how that one ended, but I hoped for the best. They reopened the guestbook as they were leaving. I could tell they were puzzled with what I had written. It wasn't much.
Baba Rhea.

'You only have power over people so long as you don't take everything away from them. But when you've robbed a man of everything, he's no longer in your power- he's free again.'

Aleksandr Solzhenitsyn

Soap

'I came to Bucharest two years ago with a legion of conquering heroes.
I <u>leave</u> with a troupe of gigolos and racketeers.'
                    German Field Marshal August von Mackensen

The new direction of the train woke me. Vertical. I looked out the pitch-black window. I could see the orange glow of the crane operator's cigarette, thirty feet below. My balance played catch up with the aerobatics. No one told me they would be hoisting all the carriages onto new flatcars. The Romanians had narrower gauge railroads. But there were still two big wide Russian sets of tracks, going all the way to Bucharest. Just in case.

The moment my coach landed on its new bed, I was dragged out of mine. This time it was the Romanians. For three o'clock in the morning, he was dapper. Short, dark moustache, slicked-back hair, three piece suit, and Italian shoes polished to such a shine, you would have seen his reflection, if he hadn't been a bloodsucker. Dollar Dracula. His shiny head was crammed with broken French, and his battered briefcase with *valuta*, for my mandatory currency exchange, from US greenbacks to worthless lei. He drooled, when I pulled real money out of my belt. Whenever I asked a question, he would cock his head, grin, and snap his fingers. *Prest-o change-o*. Tilt. Smile. Snap. Slide. Voila. I swear he changed into a bat while leaving.

They woke me at six a.m., to change for a train to Rădăuţi, the town the other grandparents emigrated from. It was listed as my destination. It was in the middle of nowhere, in Bukovina. After the night I had just been through, I decided to see Bucharest first. Romania was different from the Soviet Union. They didn't just throw me off the train. When I next awoke, it was after seven. The peasants farming outside my moving window, looked like they were playing through the world's biggest golf course. We pulled into Bucharest midmorning. The Soviet piglet who cut in front of me, in the Information booth queue, got a mouthful of the Russian words I had cultivated, for such occasions. It brought a head tilt, grin and a finger snap from the old Romanian woman behind the counter. She booked me into the Marna, a 'special hotel.' Five stories up, a bald eagle with thick spectacles, showed me to the special unmade closet, with a view of the adjacent brick wall. I'm usually thankful for an upgrade. I met Stefan in the Hungarian Embassy, who invited me home to meet his three dogs and three 'assistants.'

"This is a house with no women." He said. And all the alarms went off so loud, I'm sure they must have heard them. He scrambled to show me a picture of a girlfriend in Esbjerg. I made a graceful exit, careful not to appear too graceful, and caught a bus back to the Ritz. Later, through unlit streets, I found a buffet express, for a salad and a memory. Mămăligă is the same as polenta, but not the way the Romanian side of the family made it. Cornmeal in the old Austro-Hungarian Empire wasn't a hoity-toit splash of color for some Piedmontese pheasant and matching Barolo, it was staple peasant soul food. What potatoes were to the Irish, and rice was to the Chinese, Aztec corn Mămăligă was to my father's parents, Jacob and Rose. And I was heading to that part of old Austro-Hungary, where they had been born.

But I had diverted to Bucharest to see the place. Between the two World Wars, it was known as the 'Little Paris of the East,' because of its architectural elegance, and the sophistication of its elite. Both of those had changed dramatically. The only thing Bucharest had in common with Paris the year I was there, was that I was there. The man most responsible, for both the architectural and hierarchical misfortunes, was still running the country.

Nicolae Ceaușescu had created a pervasive personality cult, bestowing on himself the titles of 'Conducător', *Leader*, and 'Geniul din Carpați,' *The Genius of the Carpathians*. Salvador

Dalí sent Ceaușescu a telegram, congratulating him on his introduction of the 'presidential scepter.' The Communist Party daily, Scînteia, published the message, unaware that it was a work of satire. Ceaușescu razed an entire historic quarter of the city to build a megalomaniacal 'Palace of the Parliament.' He made abortion illegal and divorce difficult, creating a crisis of child abandonment, and the overflowing of orphanages. He compounded this by allowing transfusions of untested blood, creating an epidemic of pediatric AIDS. He bought into the Juche philosophy of North Korean President Kim Il Sung, and initiated a hard line ideological remodeling of Romanian society, into a Socialist Realism nightmare. After borrowing thirteen billions dollars from the West, he decided that it needed to be repaid quickly, regardless of the consequences. During my time in Romania, there were already electricity blackouts, and long breadlines in front of empty food shops. Ceaușescu was shown on state TV, in staged scenes of plenty. The produce he inspected was from Hungary, or made from painted polystyrene. Well-fed cows were transported across the country, in anticipation of his farm visits. Unfortunately, Romanians would have to wait another six and a half years to shake him off. The image of his uncomprehending expressive response to boos and heckling, during a mass meeting on December 21, 1989, was a critical portent of his vulnerability. The firing squad soldiers that had volunteered to execute him and his wife, on Christmas day, didn't even wait for the order. They were just opening their presents early, feeling the love.

Bucharest's version of the Arcul de Triumf had only three broken down Dacias drive around it, during the time it took me to walk by my way back from the curved shingles, spires and thatched roofs of the relocated houses, churches and windmills, in the Village Museum. I ended up among the artists and vendors on Calea Lispani, eating meatballs and bread. Down the street was the Historical Museum, with thirty four rooms of Romanian crown jewels, the Pietroasele treasure, and Vlad Dracul and his son, Vlad Țepeș. At that time, there were also ten rooms of Ceaușescu.

Stefan's assistants, Basil, Kiss, and Dominici intercepted me on my way to the post office. They went to great pains to convince me of their heterostatus, and we went for a beer in a sunny café, to celebrate. We spoke of East-West politics, the horrors of their recent attempt to emigrate, and their plans to try it all over again. The shorthaired eavesdroppers who took adjacent tables kept their voices low. We agreed to meet later. I returned to the Marna in a blackout, and hiked the five floors for a rest.

The Bucharest evening escorted me to the Architect's Club. Stefan and his assistants were already there, sitting with other friends. All of them spoke English, and were planning to emigrate. We drank vodka, and danced to the disco music until late. One sad but memorable young girl told me she loved me, out of the black and blue, much to the silent chagrin of her boyfriend. I told him that vodka and *valuta* were a dangerous mixture. He nodded.

There was no breakfast at the Marna next morning. Perhaps that was part of what made it special. I had paid for a first class ticket on the Bucharest-Brașov 'Rapid.' It left an hour late. In my compartment was a nineteen year old bleached blonde babysitter, in a pair of well-contoured Canadian Jeans. Christina and I ate pink citroms, and she told me of her German boyfriend, her yearning for emigrant freedom, and reluctance to prostitute herself in order to obtain it. She looked over her shoulder a lot. Brașov was pretty, built by the Teutonic Knights, with a cobblestoned plaza, and Transylvanian architecture. Christina took me to the Gothic Black Church to see its clock tower and many portals, one of which led to a touching goodbye. Thanks to the Genius of the Carpathians, we had run out of doors and time.

I checked into the Hotel Sport, and went to shower. I went downstairs and asked the desk clerk if she had any soap. She cocked her head to the side, grinned, and snapped her fingers. There was a goat chewing on the door handle.

> "For though you wash yourself with lye, and use much soap, yet your iniquity is marked before me,' sayeth the Lord.'
> Jeremiah 2:21

*　　　*　　　*

> 'What soap is for the body, tears are for the soul.'
> Yiddish Proverb

I was wending my way from Baba Rhea to Baba Rose. It was going to be convoluted. The goat had left by the time I awoke. Determined, as I was, to hitchhike from Brașov to Rădăuți, the Romanians were just as determined. Two hours after I took bus number one out of the city to the route I needed, I took bus number one back. Perhaps, it was the way I pronounced the hooks hanging off their place names. Perhaps, it was because there were more horse carts than Dacias. It didn't matter. Some demented Moldavian shoulder hog had almost killed me anyway.

My first four hours, on bus number four, took me back towards Bucharest. In Plojest, a friendly old French-speaking pensioner guided me to the other station, where I watched the gypsy band until mid-afternoon. The next bus took me back towards Brașov, in the superheated peasant body odor. I ran out of water. Most of the pungent passengers disembarked in Romaw, leaving me with a loud old crone drinking wicked brandy. I was dozing in the humidity, when an actual ticket inspector thumped me awake. He stole my pen.

It was dusk when we arrived in Suceava, just in time to see my antique hardback wooden train pulling out. *Chank-chank-*

chank. It was going so slow, I had time to buy a citrom before boarding. The worse the lighting became, the bigger the crowd I drew. Perhaps the blues harmonica was a mistake but, in the darkening carriage *chank-chank-chanking* through the rolling Moldavian scenery, it just seemed right.

The last train was waiting for me in Dornesti, although the term 'train' would only be correct in a historical context. It was the size of a Chevy van, and looked like an armored car circa 1870. There were no lights. The superheated peasant smell filled up that space that wasn't already as crowded as Hell will be, when I get there. The *chank-chank-chank* became *clank-clank-clank*. The sweat poured out of me, and them. For just over an hour, I was drenched in their nasty, brutish and short lives, and what they lacked- food, water, security, freedom, dignity, and soap. Just before midnight, we *clank-clank-clanked* around the last bend, into the land of my forefathers, and stopped. I remember stumbling down unlit dusty streets, looking for a place to stay. I found the Hotel Bukovina. There was no water. I had wound down to neutral. I needed a wash. The Talmud said that there were three gates to purgatory, and one of them was Jerusalem. I could have found the second. There I was, in all my aromatic Aramaic glory- waiting for daylight, and redemption. I fell asleep in my clothes.

No man knows till he has suffered from the night, how sweet and dear to his heart and eye the morning can be. Something like water trickled out of the hand basin tap. I washed the warm moist parts, as well as I could without soap. Downstairs, there was no one. It wasn't like there was anything to steal. I rubbed my eyes, blinded by the May sunlight in the street.

I was in Bukovina. It was named after the beech trees. In 1775 the Habsburgs annexed it from the Principality of Moldavia, into what would become the Austria-Hungary Empire, a hundred years later. The new administration encouraged the influx of immigrants, including its persecuted and dispossessed Jews from Galicia and Lodomeria.

I was in Rădăuţi. On a plain between the Suceava and Sucevița rivers, its origins were as old and as murky. Some maintained the town was originally called 'Rottacenum,' named by the Roman garrison in nearby Siret. The Romans had come to Romania for gold and salt. They left their name. A boyar property document, from 1392, mentioned 'Radomir's village.' By the 14th century, the settlement was flourishing, and had become famous for its fairs. The Jews initially made a living from lumber and livestock, but by the period between the World Wars in the last century, they had established 250 diverse industrial plants, constituted most of the area's professionals, and made up over thirty per cent of the population.

Nothing in the market I walked through that morning, suggested any such form of human endeavor or influence at all. Tarpaper hung off the scalloped picket fence roofs of the long wooden empty stalls, their lichen colored paint faded, and stained with the rust of what remained of the drainpipes. Angular men, with angular suit jacket lapels and angular Tyrolean hats, were accompanied by weedy women with headscarves and soiled aprons, buying and selling onions. It seemed that, in Rădăuţi, onions were currency. Here, at least, was no hint, of the more complex flavors, that once lived on the plain between the rivers.

But around the corner, in the main square, there was. In 1880, during the visit of Emperor Franz Joseph I, a delegation of locals requested a proper plot of land, to build a large synagogue, to accommodate the Jewish population of 3,452 souls. The consent of the Emperor was followed by the dissent between the orthodox and more progressive Jews, as to which style should govern its creation. The dispute postponed construction for several years. In a final compromise, the synagogue was built in the modern style of the great *shuel* of Czernowitz, but instead of one large cathedral-like round dome, two twin towers rose instead. It was inaugurated on the Emperor's birthday, 18th of August, 1883. Both my paternal great grandmothers sat in the women's section in the western gallery that day. The new chief Rabbi of Rădăuţi, Yithak Kunstadt, gave the inaugural address, in front of the central ark. A great religious scholar and orator, he would, in subsequent years, instill in his community a great love for the renewal of Israel's sovereignty as a nation. Despite the thousand seats, the synagogue was packed. Chassidim had also come from all parts of Bukovina. From the beginning, Rădăuţi had been a hotbed epicenter of Jewish intellectual conflict. Eight years after the inauguration of the Central Synagogue, as many more prayer houses had been constructed in the township. There were twenty-three synagogues in Rădăuţi on the eve of the Second World War. Back in the 19th century, philosophical debate between the Orthodox and the more modern Jews, and the Vizhnitz, Bojan, and Sadagoran dynasties of Chassidim, gradually transformed into a contentious political argument between the Zionists, the ultra-religious, and the left wing-socialist Bund. I had tangential childhood associations with a Conservative synagogue, but I was more the product of the simultaneous intense love affair I had with the Scientific Method. For me, civilization was a Western child, the logical progression of the Renaissance, the Reformation, and the French and American Revolutions. My religion was Progress, technological and social, and my ancestors were Jurassic obstacles to enlightenment. *'And yet, unless my senses deceive me, the old centuries had, and have, powers of their own which mere 'modernity' cannot kill... Ah, it is the fault of our science that it wants to explain all; and if it explain not, then it says there is nothing to explain.'* I thought about my love of debate, and theirs. I read how much more radical some of their views about progress were, than my own. I found out that one of my Jurassic ancestors, ten generations back was Baal Shem Tov, the founder of Chassidic Jewry. It was hardwired.

A horse pulled a cart full of haphazard barrels in front of me, as I crossed the square. The white stone twin towers had dentate ornamentation above their long columned arched windows. I walked through the beech trees between the pillars under a filigreed iron gate, and up the seven stairs, to the two green wooden doors. A yellow Star of David hung on each one, loosely. I pushed on the right door. Nothing. I pushed on the left one. It swung inwards, ajar. I called out, and from the deep recesses of the house of God, an old caretaker appeared. We had the iron irony of German to communicate with. I watched his face for any hint of recognition, as I asked after Rose. His brow furrowed.

"Babi Goodman." He said, remembering. He didn't, and couldn't, remember much more. They had left a long time ago. He opened the main room for me. As he did, another piece of a three thousand year old jigsaw clicked into place. There were frescoes of musical instruments, a golden ark, and row upon row of empty seats. I finally asked the question. He didn't tell me directly. I could see his eyes filling up. He turned away for a moment and, from a nearby washbasin, handed me the answer... soap.

> 'Soap and education are not as sudden as a massacre,
> but they are more deadly in the long run.'
>> Mark Twain

*   *   *

'The clear layer is glycerin. You can mix glycerin back in when you make soap. Or You can skim the glycerin off. You can mix the glycerin with nitric acid to make nitroglycerin. You can mix nitroglycerin with sodium nitrate and sawdust to make dynamite. You can blow up bridges. You can mix nitroglycerin with more nitric acid and paraffin and make gelatin explosives. You can blow up a building, easy. With enough soap, you can blow up the whole world.'

Chuck Palahniuk

Baba Rose died when I was in Leningrad. She didn't know that I would find her hometown, and I didn't know that she died. The story of the rest of the Rădăuţi relatives was the same story as that of every other Jewish community in Eastern Europe, with differences.

In 1937, the anti-Semitic Goga-Cuza party came to power. Jews were beaten on the streets, and forced to keep their shops open on the Sabbath. Those who lived in the surrounding villages fled, leaving behind all their possessions, for the false protection of the town. In September of 1940, Cuza's government was replaced by the even more sinister *Garda de fier*, the 'Iron Guard' or 'Legion of the Archangel Michael,' a green-shirted cult of martyrdom, and violence. 'Nests' of action Death Squads traveled around Romania, singing and Roman-saluting their 'virtues', and observing rituals that included the drinking of and writing oaths in blood. 'The blood is the life!' They railed against Freemasonry, Freudianism, homosexuality, atheism, Marxism, Bolshevism, the civil war in Spain, and other 'unexpected protean forms of rabbinical aggression against the Christian world.'

By 1940, Jews were being thrown out of moving train cars, including my great uncle, a veterinarian. He took two months to die of his injuries. Homes were confiscated. Romanian soldiers, retreating from Russia, engaged in casual random murder. Jewish students were forbidden from attending public schools, and doctors from attending non-Jewish patients. Government workers were fired. Distinguishing clothing became mandatory. The pogroms began.

The final chapter of Rădăuţi Jewry commenced with Romania's involvement in Operation Barbarossa against the Soviet Union. A curfew of six p.m. was imposed on what was now a ghetto. Hostages were demanded by the military government to work as slaves. On the 11th of October 1941, the ten thousand Jews of Rădăuţi were ordered to begin a forced march towards the camps of Transnistria, within 24 hours.

'Denn die Todten reiten schnell.' *For the dead travel fast.* Those found in the town after two days were shot. The expelled were ordered to leave the keys to their houses in the doors, and put all their valuables in the National bank. They received no receipt. Only hand luggage was permitted. Ninety per cent were murdered en route, by Romanian guards; most of the rest died from cold, hunger, or disease, marching, on cattle trains, or in the camps. There were occasions when the Germans actually stepped in, to restrain and slow down the excesses of the Iron Guards, such was the enthusiasm of some of the Romanian involvement in the Holocaust. On January 24, 1941, a Legion-instigated deadly pogrom resulted in the vicious slaughter of dozens of Jewish civilians, their bodies hung from meat hooks in a Bucharest abattoir, in a gruesome parody of kosher ritual practice. Their synagogues had been transformed into cowsheds and warehouses. Their houses and possessions had been confiscated, and their cemeteries desecrated. Torah scrolls had been 'recycled' into sandals and drums.

I drifted back through the market. The acid in the pickles jump restarted my saliva. Romania, like its people, had been defined as the meeting point of three regions: Central Europe, Eastern Europe, and the Balkans- but couldn't be truly included in any of them. The Folk Art Museum was missing more than a little something. I paid for another night at the Hotel Bukovina, and boarded a crowded slug bus behemoth to Putna, to see the first of the many famous painted Eastern Orthodox monasteries in Bukovina. Everything except the priests was undergoing a frantic reconstruction, but the colored postage stamp scenes of kerchiefed women hoeing flat sun-flooded fields, and pine groves dripping down green candle conical hills, made the excursion. I bought a citrom, and some soap from a later vintage, and learned that there were bungalows further down the road in Sucevița. I took the bus back to Rădăuți, to retrieve Serendipity and my deposit. The first was easy. The second was what used to be called a 'problem' and now, in an era of political correctness, is referred to as a 'challenge.' According to the desk clerk, it was going to be a problem. In his Romanian-English dictionary, I had him look up the words 'broken' and 'liver.' Problem solved. Disarmed with a handshake, I returned to the *Autogara* for the 15:15 bus to Sucevița. Unfortunately, there was no 15:15 bus. More unfortunately, the 16:15 bus was now doubly occupied, piled to the rivets. The superheated body odor returned, in the intensity of the angled lapels of the afternoon sun. I gave up my seat, to a young girl who had fainted. It may have been the temperature, or the lack of food. Two hours and fifteen kilometers later, we rumbled into Sucevița. I inhaled real air again, stepping off the bus. A Serendipity stroll past horse-drawn Carpathian carts, fairytale lush hills, and thick emerald dipped candles, brought me to a quiet bungalow in paradise. I showered with soap and water and, just before the sun dropped into the mountains, walked to the four hundred year old fortified Byzantine and Gothic monastery. I thought it was closed, but a sweet antique nun let me in to see the 'Scale of Virtues' and other frescoes, a moving Sister of Mercy mass, the convent museum, where I bought a painted egg, and the rich ether of Eden. Crystalline perfect heady stuff. I thanked the abbess, and retraced my steps to find sustenance next to my bungalow. I ate a cutlet with fried potatoes, peas, and real bread and cheese, like I'd never seen food.

In the last rays of the Carpathian day, I opened Bram Stoker's

Dracula, and starting a new absorption. But everything I read took me back to the old guardian at Baba Rose's synagogue, chanting ancient mournful psalms in a now deserted temple, rocking away his loneliness for all those ghosts who could no longer sing with him, or light him candles, or invite him to weddings or Friday night Sabbath dinners, or say 'Kaddish' prayers for him when he died. The Irishman's book, about a fictional Romanian vampire, was transparently also, a story of soap:

'Doctor, you don't know what it is to doubt everything, even yourself... But a stranger in a strange land, he is no one. Men know him not, and to know not is to care not for... I want you to believe, to believe in things that you cannot... I have learned not to think little of any one's belief, no matter how strange it may be. I have tried to keep an open mind, and it is not the ordinary things of life that could close it, but the strange things, the extraordinary things, the things that make one doubt if they be mad or sane... I sometimes think we must be all mad and that we shall wake to sanity in strait-waistcoats... There are mysteries which men can only guess at, which age by age they may solve only in part... the world seems full of good men--even if there are monsters in it... For life be, after all, only a waitin' for somethin' else than what we're doin'; and death be all that we can rightly depend on... We are all drifting reefwards now, and faith is our only anchor... Despair has its own calms... Take me away from all this Death... welcome to my house. Come freely. Go safely; and leave something of the happiness you bring... How blessed are some people, whose lives have no fears, no dreads, to whom sleep is a blessing that comes nightly, and brings nothing but sweet dreams.'

Transfixed

'I read that every known superstition in the world is gathered into the horseshoe of the Carpathians, as if it were the centre of some sort of imaginative whirlpool; if so my stay may be very interesting.'

Bram Stoker, *Dracula*

Two blankets and the Gold Kazoo didn't dent the deep frozen night in Suceviţa. Sleep had no place to call its own.
The sunstream that crashed through my window brought light, and an illusion of rejuvenation. I waited for three hours in the heat, on the side of the road that the police had told me, was the way to Moldoviţa. Not even a horse cart went by. It didn't concern me. The forest was green, and quiet, and there were birds. I sprawled out along the
Third Rule of Hitchhiking: *Wait a bit longer.*

And they came. Two microbuses brimming with thirty-three Romanian religious fundamentalists pulled over. Everyone poured out to stretch. Their tour guide was a priest of the all-embracing school. He swaggered over, with much bombast.
"Bonjour!" He shouted. I replied in kind.
"La Francesa!" He announced. My French had saved me again.
Strapped into a straddle seat in the front and centre of the first bus and, climbing into the mountains, I became the focal point for the day's sermon.
"Who created this, Nature or God?" Asked the priest in French. The only difficulty I had was in keeping my face straight. It was like shooting fish in a barrel of nitro.
"God." I said, to boisterous applause.
"What is your religion?" The sky pilot honed in. A man has to know his limitations.
"Eastern Presbyterian." I replied. The applause was still there, but it was scratching its head.
"Are you a communist?" He asked. Slam-dunk.

"Mon Dieu, non!" I said. And, if the roof of the minibus had been higher, there would have been a standing ovation.

We stopped at the top of a mountain pass and a monument of a giant hand, for a group photo, with 'La Francesa,' then carried on downstream, to the monastery of Moldoviţa.

Stephen the Great was the King of Romania, in the second half of the 15th century. He won most of his battles against the Ottoman Turks, and built Moldoviţa, and other Orthodox monasteries, as a defense against further incursions. Their rooflines were contoured like witches hats. Stephan's illegitimate son, Petru Rareş, began the tradition of covering them, inside and out, with elaborate frescoes, the 'holy scriptures in color.' I was particularly smitten with 'The Siege of Constantinople,' painted to commemorate the Virgin's salvation of the city from the Persians in 626 AD. Inside was a mural of 'The Last Judgment.' Outside too, as my bible squad broke out in joyous song, waved furiously through their windows, and headed off down the road. I passed them later, in the back of a Dacia, with four Romanian Mafiosi, they passed me again and forever, and I ended up on a mountain bridge, listening to the birds again.

Almost an hour later, I managed a ride with an elderly couple, who took me near the turnoff, to the most famous of the painted monasteries. I was hiking the last of four kilometers, when Nature took retribution for my heresy. Buckets dropped out of the sky, soaking me to the skin. I was in the town of Humor but, because of the deluge and my state of being, I didn't see it.

It was the most famous church in Romania, the 'Sistine Chapel of the East.' Stephan the Great built Voroneţ in 1488, in less than four months, to repay Daniel the Hermit's advice to chase the Turks from Wallachia, at the Battle of Vaslui.

The original decoration of the church was in yellow, brown, and green ceramic enameled discs. Heraldic motifs of rampant lions, auroch's heads, and two-tailed mermaids, decorated some of the frescos. But it was the west façade, and its 'Last Judgment,' that justified its legend. The sun returned, transilluminating the intense vivid cerulean blue background known as 'Voroneţ blue,' so vibrant that art historians swooned over it, as much as they did over 'Titian red.' It was still as brilliant as the day it was painted, still a mystery of creation. Teams of quick-handed painters had applied mixtures of ground azurite and malachite to still wet plaster, which fixed and transfixed the colors as it dried. Because, unlike frescos in which egg whites were used as a binder, no organic materials were used in the Voroneţ technique, and the pigments were as bright the afternoon I was there, as they had been on the day they were applied, five hundred years earlier. Apostles and evangelists, philosophers and martyrs, and angels and demons, jumped from the western wall into my memory.

Another cloudburst announced my return to secular Humor. It was somewhat less than comical how the hotel I checked into had no running water, when there was so much of it, just outside my door. I ventured out to what was passing for a supermarket in guardian Ceauşescu's Carpathian countryside. I found a horsemeat sausage, a jar of pastel pickled vegetables, and an Eastern block of 'halvah,' which compared not unfavorably with sawdust in blackstrap molasses. The kilogram wasp in my room when I returned was clearly getting his vitamins elsewhere. Whatever else he may have been missing, in his droning determination to stay with me, he wasn't lacking in Humor.

'When I was on my own in a hotel room in Romania,
I had the imagination to keep myself occupied.'
Rhona Mitra

*　　　*　　　*

> 'We are in Transylvania, and Transylvania is not England. Our ways are not your ways, and there shall be to you many strange things.'
>
> Bram Stoker, *Dracula*

It was taking me too long to decode the romantic names of Romanian trains. They were all about the illusion of speed. The bigger the illusion, the more tedious the transport. I took an 'Accelerat' to Cluj-Napoca next morning. We learn from failure, not from success. There was a heat wave outside the sealed compartment, but the emaciated mother across from me kept reaching across to close my window, pointing to her small mutation, as if I was somehow responsible for how it was turning out. There was a loud tape deck two seats down, that kept changing volume, when its owner bounced asleep across it. Three Romanian card sharks kept trying to entice me into a game. Because that would have been some rhapsody. I tried to break the superheated body odor monotony by nibbling on my hardwood halvah, and turning the pages in my India guidebook. I stared out the window, searching for the Taj Mahal, reasonably certain that some local patriot had lifted it.

I traded down in Cluj-Napoca. My train to Sighişoara was a 'Rapid.' I had the data from my 'Accelerat' excursion, and the remaining distance, but the math was too depressing, to want to know the answer. I was just nodding off, when the 'chef' stopped by to check my ticket. Quelle surprise, I hadn't paid enough, and there was a ninety lei surcharge. The passenger across from me handed me a lemon. The day passed through belching factory smoke, groups of teenage boy scouts toting AK-47s, and heat and dismal boredom, until we finally docked in the capital of Transylvania, around seven in the evening.

I carried Serendipity along the cobblestones to the category one Hotel Stella. Someone's angry daughter told me they had no vacancies. I told her how beautiful she was. Room 204 had two concave beds, a television with no television inside it, a bathtub with running water and, half a hour after my proposal, a weeks worth of laundry hanging through it, like Vlad Țepeș' impaled Turks. I could have gone anywhere I wished, except where the doors were locked, where of course I would not wish to go.

In the last light, framing the Citadel on the forested hill above, and the peasant stone huts and pebbled streets below, I gazed out the window at the rain. Within the deluge, streaks of lighting flashed across a skyline of silhouetted tall thin fluted spires rising from the witch's hat rooftops, and their smaller offspring. Loneliness sat over them with brooding wings. There was shade, and there was shadow. The howling, of a dog down the road was taken up by another dog, and then another and another, music of the children of the night. I was transfixed.

Transylvania had always been one of those nasty crossroads. Even before Bram Stoker reinvented him, he was real enough. The history of conquest through his forests had been a long and continuous one. Dacian Carpi were crushed by Romans, then Visigoths, followed by the Huns, Gepids, Avars, Bulgars, Vlachs, the Mongel Golden Horde, the struggle between Romanian Orthodox and Hungarian Roman Catholics, peasants and boyars, and the unremitting Ottoman oppressions.

His father Vlad II, or Vlad Dracul, '*Vlad the Dragon,*' was a voivode of Wallachia. He murdered his rivals, paid tribute to the Ottoman court, and fathered several illegitimate children. All four of his sons, Radu the Handsome, Vlad Călugărul, Mircea II, and Vlad Țepeș, would rule Wallachia, at some time in their lives. But Stoker took Vlad Țepeș, known also as Vlad III, 'Vlad the Impaler' or Dracula, Son of Dracul, as a prototype for his vampire. There had been a veritable plague of 'strigoi' Southern Slavic vampirism stories in the late 17th century that had spread from Hungary and the Balkans. But Vlad Țepeș, although a natural candidate to bolster the legend of the undead, was scary enough all by himself.

He was born in Sighișoara, in the winter of 1431. Under the tutelage of well-educated scholars from Constantinople, Vlad learned combat skills, geography, mathematics, science, Bulgarian, German, and Latin, and the classical arts and philosophy. In 1442, his father sent him, with his brother Radu, as hostages of his loyalty, to the Ottoman court, in return for the military support he received, to regain Wallachia. This formed him. Vlad was stubborn, imprisoned and beaten, for the verbal and physical abuse he heaped on his trainers. While Radu converted to Islam and was eventually given command of the Janissary contingents, Vlad grew angry with his father, vowing to fight the Ottomans, if he ever returned to Wallachia. In the meantime, he absorbed lessons in logic, the Quran, Turkish, Persian, and Islamic literature. He learned their warfare and horsemanship. When the Hungarian regent, John Hunyadi, killed his father in the Bălteni marshes, Vlad was place on the Wallachian throne by the Turks. He fled in stages, until he met and was befriended by Hunyadi, the man who had murdered his father.

In 1456, Vlad invaded Wallachia, and killed the Ottoman voivode in hand-to-hand combat. His rule was, for the times, reasonably fair-handed and, even today, he is often glorified as a Romanian hero. He restored order and prosperity, built new villages, raised agricultural output, limited foreign merchant trade, gave council positions to knights and free peasants rather than boyars, introduced and enforced new laws punishing thieves, and established a peasant militia. He built new churches, and contributed to existing monasteries.

It was his contrasting behavior that ruined what might have been an otherwise noble reputation. He tortured those caught stealing, by skinning their feet, adding salt, and letting goats lick it off. Lying and adultery were punished as well, with drowning, decapitation, amputations, boiling, or roasting the offenders, regardless of age, religion, or social class. He fed others the flesh of their friends or relatives. He destroyed fortresses, and had whole villages burned to the ground. He may have killed as many as eighty thousand people.

Vlad's preferred method of torture and execution was impalement. He attached horses to his victim's legs, and a sharpened stake was forced up into their bodies. Death was slow and agonizing, sometimes taking days. He arranged multiple impalements in geometric patterns. His favorite was a ring of concentric circles. The height of the pole indicated the victim's rank. On one occasion, in the 'Forest of the Impaled' outside Braşov, one of his servants held his nose, while Vlad was feasting. Vlad asked him what he was doing. He told Vlad that he found the stench unbearable. Vlad had him impaled higher than the rest, where the smell wouldn't reach him. Playing high stakes poker with the principal stakeholder got you transfixed in Transylvania.

Throughout his reign, he systematically eliminated the Wallachian boyar class in the same manner. Those he didn't impale were sent to rebuild Poienari Castle in the mountains. They were forced to labor until their clothes fell off their bodies, then naked, then until they died. In 1459, Mehmed II sent envoys, to collect what he considered to be overdue Ottoman tribute. Vlad nailed their turbans to their heads. When Mehmed invaded in 1462, he arrived to a wall of twenty thousand rotting Turkish soldiers, impaled outside Vlad's capital of Târgovişte. He was so upset and sickened by the spectacle, despite his better equipment and three-to-one numerical advantage in troops, he turned his campaign over to his subordinates, and returned to Constantinople.

It was Vlad's brother, Radu the Handsome, who chased him out of Wallachia the first time. Vlad ruled twice more, before being killed in battle by the Ottomans near Bucharest, in 1476. Some say that his head is in Istanbul.

I was apparently in the wrong establishment for breakfast next morning. The Tourism 101 final exam in session should have been the tipoff. The officials monitoring it were too paranoid to deal with me, as if the stakes were too high. Ultimately, the local Tourist Office representative was summoned to the Stella, and showed me where to eat. I told him that I would have flunked the ones taking the exam. The paranoia continued with my waiter, whose vocabulary consisted of 'omelet and chai.' I told him I was happy with the omelet, but I preferred coffee. Some petrochemical egg concoction arrived with a cup of tea. He insisted it was coffee.

I climbed to the History Museum. The tower was more interesting than its contents. Vlad's house was empty, and the church was now a school. Sighişoara all by itself was more captivating, with its rows of squat ochre Germanic monopoly houses, exotic rooftops, and quiet cobbles. I wander the lower town along the Târnava Mare River.

Back at the Stella, I watched the pencil-thin mustached desk clerk court three girls in fifteen minutes. One of them modeled her new contraband jeans. I nursed the bottled yogurt I bought, until I bought another one. My train to Hungary was an overnight 'Express,' and they had refused to sell me ticket before ten p.m. I sat in the Stella lobby, contemplating my navel, the clock, and self-mutilation. In the late afternoon, I couldn't take it anymore, and hoisted Serendipity for the trek to the station. In the second-class salon, I learned that a 'salad' in Transylvania, is pickles. Around seven thirty, a gypsy elder with and angled Tyrolean hat and a gigantic handlebar moustache entered, with his two orphaned grandchildren. I spent the next two hours watching them smile at my harmonica.

At the appointed hour, the ticket lady refused to sell me passage.

"Bucharesti!" She kept yelling. "Bucharesti!" There was no way I was backtracking seven hundred kilometers, to leave a country my great grandparents simply walked out of. They had taken enough blood.

"Capitalist!" She screamed. "Capitalist!" Had me there.

I did my Dracula imitation. Seat 101.

Just after eleven, the third incorrect train pulled into the station. It was apparently going to Hungary. I climbed on, over a sleeping soldier, and a snoring drunk, drooling in my seat. I tapped his shoulder and showed him my ticket. Seat 101. He held his up. Seat 101. The soldier next to him held his up. They must have only one number in Romania, I thought, and sat on Serendipity. The cabin overflowed.

Hours later, carriage empty, compulsive passport checking began, as we neared the border. They nudged me seven times, to make sure I hadn't lost it, between nudges. I swore I was going to drive a stake through the heart of the next one. It was just as well that I held my fire.

The next one wore a funny little cap. The sun poured into the uninhabited Pullman. He was Hungarian. I could see he was a little confused about the hug. I snuggled into the Gold Kazoo for the remaining couple of hours, thanking Baba Rose on my way down, for finding the way out, in time.

> "'Take care,' he said, "take care how you cut yourself.
> It is more dangerous than you think in this country.'"
> Bram Stoker, *Dracula*

Iron Curtain

'If the German people lay down their weapons, the Soviets, according to the agreement between Roosevelt, Churchill and Stalin, would occupy all of East and Southeast Europe along with the greater part of the Reich. An iron curtain would fall over this enormous territory controlled by the Soviet Union, behind which nations would be slaughtered."

Joseph Goebbels

'Even an iron barrier cannot separate the people of Israel from their heavenly father.'

Babylonian Talmud, *Tractate Sota 38b*

In my relatively soft landing, in the 'happiest barrack' of the Eastern Bloc, they still only dealt in hard currency. The materially superior life behind the Iron Curtain seemed to paradoxically thrive on American dollars. I changed the requisite daily requirement into forints at IBUZC, and they arranged for me to meet Beke, all the way down the route of bus 73E. She put me in a shower, and I slept the day away.

When I finally woke about six pm, my hunger drove me across to Buda for an eagle's view of the wide Danube, on a random terraced restaurant. I devoured magnificent venison, schnitzel and potatoes, soup, salad, and réte *strudel*, accompanied by decent wine, and well-dressed waiters. All, for six evil dollars, at the official exchange rate. If you had gone from Moscow to Budapest, you would have thought you were in Paris.

The original Celtic settlement on the river here became the Roman settlement of Aquinum, only to be later invaded by the Mongols, the Bulgarians, Árpád's Hungarians, the Tatars, the Ottomans, and the Habsburgs. In 1873 Buda and Pest were merged into what became the 'Jewish Mecca,' with almost 23% of the city's population so constituted. At least a hundred thousand Jewish inhabitants died in the Nazi and Arrow Cross collaborator genocide, in 1944.

Miriam and Istvan, the old couple from Budapest who I had met in Bukhara a few weeks earlier, were two of the fortunate. I called them just before I left, to tell them I wouldn't have time before I left. They seemed heartbroken. So, I was too.

But after a month behind the Iron Curtain, I was looking forward to the day that it would go up for the last time. There were fascinating things to see and learn in the Evil Empire, but they were too easily discolored, by the grey cement hues of oppression that smothered their vitality.

After yoghurt in Kertali, I spent the morning in the old town of Buda, the ruins of the old synagogue, Andrássy Avenue, and the Szépművészeti Múzeum National Gallery, in Heroes' Square. I hadn't expected such a superb collection, over a hundred thousand pieces, of fine European artworks. I took extra time with the painted mummy sarcophagi, in the second largest Egyptian collection on the continent, the beauty of the 3rd century marble 'Budapest Dancer,' and the memorable alien-eerie sculpture of a skeletal Hungarian King Stephan.

The climb to the Citadella plateau, a quarter of a kilometer above the Danube, brought me to a fortress that had been used more against the citizens of Budapest, than to protect them. Built by the Hapsburgs in 1851, its most sinister employment was by the Soviets, during the 1956 Hungarian Uprising. Tanks fired down indiscriminately, from the Citadella into the city. They killed twenty thousand Hungarians, including the legal Prime Minister of the country, Imre Nagy. Both views were nonpareil.

Despite the solitary nature of my sojourn, I felt the ruby warmth of Art Nouveau Budapest, above its thermal subterranean waters, and beyond the natural ardor of its spring days. Its Renaissance humanism shone bright through, chasing all the barbarisms that had galloped through its crossroads, back into the darkness. Budapest was *rapturous blues-nursing, jazzed up with rhapsodic manic-depression.* I could taste it in the paprika of the Fortuna goulash, and the Borsodi beer, and the Liszt Liebesträume, playing in the background.

I had reserved my last day in Budapest for business, and a perverse pleasure. The business part was the Czech visa that would allow me to board a train for Prague that evening. This was accomplished at the embassy in just a few minutes, with a minimum of fuss and expense. The perversity occurred in the Romanian embassy. A melancholic mob fidgeted in the main room. An official was requisitioned to meet me. I handed him the eighty lei they had refused to change back into dollars as I left the country, and politely requested a reconversion.

"This is not a bank." Said the dapper moustache.

Short, dark, slicked-back hair, three-piece suit, and Italian shoes polished to such a shine, you would have seen his reflection. He cocked his head, grinned, and snapped his fingers. *Prest-o change-o.* I asked him again.

"Maybe you could write a letter." Tilt. Smile. Snap. Slide. One more time.

"It is not possible." I knew this answer to be incorrect. An elderly acquaintance had been in Auschwitz, and attributed her survival to phrasing immediate needs in the form of a question which no one, not even a monster, could answer in the negative. *'Is it possible?'* It was truly bad form to claim that anything was impossible. One never know, do one.

But this guy had ruined the karma.

"The problem," I said, "is that Romania will never be free, until you learn that anything is possible." I slowly tore up the notes, and turned, and left.

He called after me.

"Please, I want your name!" He shouted. I turned back. The mob wasn't quite so dejected.

"Vlad." I said. "Vlad Țepeș." And changed into a bat while leaving.

Back at Beke's, I retrieved Serendipity, and kissed her two cheeks. My train wouldn't leave until late. I had many hours and forints to spend, on goulash and gypsy bands and glasses of Tokaji, before I had to be at the station. The wild music and dancing were like the sour cherry soup.

The English word for 'coach' comes from the Hungarian '*kocsi*,' a wagon from Kocs, the village where they were first made. The fellow cellmate in mine was an aging Hungarian Egyptologist, named Laslo. He told me that a Hungarian invented the noiseless match. I told him I wasn't quite sure how much of a strategic advantage that would have been, against Soviet tanks. Hungarian Rhapsody No. 2 in C-sharp Minor percolated through the speakers, as we jerked out of our platform, into the night. Lazlo asked me what I did.

"I'm the King of the Gypsies." I said.

'Those who were thinking logically in Hungary, always despaired.'
Antal Szerb

*   *   *

'From behind the Iron Curtain, there are signs that tyranny is in trouble and reminders that its structure is as brittle as its surface is hard.'
Dwight David Eisenhower

The big thieves hang the little ones. At least, that was how the proverb went. I arrived in the downpour of a Prague spring, fifteen years after Alexander Dubček had announced his 'socialism with a human face.' The big thieves were still hanging the little ones, same old face.

I tried two acronyms of courteous communist congeniality, Čedok and Pragatour, for accommodation, but both of their offerings were far too expensive for a downtrodden victim of capitalism, such as myself. Czechmate. A lady, far too sympathetic not to require some form of reeducation, finally told me of a hostel that opened at six p.m. I thanked her and went off into the storm, to see the attractions.

The Prague Orioj medieval Astronomical Clock in the Old Town Hall was originally installed in 1410. It had undergone several repairs, understandably, down and over the centuries. But its three components still worked, with no small precision and sophistication. The clock was instrumental in corroborating the exact time that Charles IV laid the foundation stone for the Charles Bridge, based on the auspicious palindrome recommended by his astrologers. The number, 13579531, was carved into the tower, July 9 1357, at 5:31 a.m. The astronomical dial was an astrolabe planetarium, demonstrating positions of the sun and moon, local Earth sky view and horizon, lengths of days, and vernal equinoxes; the calendar dial had medallions, representing the months; and a clockwork parade of moving sculptures. In addition to the 'Walk of the Apostles,' four additional flanking figures were set in motion, on the hour. These effigies represented the four things most despised, at the time of the clock's construction. The first was Vanity, personified by a character, admiring itself in a mirror. Next, a Turk, symbolizing pleasure and entertainment. The third was Death, a skeleton that struck on the hour. And finally, there was the stereotypical Jew holding a bag of gold, the epitome of greed and usury. Precision and sophistication.

Jews had been in Prague since 965 AD, as recalled by the merchant and traveler, Ibrahim ibn Ya'qub. I was captivated by the large serrated leaf roofline of the chunky Old New Synagogue, built in 1270. During Easter 1389, the entire Jewish population of this Holy Roman Empire capital was annihilated by a mob, encouraged by clergy who had declared that they had desecrated the host wafers of the Eucharist.

By 1708, the Jews returned, forming around a quarter of the population. The pendulum swung back sharply again during World War II, with the establishment of a concentration camp at Terezín, just north of the city, and the extermination of over a quarter of a million Czech Jews. Non-Jewish Czechs were also considered *untermenschen* by the Nazi state, and would have faced the same fate, had the Germans prevailed. When Reinhard Heydrich was assassinated, the Nazis murdered the villages of Lidice and Ležáky, in reprisal.

What I hadn't expected was the eeriness of the cemetery, jagged and heavy under a tall treed canopy. Hundreds of fractured headstones were jammed tightly into and on top of each other, like an Arctic river ice collision, in a Prague spring. There was no space for flowers, and no one to bring them.

I stopped for a Pilsner Urquell in a worker's club, on the way to the hostel. There I met Jans, a seventeen year-old East German aspiring graphic artist, and Lalo, a thin bearded Mexican, studying Czech. I'm sure he had a reason, but my courage failed me. We went out for good schnitzel and bad slivovitz, returning to the ten bunks in our room, just before curfew.

I woke to an earth tremor of shaking. It was six in the morning. Long black hair hung over my face, and gray irises looked down. Her name was Nadia. She wanted to know if I had a cigarette. At least I think so, because Lalo looked down from the top bunk.

"That's Nadia." He said. "She wants to know if you have a cigarette." We all went for coffee. I left them to go visa hunting.

The Poles made it too difficult. They wanted me to pay for a telex to Warsaw, and return in seven days to find out the answer. I told them it was too slow. It would be almost thirty years later before opportunity and solidarity reconverged, and allowed me to see the place. The East Germans were surprisingly more compliant although, in the arena of the pursuit for hard currency, there was definite anabolic steroid use. I paid twenty dollars for a visa that allowed me to camp. In their antechamber, an elderly American talked my ear off about how westerners were too judgmental. He decided that we needed to spend some more time together, exploring his thesis further. I made a judgment.

Instead, I explored the Bethlehem chapel where Jan Hus taught, before he was burned as a heretic, for pointing out the contrast between the poverty of Christ and the riches of the Catholic Church. The big thieves hang the little ones.

Lalo met me at Čedok, where I bought my onward train ticket. He walked with me through the streets of Prague, with a first generation Walkman strapped to his head. It looked out of place. We picked up Jans, and a new companion named Knudel, and returned to the scene of the previous night's indulgences. Lalo's natural Latin animation was turbocharged by two girls from the DDR, sitting across from us. The battle between his ardor and his timidity was torture for him, and an infinite source of amusement for us.

Nadia was on me again next morning. I had bought cigarettes and asked Lalo to translate that she could take a couple, and leave me alone. She took the pack. Big thieves.

I spent the morning across the Vlatava River at Prague Castle, roaming through the Tresor, and the Museums of Bohemian and Castle Art. There was something about Repin. I loved Repin. In the National Gallery was a nice Durer, but the work that speared me through the breastbone, was Gustav Klimt's 'Judith I,' painted in 1901. It was an allegory of the beautiful widow of Bethulia, who had entered the tent of the Assyrian general, Holofernes, and cut off his head. Klimt's version showed Judith holding Holofernes head, off and down to the right of the painting. It was a long time before I even knew he was there, because of the way Klimt had portrayed her. Out of the gold leaf background, she came at me with an open shirt. Her dreamy, sensual expression overwhelmed whatever slaughter had been committed. She was a Belle Epoque Viennese Jewish upper class femme fatale, better, and long before, the vamp airs of Greta Garbo and Marlene Dietrich. Until that moment I had never associated Jewish women with eroticism. But standing before this Klimt temptress, drew me right into the studio he had painted her in.

After Judith, the Military Historical Museum was a waste of time. Lalo and Jans and I went out for steaks and pilsner, until my train left later that evening. We waved, and promised to keep in touch but, as it usually happens, the waving was all that mattered. I was in a compartment with some Czechs celebrating something, although I was sure it wasn't necessarily our destination. They had guitars and slivovitz, and I played both of them badly.

'When I was first in Czechoslovakia, it occurred to me that I work in a society where as a writer everything goes and nothing matters, while for the Czech writers I met in Prague, nothing goes and everything matters.'

Phillip Roth

*   *   *

'My greatest trouble is getting the curtain up and down.'
T. S. Eliot

Camping in East Germany was like celebrating Mardi Gras at the Vatican. By the time I had taken three trains, a bus, a tram, and the two-kilometer hike to my campsite, there wasn't a lot of time to commune with the communists. As far as pity went in the DDR, I think the camp oberfuerer took some, in exchange for a small trailer and my voucher. I bought some wurst and mustard and bread, and camped.

The sky was overcast. You could see the guard towers that separated me, across the militarized buffer zone, from the West. I had no idea that these same towers would someday be used for other types of hunting. The no-man's land, along the route of the Iron Curtain, had evolved into a large de facto nature reserve, and the recreation of an amazing wildlife corridor across Europe. I remember the same kind of phenomena occurring in war-torn parts of Africa. When humans fought each other, other more neglected species could make a comeback. Peace for us meant curtains for them.

I broke camp early next morning, untying the Gordian knot that got me there. My first stop was the Pergamon Museum, to see the Pergamon Altar, the Market Gate of Miletus, and the monument I had dreamt of touching since my deep freeze internship year, before the first cartwheel. The Altar was a four hundred foot frieze of Gigantomachy, depicting the battle between the Giants and the Olympian Gods, built in the 2nd century BC by the Hellenistic king, Eumenes II, in what is now Bergama, in Asia Minor. Orion was represented here, on the North Frieze, his large club held aloft. What I had really come to see, however, were the navy and gold embossed tiles of the fabulous Ishtar Gate, the Babylonian portal under which Nebuchadnezzar marched the Israelites, during the first Diaspora. There was jasmine perfume.

My path weaved through the Egyptian collection at the Bode Museum, the National Gallery and Altes Museum, to the 13th century St. Mary's Church, at the foot of the Fernsehturm television tower, in Alexanderplatz. Here, in the hall of the tower, was the 75-foot long Dance of Death fresco, painted in observance of the plague year of 1484. In 1983, there was still no graffiti on the 'Fountain of Friendship Between Peoples,' but there were no linden trees lining Unter den Linden, and no history in the Historical Museum, either. It had all drained, from the burnt out cupola, of the Kristallnacht synagogue.

In 1936, Chaim Weizmann wrote that 'the world seemed to be divided into two parts — those places where the Jews could not live, and those where they could not enter.' Two years later, at 1:20 a.m. on November 10, 1938, Reinhard Heydrich, the same Nazi officer that would be assassinated in Prague, unleashed the Night of the Broken Glass, with an urgent secret telegram of instructions to the state police and SA, coordinating the riots. Police were instructed to seize Jewish archives, and to arrest 'healthy male Jews, who are not too old,' for transfer to concentration camps. Over 7500 storefronts were smashed, 1500 synagogues destroyed, and a quarter of all Jewish men in Germany taken to the *konzentrationslager*. Almost a hundred were ghoulishly beaten to death. *'The eyes of some had been knocked out, their faces flattened and shapeless.'* Insurance payments for property damage was confiscated, as 'damage to the German nation,' and an additional *'Judenvermögensabgabe'* collective fine was imposed, resulting in the confiscation of twenty percent of all Jewish property. In one night, the Nazis managed to achieve all three targets they had set for themselves: expropriation of Jewish belongings to finance their military buildup to war, separation and isolation of the Jews, and the move from the discrimination to physical damage, which set the stage for the legitimization of the Final Solution. It must have been a beautiful synagogue.

My last stop behind the Iron Curtain was the twelve Doric columns of the Brandenburg Gate, topped by the Roman goddess of victory, and the hammer and sickle flag of the DDR. Ronald Reagan arrived four years later, and told Mikhail Gorbachev to open it. Two years later, he did.

But I was moving like Erich Honecker, the DDR's last president, 'always forwards, never backwards.' I disappeared into the U-bahn and, through all the other right gates and subway cars, eventually rode the up escalator to the final curtain call. I had to rub my eyes, in the brightness of West Berlin. My first view was of a vaguely remembered aversion.

In my former life, I wouldn't have been caught dead near the place.
I had crossed the Iron Curtain for Golden Arches. My mouth hit the Big Mac like a crocodile taking a wildebeest at a watering hole. It tasted like... freedom.

'In necessariis unitas - in dubiis libertas - in omnibus caritas.'
'*Unity in unavoidable matters — freedom in doubtful matters — love in all things.*'

Iron Curtain Memorial, Fertőrákos, Hungary

Goosestepping

'I didn't like the play, but then I saw it under adverse conditions- the curtain was up.'

Groucho Marx

Twenty years after John Kennedy had mangled 'Ich bin ein Berliner,' I was fiddling with the lock on my door, at the Pension Aachen. Lalo had given me the names of some friends, but they were away. It was Saturday night in West Berlin and, because the Germans who lived here were exempt from the Federal Republic's compulsory military service, it was the countercultural epicenter of the continent. But I was too old to rock n roll and too young to die, and the cheapest place I could find to stay, still wanted twelve dollars. And for that, they had given me the wrong key.

I had promised Bente that I would call her when I crossed back into the West. The next morning was Sunday, and I phoned her in Esbjerg, moments before she was leaving for work. Time off had been arranged in advance, and she told me to meet her in Munich, in five days time. The connection was soldered with tears.

I strolled a relaxed tour of the city, beginning with its bizarre cultural icon, at the Egyptian Museum in the Charlottenburg Schloss, the 3300 year-old limestone bust of Nefertiti.

The Great Royal Wife of the Eighteenth Dynasty Pharoah Akhenaten, the sculptor Thutmose had carved her image in 1345 BC, a most beautiful woman, with serpentine neck, elegantly arched eyebrows, high cheekbones, slender nose, and red-lipped enigmatic smile. She was fashioned as a heavy flower, on a slender stalk. One eye was adorned with black quartz and beeswax. She wore a blue crown and broken cobra on her brow. Nefertiti's name was literally 'the beautiful one has come.'

The Antiquities Museum, the historical war photos at the

427

'Bilder von Krieg' exhibition that Lalo had recommended, and the Durer and amazing Rembrandt collection at the Gallery of Fine Arts, led to a bratwurst at the zoo, and my late withdrawal to the Aachen.

I needed south. My climb up through the guts of the COMINTERN had Eastern-blocked my natural freehand curve to Asia, and Warsaw-packed frustration into the delay. I was craving the open road and new adventures, weary of catalogue box-ticking the dead mementos in the museums and churches and cemeteries of Europe. I ached for the turning of the next Cartwheel, but it was still two months away.

I settled for an inflection point, and south. The bright early sun and a few Deutchmarks drew me along, through the subway to the zoo, the #94 bus to the #66 bus, and a two kilometer walk to a scene of fifty duffel-bagged hitchhikers, under the sign. I looked up at it. *'You are now leaving the American Sector.'*

The single crossing point for foreigners and allied forces to get through the East German corridor, from West Berlin to West Germany, Checkpoint Charlie was the holy hole in the Berlin Wall. Le Carré spies hung out at the Eagle Café, with its strategic view into and out of East Berlin. Originally, Checkpoint Charlie was blocked only with a gate, until some determined East Germans crashed the communist party. The *Stasi* put a strong pole across it. More enterprising departees took down homemade collapsible windshields in their convertibles, at the last moment, and drove under it. That's when they started shooting. Steroid use makes sore losers.

On 17 August 1962, Peter Fechter, an East German teenager, was shot in the pelvis by East German guards, while trying to escape from East Berlin. His body lay bleeding and tangled in barbed wire, in full view of the world. American soldiers couldn't rescue him because he was meters inside the Soviet sector. East German border guards wouldn't get involved, afraid of provoking Western soldiers, one of whom had already shot an East German border guard, days earlier. It took him hours to die.

Judging by the force field of freaks and freeloaders, competing for the few rides coming out of the city, I wasn't destined to fare much better. Hitchhiking was called *Autostop* in Germany. Studying the ratio of contestants to the number of decelerations, it had been misnamed. I was surrounded by highly motivated well-dressed sophisticates, with imaginative signs to everywhere. I observed the *polizei* hassling those with inferior fashion statements. What chance would I have of getting a ride?

I caught the engine sound a reflex split second before he became physically manifest. My thumb carved an arc, through the inexperienced timing, through the slow chic feigned conviviality of the crowd, and through the air. Few things are more dangerous than a bunch of incentive-driven individuals trying to play it safe. But I was one of them.

The Alfa Romeo downshifted five times in as many seconds, to pick up my Travolta. In as many more, Serendipity was in the back, I was in the passenger seat, and he was stick dancing back up the clutch to warp speed. I stole a quick glance in the rearview. Their mouths were open wide, like a choir singing Beethoven's 'Ode to Joy.' I blew on my thumb.

Renaldo was a 24 year-old Italian guest worker, heading all the way to Taranta, in southern Italy. I bought a five Deutchmark transit visa at the border, some salami sandwiches and cola for our passage, and Revvin' Renaldo did what he did best. The East German highway patrol either never saw us, or looked like keystone cop dust, on the side of the road. By the time we hit the Bundesrepublic, it was 200 km an hour, all the way to Munich. Now that's what I'm talking about.

My last view of Revvin' Renaldo was lighting up his third pack of Marlboros, into a cloud of smoke and dust and dusk. I caught a bus to Marionplatz and the S-bahn to the Youth Hostel in Pullach, meeting a young American on the way. Len was a 22 year-old math senior from Albuquerque. I teased him about making a wrong turn. We checked into room 313, and went for an omelet and a beer.

The youth hostel in Munich had the same labor requirement as other IYHF facilities around the world. Everyone had to perform a duty as part of the accommodation. Their work ethic hadn't entirely recovered, from the mentality that had dominated nearby summer camps four decades previously. It took me three hours to clean the lounge stairways, sweeping and mopping repeatedly, until my efforts finally met with the approval of the commandant. I told him I hadn't seen the sign, on my way through the entrance.

"What sign?" he inquired.

"Arbeit macht frei." I replied. His amusement was immeasurable.

But that was the gate I walked under that afternoon. I took two S-bahn trains and a bus, to Dachau. 'Lieber Gott, mach mich dumm, damit ich nicht nach Dachau kumm.' *Dear God, make me dumb, that I may not to Dachau come.*

It was a pretty place. The memorial chapels were almost Zen-like. Even the crematoria were cozy and clean. Dachau was a concentration camp, not an extermination camp, although the difference was ultimately in the degree of passive versus active annihilation. The prisoners that escaped being shot, for target practice and sport, were treated to the finality of typhus or starvation, or typhus and starvation. The American troops that liberated the place were so horrified by the conditions they found, that a few of them thought it would be fun to kill some of the camp guards. It is now referred to as the 'Dachau Massacre,' but I'm not convinced it's the right descriptor. Despite the sanitation, I could still feel the barbed wire in my lungs. The former SS barracks are now occupied by the *Bavarian Bereitschaftspolizei*, the police rapid response unit. Ours is a thin veneer of civilization.

'I dream of it. Inside I will build a chamber, crowned by a large dome. In the middle, this wonder, Nefertiti, will be enthroned. I will never relinquish the head of the Queen.'

Adolf Hitler

*   *   *

'The goose-step, for instance, is one of the most horrible sights in the world, far more terrifying than a dive-bomber.'

George Orwell

Three days later, I woke the commandant at five am, to open the gate. My offer to clean up around the place was refused. It seems he just wanted to get back to bed. I had spent most of my time at the old castle in the forest, or on the Isar River, admiring the swans. But I needed an early start, to meet the number twelve train, at the Hauptbahnhoff.

The beautiful one had come. Bente was still magnificent. I called around and found a pension, the 'Tiroler,' and the gruff old Bavarian matron that told us she had a room. Too much lipstick greeted us on the other side of the chime. She appeared to be hard of hearing. It was a good thing.

Saturday we walked through the Englischer Garten, to the Chinese pagoda. Massachusetts-born Sir Benjamin Thompson, who later became Count Rumford, created one of the world's largest urban parks, the thousand-hectare English Garden in 1789. I hadn't expected the monkeys, especially the one who tore up and ate our map. I hadn't expected him to bite my left foot, when I tried to retrieve it. But it didn't matter, at the time. It was a summer day at the five-storied 'Chineseischer Turm,' and there was room for seven thousand more in the beer garden. Bente and I had bratwurst and salad, steins of Helles, sunshine, and oom-pa-pa. Her eyes sparkled, like black quartz and beeswax. Later in the afternoon, we stumbled past a plaintive Bolivian troubadour, through the nude sunbathers in the Schönfeldwiese, to our own naked penchant for natural perfection in the pension.

My foot was sore next morning, with an area of inflammation. But I wasn't going to let a monkey ruin our reunion. Bente and I walked, too far in retrospect, to find the only apotek open on Sunday. I convinced the pharmacist to sell me a week's worth of ampicillin and some aspirin, tossed back the first installment, and set off to see the art museums. We visited the new, the old, and the in-between, the 'Neue Pinakothek', the 'Alte Pinakothek', and Hitler's 'Haus der Kunst.' I preferred the works of Cranach, Durer, Rafael, Rembrandt, Tiepolo, El Greco, Rubens, Hieronymus Bosch, and the da Vinci, in the Alte, to the images in the Neue, although it had a lovely Gainsborough. Beyond the swastika-motif mosaics in the ceiling panels of the Haus der Kunst, was an exhibit of modern art that would have lent credence to Hitler's assertion of its inherent 'degenerateness.'

My foot was electric pain by the time we had limped back that evening. Even Lipstick was nattering away, about the need to seek attention. Munich's motto was 'Weltstadt mit Herz,' *Cosmopolitan city with a heart*. In 2006, they changed it to 'München mag Dich,' *Munich likes you*. They didn't change it fast enough. For me, or the Israeli Olympic team, ten years earlier.

The 'Tiroler' had no hot water that night. About half way through the darkness, my almost unbearable torment turned on the bathroom light, to find a red streak running up my left leg, and a yellow swelling. I stuck a knife into it. The exuding pus seemed to flow forever, but my agony abated, just enough for me to fall back asleep.

I awoke to Bente and Lipstick looking down at me. They both had their arms crossed. It was going to be like that. Bente and I took a cab to one of the *tagklinikplätze,* at the Schwabing Krankenhouse. After a two-hour wait, a young Czech exile intern told me what I already knew. If some idiot had rocked up in my ER, with a full-blown lower extremity cellulitis, draining abscess, and lymphangitic involvement, I would have committed him as insane, if he refused admission. I refused admission. Even when Dr. Schwartz, the consultant arrived, I refused admission. He was furious, and asked me how I could be so stupid, especially as a physician. I told him that I didn't have three hundred dollars a day, and I didn't have insurance. He wished me luck. Sixty years after Hitler first tried marching himself into power in the Munich Beer Hall Putsch, I goose-stepped out of the clinic, stopped by another pharmacy for a double-whammy antibiotic to compliment my ampicillin, and returned to the Tiroler. Lipstick was apoplectic. I told her I had no intention of dying in her pension, but I needed a few days more.

Bente nursed me through it all and, in return, I abandoned her, again. And she knew all that, and did it anyway.

For four days I lay within the pink wallpapered walls of the Pension Tiroler, watching my left leg go through the rainbow, as the sun rose and descended. If I had lost an arm, or an eye, I could have regained my freedom of movement, and my Gypsy crown. But I was stuck in a slow motion microbial massacre, goosestepping in Munich. Hitler had been imprisoned because he had tried to overthrow the Weimar Republic, and take over the country. He wrote about his struggle in *Mein Kampf*. I was incarcerated because a monkey bit my foot. I wrote a prescription for tetracycline.

And then, on the morning of the fifth day, my toes awoke a shade lighter than the wallpaper. Bente and I took them on a test drive to the Deutches Museum, and back to the Tiroler, for a final night of a familiar suffering. The next morning, I would leave Munich with as much as Neville Chamberlain left with, white paper flag fluttering in the wind. Nothing.

"So what is the third act of the hero's journey?" Asked Sam.

"The road back, Sam. The resurrection, and the return with the elixir. But it's never that simple. The hero initially refuses to return. Why, he thinks, after everything that he has accomplished, the ambrosia he has tasted, the gods he has conversed with, should he return to his original mundane existence, with its fear and cravings. Sometimes he needed to escape with the object of his quest, if the gods had been jealously guarding it. Sometimes the return was just as dangerous as the departure. Sometimes the hero needed a guide to help him realize the road back, or that he needs to take it. There is a return threshold that he needs to cross, to reintegrate the wisdom into his more human life, and to adjust to the idea that the end of the hero's journey is not the aggrandizement of the hero. If he is very lucky, he returns able to master the two worlds, comfortable and competent with both the inner spiritual and outer material. This leads to the freedom from the fear of death, which is the freedom to live in the moment, neither anticipating the future nor regretting the past."

"Was that the story of your journey, Uncle Wink?" Millie asked. The moon was still.

"Every day of it."

Gemütlichkeit

'If you start to take Vienna- take Vienna'
Napoleon

Bente and I kissed Lipstick auf wienerzehn at the pension, and ate Weißwürste at the Hauptbahnhof, before saying our last goodbye. Hungry Butterfly would have seen the white sausages as chrysanthemums. Her train wouldn't leave until nine p.m. We were both numb.

In German, a Wiener is someone from Vienna. In Frankfurt it's also a sausage. In Vienna they call it a Frankfurter. I was heading to Vienna to sort this out.

I took the S-bahn to the Ostbahnhof, and bus #25 to the Innsbrucker Ring, where a young Frankfurter gave me a lift to an autobahn service station. A family of four squeezed me into their wagon, and brought me nowhere in particular. I ended up spending the day in the Bavarian Alps, watching convoys of Italian trucks, puzzling at why my thumb was pointing in the wrong direction. The highway polizei were less than gracious hosts, checking my passport without providing any additional navigational information. My foot was still sore. I still needed it, to hump to the next gas station. An attendant told me of a bus. I waited for over an hour and asked another. He told me no such bus existed. I walked.

Hours later, I came to another turnoff to Salzburg. An earthy Greece-bound German couple shared a Fanta. The sun was leaning hard on the horizon, when a brand new shiny black Mercedes finally pulled over. Bram was a doctor, my age. He was headed to Salzburg, to gamble away another thirty thousand Deutschmarks. I thought we had a lot in common, except for the part about the brand new shiny black

Mercedes, thirty thousand Deutschmarks, and a different destination.

Bram was definitely a gambler. He played elaborate games of chicken, at 200 km/hr, through the most fairytale Alpine magic. Smooth operator. At the Austrian border he selected a macerated Mazda with Viennese plates, rolled down his window, and spoke in perfect English.

"Can you take my friend to Wien?" He asked. The blond hair waltzed out of the other vehicle's driver side.

"Ja." She said.

And I was off, with Effie and Margit, two 24 year-old gymnasts and sports medicine students, to the city of Freud and Strauss, and schnitzel and Sachertorte. Big green eyes to the big Blue Danube. We drove through the night, past the magnificence of Melk. Some other time, I thought. We told stories and eased apprehensions. It was a late arrival. We had tea at Margit's, and Effie took me home for a shower, sweet nothings, and a restless night on three cushions, a painful foot below, and beside, her bed.

She woke me with a special Sunday brunch. We picked up Margit, and drove to a secluded spot on the Danube, for a lazy day of sunbathing, swimming, and watching them study for their final exams.

"Was ist 'training?'" Asked Margit. And Effie would toss her goldilocks, and provide the rote recitation of their professor's correct definition.

They swam topless, and I threw them Frisbees from the riverbank, mesmerized by the fluid dynamics. The British Army had named its first nuclear weapon 'the Blue Danube.' They were definitely on to something.

The day became more tactile. We went to the 'Fantasy Exhibit,' a folksy museum where all the signs said 'please touch.' I had trouble looking at Effie, without seeing the same sign. We ate ice cream and touched. In the late afternoon, they drove me on a whirlwind tour of Vienna, to an Italian café in a soft sunlit flower garden, for spinach pizza and Chianti. After coffee at Margit's, Effie took me home again. We sat in the dark drinking Campari and orange juice, playing cards by candlelight, and playing for time. Despite the electromagnetic energy in the Viennese air, we weren't ready for each other. I hadn't left Bente, and Effie hadn't abandoned her upbringing. She told me she was a virgin. I had forgotten how Catholic the Hapsburgs had been. Freud's fine form was hanging in the rafters. Even so, the forces of repulsion were having a tough time of it. Effie was an Austrian Aphrodite, and I was still throwing her Frisbees. We spent the night frustrating each other.

Coffee and concern received the morning. She needed to study, and I needed to see the city. Separation would cool the ardor. Effie went to take a shower. I emerged from the bedroom to begin my excursion, to one of Effie's friends who had just entered. Her expression was one of Habsburg horror.

My first stop was the Bulgarian chancellery, where I arranged to pick up my visa approval in Belgrade. I walked to the oval Baroque of Karlskirche, with its Greek temple portico, and the two spiral relief columns, modeled after the Boaz and Jachim pillars that stood in front of the Temple in Jerusalem. It was built by the Holy Roman Emperor, Charles VI, in homage to Charles Borromeo, revered as a healer of plague.

The Vienna State Opera House had originally been unpopular with the public. In 1945, the Americans firebombed away the back half, destroying the stage, and the entire décor and props for more than 120 operas. Over 150,000 costumes went up in smoke. Unfortunately, I didn't have tickets for the opera ball, and I had forgotten my tux.

By the end of my perusal of the million master prints at the Albertina, and the beautiful Ottoman Austria history exhibit in the richly veneered Bibliotek, I was in need of a pick-me-up. Just down Kohlmaarkstrasse was the Hofzuckerbackerei Demel, the most famous pastry shop and chocolatier in Vienna. A horse drawn jade green gilt-trimmed carriage, with a jade green gilt-trimmed top-hatted driver, was parked outside. The waitress addressed me in the third person.

"He wishes a coffee and Sachertorte?" She asked, in the historical polite form of attendance. I looked around. Nobody there. I told her that, for eighty shillings, she should have called me sweetheart. Both her smile and the pastry were delicious.

In a nearby bookstore, I bought 'West Asia on the Cheap' by Tony Wheeler. It was the dawn of 'Lonely Planet,' and a sign that the mystical places of the world would become a whole lot less lonely, long before the Internet would exterminate them all, forever. Wheeler had introduced the equivalent of the first rabbit to Australia, and the writing was on the wall.

My tour brought me to the multicolored tile roof and black façade of St. Stephens Cathedral. When it was originally built, the façade had been white. It was here that Beethoven discovered the totality of his deafness, watching birds flying frantically out of the bell tower. He hadn't heard the bells.

One of my last stops was the small Gothic Maria am Gestede church. I sat in the park in front of the Art School, confined by the dogs and pigeons and the old ladies, and the sunlight, slipping slowly along. I needed to flow again, space to move, without all the masonry getting in my way. The wanderlust was biting, harder than the monkey in the Englischer Garten in Munich. At that moment, a single dirt track was worth more to me, than all the asphalt in the universe.

I had been waiting for another chance to call my parents. The telephone worked this time. My mother told me that they had emptied my bank account, to pay off my student loans. She wanted to know when I would be coming home. I told her about the Swiss bank account. I didn't tell her about the seventy-five dollars.

I bought a bottle of Grüner Veltliner, some Camembert, a Toblerone, and a kiwifruit, for Effie, from a happy drunk shopkeeper, and took a tram back to her apartment. Effie's exam was the next day. She introduced me to her cousin,

Ingrid, and in the evening she pretended to study, while Ingrid and I played cards. She continued to pretend to study when Ingrid left, and I pretended to read my new book. Then Effie turned out the lights, and we stopped pretending.

*   *   *

'The word that allows 'yes', the word that makes 'no' possible.
The word that puts the free in freedom and takes the obligation out of love.
The word that throws a window open after the final door is closed.
The word upon which all adventure, all exhilaration, all meaning, all honor depends.
The word that fires evolution's motor of mud.
The word that the cocoon whispers to the caterpillar.
The word that molecules recite before bonding.
The word that separates that which is dead from that which is living.
The word no mirror can turn around.
In the beginning was the word and the word was
CHOICE.'

Tom Robbins, *Still Life with Woodpecker*

The third Viennese sweet thing I awoke to next morning, other than the coffee, was the millirahmstrudel pastry. Vienna was the pastry capital of the world, and the birthplace of the crescent-shaped croissant and the bagel, both created to celebrate the defeat of the Turks. The Ottoman armies were stopped twice outside the city, first during the Siege of 1529, and then at the Battle of 1683. The bagel-makers were stopped once. In 1923 there were 201,513 Jews living in Vienna, the third-largest community in Europe. They had given the world the philosophy of Wittgenstein, Freudian psychoanalysis, the economics of Hayek, the literature of

Kafka, and the music of Strauss, Brahms, Bruckner and Mahler. All gone now, Austrians had constituted forty per cent of the staff at Nazi extermination camps. There hadn't been any measurable resistance to the *Anschluss* reunification with Hitler's Germany, in 1938.

I wished Effie luck with her exam, and went to pay her parking fine. The Kunsthistorische Museum held, in addition to roomfuls of Dürer, Brughel, Veronese, Tintoretto, and my favorite, Hieronymous Bosch, the crown of the Holy Roman Empire. I took a series of trams to Schönbrunn Palace, and then to the Belvedere. I spent my medical school years living in the Belvedere in Kingston, but I would have preferred the décor of this one. In 1770, it hosted the commemorative ball for the marriage of Princess Maria Antonia, to the French Dauphin, who would later become Louis XVI. They invited sixteen thousand guests. Every notable noble of note fleeing Napoleon ended up with an apartment here. Mine was ninety dollars a month, and had no kitchen, or paintings by Gustav Klimt.

I met Effie back at her flat, but she was too agitated about the final test, for her English to work properly. She left for the examination hall a few minutes later. Moments after that, Ingrid arrived with a guitar, and her psychotic boyfriend. Peter had one motorcycle, two divorces, three earrings, and four tattoos, in the days when transdermal metal and subdermal ink were not quite yet just a matter of casual choice. We went off to a wine cellar. At the end of the night, Peter confided that my German had improved considerably. I think that's what he said.

My last day in Vienna was spent celebrating Effie and Margit's successful examination results. After lunch in a quaint little café, I said goodbye to Margit, made coffee for Effie, and went out to buy her groceries and flowers, while she slept. If training was defined as the action of teaching a person a particular skill or type of behavior, Effie was an honor student.

She drove me to the highway next morning in the rain. It wasn't a good spot for hitchhiking, but it was more important to say goodbye properly. I was soaked to the skin for the next three hours. The hypothermia became only marginally less lethal, after a bean soup at the gas station. I tried several more spots in the downpour without success. Finally, around three in the afternoon, a portly middle-aged lawyer named Hans, pulled over to give me a ride. He was headed to Klagenfurt, near the Yugoslavian border, and knew a lot of local history. I was lucky he stopped. Hans drove through the Alps to a 12th century Romanesque church, and then to the Benedictine monastery of St. Paul's in the Lavanttal. In addition to the coffins of thirteen members of the Habsburgs, the abbey had one of the largest collections of art in Europe, including paintings by Rubens, Van Dyck and Dürer.

When we arrived in Klagenfurt, Hans offered me the other bunk in his room. After a small interrogation to ensure his electrical neutrality, I accepted with thanks, and bought us curried bratwurst.

Two brave local heroes, who killed the winged dragon that inhabited the lake, had founded Klagenfurt. The 'Lindwurm's' staple diet was rumored to have been virgins but, on this occasion, it failed to reject the fat chained bull the men had mounted on a tower.

In a world of virgins and dragons and heroes, choice was sometimes a chained bull.

Balkanized

'All roads do not lead to Rome.'
Slovenian Proverb

It no longer exists. When I said goodbye to Hans next morning, I was heading to a country that no longer exists.

It was a six-kilometer hike past a baroque parish church, along fields of wildflowers enclosed by volcanic mountains, and a cotton sky. The young Austrian, who picked me up, related stories of his travels in Asia, and dropped me at what he considered a better hitching post, a classic inside curve with a 5° incline. In less than a minute, I had captured the eyes of Marion, a 34 year-old Yugoslav welding engineer working in Dortmund, on his way home. He maneuvered us through good music, sunshine, and the winding curves of the most precipitous breathtaking mountain passes until, after a twenty minute suffocation in a carbon monoxide tunnel, we surfaced at a Yugoslav border for another half hour, while I obtained my visa. Apparently, I had needed one from the consulate.

"Next time." She said.

"Next time." I echoed.

Winding down to more level ground, Marion diverted almost twenty kilometers, to show me the Assumption of Mary Pilgrimage Church, on a rock, on an island, in glacial Lake Bled in the Julian Alps. I rang the bell for good luck, and walked the 99 steps, that Slovenian bridegrooms are required to climb while carrying their brides. The new wife is required to remain silent. There was a message there for both of them. We ate rum ice cream. I was going to like it here.

Marion turned up the tunes, and we roared by castles and local pulchritude, grading them out of ten, on the 'Marion Scale.' We stopped in Brežice, where his wife and mother-in-law prepared a repast of soup, eggs and homemade cheese, and salad, accompanied by slivovice, coffee, and Metaxa. Sated, he took me back out the highway where, after an hour in the solar tangent, a doctor named Marislov, picked me up. He shared the nasty bus accident frustrations he was returning from attending to and, by the time we had finished reworking each case together, along the Sava river, let me out at the youth hostel in Zagreb.

Four dollars got me a bed and the acquaintance of Luis, from Malaga. The meal we had in 'Mosop' was a contest between the grease in the chicken and the mashed potatoes. The potatoes won. It was forgettable. We had a new roommate in our room back at the hostel, a chain smoking, hard drinking Sikh, running cars from Switzerland to Turkey, who changed my money, and got happy on candy-flavored rum. He snored like a buzz saw cutting through gravel, and was upset with the cleaning staff waking him at six in the morning. I told him he was a very lucky man.

Thick espressos brought me awake, in the market next morning. The light filtering through the blue and yellow umbrellas guided my path through the narrow alleyways. Deep voices of the mass in session, rolled out onto the vendors, down the steps of the spiked Gothic cathedral, on the other side. The colored tiles of the two coats of arms on the small roof of the Church of St. Mark, were a poorer cousin to St. Stephens in Budapest. The white castle on the red background was the symbol of Zagreb; the other represented the Triune kingdom of Croatia, Slavonia, and Dalmatia. Hungarian king Bela IV had given Zagreb a cannon. They fired it every day at noon, so it wouldn't rust. I took in the 14th century apotek and the Archeological museum, on my way to catch the mid-afternoon train for Split. I spotted Canadian flags on two backpacks, but the owners were too cool for conversation. Much warmer were a young South African couple, Sandra and Dietrich, on a year's sabbatical from their day planners. They had hooked up with Tainia, a 19 year-old Finnish girl, on a shorter Dalmatian holiday. I didn't see any of them on the train, but the nine hours passed quickly, reading and dreaming of India, eating crackers and drinking coffee, playing with a little girl in the lap of her mother across from me, and watching the mountains dissolve into Adriatic blue streams of consciousness.

Entering Split around nine thirty that night, we were met by a wiry little grandmother for 'sleeping.' She was persistent, and led us up through a maze of convoluted steep alleyways, to a Tito duplex of simple beds, and no other furniture. We left our packs, and hurried out before everything closed, for a cheese sandwich, and wine mixed with mineral water. The rest of the night kept dumping me out of my sloped bed, and onto the floor.

Split was the largest city in Dalmatia, located on the site of the ancient Greek colony of Aspálathos, named after the Spiny Broom shrub that grows so well in the area. Diocletian, the first Roman emperor to successfully extricate himself from office, built an opulent palace to retire into, in his home Dalmatia. When a group of Roman Senators came to implore him to return, Diocletian pointed to his cabbages.

Split was also the hometown of Marko Marulić, a classic Croatian author. In 1501 he wrote his most acclaimed work, *Judita*, an epic poem about the same Judith that Klimt had painted in gilt.

Dietrich and Sandra woke Tainia, and we wandered into the marker for cucumber, wurst, bread and coffee. A young Slavic beauty sold us tickets on the night boat to Hvar. The damp, dripping subterranean halls of Diocletian's palace inadequately conveyed the original magnificence of the place, but the spontaneous male ensemble in the courtyard would have likely rolled the last Jupiter-worshipping Roman oppressor of Christianity, over in his grave. The Split-Beograd soccer match scheduled for that evening was primed by a raucous rally at the wharf. Under the lengthening shadow of a large phoenix palm, we savored our ceramic and beer, on the terrace of an adjacent little restaurant overlooking the revelry, until our boat left. At least until when we thought our boat left. Instead of the 19:30 postponed to 21:30 boat to Hear, we found ourselves on the 20:30 postponed to 21:18 boat to Stalingrad.

A middle-aged Croat named Domain met us at the dock, and offered accommodation. He was wearing a tie. I pointed out to Dietrich that the necktie had been invented in Croatia, and that I hadn't quite forgiven them for that. We got into Domain's television-equipped stretch car and drove around to the other side of town. He had a magnificent house in a vineyard, surrounded by Holm oak, Aleppo and Black pines, olive trees, lavender, and a swimming pool, shimmering under a three-quarter moon. I wondered why Domain would have to take in boarders. He settled us in with a bottle of his own white wine, and left us two spacious double rooms, replete with enquires and ocean views. Dietrich and Sandra vanished into one. Tania and I shrugged, and took the other. Sometimes you got lemons. Sometimes you got lemon meringue pie.

> 'We have spilt an ocean of blood for brotherhood and unity of our Peoples and we shall not allow anyone to touch or destroy it from Within.'
>
> Tito

> 'It was from Tito that I drew inspiration while searching for the best Road to take and when making crucial decisions during our liberation Struggle. I often thought, what would Tito do at that moment?'
>
> Robert Mugabe

*   *   *

> 'I am always killing boars, but the other man enjoys the meat.'
>
> Diocletian

This much the Roman emperor had in common with the Marshall that ruled for thirty years, from the year I was born until three years before I arrived in Yugoslavia. Taking his name from another Roman emperor, Titus, Josie Bras Tito used to hunt wild boars with Nicolai Ceausescu, but the other man, because he broke the rules and cheated, enjoyed the meat. Ceausescu once shot at a boar and, having missed it, fired again, after the pig had moved out of Ceausescu's, and into Tito's, line of fire. Tito then killed the boar with his first shot, but Ceausescu claimed that he had done the same.

"In that case, your shot must have gone up the hole under the boar's tail." Tito commented. The same thing happened at least twice. The question was who to believe. Tito was the youngest Sergeant Major in the Austro-Hungarian army, a fencing silver medal winner in Budapest, wounded in Bukovina and sent to a work camp in the Urals before he could receive his Silver Bravery Medal for valor, participant in the October Revolution in St. Petersburg, prisoner in the Petropavlovsk Fortress, member of the Omsk Red Guard, test driver for Daimler, machinist, mechanic, and shipyard and train coach factory union leader, head of the Yugoslav Partisans in World War II, and an escapee from a Russian prison train, the Nazi *Operation Rösselsprung* airborne raid on his Raid on Drvarhe headquarters, and Stalin's various attempts to assassinate him. Tito had written openly:

> 'Stop sending people to kill me. We've already captured five of them, one of them with a bomb and another with a rifle... If you don't stop sending killers, I'll send one to Moscow, and I won't have to send a second.'

Tito had ordered his forces to assist escaping Jews during the war, spoke six languages, and founded, and was the first Secretary-General, of the Non-Aligned Movement. When he

447

died of gangrene on May 4, 1980, three days short of his 88th birthday, he commanded the largest state funeral in history, with four kings, 31 presidents, six princes, 22 prime ministers and 47 ministers of foreign affairs. A boar's brain is the size of a walnut.

Or you could have believed Ceaușescu.

Breakfast was sumptuous for all the right reasons. We all walked the harbor and along the winding boardwalk to the Tri Palmas, for a lazy late lunch of schnitzel, salad, and wine. The day was Venetian, and languished along with us, playing ping-pong, doing laundry, and catching the beach rays down below. We bought victuals at the local grocer, and returned for a collective creative collation. Domani breezed through just long enough to lay on another couple of flasks of his best libation.

Dietrich confided in me his concern that Tainia hadn't contributed anything to the communal pot. I told him that I thought of her as MFF, *Meine Finnische Frau*. He told me to be careful. I told him I thought she was just young, impecunious, and nervous. He wasn't so sure.

The next morning was as idyllic as our first. Beachfront cavorting retreated to a harborside café indulgence of burek, yoghurt, ice cream and coffee. The sleek fishing boats bobbed happily beside us. After lunch we took the sun bus, through lavender fields, along azure Adriatic views from the stone-skirted winding roads, to Hvar, another picturesque Venetian town. At the top of a limestone-lined alleyway near the castle, Tainia and I found a twin room next to Dietrich and Sandy. We bought sardines, cheese, cucumber, bread and wine for a climb up the castle walls, and a picnic in the sunset over Hvar. I had a hot and cold shower, and was about to fall asleep, when MFF asked me.

"Hey man, will you massage my neck?" Hot and cold lemon meringue. These Finnish girls were unusual creations.

I needed to go to Korčula. No matter what was happening in the rest of the world, I needed to go to Korčula.

Dietrich and I tanned behind our sunglasses on the deck of the boat next morning, discussing the fiscal and thermal regulatory dysfunction of MFF.

"Dalmatians don't change their spots, Wink." He said.

"She's Finnish." I replied.

"What's the difference?" He asked. I noted my observation of the three national characteristics, and how Finns were the product of a harsh geography and climate, fond of their liquids, and fiercely independent.

"What's that got to do with Tainia?" He asked.

"I have no idea," I said. "But I don't think its love."

We arrived on an island of the dense pines that originally supplied timber for the walls of Venice, in return for the stonework that distinguished its architecture. Korčula was also an island of Greek artifacts, Roman villas, Byzantine suzerainty, Neretvian pirates, Ottoman resistance, Habsburg monarchy, French Empire, Austro-Hungarian domination, Nazi invasion, and Yugoslav partisan hideouts. None of this was why I needed to go to Korčula.

It was one of the most romantic places I had ever seen. The Adriatic sun penetrated tight cobbled alleyways of flowerboxes, brimming with red and yellow blossoms. We gorged on red plums and the sweet purple juicy fruit of mulberries, right off the trees, along the rocky path from the beach.

Right on cue, a little old Dalmatian lady reversed direction and spotted us. We followed her home and stored our packs. In the stunning stone square near the market, a café lunch of scampi, salad, and beer had been waiting just for us. Sated and slaked, we strolled past white dolomite outcropped hollows of nude Germans, to find our own sunny refuge, further down the shore.

In late afternoon, we returned via the market, and found legumes and lemons and wine, and freshly caught sardines, for our dinner. On the next street over from our shelter, was the reason I had come. It was a stone house similar to others

449

in the maze, under a red-tiled terra cotta roof, with a small Venetian column, above a stone arch. A small sign said 'Koca Marka Pola,' the *House of Marco Polo*. According to local tradition, Marco was born here in 1254 AD, to an established family of merchants. The Italians had contested this, unconvincingly. What was quite certain, however, was that, in 1298 in the Battle of Korčula, a Venetian galley commander, named Marco Polo, was taken prisoner by the Genoese, and imprisoned. During his yearlong incarceration, he dictated the memoirs of his trip through Asia, his meeting with Kublai Khan, and his subsequent 24 years of extensive adventures, traveling over twenty four thousand kilometers in the service of the Mongol court. As a young boy, I had read a translation of the book that recorded his odyssey, '*Il Milione*.' It set the hook.

I fell asleep for a while, sometime after the grilled sardines and white wine. In the previous two days, MFF had gone embryonic. The fact that she hadn't covered her travel costs was forgivable. The fact that she hadn't contributed to, and was detracting from, the travel experience, was becoming unbearable. Dietrich and Sandra were getting impatient with her, and I needed to find out what was wrong.

But I wasn't really in the mood, and instead, snuck out under a full moon in a clear sky on a crisp evening, on an idyllic island in the Adriatic. I let myself randomly wander through the cobbled labyrinth, until I could just faintly hear the music. Then I kept going. I came out onto an alluring scene of enchantment. The lights from the fishing boats reflected on the harbor. A band, in blue and white horizontal striped shirts and fishing caps, with an accordion, mandolin, bazouki, guitar and string bass, played rich Slavic folk songs in the moonlit square. Their passion flowed into the crowd, ever so slightly faster than the wine. I didn't understand a word, but I knew it was about love and death, and that's just the way I felt too. It was powerful and beautiful, and timeless. Everyone in that warm summer night was laughing and crying to the music.

And I realized that, for the first time in almost a year, I was warm. Not hot, not cold, just warm.

It rained the next morning, and everyone was moody. Even the coffee we had in the market was sour. We all decided to split up for awhile. I went for a long wet hike in the scrub, and returned to a thick soup and ražnjići with Sandra and Dietrich, in an arbored café around the corner from Marco Polo's house. By the time we had picked up MFF and our packs, we only just made the boat back to Hvar.

Out of nowhere, Tainia bought me an International Herald Tribune, and I settled into the weekend crossword. Just before docking, I sensed that something wasn't quite right with Tainia. She was friendly, and talkative. I don't mean talking. I mean chatty and loquacious and garrulous and babbling and blathering. She said more in a minute than she had since I met her. I tried to find out from Dietrich and Sandra, what had been going on, while I was three across and one down. They told me she had had a couple of glasses of wine, but hadn't noticed anything else out of the ordinary. By the time the boat docked, MFF was incoherent, rocking her head between her legs. On two glasses of wine, she had jumped full steam into an acute organic brain syndrome. She vomited in the ship's lounge, and then hung onto me for dear life. We managed, with no small effort, to wheedle her off the boat. I exchanged addresses and said goodbye to Dietrich and Sandra, and took Tainia to the local clinic. It was closed. She had a pulse and a blood pressure, and I had an insistent old lady with a spare room, who truly wanted our patronage. It was all too much. I put her to bed and, checking frequently to make sure she was recovering, eventually went out to buy some food for dinner. I returned to a closed bedroom door, and a note:

'Dear Wink,

As you've seen its sometimes very difficult for me to say what I'd like to say. I'm not using other people. I've been very unpolite the last five days, and I'm sorry. I promise you, this is the first time I've behaved like an idiot- and the last. Sometimes love arrives in different forms.

Die Finnische Frau, Tainia'

I opened the door cautiously. To tears and flushed cheeks. She pulled me down on top of her. The only wavering was in the candlelight.

'That is the whole history of the search for happiness, whether it be your own or someone else's that you want to win. It ends, and it always ends, in the ghastly sense of the bottomless nothingness into which you will inevitably fall if you strain any further.'

D. H. Lawrence, *The Fox*

*   *   *

'If you want to see heaven on earth, come to Dubrovnik.'

George Bernard Shaw

In the black ice tundra city I trained in my internship year, there had been a restaurant named 'Dubrovnik.' The philosophy professor from Sydney in the ticket booth at the dock, with the leftover pieces of toilet paper stuck to his face, was just as lost. Tainia and I were headed to the most magnificent white walled fortress city in the azure Adriatic, just a few years before it came under fire, from the Balkanized guns of the self-dismembering states that were once Tito's Yugoslavia. Between its frozen facsimile in Manitoba, and the blasted remnants of the secessionist war, we came to George Bernard Shaw's Dubrovnik, while it was still heaven on earth. It was here meine Finnische frau left me, heading south to Greece, for the rest of her holiday. She was quiet again.

I hiked the two kilometers around the rook-like stone walls of the city. They were twenty feet thick in some places. I was the same way. In 1192, Richard the Lionheart was washed ashore here, after being shipwrecked. I was the same way. Skinny cats and hanging washing and bougainvillea punctuated my exertions. I bought a 'gemichte' ice cream, served up by a young juggler who scooped the balls into the air, and whistled as he caught them in the cone.

Under the fluent triple arches of the 14th century Dominican Friary, I found a lovely Gothic cloister, tranquil gardens, an unsurpassed library of over two hundred incunabula and illustrated manuscripts, and an ancient pharmacy. In May of 1544, a shipload of Jewish Conversos, fleeing persecution in Spain and Portugal, landed here. The synagogue and museum were padlocked; the Rabbi had died. I bought comestibles in the market, and retired to the youth hostel, where I met John, a twenty year-old San Franciscan, who had just returned from Turkey. I shared my bread and cheese and sausage and cucumber, in exchange for Turkey tips.

I was on the early bus to Mostar next morning. It took three hours, and I was the only one to get off. In Moslem Bosnia, I had arrived with the paranoia. There was only one thing to see. It had been commissioned by Suleiman the Magnificent in 1557, and had stood for 427 years over the Neretva River, until the Croats blew it to smithereens, ten years after my visit.

It had taken nine years to build the perfect semicircular stone archway of the Stari Most. A 17th century Turkish traveler had remarked that it was '*like a rainbow arch soaring up to the skies, extending from one cliff to the other. I, a poor and miserable slave of God, have passed through 16 countries, but I have never seen such a high bridge. It is thrown from rock to rock as high as the sky.*'

I walked across the glass-smooth cobbled corrugations, to

find out where there might be accommodation. I hadn't considered the possibility that, despite the near emptiness of the town, there might not be. I was advised to board the afternoon bus to Sarajevo. It took an hour longer because of the construction work underway for the 1984 Olympics, and that would be the last feel-good moment in Sarajevo, for a long while.

I arrived just after six p.m., and asked for directions to the hostel. Up a long flight of stairs, there was a coldwater shower and two hyperthermic French Canadians, George and Pierre, to greet me. I played victorious games of chess with each of them, and crashed early.

Before 1914, Sarajevo had been called the 'Jerusalem of Europe,' because of its long and rich history of religious diversity. It had a large Sephardim population, and was home to the oldest Sephardic document in the world, issued in Barcelona in 1350 AD.

The beginning of the end of all the brotherly love occurred sixty-nine years, to the day, before my arrival. I walked through the hot early morning sun *'where minarets have twisted up like sugar, a village like an instinct left to rust, composed around the echo of a pistol-shot,'* to locate the exact spot on the bridge, where Gavrilo Princip shot Archduke Franz Ferdinand, and his wife Sophie. The Archduke's last words were apparently 'It is nothing.' He was wrong for the second time that day. His assassination triggered all the tectonic events of World War I. Otto Von Bismarck had been right in his observation that 'if there is ever another war in Europe, it will come out of some damned silly thing in the Balkans.'

I joined George and Pierre for a walk through the coppersmiths in the Turkish quarter, and a visit to the stalactite ornamentation inside the Gazi Husrev-Beg mosque. We dodged the collection trays in the old Serbian churches, and returned to the hostel for Turkish coffee, and more games of chess, until it was time to leave for my train to

Beograd. I noticed that Serendipity's handles were beginning to fray.

There were two gorgeous Norwegian girls in my carriage, heading to Budapest. They offered to take me along as their toothpaste. My restraint was both praiseworthy and regrettable.

In Belgrade, I boarded tram #9 to the youth hostel. The number nine was actually the number of kilometers out of town, and the unfriendly driver took me ten. Backtracking, an obnoxious warden told me the hostel was full, and I reboarded the tram, heading back into town.

Beograd had been fought over in 115 wars, and razed to the ground 44 times. I was trying to be sensitive.

In front of Hotel Astoria, I encountered Ivan, a lanky middle-aged bank teller, nervously jingling the keys in his pocket. His French was terrible, but better than my Serbian. Ivan asked if I needed a place to stay. He quoted a reasonable price. We took tram #3 to a rather rundown roach-infested central apartment, but Ivan made up for it, in hospitality. He made me a raspberry drink, and provided bread, cheese, and milk coffee, gave me a map of the city, and bid me goodnight.

Coffee and bread were already set out for breakfast, by the time I finished my shower next morning. We took tram #42 to Ivan's bank, where he pointed me in the direction of the park. I wandered the ruins of the massive old fortress, and then headed to the Bulgarian Embassy. Twenty minutes after it opened, there was already a long queue.

The German guy in front of me was nervous. I tried to calm him down. John had been a taxi driver in Munich until he decided, only the previous week, to become a truck driver, on the long road to Iran. I helped him with his visa application, and, in exchange, John agreed to drive me through Bulgaria to Turkey. We grabbed a cab to Ivan's bank, pulled him out of work to fetch Serendipity, brought him back to work, and flew across the river to the National Hotel. Here, waiting, were an ex-hippie chef, Michael, and Horst, a fat Bavarian with a nose for self-sufficiency, guarding our orange and green Mercedes dump trucks.

We roared out of Beograd, through spectacular mountain curves and tunnels, and arrived at the near side of the Bulgarian border by dusk. I bought bread and sheep cheese and cucumbers and beer, and played chess with Michael until last light. Sleep came easy inside the Gold Kazoo, flung out over my homemade straw pallet.

These were exhilarating diesel days again. I was heading to Asia, out from between the cartwheels, and I could smell spices and shit.

Beyond the Pudding Shop

'And therefore I have sailed the seas and come
To the holy city of Byzantium.'
William Butler Yeats

Eccentric behavior is not the result of ignoring logic, but of pursuing it to unusual extremes. My horse sense had planned a gallop to Istanbul to pursue an Iranian Visa, followed by a trot across Mesopotamia to the Indian subcontinent. Its blinders unfortunately had blocked out the psychotic cleric that had just flown in from France, and the suicide potholes that were germinating along Sadaam Hussein's picket fence. Plus, the horse was crazy.

Michael woke me around five, for the crossing into Bulgaria. My immigration official was playing some kind of word association game with 'doctor' and 'capitalist.' I never did find out what the prize would have been if he had won. Across, I bought breakfast for the boys at the communist truck stop, which seemed far too Western for the Bulgaria of the time. While we were enjoying our bread and olives and sheep cheese and coffee, a local inebriant sold me his local currency, at an overly favorable black market exchange rate. Hard currency is a hard taskmaster. John and I left in our truck, with Michael and Horst to follow. Shortly before Plovdiv, we lost them, and parked for a couple of hours on the side of the road, drinking Bulgarian *Repoorit* soda. We finally decided to head off anyway, past white kerchiefed peasant women, hoeing fields of deformed green lines that came together in communal joy, on the solar horizon.

John and I had become good friends by now, singing, joking and sharing road stories. We stopped to pick green plums. When we finally made the far frontier, to our surprise, we found Horst and Michael in the company of a thousand other trucks from all of Europe, heading to Iraq and Iran. The

457

Bulgarians had a captive audience, and were in no hurry to process us across. We drank water and ate peanuts, and cursed in German, until they finally let us through just after seven in the evening. It was Ramadan on the Turkish side, and we had to wait until the sun was properly disposed of, before the Turks would properly dispose of us. It was late when we pulled into our campsite, and the first evidence of my intrusion into the Ottoman invasion of Europe. Someone had stolen the toilet out of the toilet, and left their footprints in porcelain over the hole. *Salaam Aleichem.* The restaurant had too many beers and stuffed peppers, and *Papillon,* dubbed in Turkish, playing on the video above the bar. I rolled out the Gold Kazoo in the back of the dump truck, and slept in the land of the Sultans for the first time.

It was the sobbing that woke me next morning. A Finnish girl was wandering the campground, frantic with fear. She had apparently come close to being raped the previous night, and was uncertain where sanctuary was, on a sea of truckers in an Islamic island. I bought coffee and sat with her until she was calm enough to rethink her priorities. *First, your safety, then your possessions, and then your journey.* Like I was a paragon of precision.

We mounted up, and stopping only once for chai and the smell of fresh roses, drove past the immense mosque in Adana, across the Bosphorus and its union with the Golden Horn and Maramara Sea. *If one had but a single glance to give the world, one should gaze on Istanbul.*

I waved to the Germans, and wished them well. None of us knew that they were heading into the eye of the Iranian Revolution. I caught a dolmus to Akerserai, and hiked with Serendipity high on my back, whistling, three kilometers to the most famous overland traveler's landmark on the 'Hippie Trail,' the watershed between East and West, the Mecca in the middle. This was the place you fattened your VW van, if you had one, or scoured the bulletin board if you were looking for a ride, on your compulsory consciousness-raising pilgrimage to India and Nepal, and beyond. This was the end of menial monotony, and the beginning of *Midnight Express*. This was where you countered your culture, and counted your change. This was where you left passive consumption, and embraced active experience. This is where your superior social status was validated.

This was the Lale Pudding Shop. I came through the door, to some of the original hippies, still planning their route to self-discovery. They were curled up on couches, and in large booths, pouring over maps, playing guitars, or both. *Led Zeppelin* hovered overhead. There were white walls, piles of books, and the most amazing view of the Hagia Sophia and Blue Mosque through the glass, and from the garden.

I sat and ordered the signature dish of departure, *tavuk göğsü*, pounded chicken breast, prepared with rice flour, milk, and sugar, and topped with cinnamon. The juices flowed into the Bosphorus. I studied the bulletin board, searching for any sign of me, and finding none. Here was love and death, messages for family, friends, and lovers. There was a note from Megan to Malcolm, apologizing for '*that business down in Greece*,' and another, seeking '*the girl in the green dress who waved to me on the Ganges*.'

It was all a trap, of course. Backpacker culture was just as rigid as the one you were escaping from. Its central tenets avowed independence, frugality and acceptance of the locals, and were your ticket into a travel community.

But this is where you lost the moral high ground. Because, in your search for community, you became influenced less by the exotic surroundings, than by the social dynamics of home. The community, and not the new culture, became the focus of travel. Independent travelers sought each other out and, instead of looking for nuances and complexities within the host custom, frequently clung to signs of subcultural authenticity in each other. Faraway places and their societal differences, no longer required active experience, but mere passive consumption. And wasn't that what you had contemptuously left behind, as the hypocrisy you were escaping from?

The food was good. I had another pudding, with hazelnuts, barley, figs, raisins, and yoghurt. I got to speak with a nuclear physicist from Louisiana, who asked me if I knew where he could get some morphine.

I left the Lale landmark, for another. I had heard of the Yücelt Hostel, and checked in, behind a bearded young Canadian with a red baseball cap. Uncle Albert was from Saltspring Island in British Columbia, and had just returned from Africa. We shared a room, and showed each other maps and plans. He was heading south along the Aegean coast, as was I. It was a natural.

We spent the evening writing postcards, eating stuffed peppers, and charting our course through Anatolia under bare light bulbs. Below in the courtyard, a drum and shaz twanged in rhythm to the handclapping, and the cats and seagulls moaned along, in a minor key. The silhouette of a minaret from the Aya Sophia looked down. There was cool in the night air, warm glue in sticky clothes.

After one and a half years I was finally leaving Europe. The feeling was one of indescribable ecstasy. I fell asleep in the only metropolis in the world that had served as the capital of the Roman Empire, the Byzantine Empire, the Latin Empire, and the Ottoman Empire, and spanned two continents. The dreams were just that wide.

*   *   *

'Either I conquer Istanbul or Istanbul conquers me.'
Fatih Sultan Mehmet

My horse sense took me to the Iranian consulate early next morning. I gave them four photos and four application

460

forms, and they told me to check in Ankara, in four weeks time. I asked if they could skip the fourplay. They quoted me a Turkish proverb. *'If you are an anvil, be patient; if you are a hammer, be strong.'* It looked like I was going to be an anvil.

I returned to the Yücelt to get Uncle Albert, but he was destined to have a frustrating day of sightseeing. We walked through the bazaar to a shady university café for a cola, and then to the Sulemaniye mosque, the second largest in the city. It was built in 1550 by Süleyman the Magnificent, referencing the Dome of the Rock, and his belief in himself as a 'second Solomon.' It was only slightly less egotistical than Justinian's boast, upon completion of the Hagia Sofia: 'Solomon, I have surpassed thee.'

The descendents of Solomon had lived in the city for over half a millennium. During the Spanish Inquisition of 1492, the Ottoman Sultan Bayezid II sent a large fleet to Spain to save the Sephardim. The Caliphate was, at first, a beacon of tolerance in an otherwise intolerant world, and there were over twenty synagogues in Istanbul. A Jew traditionally held the office of the Chief Physician of the Sultan. Under his supervision, palace drugs were prepared, mixed and sealed. He was a companion of the Sultan outside the palace, and accompanied him into battle.

Uncle Albert wasn't allowed inside the Sulemaniye mosque, because his short jeans cutoffs were cut off too short. He took note, so as not to be turned away from future Turkish delights.

The next day was Dominion Day, changed that very day to Canada Day, the homeland's birthday. Uncle Albert and I began our celebration with breakfast at the Pudding Shop. The nuclear physicist had been renarcotized. I cured his German friend's gonorrhea, over a hard-boiled egg and a Turkish coffee. The German friend told me it was supposed to be 'black as hell, strong as death, and sweet as love.' I told him he oughtta know.

Uncle Albert and I left to see Istanbul. Just around the corner was the Hippodrome, built by Septimus Severus in 203 AD, for chariot races. The remains of the Karnak red granite Egyptian obelisk of Pharoah Tutmoses II, transported by Theodosius, were still there. When Constantine moved his Byzantine capital to what would become Constantinople 120 years later, he renovated it to hold a hundred thousand spectators. The Blue and Green team sports rivalries that came out of the Hippodrome, caused riots and civil wars, one of which destroyed the Hagia Sophia, and killed 30,000 people. The only horse racing the Ottomans ever did, were to see who could sack the city soonest.

Across the street was the Sultan Ahmed 'Blue' mosque. More than 200 Venetian stained glass windows shone colored light onto 20,000 handmade blue ceramic interior tiles. The blue had faded with time. Ostrich eggs sat in the chandeliers, repelling spiders from rappelling spider webs. I was fascinated by the heavy iron chain in the upper part of the court entrance, designed to force the horse-mounted Sultan to lower his head, to ensure the humility of the ruler in the face of the divine. Uncle Albert suggested a few of them hang in the Canadian parliament. I thought he was referring to the chains. He told me he was talking about the rulers. Happy Dominion Canada Day.

Over the road was the largest failure of Christianity, before the onslaught of Islam. The earlier efforts by the Latin Crusaders to rescue Jerusalem had been so dysfunctional that, in 1204, they passed through and treated Constantinople as collateral damage. The angry Byzantines who recaptured the city fifty years later spat on the tomb of the Roman Catholic Doge of Venice, buried inside the church.

The Hagia Sophia had been the world's largest cathedral for a thousand years, until the cathedral in Seville was completed in 1520. Beginning in 532 AD, Emperor Justinian employed ten thousand people in its construction, and imported Hellenistic columns from the Temple of Artemis at Ephesus, large quarried stones in porphyry from Egypt, green marble from

Thessaly, Corinthian pillars from Baalbek in Lebanon, black stone from the Bosporus, and yellow stone from Syria. The largest columns were granite, and weigh over 70 tons apiece. It was the masterpiece of Byzantine architecture. When Sultan Mehmed II conquered Constantinople in 1453, he promised his troops three days of unbridled pillage. That didn't help. The looters even enslaved the congregants inside, except for the elderly and infirmed, who were considered without value, and killed.

The large haunting Madonna and Child mosaic looked out quizzically at Mehmed's mosque conversion of Justinian's dream. The guards left stone depressions where they had stood. Uncle Albert and I were underwhelmed by the Mosaic Museum, especially since the price of admission also required a photo of the ticket vendor's bearded uncle, a man whom, except for the purple toque, looks surprisingly similar to the way I do now.

The afternoon was devoted in its entirety to the Topkapi Palace, the offices and primary residence of the Ottoman Sultans for two thirds of their six hundred year reign. As Uncle Albert and I made our way into the more interior and intimate of the four courtyards, the life stories portrayed inside the Seraglio, grew progressively more mysterious, silent, reclusive, ceremonial, decadent, and bizarre.

Visitors were required to dismount from the horses, between the First and the Second Courtyard, since only the Sultan was allowed to enter the gate on horseback. Court officials and Janissaries lined the path in their best garb, waiting. Hundreds of turbans inclined together, like a field of ripe corn, moving in synchrony, under a fast wind. Their hands were joined in front, and silence, for hours, in the manner of monks, or statues of monks. One then passed the Fountain of the Executioner, where the executioner washed his hands and sword, after a decapitation.

The Third Courtyard was surrounded by the quarters of the Ağas, young pages learning music, painting and calligraphy.

Inside, the chamber walls were covered with mosaics, spangled with azure and gold. The Emperor was seated on an elevated throne covered in gold brocade, sown with emerald and ruby plaques and pearls, and cushions of inestimable value; the fireplace was solid silver and covered with gold. At one side of the chamber a fountain of water gushed from a wall. On the lacquered ultramarine blue ceiling, studded with golden stars and jewels, were foliage patterns accompanied by a depiction of the fight of a dragon with the *simurg*, a mythical bird. The main door was surmounted by an embossed *besmele,* 'In the Name of God the Compassionate, the Merciful,' dating from 1723.

Outside the Sultan's window, a small gilded ball hung from the ceiling, representing the earth, and symbolizing his dispensation of world justice, and limitation of his viziers' power. They came to present their individual reports. Depending on performance, the sultan showed his pleasure by either showering them with gifts and high offices or, in the worst case, having them strangled by deaf-mute eunuchs. Officials entered without knowing if they would leave alive.

But it was inside the Fourth courtyard that intrigued.

The Imperial Harem contained more than 400 rooms, home to the sultan's mother and her forty rooms, his wives, children and their servants, his fenced bath, and the staircase, the 'Forty Steps,' that led to the dormitory of his concubines. Black eunuchs stood guard with their 'beating sticks,' along the staircase. The door to the right lead through the Golden Corridor to the sultan's quarters, where, once a year, the sultan showered his 400 concubines with gold and silver coins. His entertainment room must have been the inspiration for 1001 nights, with its sophisticated seating and small ruby colored glass bulb suspended over the throne, the reward for the best dancer to touch. Here, as well, was a gilded cage with stained glass windows, the prison of each of the Sultan's successors. One was driven mad, after forty years in the small confined space.

There were also, it seems, treasures. The most holy relics of the Moslem world were here, the Prophet Muhammad's cloak, two swords, a bow, one tooth, a hair of his beard, an autographed letter and other relics, which are known as the Sacred Trusts. The swords of the first four Caliphs, The Staff of Moses, the turban of Joseph, the arm of John the Baptist, and a carpet of the daughter of Mohammed, were also part of the Privy Chamber collection. There were over ten thousand pieces of Chinese, Japanese Imari, and Turkish porcelain, one of the finest collections in the world, including 3,000 pieces of Yuan and Ming Dynasty celadons, valued by the Sultan because they were supposed to change color, if the food or drink they carried was poisoned.

Here I found one of the richest assemblages of Islamic arms on the planet, spanning a period of 1,300 years, and including Umayyad and Abbasid swords, Mamluk and Persian amour, and helmets, swords and axes. Clocks and robes and miniatures and calligraphy and Treasury jewels of every description, it just went on and on.

"Do you know what he didn't have?" Asked Uncle Albert.

"What?" I asked.

"Beer." He replied. And he was right.

We retreated to the Yücelt for Tuborg, and began our own collection. In our dorm room were an economics major from Stanford, named Joe, Brian from Illinois, and two Germans that had just returned from Tehran. We all went out for chicken and stuffed peppers, rice, tel kadyif, and salad and tea. Two English docs, Rob and Gary, joined us, on the way. Gary asked me what my specialty was. I told him Internal Medicine. He asked what I was doing in Turkey.

"Stepping outside." I said.

*   *   *

465

> 'To a Turk, the inside of a town is a prison.'
> Osmani Proverb

The next morning Uncle Albert and I went beyond the Pudding Shop. Down past the train station, we flagged a taxi to Kabatas, for the ferry to Yalova. Chai, yoghurt, and the big brown eyes of a young Turkish girl, took us through the Maramara sea haze and, on the other shore, onto an instant bus to the slopes of Mount Uludağ, and the hometown of Mehmet I.

The route to Bursa looked a lot like the road through Morocco. At the Hotel Hasel, we traded our packs with the grumpy Bulgarian clerk, for a restaurant recommendation. The rose's rarest essence lives in the thorn. The Ugadaya Locanta was the Taillevent of the Orient: stuffed eggplant, beans and pilaf, a peppery pepper salad, cacik, and fresh peaches, for a dollar. Uncle Albert took a photo of me having my first *salaamic* shave since Essouira. Along the caliphate trail, they were infrequent but wonderful small indulgences. Others were closer than some. It was worth the price of admission for the series of scents alone.

We moved through the bursting market, to the first great Ottoman mosque of Ulucami. A local graphic artist gave us a tour in German. The gilding on the mihrab was blinding. On and up to the Yeşil Cami *Green Mosque*, the perfect blend of architecture and embellishment, we crossed the street to the matching mausoleum of Mehmet I, fifth of the Ottoman Sultans. It reminded me of Tamerlane's tomb in the Gir Emir, in Samarkand. Back in the market, we bought a watermelon. Our enthusiastic applause, for the live soap powder demonstration from a microphoned moustache, caused a frenzy of buying. Away from the brightness and molten heat, back in our room at the Hasel, we ate watermelon and napped.

I took a cold shower, to bring me out of the setting haze. Uncle Albert wanted 'a night on the town.' Our first stop was a dollar dinner at the Ugadaya, of İskender kebap, aubergine stew, and candied chestnuts. A few doors down from our restaurant, was the kind of establishment that Uncle Albert had been looking for. We entered the 1001 nights of the 'Kapri night culiip,' and, oh my. Everything that wasn't painted black was flashing red, including the ten Harem girls. Lady Montagu had described the greatest ornament of a Turkish woman as simply being Turkish, as each was already an 'alive priceless jewel.' Lady Montagu hadn't been in the Kapri for a while. The jewels were, to be as kind as possible, Rubenesque, and their swallows of Efes pilsen were punctuated, by long exhalations from their continuous cigarettes. I had hoped that we hadn't been noticed, but it was too late. The even more portly singer was wearing a leopard skin, or two. She began to direct her heartfelt moaning towards Uncle Albert.

"There ain't nothin' like this on Saltspring Island." He observed.

"You remember Gallipoli?" I asked. He nodded.

"These are the girls they went home to." I said. We slowly backed towards the exit. In the shadow of the Sultan, and the incessant noise of the motorcycle traffic outside our window, sleep was intermittent.

Uncle Albert and I were on the ten o'clock bus to Çanakkale next morning, heading into six hours of heat, wheat fields, and camels. We were greeted by storm clouds, and an imaginative but touristic mockup of a giant wooden horse. Almost a year and a half earlier, Steve and I had been across the Aegean, in Mycenae, where Agamemnon had gone under the Lion Gate, in pursuit of his sister-in-law, Helen, who had run off with a Trojan, named Paris. According to Homer's epic, it had all ended badly here for everyone, ten years later. Agamemnon's troops came out of the horse to demolish Troy and, in return, the Greek Dark Ages invaded Mycenae. Beware of Greeks bearing gifts. We passed under the gate of Troy VI, the layer that Heinrich Schliemann identified as Ilios, the fabled city for which the *Iliad* had been named.

The lightning streaks across the ruins added to the atmosphere, but the atmosphere crackled ever more frightening flickering images from the Trojan War, before the rest of the sky opened up everything it had been holding in reserve. Albert and I plodded through the downpour and the mud, until a dolmus pulled alongside. The driver seemed to be studying Uncle Albert. He rolled down his window.

"J. R?" He queried.

"Huh?" Replied Albert.

"J. R. Yuwing?" The driver asked again. I turned to Uncle Albert.

"He thinks you're 'J. R. Eweing,' from *Dallas*." I said. "No matter who else you want to be, right this moment, you're Larry Hagman." Albert ran with it.

"Howdy." He said. The driver welcomed us into his vehicle, and drove us into Çanakkale to the Hotel Truva. He wouldn't take any money for the ride. Uncle Albert gave him his autograph, or one from somebody who looked like him.

Later we went out to a seafood restaurant with a view of an Ottoman castle across the Dardanelles Strait. We were joined by Kehmit, a tipsy local businessman, who made us feel welcome, and ordered us sea bass, minced aubergine, and baklava. He sent watermelon to the table as he left. When we went to pay the bill, there was no bill.

We boarded a bus to Bergama, just before noon the next day. It was the 4th of July. This meant absolutely nothing to any of us. Just before boarding, I was play wrestling with the driver's helper. This was a silly idea. Wrestling was not an avocation in Turkey; it was a religious observance. I turned to find a crowd, gathered in sharp anticipation of a match. I turned back to find the driver's helper, removing his shirt, and stretching. It was Napoleon who had made the observation, that you could kill a Turk but you could never defeat him. I wasted no time in trying to win, my pain undoubtedly lessened for doing so. In return, the driver's helper brought me an epiphany as we pulled out. Albert and I were getting used to the towels, the free face-slap of cologne and the sodas, but I had never tasted anything like this. The label on the bottle said 'Aroma visne suyu,' and the contents were blood red.

"It's cherry juice," said Uncle Albert.

"Nope." I said. "That, my friend, is sex." We were both technically correct, and spent the rest of the trip watching the Aegean coast go by, playing chess, and catnapping. It was raining when we were finally ejected from the bus, at a dolmus stand on the edge of town. We boarded one such conveyance to the Hotel Park. Uncle Albert was relieved to find chickens, rather than the traffic from previous nights, outside our window. I told him to wait until four the next morning. Our backpacks secure, Albert and I wandered outside. A stall owner in the market handed us two delicious pastries as we walked by. We learned the Turkish gesture for 'no,' an upturned head and a sucked-in flick of the tongue against the palate, when we tried to pay. There was no hospitality greater than that in a small Turkish town.

Within the fascinating ruined brick walls, of the 2nd century red Roman Temple of Serapis, were shards, and sheep. The basilica had been built for the Egyptian Gods of Hadrian. It straddled the Selinus River. Outside were ancient heavy white tombstones, inscribed in Hebrew.

The evening brought us to the Selami restaurant, for scrumptious aubergines and peppers in yoghurt, shishkebabs, and Aroma visne suyu. It is still impossible for me to return to Turkish memories, without closed eyes and saliva. Uncle Albert and I ended up in the cay shop, smoking hookahs, drinking strong sweet chai, and listening to the Oriental music moaning from the suspended speakers. As any Trojan horse would have told you, patience is the key to joy.

*   *   *

The ruby and the sunrise are one. The roosters and Uncle Albert were another. It was the last ruby sunrise for the one that connected with his hiking boot.

More recently know for its cotton, gold and fine carpets, Bergama had been the ancient Greek and Roman cultural center of Pergamon. Just after the rooster became one with the sunrise, Uncle Albert and I went to the bus station for coffee, and took a taxi to the locked Pergamon gate. We climbed above it, up the rest of the mountain promontory, overlooking the Bakırçay River. Our ascent took us past the dramatic theater carved into the Western steep hillside, and the temples of Dionysus and Athena, to the Acropolis. It was all here, minus the homesick Altar, which I had seen in East Berlin, and the two hundred thousand books of the Library, which Anthony had given to Cleopatra as a wedding gift. I wouldn't have thought she got much reading done. Our reward was a delightful view of the sun-scorched valley, shadow casting long patterns off the olive and pomegranate orchards below. Our punishments were the large sleeping cranes involved in the German reconstruction of Trajan's temple, and the arriving cruise ship tourist hordes pouring out of the matrix of buses, beneath us. In my head I began designing improvised explosive devices.

We beat the crowds to the Asklepion, similar to the ones at Epidaurus and Kos, but different. This medical center was the home of Galen, one of antiquity's most prominent physicians. As a young man, he had traveled extensively, and held the view that the best physician was also a philosopher. His methodological preference of direct observation, using dissection and vivisection, represented a complex middle ground between the two contending schools of rationalism and empiricism. At the age of 28, he returned to Pergamum, as physician to the gladiators of the High Priest of Asia.

Galen was chosen from several candidates for the position. He won, after eviscerating an ape, challenging the other contenders to repair the damage, and when there were no takers, did it himself. He later became the personal physician to several Roman emperors, and was particularly prominent during the plague that devastated the city in 166 AD.

The other plague was catching up fast, and we diverted into a local locate for lunch. I made the mistake of ordering brains, to Uncle Albert's sheer delight. This softened substantially, when I provided a Hannibal lecture of the neuroanatomical details, after Galen. After lunch, at the Sacred Spring, we were buffeted by the buffet rabble. One couple from Philadelphia looked at us disdainfully.

"What are you doing here?" Asked the one with the big Nikon. I told him of my interest in archeology.

"I don't believe that." He said. Uncle Albert began to cite the sites and sights we had already visited in our short association.

"You could have just memorized that." Replied the other ugly American.

"He's a physician. He had brains for lunch. Must have been yours." Albert finally said.

Our bus to Izmir didn't leave until three. I played numerous games of backgammon with Mehmet, the owner of the adjacent chai shop, losing every one. He kissed me on both cheeks when I left. Albert suggested that something had been lacking in my lunch.

Izmir had been Smyrna, when it was captured and burned by the Turks in 1922. Over a hundred thousand Greek and Armenian Christians were murdered. We fared better. A convoy of tanks and other military vehicles rolled by the station. A young cat lay starving outside, for shade, food, and affection.

Albert and I were heading to Selçuk, the site of the annual camel wrestling championship, and the jumping off point for visits to Ephesus. We decided it was safer to work on my

471

archeological reputation than my wrestling skills. In Selçuk, we were met by Mustafa, a local carpet salesman who chose our pension, regaled us with a dinner of aubergine, pilau and visne suyu, and brought out his twenty-five photo albums of vacationing girlfriends. Mustafa was reliving the Ottoman dream of European conquest, one tourist invasion at a time.

Uncle Albert and I had just walked the three kilometers from our pension. If the cruise ship tourist hordes at Pergamon were annoying, the megaton swarms at Ephesus were maddening. Acres of foolish flesh flowed under the merciless heat, behind closing throngs of Turkish hustlers and touts.

"What are you interested in?" Demanded one particularly uncouth specimen.

"Nothing." I said.

"I don't believe that." He said. I turned to Uncle Albert.

"Do I need a change of wardrobe, or something?" I asked.

"Not to my eyes, brother." He replied.

"Then this coast is just crawling with snakes." I said.

But we could understand why they came. One of the twelve cities of the Ionian League, Ephesus became the second largest city in the world when the Romans took over. Its Temple of Artemis, one of the Seven Wonders of the Ancient World, was only evident, in its one remaining inconspicuous column.

We found green peaches and ate them along the peasant life, on the way in. We found the library of Celsus, a theatre for 25,000 spectators, a large gladiator's graveyard, Hadrian's bathroom and well-constructed communal toilets, geckos, marble roads, and delicious fennel with visne suyu, and two lovely rose-cheeked medical students from Bristol. The terra-cotta statuette of Priapus in the frescoed museum made their cheeks rosier, and we laughed at the two multibreasted images of Artemis next to him. Then I remembered that Artemis had killed Orion. Uncle Albert tried to convince the English girls to come with us to Bodrum, but they were heading to Kusadasi.

Our Karadeveci otobusleri bus curved on through dusk, tranquil pine glens, and southern mountains. The deepening blue Aegean gradually emerged on our right side. A little after eight, we were greeted by Levant, who took us home to two beds on the roof of his family's pension. On the roof, we were open to the night sky. It was one of those rare places where you could see all the nameless stars above, and the multicolored courtyards lit up down below. There were spotlights on the Crusader's castle, and a fluttering blood-red Turkish flag descending between its turrets. We crashed tipsy. Closing my eyes, the universe and the light of the stars came through me.

On July 7, 1983, I woke in ancient Halicarnassus, and helped Uncle Albert get ready for his boat to Kos. We said goodbye at the dock. He gave me his red baseball cap.

"It's been a slice." I said.

"I don't believe that." He replied. And we laughed, and did the man hug thing.

*   *   *

> 'If the sun were not in love, he would have no brightness,
> the side of the hill no grass on it.
> The ocean would come to rest somewhere.'
>
> Rumi

It was a long smooth ride through flowered ravines filled with olive trees, setting sunrays, and olive-colored everything, river included. I sat beside Guazin, a 25 year-old pharmacist from Ankara. She sang me songs and bought me a soda, and I fell into her eyes. But too many times, a twist of fate winds up as an exchange of addresses, and oblivion. We said goodbye, just before midnight, when our bus pulled into Denizli. I was too late for any decent accommodation, and ended up on the exposed rebar concrete roof of a rat hole.

Early next morning, I left on a dolmus, to Pamukkale. Its name in Turkish means 'cotton castle.' The calcium crust terraces were extraplanetary. There had been similar terraces in Tarawera. New Zealand, but they had been blown away by a volcanic eruption a half-century earlier. It was the same surreal landscape of dripping white dental impressions, and there were tadpoles.

I had breakfast at the hotel, overlooking the formations. A noon bus to Antalya ground along slowly in the blast oven heat. It got merciless in Burbur, when boarding masses of Neanderthal soldiers, with keen crewcutted Koranic enthusiasm, displaced the remaining oxygen in our bus. Even Albert Einstein had recognized Turkish soldiers as 'very brave.' I bought a salted cucumber, to counter the odor it generated.

In Antalya, I took my last ride of the day. The city's Anatolian name meant 'pomegranate.' It fell without a struggle, to Alexander the Great in 333 BC. The single garrison he left behind populated and peppered the place with Hellenistic culture. They had defeated the fugitive Carthaginian, Hannibal, and removed itself from the yoke of the Seleucid empire. My free ride into Side came compliments of an American military couple on vacation, with a cold Budweiser and a zoom through the tight Roman gate into town. I thanked them and set off to find a place to stay. A demented Turk, with a glass eye, tried to rent me a ground level tree house, but I was looking for where the ocean had come to rest. An hour later, I came across a scene of grass-woven huts, strewn Corinthian columns, gourd lampshades, pomegranate tress, and flowers. The columns, and the other ancient Greek temple detritus, were real. It was a campground on the Illyrian sea. It was called the 'Winter Palas.' There was Tuborg. The bar was playing *Rolling Stones*. I set Serendipity down. The sun was in love.

Sufi's Paradise

'We come spinning out of nothingness, scattering stars like dust.'
Jalal ad-Din Muhammad Rumi

Coral blocks and beach Medusas littered the littoral. The next morning was for washing the road dirt from my clothes, in an old Roman stone tub. After yoghurt and a visne suyu, I walked along the blue-white line of the seashore. Through the ruins, under an umbrella, I caught a splash of wavy red hair and sunglasses. Despite the breeze, the heat from the sun pulled at my breath. The face that emerged, as she pulled off her sunglasses, stole the rest of it.

Jane was a nurse from Queensland, twenty-two, like Katherine Hepburn would have looked, if she'd had estrogen. She was traveling with her friend, Trish. We compared maps, and agreed to meet at the Soundwaves restaurant later. After she left, I cakewalked down the rest of the beach. The guardian at the museum opened steel doors, to show me the statue of Hermes. Later, I found several puppies, suckling a dying mother in the ruins.

Back at the Winter Palas, the owners, Attaturk and Shazam, asked me to babysit the place for a couple of hours. They arrived late, and I hastened down to the Soundwaves. The views out over the Mediterranean were stunning, as was Jane. She made introductions to new friends, around the table. There was Trish, darker and more extroverted, Hans and Adrian, a Dutch and English homogeneity, and Meg, the quiet sister of Ali, the restaurant owner's wife. Chemical bonds formed, between the gin and tonics. We ate shishkebabs, and drank wine. Trish and Jame wanted to dance, so we walked to the beachside disco, and danced. *In your light I learn how to love. In your beauty, how to make poems. You dance inside my chest, where no one sees you.* We danced until we closed it down, at two am. Waltzing Matildas.

Trish and Jane wanted a swim. I didn't blame them. It was a full moon, and the water and breeze were both warm. Clutching onto me from both sides, we stumbled through the dark Roman gate, onto the starlit, wave-whitened beach, until there was no need for stumbling. *Thirst drove me down to the water, where I drank the moon's reflection. Silence is an ocean. Speech is a river.* It became suddenly silent, as we stripped off our clothes, and ran into the ocean. We swam and then lay on our backs. Trish fell back onto me. And there were mouths and breasts, and salt water dreaming. Flashlights appeared on the shore. A brigade of soldiers, M-16s shoulder-slung, challenged our pretense.

"Stay in the water." I said, wading through the undulating appendages, streaking out of the water. I'm sure they dreamt of the harmonics for months. It was three am, when we finally returned to the Palas for showers, to wash off the salt. I was the last.

"Stay in the water." Trish teased, pulling my towel away from the rest of me. *Love is the water of life. This is love: to fly toward a secret sky, to cause a hundred veils to fall each moment. First, to let go of life. In the end, to take a step without feet.* It was nautical and aerobatic. I slept laughing.

"We want to go to Cappadocia with you." Jane told me during our 'breakfast of sheep cheese, bread, melon, and yoghurt, at the 'Terminal' restaurant next morning. Loved the name.

"Sure." I said. Whatever.

We met up with Hans and Adrian, Meg, and caught a dolmus to Managu's market. Vegetables and alms to Allah were on offer in the heat of the midmorning sun. I introduced them to visne suyu. *I will soothe you and heal you. I will bring you roses. I too have been covered with thorns.*

We took cabs to the waterfall. On a dare, I jumped in, without realizing the force of the undertow. Most of the concern about how long I was submerged, was mine. Trish and Jane and I left, to catch our bus to Konya. The little girl sitting next to us was a darling, kissing my hand and putting it to her forehead. We arrived after midnight, and found the three bedroom top floor of the Hotel Azzizye.

The morning heat woke us. We dressed, and climbed Allaedin hill, for visne suyu on a café terrace. There were lush turquoise tiles in the Karatoy ceramic museum, and a highly ornamented façade on the stone portal of the Ince Minaret Medrese. We ate biscuits and drank Turkish coffee. Around the other side of the hill, we were unsuccessful in our attempt to persuade the guardian of the Archeological Museum to let us in to see the Heracles sarcophagus. Better fortune awaited under the enameled turquoise tower dome of the Mevlâna Tekke, bulging at the rafters with exquisite Islamic art. There were Korans from the ninth century calligraphed on gazelle skins, carpets, weapons and a nacre-decorated box, containing the Holy Beard of Muhammad. Judging by how many others I had seen between the cartwheels, he must have grown a long one.

But it was who was buried here, and not what he was buried with, that made us pilgrims. This was the mausoleum of the 13th-century Persian Muslim poet, jurist, and Sufi mystic, Jalāl ad-Dīn Muḥammad Balkhī. Since he lived most of his life in an area called Rūm, he became renowned as Rūmī, the Roman. His 'tekke,' or lodge, was the home to the Whirling Dervishes. The whirling was the mystical embodiment of man's spiritual ascent through mind and love, the abandonment of ego, and his arrival at perfection. He turns towards the truth, and returns mature, and capable of loving and being of service to the whole of creation. I remembered the Sudanese version I witnessed in Omdurman, almost two years previously:

'The creation of Mevlevi Dervish whirling, indeed the very order itself, is attributed to the Persian poet, Rumi, who was walking through a market

477

place one day when he heard the rhythmic hammering of the goldbeaters. Entranced in the happiness of the alliteration he thought he was hearing ("There is none worthy of worship but Allah"), he stretched out both his arms, and started spinning in a circle. In so doing, he discovered his bliss. When it started from where I was watching, the gold beaten was far better in Arabic:

'La elaha ella'llah'   'الله رسول محمد الله الا اله الا ل'
'La elaha ella'llah'   'الله رسول محمد الله الا اله الا ل'
'La elaha ella'llah'   'الله رسول محمد الله الا اله الا ل'

The Sufis in the line began to stomp their feet, as the tempo and the amplitude of their swaying increased. And then the drums kicked in. One at a time, almost, it seemed, by divine invitation, men broke off from the line and began to twirl and spin, looking skyward. Their eyes performed crisp saccadic returns, focused perhaps on a cloud that wasn't there, or a deity that was. They would whirl until their souls entered Allah's chatroom and were cleansed of evil, or were called to evening prayer, whichever came first. Every so often, ballistic out of no special place in the donut, another enraptured giant would fly into the inverted cyclone, bringing even more rotational energy into the energetic centre of this Sufi storm of ecstasy. A crazed black man with bulging eyeballs, dressed more like a witch doctor than a wizard, leapt over the crowd and begin to spin wildly on one leg, shaking a rattle in time. Saliva spilled from his mouth. A year and a half later I would get to see the more refined Mevlana version of whirling dervishes in Konya, in Turkey, pale thin moustached men with tall red fezes and white spinning inverted martini glass dresses. The difference was startling, but understandable. Dervishes danced differently in Africa.'

The Mevlevi were founded in 1273 AD, but had been banned by Attaturk in 1925. I saw them spin. The dervishes wore a white gown, symbolic of death, a wide black cloak, symbolic of the grave, and a tall brown hat, symbolic of the tombstone. Removing their black cloaks, they twirled on the right foot, right palm upward, left hand pointing at the ground. There were four highly ritualistic parts to the ceremony. It looked like bliss. Which was Rumi's theme, the spiritual need of *tawhīd* - the longing to reunite with the divinity from which you emerged, and from which you had been separated from. For me, he was light and love and loss and longing and life force and loveliness and 'la elaha ella'llah' 'الله الا اله الا ل محمد'

الله. رسول.' *Whoever brought me here will have to take me home.*
Rumination.

$$* \qquad * \qquad *$$

> 'Come to the orchard in Spring.
>   There is light and wine, and sweethearts
>   in the pomegranate flowers.
>   If you do not come, these do not matter.
>   If you do come, these do not matter.'
>   Rumi

According to Acts 2:5, the Cappadocians were 'God-fearing Jews.' From the appearance of the Cappadocians on the bus to Nevşehir, it had been a while. The soft volcanic rocks of Cappadocia had eroded into hundreds of fairy chimneys and morel pillars that the villagers, in the heart the region, had carved out to form houses, churches and monasteries. Fifty per cent of them would die of mesothelioma, from the asbestos within. I played backgammon with Jane, as pieces of cloud dissolved in sunlight. *This is how I would die into the love I have for you.*
A lanky local gave us a free dolmus ride into Ürgüp, and a hard sell to stay at his establishment, the Hotel Sefa. He showed us a three-bed room upstairs, and offered a bargain rate. Jane, Trish, and I checked out every other place in town, and returned to accept his offer. Lanky and his sidekick invited us for an Efes around the corner, and to another 'Terminal' Restaurant, for aubergine and pilau. He entertained us with abracadabra hocus-pocus magic tricks. We returned to our room, and wished each other sweet dreams. Jane fell asleep, or seemed to. Trish came over for 'just a massage,' or seemed to. *Good and bad are mixed. If you don't have both, you don't belong with us.*

479

The cold shower next morning was unnecessary. We figured that Lanky was named after the dried bread, tea, and sour cheese he served for breakfast. Jane and Trish accompanied me up the hill overlooking Ürgüp, a hasty exit from a private path, a dead donkey, and a warm sit-down with a 30 member Turkish family. We had donor kebab and drank *ayran* and played backgammon, in the nude-decorated draft house.

The afternoon sun at the Sefa was only good for an afternoon nap. The flies and noise and heat ruined any chance of sleep, and the heat from Jane made it entirely out of the question. *When I am with you, we stay up all night, When you're not here, I can't get to sleep. Praise God for these two insomnias! And the difference between them.*

We all dressed and began a beautiful four kilometer walk up and out of town, picking apricots and cherries and apples, watching the sun sink through the clouds, and admire the Martian chimney and troglodyte landscape. A French-speaking Belgian Turk stopped to give us some cold grenadine. Back at the Terminal, we ate eggplants, taken to their ultimate evolutionary level. And withdrew to our room, and ourselves. The kitty-corner windows admitted the sounds of Turks in the air and breezes. And it started to come out of the deepest recesses of my brain. '*Who'll come awaltzing, Matilda, with me.*'

In the morning we caught a dolmus to the Ortahisar Citadel, for a climb up the sandstone stronghold. An old farmer on a tractor gave us a lift down the hill to Göreme and, even though Jane and I flanked Trish on the right fender, we had to pull him off her, at the end of the ride. No tip. While Jane was changing money at the museum bank, we met Nuri, a 30 year-old barefoot guide, who we hired on the spot. He took us in a rather uninformative but enthusiastic fashion, to the main area attractions.

The Apple Church had a frescoe of the Last Supper with a symbolic sign of the fish, and apple trees in the courtyard below. Up a five-meter chimney, in the tallest central rock formation, was the Sandal Church. The Ascension fresco at the entrance was an exact copy of the one contained at the church of the same name in Jerusalem. Standing in the foot impressions of the Saints, was the gift of a spectacular view of the valley. The most exciting adventure, however, was the more dangerous access to the Church of Maria, along a bottomless ravine, through a narrow tunnel, along a ledge, and into an amazingly frescoed 7th century church, still magical.

We all descended eating green chickpeas, for an orange soda at a roadside rest stop.

We passed quickly through an onyx factory, the Zelve Monastery, and a three kilometer walk back to the main road, picking apricots and flowers, turning down lifts, exposing my roll of film with all the fairy chimneys. A broken down old truck, with seven Turks and two 17 year-old guys from West Berlin, slowed down even more to let us on. We all had to get off at the bottom of the Göreme hill, so their truck would make it. The back of a pickup soon after, took us the rest of the way. We stopped for a melon at the top of one hill, and played sasz and sang rock 'n' roll, all the way back in the troglodyte city. After a shower, back in our room at the Sefa, we went out to the Terminal for 'iman bayaldi,' *the priest fainted*, stuffed eggplant in olive oil, an expensive ingredient that apparently caused stress in a particularly frugal iman. We shared travel tales with the West Germans, and Jane and Trish and I went home to bed. Trish snored off immediately, but Jane and I could sense each other across the room. *There is some kiss we want with our whole lives, the touch of spirit on the body.*

"Would you like to have an affair for a night?" She asked. *Out beyond ideas of wrongdoing and rightdoing, there is a field. I'll meet you there.* Then I really couldn't sleep. I went downstairs, but that was a mistake. It appeared that Lanky and his sidekick were wondering which of the ladies they could rescue from me. Abracadabra.

The backpack straps and snaps were angry next morning. Jane had clearly spoken to Trish, and Trish was clearly not speaking to me. *Love said to me, there is nothing that is not me. Be silent.*

Two silent dolmus rides took us to the underground city of Denemkuya. The peaches we bought to eat went quietly, down 55 cool meters. A late bus drove us into a singsong, and down into a hot plain, past snow-capped peaks. It eventually emerged from under Mount Erciyes, Kayseri, the city of carpet-sellers. It was almost midnight. I got a separate room from Trish and Jane. It was for my own protection. The beer in the bar wasn't as frosty.

*   *   *

'I would love to kiss you.
The price of kissing is your life.
Now my loving is running toward my life shouting,
What a bargain, let's buy it.'
Rumi

Trish awoke next morning with a case of Turkish tummy. I brought her some cay, and Jane and I left on a carpet-buying mission, stopping for breakfast soup at a locanta, and a heart-to-heart on the way. But she had become paralyzed by divided loyalties, and couldn't decide. Our quest took us down the end of a bazaar street, to a cool dimly lit Ottoman dome. Mustafa the Elder was there, waiting like a funnel spider. Tea and multicolored kilims and the webspinning came out simultaneously. We escaped to Cas' shop, and then to Joseph's, but she couldn't decide. We left to bring Trish yoghurt. She had improved enough to come out for a kebab, and accompany us back to the bazaar. I bought a Turkish camel saddle. At the fourth place, Jane came up with a decision, but she was forty dollars short of a compromise. Instead she put it towards a trunk call to Australia at the post office. The employees, smittened, patched her through for nothing, and brought visne suyu and peaches, as a further demonstration of their affection.

The day faded into aqua and aubergine. Jane and Trish and I ended up in the second floor lounge of the Hotel Ergodan, watching an old black and white film dubbed in Turkish, '*Land of the Pharoahs.*'

I said goodnight, and climbed the staircase to my small corner room. I stared at the patterns the moonlight made on the ceiling. And then she decided. My door opened just wide enough to allow her to enter. She slid across the room to sit beside me, and cut loose all the poetry in Rumi's universe. *I begin the Night Journey in your eyes toward the wild desert fragrance I longed for all day. Watch the dust grains moving in the light near the window. Their dance is our dance. I desire you more than food or drink. My body my senses my mind hunger for your taste. My face became all eyes, and my eyes all hands. Your hand opens and closes and opens and closes. If it were always a fist or always stretched open, you would be paralyzed. Your deepest presence is in every small contracting and expanding, the two as beautifully balanced and coordinated as bird wings. There is a candle in your heart, ready to be kindled. There is a void in your soul, ready to be filled. You feel it, don't you? Because your sighs have fermented my blood I need no wine. When dawn comes, we'll whisper which of us was stillness, which the dancer.* It was an orchard of ripe peaches in a warm rain.

But later, there were sobs down the hallway. We both felt her pain. There was no solution. *Dance, when you're broken open. Dance, if you've torn the bandage off. Dance in the middle of the fighting. Dance in your blood. Dance, when you're perfectly free.* But freedom isn't freedom if your one desire is captivity. Is it? Jane left, guilt-ridden, at dawn.

The desk clerk woke me in German. Jane was on the phone downstairs, wanting to know if I wanted her to buy a ticket

483

for me to Melatya. It was supposed to be our next stop, but I guess she just wanted to make sure. A wall of abuse came out of the shower.

"When we get to our destination, I'm going to travel alone." Trish said. "You don't know the value of friendship."

I didn't know our destination, but I did know about friendship, and that wasn't what she had valued. *Love so needs to love, that it will endure almost anything, even abuse, just to flicker for a moment.* I went downstairs for a cay, and caught her tears falling down the banister behind me. We spent time in the common room, for we still had that to spend. *Do not grieve. Anything you lose comes round in another form.*

Jane met us at the otogar with the tickets. *Gule gule.* Trish and I played backgammon through the canyons of the landscape, and the day. We were flowing from ripe peaches to the city of apricots and honey.

Melatya was the staging point for the sunrise climb to the monuments on Nemrut dagi, a day away. We rolled in around seven pm, greeted by a forest of commission hustlers. I pretended to speak only Danish. The tout switched to Danish, like he was downshifting on an incline. Slashing through the crush, we hiked for twenty more minutes to the Hotel Camir. Our three-bed room was just inside the motorcycle rank, but it couldn't be helped. The internal combustion continued, long after their drivers were asleep, long after the delicious aubergines and peppers and yoghurt and dolma and kagit kebabi and clove rice, at the Burc Locanta on the other side of the night.

*   *   *

Guide Leader for Tourists
DEAR TRAVALLERS
If you have come to see- 8th wonder marvel of world
You have to come Nemrut mountain.
We shove you the shortest way to go to Nemrut mountain
You can rent A dodge or jeeps. We always at your service
With our helps. You can see sunset sunrise on the Nemrut mountain
Than you can see the Hercules zeus apollu
Comangenes statues, in saim time it wellbe goad tours
Because- interesting willages, colt water, frash air,
sleping place, Deliciova silages meals
Place come aur address Malatya

The card had been slipped under our door in the darkness. We were going to need a sleping place. It was settled.

Antiochus I had been the ruler of the central Anatolian Kingdom of Commagene, during the Roman wars between Caesar and Pompey. He was the direct descent of five generals of Alexander the Great, and managed, through his diplomatic skill, to keep his hybrid realm independent of the Romans. Antiochus created his own royal cult of Zoroastrianism, assuming a position of divinity alongside a syncretism of Greek, Armenian, and Iranian gods, such as Hercules-Vahagn, Zeus-Aramazd, and Apollo-Mithras. He devised a new calendar based not on solar and lunar movement, but on 'Hayk,' the same star of Orion the Egyptians used as the template for their year.

His most famous accomplishment, however, was the impressive religious sanctuary on Mount Nemrut. Here he built colossal limestone effigies of himself and his gods, with Greek physical features, and Persian clothing, headgear, and scale. At some point the giant heads had been separated from their gigantic bodies, spread across the face of the mountain, their noses bashed in. The oldest known bas-relief of two figure shaking hands received similar treatment. Someone hadn't appreciated his iconoclasticism.

That was our destination of the day. We found the address on the card, in an obscurely located second floor office up the hill from the Hotel Camir. Hussein, a chubby, gregarious 25 year-old, was the boss. His poor command of English required a French hypochondriac and a German paranoid-schizophrenic to handle customer relations. Judging by their equally poor command of English, and Turkish, Hussein's business potential might remain just that. We signed up to be shoved the shortest way to the interesting willages, colt water, and frash air, and set off in an old faded red truck for our sleping place on Nemrut dagi. We hadn't counted on any other passengers, especially the one we stopped at the bus station for.

Danielle was just about the most talkative, authoritarian, obnoxious, know-it-all, any of us had ever met. She told us she was a French teacher working in Istanbul, and then she told us what to think, and what to do, for the rest of our collaboration. It was a five-hour climb through the mountains to our sleping place, and Danielle never stopped talking long enough to draw breath. There were magnificent views of Bogazy village near the base of Mount Nemrut. Danielle was eager to lead a climb to the ruins, for a sunset survey of the monuments. Apollo, Zeus, and hypoxia were waiting at the top. An eagle flew over the sun fading on the surrounding peaks, and as dusk melted into darkness, Venus shone. The milk of the moon shadowed our descent to a Kurdish family's hut, still near the summit.

They served us a delicious meal of eggs and flat cornbread and cay around an open fire. Horses grazed nearby. The water was colt, the air frash, and the sleping place was a ruin of a crossbeamed stone barn, open to a universe of night sky. The guardian with the cane brought me a mat. I lay gazing at the stars and silhouetted mountains, warm within the Gold Kazoo. Jane asked me if I was asleep. We snuggled and giggled, until fatigue and prudence overcame us.

My alarm forced me into my clothes at four am, and we scampered back up to the stone sentinels at the top. Trish was the first to notice the fifty tourist buses, already there.

Danielle started winding up about how fortunate we were, to have had her encouragement to see the place, the evening before.

We descended, to Kurds and whey, to corn bread and sheep's cheese mixed with butter, and tea, and the long bumpy ride back to Malatya, interrupted by every local's shopping list, a lunch of lamb pilau in a larch-lined roadside locanta, and the tears and retching of a newly-betrothed black-garbed Turkish girl, on her way to an unseen bridegroom in Istanbul. Every woman in the village was crying for and with her. Danielle explained how purely natural it all was. When Hussein met us at the cay shop, she refused to pay the price we had all agreed to.

Hussein had booked us two rooms in another hotel for our return. Danielle told us that her and Trish would take the big one, and Jane and I would sleep in the small, hot, noisy corner room down the hall, presumably as some form of punishment. *Love is the water of life.*

In the shower, we were like melting snow, washing ourselves with ourselves, and of ourselves. Our faces became all eyes, and our eyes all hands. *Let us fall in love again and scatter gold dust all over the world.* The St. Christopher's medal between her breasts traveled in crescentic arcs, hunting for the diamond necklace that was already around her neck. We became each other's search, for what was between our mirrors, and the light that touched the sky.

Jane and I eventually joined the others at the Burc Locanta. There were still more basic kinds of hunger. Here we found Trish and Danielle, and Hussein and his Tower of Babel boys. Danielle ignored them, picked all the dishes, and monopolized the conversation. It was the third anniversary of the first day of my journey. We celebrated with fried melon rinds in tomato sauce, aubergines and peppers and yoghurt, dolma, cicik, kebabs, wine, baklava and cay. Hussein and I smoked hookahs, and spoke like Turkish men speak, with backward head snaps and sucked-in flicks of the tongue against our palates. We decided that Danielle should be strangled by one of our deaf-mute eunuchs, a considerable number of whom she seemed to have created, in her wake.

Jane and I initially slept in separate beds because of the heat. But the moonshadows danced out of the silence, whirling us through our Sufi's paradise, 'la elaha ella'llah' 'لا اله الا الله رسول الله.' *The breeze at dawn has secrets to tell you. Don't go back to sleep. You must ask for what you really want. Don't go back to sleep. People are going back and forth across the doorsill where the two worlds touch. The door is round and open. Don't go back to sleep.*

Exodus

'I have never seen a man lost who was on a straight path.'
Saadi of Shiraz

I was lost. My new plan had been to continue into Syria, and pick up my Iranian visa in Damascus, on my overland route to India and the Far East. Not long after we didn't go back to sleep, I kissed Jane and Trish goodbye at the Burc, and took a cab to the otogar. Waltzing Matildas and Whirling Dervishes. *And his ghost may be heard as you pass by that billabong,* الا اله ال الله رسول محمد الله. I looked up at the bus company sign, in the queue to buy tickets for Gazientep. 'Findikli Toros.' It wasn't a question, unlike the words I saw on the side of the road in New Zealand, years later. 'Mind wandering?' Not at all.

It was so steamy inside the bus, the mountains outside my window travelled backwards. We stopped for a moment in an oasis, filled with the sound and fresh air of running water. The elderly driver's helper handed me a cay with most of his right hand, without losing a beat in the rhythmic counting of his worry beads, with the last two fingers.

Gaziantep was the pistachio capital of the world, and the home of baklava. I couldn't linger. My destination was the Syrian border town of Kilis. Serendipity went onto the top of a crowded microbus, and I squeezed inside for the sixty-kilometer sauna sojourn. Kilis was a haven for smugglers and drug traffickers, and lisping young men on mopeds. I found the Hotel Paris, as far as possible from where it should have been. The shower was as cold as the hospitality was warm. The waiter in the restaurant shooed away the birds, and brought Kilis Kebabi, pistachio yogurt, cicik, visne suyu, and his seven brothers to keep me company. Mopeds, and my Damascene anticipation, kept me awake.

A Syrian motorcycle driver was waiting in the Parisian lobby early next morning. I climbed on the back of his BSA bike, with Serendipity on mine, and we rode like the wind, through cool counter breezes, past yellow flat fields, donkeys, minarets, and veiled women. My passport was stamped out of Turkey. I walked the last barbed-wire kilometer to the final frontier, and straight into two surly swarthy Syrian border guards.

"Bonjour." Went the greeting. Au revoir. Went my prospects. "You must go back to Ankara for visa." Said the one with the five o'clock shadow on his five o'clock shadow.

My *'West Asia on the Cheap'* said that Canadians didn't need visas to enter Syria. I showed them the passage. They were underwhelmed. They began cleaning their guns. Time to leave. It was, in retrospect, for the best. My ignorance of the requirements for Syrian entry, was surpassed only by my ignorance of the 'human wave' assaults that the Iranians were throwing across the border into Iraq. Sometimes it is better to be lost, than on a straight path.

The Turks welcomed me back like I'd been gone forever. They took me back to the otogar in Kilis, and put me in a lawn chair, in the very front of a bus to Adana. In the blistering heat, I fell asleep. The driver woke me for an ice-cold ayran, and again at our destination. The day merged into a series of short rides, past a sea castle and a land castle, and thousands of orange and blue tents, to Silifke, and the port of Tesecu, ten kilometers further down the road. I found the rooftop of the Pansiyon Tekim. It came with an old dog, smiling daughter, cold shower, mosquito net, frosty Efes, and homemade meat and bulgur kebbeh.

The first merciless rays of the sun baked me awake early enough. Back in the otogar in Silifke, I purchased a ticket for the eleven a.m. bus to Ankara, and settled into the terminal's cay shop with a visne suyu, and a hazy view of the castle on the hill. I was heading to my bus later, when a petite blonde American cycloned through the café.

"Do you speak English?" She asked. And then she asked where I was going.

"Ankara." I said. She inquired when I was leaving.

"Now." I said. She told me to wait while she bought a ticket. Note to self.

Marilyn was divorced, unemployed, and living in Athens. She told me she was headed for a vacation in her 'old stomping ground.' I asked her where that was.

"Beirut." She said. That should have been the third clue. Ankara was known for, among many other things, a special breed of cat, and goat, and rabbit. There would prove to be a little of each in my new travel acquaintance, but eight hours rumbling through surreal altiplano softened my considerable reserve, considerably. We arrived just before sundown, and found twin beds in room 301, at the Hotel Oba.

We found an open patisserie for a breakfast next morning, and strolled downhill, past the excavated hillside image of a man on a horse, to the tourist information office. The woman who arrived to open it an hour late spoke only French, so I translated for Marilyn, an Irish-Australian couple, and a Bostonian, who made Danielle seem demure. We left enlightened, to a sidewalk terrace café, for döner kebab and yoghurt. I left Marilyn to run some errands, and returned to the Oba late afternoon. In the foyer, I met Sa'ed, an expatriate Iranian Air Force officer, who wanted to move all his worldly assets into Canada. He wanted to come with them. We discussed politics and human relationships. For an exile, Sa'ed seemed somewhat overly enthusiastic about the glorious Khomeini revolution. He told me that the American rescue mission had been destroyed by Russian laser-guided missiles, that Revolutionary guards would actually give me money to participate in the new black market in Tehran, and that women returned to the veil with joy in their hearts. He was homesick.

Marilyn arrived with bread, and wine, and *findik ezmesi*, Turkish hazelnut butter. It was delicious. We talked until late.

491

I told her that, someday, I would have hazelnut trees, and make findik ezmesi. She told me we should go to bed. I didn't realize she meant together, and got up to turn off the light. She was there before the room was dark, like a cat, and a goat, and a rabbit.

*　　*　　*

'It's over, and can't be helped, and that's one consolation, as they always says in Turkey, when they cuts the wrong man's head off.'
Charles Dickens

I paid for room service in Bulgarian currency. No one seemed to mind. Marilyn and I strolled up to the Citadel for visne suyu and Turkish coffee, the Hittite collection of antiquities at the Archeological Museum, and the Arslanhane mosque. Tripe soup and sawdust pie revitalized our blood at the Rumeli restaurant. Back at the Oba, a science fiction film, on the small black and white television, was interrupted by the live action Technicolor feature in the foreground. Every performance that night was impromptu, unscripted, and unique.

The next morning I put on my ugly long pants, for the first time in weeks. Sa'ed had offered to accompany me to the Iranian legation, so I could redeem my anvil status.

"My name means 'helper' in Farsi." He said, but it turned out that there wasn't much we could do for each other at our respective embassies. I didn't even get through the Iranian gates, and had to settle for an anonymous voice over an intercom. It told me I could be issued with a ten-day transit visa, if I produced a letter of endorsement from my embassy. This I duly provided, after another trudge up the hill.

"Come back tomorrow." It said. I was still an anvil. Sa'ed and I retreated to a kebab café to lick our wounds, and eat a late lunch. After cay, I left him, for room 301 at the Oba, and Marilyn. But Marilyn wasn't Marilyn any more.

"How alone have you been?" She asked, as I entered.

"What?" I said, surprised.

"I don't know if I can trust you." She said. I asked her why she felt that way, what this was all about.

"I may have done something wrong." She said. I asked her what that might have been.

"I may have read your journal." She admitted.

"You may have?" I asked. "Why did you do that?"

"I was curious." She said.

"And you don't know if you can trust me?" I asked.

Turkish proverbs rained down on the twin beds. *Thorns and roses grow on the same tree. Stretch your feet according to your blanket. No matter how far you have gone on a wrong road, turn back. If you speak the truth, have a foot in the stirrup.* My worst fears won over my best intentions, and in the end, there was only one thing to do.

"I'll pay for the room." I said. Down at the front desk, I found out that there were no others available. The hotel was full. Reluctantly, I called Sa'ed, and told him of my situation.

"My name means 'helper' in Farsi." He said. I would sleep on his floor. And beat him in backgammon and his roommate in chess, over and over. We would drink twenty glasses of tea, and speak of Sa'ed going to Canada, and me going to Iran. We were not the country we were in, but the countries we were going to. And for me, *Insha'Allah*, it would be the very next day.

I awoke optimistic and determined. Serendipity rode on my back to the embassy, and Sa'ed rode the bus, at my side.

The first Iranian hostage crisis two years earlier, had ended in an entanglement of 'vengeance and mutual incomprehension.' Two years turned out to be an inadequate amount of time for learning, and the second Iranian hostage crisis was destined to have the same outcome. The intercom was a hammer.

493

"If you want to wait for two months, we won't cancel the 22nd page of your passport. If you don't, we will cancel your visa stamp." It said, bluntly. My anvil had run out of patience. I sent him the following note:

'I have waited six weeks for a visa, after applying in Istanbul. Only yesterday, I was promised a transit visa for today. I have given you a page in my passport, six photos, and the requested letter of endorsement from my embassy. I would like to speak to you.'

They sent back my passport, with the 22nd page cancelled. I stared at the revoked visa in disbelief. Khomeini's words rang across the page. 'There is no room for play in Islam... It is deadly serious about everything... You all have to obey the Islamic Republic. And if you don't, you all will vanish.' I would vanish, but not before I sent a last message past the intercom. It should have been 'The earth is but one country, and mankind its citizens.' from Baha'ullah, the Persian founder of Bahai. But it was from me, and I was young, and rather than going to Iran, I was going quite Irate. 'Fuck the Ayatollah.' It said. Not my finest moment, but I was lost.

The sudden realization, that there was no longer an overland route to India, hit me like a hammer. To get past Syria and Iraq and Iran, I would have to fly. And the cheapest place to fly from wasn't Turkey. It was Greece, the Cradle of Western Civilization. I needed to return to Athens.

Sa'ed and I embraced, and said our farewells. Serendipity was hoisted, for the hike to the otogar, and the seemingly endless bus trip back to Istanbul. The day was long and tedious, punctuated only by the wonderful mint-stuffed peppers I ate, between the sprays of perfume and the *nyah-nyah* music, en route. But now I was on a straight path.

The Yücelt was full, by the time I arrived in the late darkness. They let me sleep in the flagstones in the garden, under the rowdy Germans, singing on the first floor. The ground was hard and unforgiving, but I was tired and defeated. My last image was of a black-garbed Medusa wearing sunglasses, fading through the garden, accompanied by a young Turk. Then I vanished too.

'A man can have sex with animals such as sheeps, cows, camels and so on. However, he should kill the animal after he has his orgasm. He should not sell the meat to the people in his own village; however, selling the meat to the next door village should be fine.'

Ayatollah Khomeini, *Tahrirolvasyleh*

*   *   *

'Santorin,
  Curling and smoky and satanic,
  Fires a spiral ladder in the air
  And balances a town among the birds.'
  Patrick Leigh Fermor, *Greek Archipelagoes*

She came down the stairs and walked across the foyer next morning. I was working on a Turkish coffee and omelet, on a breakfast table that had replaced where the Gold Kazoo had been, an hour earlier.

"Hi, Wink." She said, like there had been no space or time in between. I looked up into the green-eyed Malawian memories of Carol, still all poise and beauty. She had been traveling alone through Africa, to rendezvous with Jean Guy in Paris, from where they would return to Montreal. She didn't say why they weren't doing this together. I didn't ask. We agreed to meet later at the hamam baths. I wandered out to check the messages at the Pudding shop, and met Horst on the way. Michael had abandoned him at the Iranian border. I didn't ask. Back at the Yücelt, I played a guitar in a corner of the garden, and drew some new friends. One of them was the dark Medusa of my twilight. Helene was also from Montreal. She was heading to Athens to meet her boyfriend. I told her I was bound for Pakistan, to meet my wife. She asked me what

495

her name was. I told her I didn't know. I hadn't met her yet. She laughed. She shouldn't have.

The Turkish bath at the Cavaglu was a magnificent experience. Sweat cascaded off me in the hot room. The short, wiry Turkish masseur, in the next room, got that way by doing what he did to me, to others. He started by cracking every joint in my body, loosening every muscle, and pulling every ligament and tendon out of their insertions. Left to his own devices, he would have moved on to bones. After a cup of cay, I met Carol outside. We walked back to the Yücelt to change.

Helene was in the laundry room. She told me she had decided to accompany me to Athens. I told her I wasn't sure I was leaving just yet. She asked me if I had met my wife. I told her no, someone else's. She said she would wake me at 6:30 am, for the bus to the border.

Carol and I walked up Caddesi, looking for a place to satisfy her craving for cheese. Instead we had kebabs at my old kebab hangout, pastries at the hippodrome, *son et lumiere* at the Blue Mosque, and a beer back at the hostel. She told me about the plans she had in the next few days.

Helene resolved my dilemma, by shaking me awake. We fell asleep against each other, on the bus to the border. On the Greek side, there was no transport, no bank open, and no hope of getting to Athens that day. We managed to get a late bus to Alexandropolis and, just before midnight, the night train to Athens. We held hands, across the bottom bunks.

The conductor took our sheets about seven next morning, and the day dissolved into the passing mountains of northern Greece, and a long hot afternoon of propping each other upright. By the time we made it to Syntagma Square, it had been almost forty hours since we left Istanbul. The only available accommodation was in the form of dorm beds at the Thisseus Inn. We held hands, across the bottom bunks.

I was up before Helene next morning, waiting in the entrances to a half dozen bucket shop travel agents, until they opened. My least expensive option appeared to be a one-way red-eye Egypt Air ticket to Karachi, with a stop in Cairo in the wee hours of the morning. I told all of them I would sleep on it. That ended up like most of my other intended objectives. Helene and I commiserated over dinner at the same Garden of Eden vegetarian restaurant that Frank and Bev, and Jacki and her mother and I had eaten at sixteen months earlier. Like Jacki, Helene was 'all eighteen and ethylene, ripe peaches and open flowers.' We talked.

"Maybe I'll find a Swedish girl on a beach somewhere and forget all about you." I teased. Or tried. She cried in her salad. And we would say goodbye forever in Syntagma next day, after a sleepless night holding hands in the heat and mosquitoes, across the bottom bunks. I returned to the bucket shops, and bought my ticket to Karachi from 'Viajes Mexico,' just because it made as much sense as anything else that had occurred in the previous week.

I had another three days before my night flight to Pakistan. The train got me to Piraeus, and my remaining drachmas got me a spaghetti and salad lunch, and deck passage on the five o'clock boat to Santorini. I boarded the *Kyklades* half an hour before it departed, and staked out a place in the bow beside the anchor chain motor, with Serendipity and the Gold Kazoo.

A trio of beautiful Italian girls claimed their spot on my starboard flank, and three beautiful Swedish girls rolled out their sleeping bags, on the port bow beside me. I just knew that this was going to be its own punishment, and fell asleep as we pulled out of the harbor. For an hour.

"Excuse me, do you know when the boat arrives in Thera?" Woke me with a Swedish lilt. Her name was Elisabeth. It took me a few seconds to focus on her soft setting sun loveliness, and another few to accept her as real.

"I think it's supposed to take five hours." I said, confidently. I was wrong, of course. It was thirteen. Neither of us cared. We made small talk, I played harmonica, and we all watched big dolphins leaping beside and ahead of the bow. We tried to sleep but the rain came, forcing a grab for our belongings, and a headlong hurdle into the lounge.

The Swedish girls commandeered a table, and then found an extra chair for me. Elisabeth was on holiday with her friends, Anna and Ingrid, who they called 'Ia.' Ia was stunning. I tried to keep up in Swedish, until they took mercy on me. A little later Ia found me a place to roll out the Gold Kazoo, beside the exhaust vent, and Ia. Elisabeth woke me about four am, thinking that we had arrived. We hadn't, so we went for a coffee. The view woke all of us up at sunrise, a Greek eternity of water, rocks and wind. We were entering the remnants of a volcanic caldera left over from the Minoan eruption, 3600 years earlier. We were entering the harbor of the southernmost Cyclade, the reputed legendary site of Atlantis, or Kallístē *the most beautiful one*, or Thera, or the Latin '*Saint Irene*,' Santorini. They came for the hot desert climate, and the solidified lava pebble beaches of various colors, red or black or white. They came for the white eggplants, yellow cucumbers, intense red tomatoes and amber-orange dessert wines. They came for the bone white architecture, high above the turquoise of the Southern Aegean. And they came for the kind of passion that could only be found in such a place.

We sailed along sheer volcanic-faced cliffs, dotted with coast hugging whitewashed villages and blue-domed Orthodox churches, their lights like stars, against the struggling first rays of the rising sun. We raced off the pier for the bus to Kamari. Tops came off, and we swam in the Aegean as the sun hit horizontal. Omelets were folded in the Sunrise café, before the tops came off again for the afternoon. We had planned to sleep on the beach. Why would you sleep anywhere else? The mistake we made was to eat in the self-service restaurant for dinner. We all had moussaka except Ia, who ate chicken. It ate her back.

We hadn't made it far down the beach with our sleeping bags, when she became ill. Her initial cramped fetal position only relaxed with fatigue and time and deepening darkness. We spread out under the night sky. I distracted her with jokes, and astronomy lessons, pointing out shooting stars and constellations. Orion beckoned. I told her of his first cartwheel, and the one to come. Anna watched and listened. Elisabeth curled up in a ball, facing away. She and the meteors and I missed each other by a narrow margin.

*　　*　　*

> 'They were stepping stones to Troy
> Trireme harbours, milestones to Odysseys
> A night's sleep for Argonauts.'
> Patrick Leigh Fermor, *Greek Archipelagoes*

When Moses led the Israelites out of bondage, he may have made the journey through an area drained by tsunamis, and caused by the caldera collapse of the Minoan eruption. Thera's volcanic explosion may have also been responsible for all the precursory biblical plagues afflicting his Pharaonic oppressors. His Exodus out of Egypt, across the Red Sea, may have been preceded by what happened in Santorini. Like mine was to be.

Ia felt well enough at dawn to go for a run with Anna, while Elisabeth and I had a swim. Late morning, we left on an island day tour narrated by an elderly Greek lady, in a languid monotone.

"On... the island... of Santorini..." She droned. The girls modeled monastic robes imprinted with large crosses, at the monastery. As religious novices, they were unconvincing, particularly when the priory's brandy came out. I handed them carob pods, picked off the monastery trees. We reboarded the bus to the ancient Minoan ruins, protected by a prefabricated roof, which only served to increase the already

499

high heat and humidity, and the speed of the striped skinks underneath. Perissa beach came as a refreshing stop, and a chance to work on what Elisabeth had called my 'Pakis tan.' I had to pull them back, from pulling off their tops. Calamari and Greek salad was lunch. We finished the tour with wine tasting and pistachios, at one of the local vineyards. Back at Kamari, Ia and I rode the volcanic tremors. We spoke of love, and life, and traveling in India, together. We ate spaghetti at the Sunrise café, and belted our packs on tight, to walk further on down the beach in the dusk. The light went oblique on the fissured rock promontory, and Venus arrived above the horizon. She made room for the stars, and the sound of the waves, and kisses in the cool night air.

I awoke feeling like I'd been sleeping on the beach my whole life. The sensation was sensational. We decided to move to Perissa beach, but the second bus we took was bursting. Elisabeth sat in my lap. Anna was sick. We exploded onto the beach like the Minoan eruption. Ia and I swam out to a sleek wooden fishing boat, and back. When we emerged from the water, she told me she needed to tell me. I asked her what. She told me. About the reason for the trip, the recent separation after the relationship, about her need for caution. It wasn't a problem. I told her I was leaving the next night for Karachi, and that all this was happening far too fast, not only because of who it was happening with, but likely because of where it was happening as well. I kissed her goodbye, and went to the tourist office to buy my return ticket for the next day. I left Serendipity at the base of a volcanic cliff face on sunset, and sat in a little café, reading my India book. Later, I went to check on my knapsack, and returned to find Ia, beaming.

"On... the island... of Santorini..." I droned. We sat on the wall lining the boardwalk, until she told me how all the pressures she had felt before were illusions. Where we went after that wasn't a place. I remember her telling Anna and Elisabeth, and fetching her bedroll. I remember the pebbled beach behind the large boulder. We went to her laughter and kisses and breathing. We buried ourselves in each other, and our heads in each other's necks. The space between the night sky and the black sand became firelight.

The packed bus that wound down the pencil thin road to the port next day was slow. It had a furnace inside. The ticket office told me that my five p.m. boat to Piraeus had been cancelled, but that I had been rebooked on the *Santorini*, scheduled to leave two hours later. I spent the time reading about India, desperately avoiding any form of company. When the ship finally docked an hour late, an army of young backpackers attacked the gangplank. I was heading in the right direction. I found myself a piece of flooring on the windblown upper deck, and watched Atlantis sink into the southern Aegean behind me. After we docked in Ios, there were bodies strewn everywhere. I took the train to Monasteria, had a last coffee in Syntagma, and picked up my ticket at Viajes Mexico. I drank water in the bar at the East Airport, until they boarded my flight on sunset. I sat beside an Israeli karate black belt, bound for Japan. He asked me where I was going.

"Asia." I said.

"Which part?" He asked.

"All of it." I said. He told me I was overly ambitious. I told him that he was the one with the black belt, heading to Japan. I told him about how I got here, to tell him about where I was going.

"Shalom." He said, when we disembarked in Cairo, two hours later. Shalom. Right back at you.

*   *   *

'For I will pass through the land of Egypt this night...'
Exodus 12:12

It was a smoky night in Cairo. The last rays of the blood red sunset streamed sideways through the windows, in the long corridor. I floated through a sea of black African Muslims, on the way to my connecting flight.

It had been over three years since my thumb first carved an arc in the prairie sky, and eighteen months from the day I last passed over the edge of this city, on my way to the crucibles of Western Civilization. I had come out of Africa like Early Man, and would be leaving again, this time with a history of Europe. The road had taken me across and along the paths of old explorers and poets, new friends, and ancestors. I'd found the extremes of human endurance and emotion, and cruelty and kindness. There had been art and literature and history in abundance.

I arrived at the portal to the Hind Cartwheel, knowing that, beyond the transit lounge entrance, was a ramp way to an Egypt Air 707, refueling for my red-eye flight to Karachi.

What I didn't know was that, sitting on the other side of that door, was something more.

Destiny.

The Milky Way was slowly splitting the blackness above us.

"Is that the end of the story, Uncle Wink?" Asked Sam.

"No, Sammy. Just the end of the second part. And way past your bedtime."

"So why did you tell us about returning if you haven't returned yet?" Asked Millie.

"Because you wanted to find out about heroes. But the end of your quest may not have been the same as the end of mine."

"So when can we find out what happened to you?" She asked.

"Soon." Said Uncle Wink. "Hopefully, soon."

Other Works by Lawrence Winkler

Westwood Lake Chronicles

Cartwheels Quadrilogy
Orion's Cartwheel
(Between the Cartwheels)
Hind Cartwheel
The Final Cartwheel

Stories of the Southern Sea

Wagon Days

Samurai Road

Stout Men

Fire Beyond the Darkness

*   *   *